UNITED NATIONS CONFERENCE ON TRADE AND DEVELOPMENT
GENEVA

TRADE AND DEVELOPMENT REPORT, 2012

Report by the secretariat of the
United Nations Conference on Trade and Development

DÉPÔT
DEPOSIT

UNITED NATIONS
New York and Geneva, 2012

Note

- Symbols of United Nations documents are composed of capital letters combined with figures. Mention of such a symbol indicates a reference to a United Nations document.

- The designations employed and the presentation of the material in this publication do not imply the expression of any opinion whatsoever on the part of the Secretariat of the United Nations concerning the legal status of any country, territory, city or area, or of its authorities, or concerning the delimitation of its frontiers or boundaries.

- Material in this publication may be freely quoted or reprinted, but acknowledgement is requested, together with a reference to the document number. A copy of the publication containing the quotation or reprint should be sent to the UNCTAD secretariat.

UNCTAD/TDR/2012

UNITED NATIONS PUBLICATION

Sales No. E.12.II.D.6

ISBN 978-92-1-112846-8
eISBN 978-92-1-055401-5
ISSN 0255-4607

Contents

List of tables

List of boxes

List of charts

Classification by country or commodity group

The classification of countries in this *Report* has been adopted solely for the purposes of statistical or analytical convenience and does not necessarily imply any judgement concerning the stage of development of a particular country or area.

The major country groupings used in this *Report* follow the classification by the United Nations Statistical Office (UNSO). They are distinguished as:

» Developed or industrial(ized) countries: the countries members of the OECD (other than Mexico, the Republic of Korea and Turkey) plus the new EU member countries and Israel.

» Transition economies refers to South-East Europe and the Commonwealth of Independent States (CIS).

» Developing countries: all countries, territories or areas not specified above.

The terms "country" / "economy" refer, as appropriate, also to territories or areas.

References to "Latin America" in the text or tables include the Caribbean countries unless otherwise indicated.

References to "sub-Saharan Africa" in the text or tables include South Africa unless otherwise indicated.

For statistical purposes, regional groupings and classifications by commodity group used in this *Report* follow generally those employed in the *UNCTAD Handbook of Statistics 2011* (United Nations publication, sales no. D.11.II.D.1) unless otherwise stated. The data for China do not include those for Hong Kong Special Administrative Region (Hong Kong SAR), Macao Special Administrative Region (Macao SAR) and Taiwan Province of China.

Other notes

References in the text to *TDR* are to the *Trade and Development Report* (of a particular year). For example, *TDR 2011* refers to *Trade and Development Report, 2011* (United Nations publication, sales no. E.11.II.D.3).

The term "dollar" ($) refers to United States dollars, unless otherwise stated.

The term "billion" signifies 1,000 million.

The term "tons" refers to metric tons.

Annual rates of growth and change refer to compound rates.

Exports are valued FOB and imports CIF, unless otherwise specified.

Use of a dash (–) between dates representing years, e.g. 1988–1990, signifies the full period involved, including the initial and final years.

An oblique stroke (/) between two years, e.g. 2000/01, signifies a fiscal or crop year.

A dot (.) indicates that the item is not applicable.

Two dots (..) indicate that the data are not available, or are not separately reported.

A dash (-) or a zero (0) indicates that the amount is nil or negligible.

Decimals and percentages do not necessarily add up to totals because of rounding.

Abbreviations

ADB	Asian Development Bank
BCBS	Basel Committee on Banking Supervision
CCT	conditional cash transfer
CIS	Commonwealth of Independent States
EC-AMECO	European Commission Annual Macro-economic Database
ECLAC	Economic Commission for Latin America and the Caribbean
ECB	European Central Bank
EIU	Economist Intelligence Unit
EMU	Economic and Monetary Union (of the European Union)
EU	European Union
FAO	Food and Agriculture Organization of the United Nations
FDI	foreign direct investment
FSB	Financial Stability Board
GDP	gross domestic product
GFCF	gross fixed capital formation
ICT	information and communications technology
ILO	International Labour Organization (or Office)
IMF	International Monetary Fund
KILM	Key Indicators of the Labour Market (ILO database)
LDC	least developed country
MDG	Millennium Development Goal
MFA	Multi-Fibre Arrangement
NIE	newly industrializing economy
ODA	official development assistance
OECD	Organisation for Economic Co-operation and Development
PPP	purchasing power parity
SME	small and medium-sized enterprise
SOE	State-owned enterprise
SWIID	Standardized World Income Inequality Database
TDR	Trade and Development Report
TNC	transnational corporation
UNCTAD	United Nations Conference on Trade and Development
UN/DESA	United Nations Department of Economic and Social Affairs
UNDP	United Nations Development Programme
UNECA	United Nations Economic Commission for Africa
UNECE	United Nations Economic Commission for Europe
UNESCO	United Nations Educational, Scientific and Cultural Organization
UNICEF	United Nations Children's Fund
UNIDO	United Nations Industrial Development Organization
UNSD	United Nations Statistics Division
VAT	value-added tax
WESP	World Economic Situation and Prospects
WTO	World Trade Organization

OVERVIEW

The world economy, which continues to suffer from the fallout of the financial crisis that began in late 2007 and the meltdown in September 2008, has not been able to revive the growth conditions of the preceding decade. Those conditions had been particularly supportive of economic and social progress in the developing world, and the resulting momentum, especially in some of the larger developing countries, helped to stoke recovery in the world economy once the worst of the crisis had been contained. However, those countries are now losing that momentum and downside risks for the world economy are growing again.

The immediate problem is the inability of the developed countries to return to a normal growth pattern, but there is also an equally serious problem of contagion. Amidst their fragile recovery, an unreformed (and unrepentant) financial sector and macroeconomic policies that are timid at best, and counterproductive at worst, the developing countries will find it difficult to sustain their own growth dynamic, let alone that of the global economy.

In the United States, a sluggish recovery remains vulnerable to events in Europe given their strongly intertwined financial systems. Europe as a whole is on the brink of a deep recession, with some members having been stuck in reverse gear for several years. In both cases, attempts to overcome the present crisis are dominated by fiscal austerity, combined with calls to further "flexibilize" their labour markets. In practice, this means wage restraint and in some cases massive wage reductions. However, these policies are more likely to further weaken growth dynamics and increase unemployment instead of stimulating investment and job creation. At the same time, as has been demonstrated with similar structural reform policies in the developing world over the past 30 years, they will also serve to reinforce the trend towards greater inequality, which has become a visibly damaging feature of finance-driven globalization.

Therefore, a fundamental policy reorientation is needed, recognizing that healthy and inclusive growth will require a stable expansion of consumption and investment in productive capacity based on favourable income expectations of the working population and positive demand expectations of entrepreneurs. This requires a rethinking of the principles underlying the design of national economic policy and supportive international institutional arrangements.

In particular, while globalization and technological change, and their interplay, have created both winners and losers, their apparent adverse impacts on overall income distribution in many countries must be understood in the context of the macroeconomic, financial and labour market policies adopted. Those policies have caused unemployment to rise and remain high, and wages to lag behind productivity growth, and they have channelled rentier incomes towards the top 1 per cent of the income ladder. Neither globalization nor technological improvements inevitably require the kind of dramatic shift in the distribution of income that favours the very rich and deprives the poor and the middle-class of the means to improve their living standards. On the contrary, with more appropriate national and international policies that take into account the crucial importance of aggregate demand for capital formation, structural change and growth dynamics, job creation can be accelerated, inequality reduced and the requisite degree of economic and social stability guaranteed.

Global recovery: uneven and fragile

The recovery from the global financial and economic crisis, beginning in mid-2009, has been uneven and fragile. While growth has regained steam in some developing regions, it has sputtered in most developed countries, with ongoing deleveraging across the private sector, high unemployment spreading uncertainty among households and governments scrambling to consolidate their budgets prematurely. Global decision-makers, including at the level of the G-20, have lacked a clear idea of how to pierce through the thick fog of uncertainty enveloping the global economy and to "lift all boats" on to a more sustainable growth path.

The global economy weakened significantly towards the end of 2011 and further downside risks emerged in the first half of 2012. Growth of global gross domestic product (GDP), which had already decelerated in 2011, is expected to experience a further slowdown in 2012, to around 2.5 per cent.

Despite a very modest improvement of GDP growth in the United States and a more significant one in Japan, developed economies as a whole are likely to grow by only slightly more than 1 per cent in 2012 owing to the recession currently gripping the European Union (EU). That recession is concentrated in the euro zone where the authorities have so far failed to present a convincing solution to the area's internal imbalances and related debt overhangs. The chosen policy of unconditional austerity is suffocating the return to sustainable economic growth. Indeed, a further deterioration of economic conditions in Europe cannot be excluded.

Growth in developing and transition economies has been driven by domestic demand and high commodity prices

While developed countries are still struggling to reignite recovery, GDP growth in developing and transition economies is expected to remain relatively high, at around 5 per cent and 4 per cent respectively. Indeed, most developing countries have managed to regain the ground they had lost as a result of the crisis. This owes much to the adoption of expansionary demand-side policies. For example, China was able to absorb a dramatic fall in its current-account surplus with only a small reduction of its overall growth expectation and without restraining real wage growth. The contrast with Germany, which could not avoid economic stagnation despite its huge surplus, is striking.

Private consumption and wage growth have also played a crucial role in the superior performance of many developing countries. Although GDP growth is slowing down moderately in Latin America and the Caribbean, it is expected to remain in the order of 3.5 per cent in 2012. This growth stems from strong domestic demand, which is being sustained by rising real wages and credit to the private sector. Several countries have been responding to the deteriorating external environment with countercyclical policies, including higher public spending and a more accommodative monetary stance. They have been profiting from the policy space made possible by higher public revenues and active financial policies, including the management of foreign capital flows. As a result, investment rates are on the rise and the unemployment rate has fallen to its lowest level in decades.

Growth rates increased in Africa, owing to continuing expansion in sub-Saharan Africa and to economic recovery in the Northern African countries following an end to the internal conflicts in 2011. Relatively high prices for primary commodities benefited external and fiscal balances, enabling many countries to adopt fiscal stimulus measures. Investment in infrastructure and in natural resources also supported domestic expenditure and growth.

Although it remains the fastest growing region, Asia is experiencing an economic slowdown, with GDP growth expected to fall from 6.8 per cent in 2011 to slightly below 6 per cent in 2012. Several countries – including China, India and Turkey – have been adversely affected by weaker demand from developed countries and by the monetary tightening they applied in 2011 to prevent a rise in inflation and asset prices.

Given the headwinds from the international economy, they have since relaxed their monetary conditions and many of them have applied countercyclical measures. Regional growth is based on a continuous expansion of household incomes and a shift from external to domestic demand, as well as on high levels of investment.

The transition economies are expected to maintain a growth rate exceeding 4 per cent in 2012. This is entirely due to the dynamism of members of the Commonwealth of Independent States (CIS). Growth in the CIS is based on strong domestic demand, spurred by gains from the terms of trade and/or strong workers' remittances, while on the supply side the recovery of the agricultural sector has also played a significant role.

Slow expansion of global trade

International trade expansion, after a strong rebound in 2010, slowed to only 5.5 per cent in 2011, and is likely to further decelerate in 2012. In most developed economies – particularly in the euro zone – trade volumes have not recovered to their pre-crisis levels, although in the first half of 2012 they did grow somewhat in Japan and the United States. Trade was comparatively more dynamic in developing countries, but its growth has slowed down significantly even in these countries to around 6–7 per cent in 2011. The exceptions are some commodity exporters, which were able to increase their imports at two-digit rates owing to gains from the terms of trade. These countries benefited from commodity prices that remained high by historical standards in 2011 and the first half of 2012. However, those prices continue to display strong volatility and have been exhibiting a declining trend after peaking during the first months of 2011.

Considerable downside risks to global recovery

The main obstacles to global recovery and a benign rebalancing are concentrated in developed countries. Among these countries, the United States, which continues to have the largest current-account deficit by far, saw its external deficit decline to around 3 per cent of GDP in 2009 due to a marked contraction of imports. Since then, its current-account deficit has remained stable, while domestic demand growth has been sluggish. Moreover, a major risk ahead is that premature and excessive fiscal austerity by early next year could choke growth dramatically. An even greater problem for global recovery is Europe's increasing dependence on exports. Germany's external surplus is only slightly smaller today than it was prior to the crisis. So far, much of the German surplus is offset by deficits mainly in the rest of Europe. However, the ongoing crisis is reducing incomes and imports, and with most countries seeking to improve their competitiveness, the EU's external position may be shifting towards a sizeable surplus. The whole region is, in effect, trying to export its way out of the crisis. This could exert an enormous drag on overall global growth and worsen the outlook for many developing countries.

The crisis in Europe is being widely referred to as a "sovereign debt crisis", as public finances have deteriorated markedly since the start of the global financial crisis and interest rates have soared in a number of countries. However, the situation with public finances is less dramatic in most countries in the euro zone than in other developed economies such as Japan, the United Kingdom and the United States, which have nevertheless seen their bond yields fall to historical lows. Overall, in developed countries the worsening of public finances is primarily due to the working of automatic stabilizers and to the bailouts of financial institutions after the shock of late 2008, though the latter were entirely justified by the gravity of the situation. Since 2010, however, calls for an "exit strategy" from fiscal stimulus and for quick fiscal consolidation have gained the upper hand. As a result, fiscal austerity has become the "golden rule" throughout the euro zone, entailing especially draconian fiscal retrenchment in the Southern European member States. Such a measure may prove to be not just counterproductive, but even lethal for the euro and dire for the rest of the world as well.

Rising fiscal deficits in Europe are but symptoms – not the root cause – of the euro-zone crisis. Underpinning the huge divergence of long-term interest rates in the Economic and Monetary Union (EMU) are the wide wage and price differentials and the related build-up of large regional trade imbalances among the members. These imbalances started to build up at the very juncture when the most important instrument to deal with such imbalances – namely changes in the exchange rate – was no longer available. With fiscal policy ideologically blocked in many key countries and the existing monetary policy toolkit clearly inadequate, unconventional policy instruments are now needed.

Structural reforms are no substitute for a growth strategy

In general, the role of fiscal policy in developed, developing and transition economies alike needs to be reassessed from a dynamic macroeconomic perspective. Fiscal space is largely an endogenous variable which depends on a combination of policy choices and institutional capabilities. In particular, macroeconomic policies that stabilize GDP growth and keep interest rates low can contribute to securing fiscal space and achieving a sustainable public debt. Clearly, fiscal space is not evenly distributed either globally or regionally, but slowing domestic demand and GDP growth has never been a viable option to help consolidate public finances. It is crucial for the world economy and for the prospects of developing countries that systemically important countries, in particular those with current-account surpluses, make wise use of their available fiscal space to restore growth and support current-account rebalancing.

Adding to the bleak prospects for global recovery is the problem that policymakers in developed countries, particularly in Europe, now appear to be pinning their hopes once again on "structural reforms". However, those reforms are all too often coded language for labour market liberalization including wage cuts, a weakening of collective bargaining and greater wage differentiation across sectors and firms. The reasoning behind such a structural reform agenda is flawed because it is based on purely *microeconomic* considerations and ignores the *macroeconomic* dimension of labour markets and wage determination. A fixation on reforms of this kind can be dangerous in the current situation of rising unemployment and falling private demand. Moreover, asymmetric rebalancing that places the burden of adjustment solely on crisis-stricken current-account deficit countries in the European periphery is bound to further undermine regional growth.

Reforms in global governance need to be reinvigorated

The G-20 process established in 2008 to enhance global macroeconomic and financial coordination has lost momentum. It has made no progress towards reforming the international monetary system, even though exchange rate misalignments driven by currency speculation persist. International financial reform is another unresolved issue. While the crisis prompted the consideration of an agenda for placing the international financial system on a safer footing, policymakers' attention to it remains fragmentary and hesitant.

It now seems that the moment of opportunity has passed – the advice to never let "a serious crisis go to waste" has gone unheeded. The financial crisis and the bailouts have led to even greater concentration in the financial sector, which has largely regained its political clout. Short-term rewards rather than long-term productivity remain the guiding principle for collective behaviour in the financial industry, even today. There is a very real threat that financial institutions and shadow banking activities may again succeed in dodging the regulators, as vividly demonstrated by recent banking scandals.

Bank deleveraging in developed economies, even if warranted, may again have negative effects on developing countries. If the deleveraging does not occur in a gradual and orderly manner, but is forced by sudden stresses in banks' balance sheets as a result of new shocks, it may also affect international bank lending. In this regard, the availability of trade finance is of particular concern, and may require a new global initiative to make sure that developing countries are not adversely affected due to an external credit crunch.

Rising income inequality: a feature of the past three decades

Fiscal austerity, combined with wage restraint and further flexibilization of labour markets, not only causes an economy to contract, but also creates greater inequality in the distribution of income. The ensuing threat to social cohesion is already visible in several countries. However, rising inequality is by no means a recent phenomenon; it has been a ubiquitous feature of the world economy over the past 30 years, even if in some developing countries this trend appears to have come to a halt since the beginning of the new millennium.

After a long period of relatively stable distribution of income between profits and wages, the share of wages in total income has fallen since around 1980 in most developed and many developing countries. In several of the larger developed countries much of this decline already occurred between 1980 and 1995, when increasing unemployment started to exert pressure on workers and to weaken unions and average wages began to fall behind overall productivity growth. In some countries this trend continued for two decades. With wage compression pursued in many developed countries to overcome the current crisis and new records in unemployment, this trend is likely to be even reinforced. In several developed countries it has been accompanied by a dramatic gap between the top income groups and those at the bottom of the income ladder.

In developing countries the wage share has also tended to decline since the early 1980s. It has to be kept in mind, though, that in many of them data on functional income distribution are less indicative in this respect than in developed countries. Large segments of their active population are self-employed in low-productivity agriculture or retail commerce activities, and it would be misleading to consider all their revenue as capital income.

Inequality of personal income distribution increased in all regions after 1980

Personal income distribution, which reflects the distribution between profits and wages, disparities between income categories and redistribution by the State, had become more equal in most developed countries during the post-war period until the late 1970s. Subsequently the income gap widened. The Gini coefficient that measures income inequality across all income groups confirms this trend: in 15 out of 22 developed countries, personal income distribution deteriorated between 1980 and 2000, though in 8 of them this trend was reversed to some extent after 2000.

In developing countries, inequality of personal income distribution is generally more pronounced than in developed countries and transition economies. As in developed countries, the income gap narrowed during the first three decades after the Second World War, with the exception of countries in Latin America. But during the period 1980–2000 there was a general increase in inequality in all developing regions. Since the turn of the millennium, trends in income distribution have diverged among developing regions.

In Latin America and the Caribbean inequality rose during the 1980s and 1990s in 14 out of 18 countries for which relevant data are available. It reached a historical peak in the region as a whole by 2000, but has fallen since then in 15 of the 18 countries. However, overall, it remains higher than before the 1980s.

In Africa as a whole, between 1980 and 1995 inequality increased from an already high level, as in Latin America, but this increase began a few years later than in other regions. Out of 23 African countries for which relevant data are available, inequality increased in 10 countries (including several with large populations), but fell in another 10 and remained unchanged in the remaining 3 countries. After 1995, the income gap narrowed in 15 out of 25 countries, mainly in Southern Africa and West Africa, but sub-Saharan Africa still accounted for 6 of the 10 countries with the most unequal income distribution in the world.

In Asia, where inequality of personal income is generally lower than in other developing regions, it has increased since the early 1980s in terms of both income disparities across all income groups and the share of the top income groups in total income. Greater inequality is particularly evident in India, but it has also increased in East and South-East Asia, where 7 out of 9 countries for which relevant data are available saw an increase in personal income inequality between 1980 and 1995. Distinct from some countries in South-East Asia, inequality continued to rise in East Asia also after 2000, albeit at a slower pace. In many Asian economies, income from financial activities rose considerably faster than from other activities.

In China, a marked rise in inequality has accompanied fast economic growth since the 1980s, and this trend has continued beyond 2000. Despite rapid growth in the average real wage, the share of labour income in total income has declined and wage disparities have grown on several dimensions: between urban and rural areas, interior and coastal regions, and between skilled workers in certain occupations and low-skilled migrant workers. The share of the top 1 per cent incomes in total income has also increased since 1985, but it remains low by international comparisons.

In Central and Eastern Europe, income distribution was the most egalitarian among all country groupings until the early 1990s. Following their transition to a market economy, the wage share in GDP fell dramatically and inequality of personal income distribution in this region increased more sharply than in any other region, although it is still lower than in most developing countries.

In all regions growing income inequality since the early 1980s has been associated with an increase in the concentration of wealth in the higher income strata. Ownership of financial and real assets is not only a source of income but also facilitates access to credit and privileged participation in political decision-making. In many developing countries, the concentration of land ownership plays a particularly important role in this regard. It is especially high in Latin America, where income inequality is also the most pronounced, whereas it is relatively low in East and South-East Asia and in sub-Saharan Africa.

Is greater income inequality inevitable?

The shifts in income distribution over the past three decades occurred in parallel with accelerating trade and financial flows, the spread of international production networks and rapid technological change, owing in particular to progress in information and communication technologies (ICTs). This led to the widespread assumption that increasing income inequality is an inevitable by-product of structural changes brought about by globalization and technological change, or even a precondition for such change. However, structural change also occurred throughout the past century, including during periods when inequality of income distribution was considerably lower.

It is true that in the past few decades globalization has been spurred by trade and financial liberalization and the greater participation of developing countries in international production chains and in international trade of manufactures. Moreover, progress in the application of ICTs in recent decades may have been faster than technological change in earlier phases of economic development. But it is also true that there was rapid increase in productivity during the previous decades, and yet income disparities narrowed along with the simultaneous creation of a sufficient number of new jobs.

Structural change and corporate strategies in developed countries

In developed countries, which entered a period of normal "deindustrialization" in the 1970s and 1980s, structural change in recent decades has been shaped by fast growth of the financial sector, and to some extent by advances in ICTs and by increased competition from developing countries. In some countries, these have been accompanied by shifts in the demand for labour with different skills – i.e. a decline in the demand for moderately skilled workers relative to both the highly skilled and the low-skilled. The rise of imports from developing countries has accclerated since the mid-1990s largely as a result of offshoring of production.

The increasing frequency of such relocation of production is related not only to the liberalization of trade and increasing attempts by developing countries to attract foreign direct investment (FDI), but also to a change in corporate strategies of a growing number of firms in developed countries. Emphasis on the maximization of shareholder value has led managers to focus on short-term profitability and a higher stock market valuation of their companies. This approach has changed the way companies have been responding to competitive pressures under conditions of high unemployment. Instead of adopting a long-term perspective and trying to further upgrade their production technology and the product composition of output through productivity-enhancing investment and innovation, they have increasingly relied on offshoring production activities to low-wage locations in developing and transition economies, and on seeking to reduce domestic unit labour costs through wage compression. The pursuit of such strategies has been facilitated by the weaker bargaining position of workers faced with the persistent threat of becoming unemployed, which has strengthened the power of profit earners vis-à-vis wage earners. This trend has been associated with growing wage inequality between workers with different skills, and of those with similar skills in different occupations.

Structural and macroeconomic factors influencing inequality in developing countries

Widening inequality in the different developing regions and in the transition economies is associated with very different development paths. In some cases, as in a number of Asian economies, it has accompanied rapid economic growth. In others, it has taken place during periods of economic stagnation or depression, as in Latin America and Africa in the 1980s and 1990s, and in the transition economies in the 1990s.

In a number of developing countries, especially in Latin America, but also in some transition economies, the trend towards greater inequality in the 1980s and 1990s occurred in a context of "premature" deindustrialization. Labour moved from manufacturing activities in the formal sector towards lower productivity jobs with lower remuneration, such as in informal services and the production of primary commodities. Declining industrial employment, combined with large absolute falls in real wages, in the order of 20–30 per cent in some Latin American countries, led to increasing income gaps in conjunction with stagnating or declining average per capita incomes.

One explanation is that many countries with rich natural resource endowments and a nascent industrial sector found it difficult to sustain a dynamic process of structural change after opening up to global competition. Unlike developed countries, they had not yet acquired the capabilities for technological innovation that would have allowed them to seize the opportunities presented by globalization to upgrade to more capital- and technology-intensive activities. Moreover, unlike low-income countries at the initial stages of industrialization, they did not, or no longer, possess abundant cheap labour and thus could not benefit as much from the offshoring of labour-intensive activities by developed-country firms. Countries that possessed some industrial production capacity relatively early may also have been adversely affected by increasing imports of manufactured goods from other, lower-wage developing countries.

However, the main cause of deindustrialization in a number of developing countries in the 1980s and 1990s lies in their choice of macroeconomic and financial policies in the aftermath of the debt crises of the early 1980s. In the context of structural adjustment programmes implemented with the support of the international financial institutions, they undertook financial liberalization in parallel with trade liberalization, accompanied by high domestic interest rates to curb high inflation rates or to attract foreign capital. Frequently, this led to currency overvaluation, a loss of competitiveness of domestic producers and a fall in industrial production and fixed investment even when domestic producers tried to respond to the pressure on prices by wage compression or lay-offs.

In other countries, such as India and many African countries, the manufacturing sector has not grown fast enough to generate sufficient employment and a much larger proportion of the labour force has been absorbed in informal and less remunerative employment, while price liberalization in agriculture has led to lower incomes of farmers, particularly in Africa. To the extent that liberalization has brought benefits, these have accrued mainly to traders rather than farmers. Moreover, where industrialization has largely relied on integration into international production networks, as in a number of countries in South-East Asia and parts of Africa, production activities and job creation have been mainly in labour-intensive activities without igniting or sustaining a dynamic process of industrial deepening. As a result, traditional patterns of specialization in primary commodities and natural-resource-intensive manufactures have been preserved, if not reinforced.

Some improvements in income distribution since the late 1990s

Reductions in income inequality over the past decade in Latin America and in parts of Africa and South-East Asia occurred in a context of improved external conditions, especially higher international commodity prices and lower debt service burdens. However, owing to different internal structures and domestic policies their effects on income inequality were not the same everywhere. In resource-rich developing and transition economies where the concentration of ownership of land and mineral resources is typically high, rising prices of oil and mineral products tend to increase income inequality. Nevertheless, some resource-rich countries, especially in Latin America, have succeeded in translating terms-of-trade gains into broad-based income growth in the economy as a whole since 2002 and thus in narrowing the income gap. They achieved this by augmenting their fiscal revenues and by targeted fiscal and industrial policies, which helped to create good-quality jobs outside the commodities sector. Higher fiscal spending created jobs directly in the public and services sectors, and indirectly in occupations related to infrastructure development and in manufacturing industry. Countercyclical fiscal policies and more progressive income taxes were also very important. Moreover, many countries used higher public revenues for increased social spending. Several countries also adopted managed exchange rate systems and capital controls with the aim of stemming speculative capital inflows and preventing currency overvaluation.

Rapid industrialization with growing inequality in Asia

In many East and South-East Asian economies, macroeconomic and industrial policies supportive of productive investment spurred rapid industrialization and buoyed economic growth in the context of increasing globalization. In these subregions, the shifts in income distribution over the past few decades have been strongly influenced by the creation of numerous employment opportunities in high-productivity activities, mainly in manufacturing. Thus labour was able to move from low-productivity jobs, often rural, towards higher productivity jobs. Wages in these occupations rose faster than average wages as the supply of better skilled workers fell short of demand. In addition, financial liberalization caused incomes from financial activities to rise faster than those from other activities. To the extent that income inequality hinders the development of domestic markets, a move to more equal income distribution would facilitate a productive upgrading away from low-wage and low-skill specialization within international and/or regional production networks.

In China, rising inequality has also taken the form of growing regional income disparities and a widening urban–rural income gap. This appears to be due to fiscal decentralization and trade and industrial policies, including investment in infrastructure, that have favoured coastal areas closer to international trade routes and large-scale capital-intensive production over small-scale production. At the same time, disparities among wage earners contributed to overall inequality, as the distribution of wages shifted in favour of skilled workers in the high-tech, financial and services sectors, and migrants from rural areas receive lower wages and social benefits than urban workers with formal residence.

The role of FDI and relocation of production

The global production and investment decisions of transnational corporations (TNCs) have played an important role in the globalization process. They integrate the output from production stages outsourced to a specific country seamlessly into the continuously evolving total production process. TNCs typically achieve this by offshoring specific slices of their technology to their foreign affiliates, combining their advanced technology developed at home with cheap labour abroad. Over the past two decades, albeit under the specific circumstances of rather high unemployment and possibly contrary to earlier periods with low unemployment, FDI outflows at times have had the effect of exerting downward pressure on wages and employment in manufacturing, which may have contributed to an increase in income inequality in the largest developed countries.

For developing countries the evidence is mixed. However, FDI alone has never been sufficient to change the balance in the labour markets in favour of labour on either side of the flow. Paradoxically, home and host countries have displayed similar responses to growing FDI in terms of labour market policy and wage setting: home countries attempted to curb the trend towards the relocation of production abroad by deregulating their labour markets and putting pressure on wages, while host countries also made efforts to create "flexible" labour markets to attract additional FDI. In the same vein, governments have often aimed at creating locational advantages or compensating for presumed locational disadvantages by lowering taxes, thereby boosting net profits of TNCs and limiting their potential to reduce inequality with fiscal instruments.

The turning point: financial liberalization and "market-friendly" policy reforms

In order to comprehend the causes of growing inequality, it should be borne in mind that the trend towards greater inequality has coincided with a broad reorientation of economic policy since the 1980s. In many countries trade liberalization was accompanied by deregulation of the domestic financial system and capital-account liberalization, giving rise to a rapid expansion of international capital flows. International finance gained a life of its own, increasingly moving away from financing for real investment or for the international flow of goods to trading in existing financial assets. Such trading often became a much more lucrative business than creating wealth through new investments.

More generally, the previous more interventionist approach of public policy, which strongly focused on reducing high unemployment and income inequality, was abandoned. This shift was based on the belief that the earlier approach could not solve the problem of stagflation that had emerged in many developed countries in the second half of the 1970s. It was therefore replaced by a more "market-friendly" approach, which emphasized the removal of presumed market distortions and was grounded in the strong belief in a superior *static* efficiency of markets. This general reorientation involved a change in macroeconomic policies; monetary policy gave almost exclusive priority to fighting inflation, while the introduction of greater flexibility in wage formation and in "hiring and firing" conditions was intended to reduce unemployment. The idea behind this approach, based on static neoclassical economic reasoning, was that flexible wages and greater inequality of income distribution would enhance investment by boosting net profits and/or aggregate savings.

In the context of expanding financial activities, greater inequality often led to higher indebtedness, as low- and middle-income groups were unable to increase or maintain their consumption without resorting to credit. This in turn tended to exacerbate inequality by increasing the revenues of owners of financial assets. Moreover, when excessive debts eventually led to financial crises, inequality frequently rose because the costs of the crises generally had a disproportionate impact on the poorest.

While this shift in policy orientation occurred in most developed countries from the late 1970s onwards, the new thinking also began to shape policies in developing countries in the subsequent decades. In particular, a large number of countries were forced to comply with the conditionalities attached to assistance from the international financial institutions or followed their policy advice in line with the "Washington Consensus" for other reasons.

Deregulation of labour markets and tax reforms

With regard to labour markets, this new policy orientation meant deregulation and the introduction of greater flexibility. The unwillingness of workers to accept lower wages was considered the main reason for unemployment inertia. In an environment of high and persistent unemployment, the influence of trade unions was weakened in countries where they had previously been influential, and in countries where they were initially weak, they could not be strengthened. As a result, the power in wage negotiations shifted towards employers, and wage increases were kept low in comparison with overall productivity gains, leading to a widespread increase in the shares of profits in total income.

The new spike of unemployment in the context of the financial crisis in 2008–2009, rather than motivating a rethinking of this approach, has, curiously, led to a reiteration of the presumed superiority of flexible labour markets in most developed countries. Only a few governments, notably in Latin America, have not followed such an orientation. Instead, they have focused on policies that improve the economic situation of the poor and the bargaining power of workers without hampering growth and global economic integration.

In terms of fiscal policy, the reorientation of economic policy since the early 1980s towards the principle of minimizing State intervention and strengthening market forces entailed the elimination of "market distortions" resulting from taxation. According to this view, the distribution of the tax burden and the allocation of public expenditure should primarily be determined by efficiency criteria and not by distributive considerations. Lower taxation of corporate profits and lower marginal income tax rates at the top of the income scale were expected to strengthen incentives and increase companies' own financial resources for investment. Another argument in support of lower taxation of high-income groups and profits was that the resulting shift in income distribution would increase aggregate savings, since these income groups have a higher-than-average propensity to save. Supposedly, this in turn would also cause investment to rise.

In many developed and developing countries such liberal tax reforms reduced the tax-to-GDP ratio, lowered marginal tax rates and contributed to strengthening those elements of the public revenue system that had regressive effects on income distribution (i.e. a tax burden that falls disproportionately on lower income groups). In developed countries this was associated with a considerable decline in revenues from direct taxation as a share of GDP.

Reduced fiscal space in developing countries

Fiscal reforms in developing countries in the 1980s, together with the loss of tariff revenues resulting from trade liberalization also led to a reduction of public revenue, or prevented it from rising to an extent that would have enlarged the scope for governments to enhance the development process and to act to improve income distribution. This problem was aggravated by the stagnation of per capita flows of official development assistance (ODA) in the 1980s and their dramatic fall in absolute terms in the 1990s. As a result, in many countries the provision of public services was reduced or user fees for public services were introduced, often with regressive effects or leading to the exclusion of low-income groups from access to such services, especially in Africa and Latin America.

ODA disbursements recovered from a historically low level from the mid-1990s until recently. However, a large proportion of this increase went to only a few countries emerging from several years of conflict, or it was provided in the form of debt relief to a number of countries that were accumulating debt arrears, so that it had a limited effect on the current budgets of most recipient countries. An increasing proportion of

ODA was also directed towards health, education and other social purposes, with positive effects on income distribution in the recipient countries. But since the increasing share of ODA for these purposes meant a decline in the share allocated to growth-enhancing investment in economic infrastructure and productive capacities, its effects on structural change and the creation of new employment and wage opportunities were limited.

The failure of labour market and fiscal reforms

Insufficient growth of average real wages, coupled with inappropriate tax reforms, constitute the root causes of rising inequality in most countries, but they have not led to the promised outcomes of faster growth and lower unemployment. This is because any policy approach that dismisses the important contribution of income distribution to demand growth and employment creation is destined to fail. A shift in income distribution to high income groups with a higher savings rate implies falling demand for the goods produced by companies. When productivity grows without a commensurate increase in wages, demand will eventually fall short of the production potential, thereby reducing capacity utilization and profits. This in turn will typically lead to cuts – and not to an increase – in investments.

Real wage increases below productivity growth and greater job uncertainty systematically destabilize domestic demand and serve to increase unemployment rather than reducing it. This suggests that relying on the simple market mechanism cannot prevent disequilibrium on the labour markets. Indeed, just ahead of the new jump in unemployment in developed countries – from an average of less than 6 per cent in 2007 to close to 9 per cent in 2011 – the share of wages in GDP had fallen to the lowest level in the post-war era. Due to their negative effect on consumer demand, neither lower average wages nor greater wage differentiation at the sector or firm level can be expected to lead to a substitution of labour for capital and reduce unemployment in the economy as a whole. In addition, greater wage differentiation among firms to overcome the current crisis in developed countries is not a solution either, because it reduces the differentiation of profits among firms. Yet it is precisely the profit differentials which drive the investment and innovation dynamics of a market economy. If less efficient firms cannot compensate for their lower profits by cutting wages, they must increase their productivity and innovate to survive.

Equally, a possible initial improvement of international competitiveness that may result from translating productivity gains into lower export prices is not sustainable, because it adversely affects growth and employment generation in other countries. Moreover, when such a strategy is pursued simultaneously in many countries whose producers compete internationally, it will tend to trigger a downward spiral in wages. Such practices may deprive a large proportion of their populations of a share in the productivity gains. The same holds for international tax competition, especially with regard to corporate taxation.

A reorientation of wage and labour market policies is essential

Influencing the pattern of income distribution in a way that society as a whole shares in the overall progress of the economy has to be a leading policy objective. That is why, in addition to employment- and growth-supporting monetary and fiscal policies, an appropriate incomes policy can play an important role in achieving a socially acceptable degree of income inequality while generating employment-creating demand growth. A central feature of any incomes policy should be to ensure that average real wages rise at the same rate as average productivity. Nominal wage adjustment should also take account of an inflation target. When, as a rule, wages in an economy rise in line with average productivity growth plus an inflation target, the share of wages in GDP remains constant and the economy as a whole creates a sufficient amount of demand to fully employ its productive capacities. This way an economy can avoid the danger of rising and persistent unemployment or the need to repeatedly adopt a "beggar-thy-neighbour" policy stance in order to create demand for its supply surplus.

In applying this rule, wage adjustment should be forward-looking. This means that it should be undertaken in accordance with the productivity *trend* and with the inflation *target* set by the government or the central bank for the next period, rather than according to actual rates of productivity growth and inflation in the preceding period (i.e. backward-looking). The latter would only serve to perpetuate inflation without securing the desired level of real wages. Linking wages to both productivity growth and the central bank's official inflation target would also facilitate the task of the central bank in preventing inflation, while giving it greater scope to stimulate investment and growth. Collective bargaining mechanisms can contribute to a successful incomes policy.

Wage increases in line with overall productivity growth and an inflation target would primarily serve to keep the wage share from falling and prevent the emergence of large differences in wages for similar occupations. Still, when the wage share falls and inequality of personal income increases, as has been the case in most countries over the past few decades, governments may try to restore the wage share and reduce inequality. Achieving this requires an *a priori* social consensus, which may be reached through a process of collective bargaining between employers' and workers' associations, complemented by government recommendations or general guidelines for wage adjustments.

There are also other instruments that can be used to correct the market outcome in favour of those with weak negotiating power. These include creating additional public employment opportunities, establishing legal minimum wages, and progressive taxation, the proceeds from which could be used for increased social transfers. Public spending designed to improve the provision of essential goods and services and make them more affordable may also be increased.

Income supporting measures in developing countries

These latter instruments are of particular relevance in developing countries, which generally may need to achieve a more drastic reduction of income inequalities than developed countries. There is considerable potential for enhancing productivity growth in these countries by increasing the division of labour and exploiting opportunities to draw on advanced technologies. This means that there is also considerable scope for these countries to reduce inequality by distributing productivity gains more equally, thereby also fostering demand growth.

No doubt, in developing countries, which are still highly dependent on the production and export of primary commodities, the link between growth and employment creation is less direct than in developed countries. Their growth performance is often strongly influenced by movements in internationally determined prices of primary commodities. Moreover, in many developing countries the informal sector is quite large, and small-scale self-employment is rather common. In many of them, formal employment in the manufacturing sector accounts for a relatively small share of total remunerative occupations, and labour unions and collective bargaining typically play a much smaller role than in most developed countries. It is therefore important to complement an incomes policy for the formal sector with measures to increase the incomes and purchasing power of the informally employed and self-employed.

Mechanisms that link agricultural producer prices to overall productivity growth in the economy would gradually improve the living conditions of rural populations. The introduction of legal minimum wages, and their regular adjustment in line with the trend of productivity growth of the economy and the targeted rate of inflation, can have a positive effect on the investment-productivity-growth dynamic. Apart from reducing poverty among those who earn the minimum wage, this can also generate additional employment in response to higher demand, which is likely to be mainly for domestically produced goods and services. Moreover, the level of the legal minimum wage and its adjustment over time can provide an important reference for wage setting in the economy more generally. It is true that implementation of legal minimum wages is difficult in economies with large informal sectors. In those economies, it is necessary to complement such legislation with enhanced public employment, and with strategies to improve the viability of small-scale production.

Influencing income distribution through taxation

In addition to labour market and wage policies, taxation of income and accumulated wealth on the revenue side, and social transfers and the free and universal provision of public services on the expenditure side, play a central role in influencing distributional outcomes.

Progressive taxation can lower inequality among disposable incomes more than among gross incomes. The net demand effect of an increase in taxation and higher government spending is stronger when the distribution of the additional tax burden is more progressive, since part of the additional tax payments is at the expense of the savings of the taxpayers in the higher income groups, where the propensity to save is higher than in the lower income groups.

The experience of the first three post-war decades in developed countries, when marginal and corporate tax rates were higher but investment was also higher, suggests that the willingness of entrepreneurs to invest in new productive capacity does not depend primarily on net profits at a given point in time; rather, it depends on their expectations of future demand for the goods and services they can produce with that additional capacity. These expectations are stabilized or even improve when public expenditures rise, and, through their income effects, boost private demand.

Indeed, the scope for using taxation and government spending for purposes of reducing inequality without compromising economic growth is likely to be much larger than is commonly assumed. Taxing high incomes, in particular in the top income groups, through greater progressivity of the tax scale does not remove the absolute advantage of the high income earners nor the incentive for others to move up the income ladder. Taxing rentier incomes and incomes from capital gains at a higher rate than profit incomes from entrepreneurial activity – rather than at a lower rate as practiced so far in many countries – appears to be an increasingly justifiable option given the excessive expansion of largely unproductive financial activities.

There is also scope for taxation in developing countries

Tackling income inequality effectively through progressive taxation requires a relatively high degree of formal employment in the economy and considerable administrative capacity, which many developing countries do not possess at present. However, these countries (including low-income countries) have a number of potential sources of revenue that can contribute to improving equality while increasing government revenues.

Greater taxation of wealth and inheritance is a potential source of public revenue that can be tapped in many developed and developing countries to reduce inequality of both income and wealth distribution and enlarge the government's fiscal space. For example, taxes on real estate, large landholdings, luxury durable goods and financial assets are normally easier to collect than taxes on personal income, and can represent an important source of revenue in countries that have high inequality of income and wealth distribution.

In resource-rich developing countries, incomes from the exploitation of natural resources and gains resulting from rising international commodity prices are another important source of public revenue. By appropriating their fair share of commodity rents, especially in the oil and mining sectors, governments in such developing countries can ensure that their natural resource wealth benefits the entire population, and not just a few domestic and foreign actors. This is particularly important, as the revenue potential from natural resources has grown significantly over the past decade owing to higher commodity prices.

There also appears to be considerable scope for modifying the tax treatment of TNCs, and FDI more generally. Developing countries often try to attract additional FDI by offering fiscal concessions. However, competing with other potential host countries by offering lower taxes is problematic since it triggers a downward spiral in taxation that reduces fiscal space in all the countries concerned, while initial locational advantages based on taxation tend to erode over time.

Public expenditures to reduce inequality

Well targeted social transfers and the public provision of social services can serve to reduce inequality of disposable income. For example, higher spending on education may contribute to more equitable income distribution, especially in the poorer countries, but only if job opportunities are provided to those who have received such education. However, employment creation depends on overall growth dynamics and especially on the expansion of the formal manufacturing and services sectors.

Public employment schemes, such as those launched in a number of developing countries in recent years, may have a positive effect on income distribution by reducing unemployment, establishing a wage floor, and generating demand for locally produced goods and services. These can be implemented even in low-income countries with low administrative capacity, and can be combined with projects to improve infrastructure and the provision of public services. If well conceived, they may also help to attract workers into the formal sector.

Proceeds from higher tax revenues may also be used for different forms of concessional lending and technical support to small producers in both the urban industrial and rural sectors. Apart from supporting productivity and income growth in these activities, the provision of such financing can also serve as a vehicle to attract small-scale entrepreneurs and workers into the formal sector.

The international dimension

In a world of increasingly interdependent, open economies, a country's macroeconomic performance is more and more influenced by external developments and policies in other countries. Sharp fluctuations in international prices of traded goods and currency misalignments can lead to distortions in international competition between producers in different countries.

The macroeconomic shocks that arise from such mispricing in currency markets affect an economy as a whole, and therefore cannot be tackled at the level of the firm. The appropriate way to deal with such shocks is by revaluation or devaluation of the currencies concerned, rather than by wage cuts in countries whose producers are losing international competitiveness. Movements of nominal exchange rates should reflect changes in inflation rate differentials or in the growth of unit labour costs. This would also prevent beggar-thy-neighbour behaviour in international trade.

Another important aspect of the international framework is the way in which countries deal with the relocation of fixed capital. Greater coordination among developing countries may be necessary to avoid wage and tax competition among them. Such coordination should aim at obliging foreign firms to conform to two principles: to fully accept national taxation schemes; and to adjust real wages to an increase in national productivity plus the national inflation target. Both these principles would set a standard for domestic firms. The latter would not deprive the foreign investors of their – often huge – extra profits arising from the combination of advanced technologies with low wages in the host country, because their labour costs would not rise in line with their own productivity but in line with the average productivity increase in the host economy as a whole.

* * * *

All these considerations serve to show that an efficient outcome of market processes in an increasingly globalized economy does not require greater inequality between capital and labour incomes and a greater dispersion of personal incomes. Inclusive growth and development requires active employment and redistribution measures, as well as supportive macroeconomic, exchange rate and industrial policies that foster productive investment and create decent jobs. A better income distribution would strengthen aggregate demand, investment and growth. This in turn would accelerate employment creation, including in high-productivity activities that offer better remuneration and social benefits, thereby further reducing inequality.

Supachai Panitchpakdi
Secretary-General of UNCTAD

Chapter I

CURRENT TRENDS AND CHALLENGES IN THE WORLD ECONOMY

A. Recent trends in the world economy

1. Global growth

The global economy weakened significantly towards the end of 2011 and further downside risks emerged in the first half of 2012. The growth rate of global output, which had already decelerated from 4.1 per cent in 2010 to 2.7 per cent in 2011, is expected to slow down even more in 2012 to below 2.5 per cent (table 1.1). Despite a very modest improvement in gross domestic product (GDP) growth in the United States and a more significant one in Japan, developed economies as a whole are likely to grow by only slightly more than 1 per cent in 2012, owing to the recession currently gripping the European Union (EU). This contrasts with a much stronger performance in developing and transition economies, where GDP growth should remain relatively high, at around 5 per cent and 4 per cent respectively.

Developed countries have not yet recovered from the financial crisis,[1] which has left in its wake a highly indebted private sector and a vulnerable financial system, with rising non-performing loans and limited access to inter-bank financing. Significant deleveraging was set in motion as banks sought to recapitalize and the private sector was unable or unwilling to take on new debts, strongly hampering domestic demand. Expansionary monetary policies, which included huge money creation in addition to very low policy interest rates, proved inadequate for reversing this situation. High levels of unemployment and wage stagnation or compression further hindered private consumption. On top of already weak private demand, fiscal tightening has been adopted in several developed countries with a view to reducing public debt and restoring the confidence of financial markets.

These problems have been particularly severe in the *European Union*, where economic activity is set to shrink in 2012: a fall in domestic consumption and investment since mid-2011 is only partly compensated by a rise in net exports. Recently, a number of policy initiatives have been undertaken to strengthen the banking system and reassure financial investors. Among these is a new fiscal architecture that includes a requirement for national budgets to be in balance or in surplus,[2] long-term refinancing operations by the European Central Bank (ECB), write-down of part of the Greek debt, reinforcement of the European Stability Mechanism and new rules for bank recapitalization. However, improvements in financial markets and confidence indicators in response to these measures were short-lived because the underlying causes of the crisis persist.

Within the EU, the euro zone faces some specific difficulties: it lacks a lender of last resort which could support governments as well as banks

Table 1.1

WORLD OUTPUT GROWTH, 2004–2012

(Annual percentage change)

Region/country	2004	2005	2006	2007	2008	2009	2010	2011	2012[a]
World	**4.1**	**3.5**	**4.1**	**4.0**	**1.5**	**-2.3**	**4.1**	**2.7**	**2.3**
Developed countries	**3.0**	**2.4**	**2.8**	**2.6**	**0.0**	**-3.9**	**2.8**	**1.4**	**1.1**
of which:									
Japan	2.4	1.3	1.7	2.2	-1.0	-5.5	4.4	-0.7	2.2
United States	3.5	3.1	2.7	1.9	-0.4	-3.5	3.0	1.7	2.0
European Union (EU-27)	2.6	2.0	3.3	3.2	0.3	-4.4	2.1	1.5	-0.3
of which:									
Euro area	2.2	1.7	3.2	3.0	0.4	-4.4	2.0	1.5	-0.4
France	2.5	1.8	2.5	2.3	-0.1	-3.1	1.7	1.7	0.3
Germany	1.2	0.7	3.7	3.3	1.1	-5.1	3.7	3.0	0.9
Italy	1.7	0.9	2.2	1.7	-1.2	-5.5	1.8	0.4	-1.9
United Kingdom	3.0	2.1	2.6	3.5	-1.1	-4.4	2.1	0.7	-0.6
European Union (EU-12)[b]	5.6	4.8	6.5	6.0	4.1	-3.7	2.3	3.1	1.2
South-East Europe and CIS	**7.7**	**6.5**	**8.4**	**8.6**	**5.2**	**-6.5**	**4.2**	**4.5**	**4.3**
South-East Europe[c]	5.6	4.9	5.3	5.9	4.2	-3.7	0.7	1.1	0.2
CIS, incl. Georgia	7.9	6.7	8.7	8.9	5.3	-6.8	4.6	4.8	4.6
of which:									
Russian Federation	7.2	6.4	8.2	8.5	5.2	-7.8	4.0	4.3	4.7
Developing countries	**7.4**	**6.8**	**7.6**	**7.9**	**5.3**	**2.4**	**7.5**	**5.9**	**4.9**
Africa	7.9	5.4	6.1	6.0	4.8	0.9	4.5	2.5	4.1
North Africa, excl. Sudan	4.8	5.1	5.4	4.7	4.6	3.2	4.0	-1.1	3.9
Sub-Saharan Africa, excl. South Africa	12.8	5.8	6.9	7.2	5.6	0.6	5.8	4.8	4.9
South Africa	4.6	5.3	5.6	5.6	3.6	-1.7	2.8	3.1	2.7
Latin America and the Caribbean	5.8	4.6	5.6	5.6	4.0	-2.0	6.0	4.3	3.4
Caribbean	3.7	7.3	9.3	5.8	3.0	0.2	2.8	2.6	2.7
Central America, excl. Mexico	4.2	4.8	6.4	7.0	4.1	-0.2	4.0	4.9	4.5
Mexico	4.1	3.3	5.1	3.4	1.2	-6.3	5.8	3.9	4.0
South America	7.1	5.0	5.5	6.6	5.4	-0.2	6.5	4.5	3.1
of which:									
Brazil	5.7	3.2	4.0	6.1	5.2	-0.3	7.5	2.7	2.0
Asia	8.0	7.9	8.7	9.0	5.9	4.1	8.4	6.8	5.5
East Asia	8.3	8.6	10.0	11.1	7.0	5.9	9.4	7.6	6.3
of which:									
China	10.1	11.3	12.7	14.2	9.6	9.2	10.4	9.2	7.9
South Asia	7.5	8.2	8.5	8.9	5.8	5.5	7.3	6.0	5.2
of which:									
India	8.3	9.3	9.6	9.7	7.5	7.0	9.0	7.0	6.0
South-East Asia	6.5	5.8	6.2	7.0	4.0	1.3	8.0	4.5	4.9
West Asia	8.8	6.9	6.7	4.5	3.8	-1.1	6.5	6.9	3.7
Oceania	2.2	3.5	2.9	3.6	2.7	2.1	3.4	3.8	3.6

Source: UNCTAD secretariat calculations, based on United Nations, Department of Economic and Social Affairs (UN/DESA), *National Accounts Main Aggregates* database, and *World Economic Situation and Prospects (WESP): Update as of mid-2012;* ECLAC, 2012; *OECD,* 2012; IMF, *World Economic Outlook,* April 2012; Economist Intelligence Unit, *EIU CountryData* database; JP Morgan, *Global Data Watch;* and national sources.

Note: Calculations for country aggregates are based on GDP at constant 2005 dollars.
 a Forecasts.
 b New EU member States after 2004.
 c Albania, Bosnia and Herzegovina, Croatia, Montenegro, Serbia and the former Yugoslav Republic of Macedonia.

if needed, and it has to manage trade imbalances and asymmetric trends in competitiveness within the zone while individual countries are unable to resort to nominal devaluations. Policy responses so far have been characterized by fiscal tightening, especially in countries with high external and fiscal deficits, in order to reassure financial investors of the solvency of their governments and banking systems. Both of these are closely related, as public bonds account for a significant share of banks' assets. In addition, governments have been seeking to reduce nominal wages and other costs in order to achieve a real devaluation within the monetary union (a process known as "internal devaluation"). These policies have taken a toll on economic growth and employment because they have aggravated the basic problem of insufficient demand. With faltering growth, fiscal revenues have been below expectations and the stress in the banking system has intensified in several countries. In addition, since "internal devaluation" has been undertaken simultaneously by several partners, and not all trading partners can become more competitive at the same time, ultimately none of them have been able to improve their competitiveness significantly. Given the disappointing results in terms of rebalancing competitiveness and reducing sovereign and banking risks, new initiatives have been approved, or are being debated, with the aim of supporting domestic demand. One such initiative is the announcement of a €120 billion "growth pact" at the Euro Summit on 28–29 June. There are also proposals for strengthening the mechanisms for supervision and recapitalization of the banking systems.

As a result of these developments, in 2012 almost all European countries will either experience decelerating growth (e.g. France, Germany and Sweden) or fall into recession (e.g. the Czech Republic, Hungary, Italy, the Netherlands, Spain and the United Kingdom). Meanwhile, Greece and Portugal are already in the throes of an economic depression. It is only in Iceland and Norway that GDP growth seems to be accelerating.

In the *United States*, GDP is forecast to grow at close to 2 per cent in 2012 – only slightly higher than in 2011. This growth is being driven almost exclusively by domestic demand; since exports and imports (by volume) are growing by similar amounts, the contribution of net exports to growth is virtually neutral. After recovering from the 2009 recession, domestic demand has lost momentum since late 2010

owing to high indebtedness of households, lower housing prices, sluggish real wages and persistently high unemployment rates. There were some improvements in household demand in the last quarter of 2011 and the first quarter of 2012, partly due to a reduction in the savings rate and a moderate increase in bank credit, but this trend was not maintained in the second quarter. The Government has managed to avoid full-scale fiscal tightening so far, although a fall in public spending has had a negative impact on overall growth since the third quarter of 2010. This could dramatically worsen if political considerations lead to deep fiscal cuts – the so-called "fiscal cliff" – in 2013.

Japan's GDP growth rate will probably exceed 2 per cent in 2012, based on relatively strong domestic demand. In particular, government expenditure on reconstruction following the natural disasters and nuclear accident in March 2011 will help boost GDP growth in 2012. The country's monetary policy remains very expansionary, with a policy rate close to zero and the extension of the asset-purchase programme. This policy, which aims at countering deflationary pressures by setting the inflation target at 1 per cent in 2012, has helped maintain low interest payments on the public debt. However, it has not stimulated bank credit to the private sector, which remains flat.

The crisis and its fallout have accelerated the trend towards a greater role of developing countries in the world economy. Between 2006 and 2012, 74 per cent of world GDP growth was generated in developing countries and only 22 per cent in developed countries. This is in sharp contrast to their respective contributions to global growth in previous decades: developed countries accounted for 75 per cent of global growth in the 1980s and 1990s, but this fell to a little over 50 per cent between 2000 and 2006 (chart 1.1).

GDP growth has been slowing down moderately in *Latin America and the Caribbean* to reach around 3.5 per cent in 2012 (table 1.1). Growth stems mainly from resilient domestic demand and other positive factors, including only a modest current-account deficit for the region as a whole averaging about 1.4 per cent of GDP in 2011, an equilibrated primary fiscal balance, falling public and external debts (except in the Caribbean countries) and solvent banking systems. In 2011 and the first half of 2012, employment grew consistently, particularly in formal occupations, real wages and credit to the private sector increased,

Chart 1.1

REGIONAL CONTRIBUTIONS TO WORLD GDP GROWTH, 1970–2012

(Per cent)

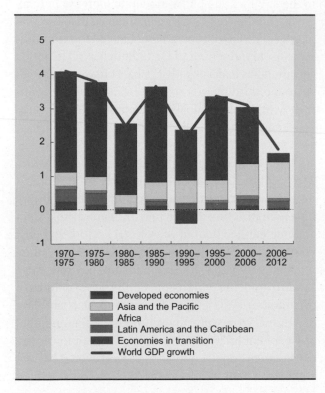

Developed economies
Asia and the Pacific
Africa
Latin America and the Caribbean
Economies in transition
— World GDP growth

Source: UNCTAD secretariat calculation, based on table 1.1;
UNCTADstat; UN/DESA, *National Accounts Main
Aggregates* database; World Bank, *World Development
Indicators;* and Maddison, 2008.
Note: Data are averages for the periods.

and the flow of remittances from the United States to several countries recovered. All these factors supported the expansion of private consumption. Regional gross fixed investment reached 23 per cent of GDP in 2011, exceeding its pre-crisis level. As a response to the worsening external environment, many countries have been adopting countercyclical fiscal policies by increasing public spending rather than lowering taxes. Indeed, some of them (including Brazil, Costa Rica, Chile, Colombia, Ecuador, El Salvador, Guatemala, Paraguay and Peru) have recently launched fiscal reforms aimed at increasing revenues to sustain government expenditure (ECLAC, 2012). Concerns about inflationary pressures that caused interest rates to rise in the first half of 2011 receded subsequently, which led to more accommodative monetary policies, particularly in the Bolivarian Republic of Venezuela, Brazil, Chile

and Paraguay. Some countries, such as Argentina and Brazil, complemented such policies with credit schemes to promote the financing of productive activities. These measures aim to safeguard the policy space generated in recent years through higher public revenues and macroprudential financial policies (including the management of volatile external capital flows), and to use it for supporting growth and employment.

Growth rates increased in *Africa* because of the continuing dynamism in sub-Saharan African economies and a partial recovery in the Northern African countries whose economies had been strongly affected by internal conflicts in 2011. However, it will be difficult for the latter countries to return to their 2010 GDP levels before 2013 owing to a slow revival of their tourism revenues, high unemployment and the recession in Europe which is an important market for them. In South Africa, strong growth in public investment continued to support economic activities in early 2012. However, private investment, and to a lesser extent household consumption, have been showing signs of slowing down since early 2012. More generally, the weaker global environment is also taking its toll on several African economies, particularly those that are more dependent on developed-country markets. In addition, some mineral-exporting countries have witnessed a cooling off of external demand from some large emerging economies, though to a lesser extent. Nevertheless, the external and fiscal balances of many economies continue to be supported by relatively high prices of primary commodities. In addition, a few African countries have also benefited from the exploitation of mining, oil and gas deposits. In contrast to the bleak external conditions, domestic economic activities remain dynamic in many African economies. In sub-Saharan Africa, public spending and the services sector, particularly transport and telecommunications, continue to register robust growth. In parallel, investment in infrastructure and in natural resources has also been supporting domestic expenditure and growth.

Although it remains the fastest growing region, *Asia* is experiencing an economic slowdown, its GDP growth rate having fallen from 6.8 per cent to around 5.5 per cent in 2012. Several countries, including China, India and Turkey, have been negatively affected by weaker demand from developed countries and by the monetary tightening they applied in 2011 for curbing inflation and rising asset prices. Given the headwinds from the international economy, they have since relaxed monetary conditions and several countries have applied countercyclical measures. Regional growth has been driven mainly by high levels of investment and by the continuing expansion of household incomes and consumption, thereby reflecting a rebalancing of the sources of growth from external to domestic demand.

Within Asia, *East Asia* remains the fastest growing subregion, even though economic activity has moderated since mid-2011. In China, the recent easing of credit amidst a property market downturn, combined with a slightly more expansionary fiscal policy stance, is projected to maintain growth close to 8 per cent in 2012. Rising real wages will also support private domestic consumption. By contrast, Taiwan Province of China is forecast to experience a marked decline in annual GDP growth in 2012, owing to its strong exposure to developed economies and its smaller domestic market. In *South Asia*, India's recent slowdown also reflects decelerating private domestic demand, particularly investment, as a result of aggressive monetary tightening. In *South East Asia*, some highly export-oriented economies registered low quarterly GDP growth in late 2011 and early 2012. On the other hand, populous economies of this subregion continue to experience robust domestic demand. For example, in Indonesia, which is one of the world's fastest growing economies, the unemployment rate declined further in early 2012. In Thailand, a large increase in fiscal spending is expected, which will support economic activity in the country, as the Government invests heavily in post-flood reconstruction activities. In *West Asia*, there are indications of a substantial slowing down of economic growth in 2012 owing partly to lower public spending in some of the countries compared with the exceptionally high levels of such spending in 2011. Moreover, conflict in the Syrian Arab Republic is strongly affecting its economy, and higher import bills in the oil-importing economies have been dragging down domestic demand. On the other hand, in the oil-exporting countries continuing high oil prices should allow them to resume strong public spending if necessary, and boost private consumption.

The *transition economies* have been maintaining a growth rate of over 4 per cent. This is entirely due to the dynamism of members of the Commonwealth of Independent States (CIS), given that the countries of South-Eastern European continue to suffer from

the impact of economic recession in the EU. Growth in the CIS is based on strong domestic demand, spurred by gains from the terms of trade and/or workers' remittances. In the Russian Federation, private consumption and fixed investment supported growth despite near record capital outflows of over $84 billion in 2011 (Bank of Russia database). On the supply side, the recovery of agriculture has also played a significant role. In the central Asian CIS economies, growth continued to be strong as a result of relatively high commodity prices and increased public spending on infrastructure.

Summing up, most developing and transition economies have supported their GDP growth by encouraging domestic demand, and pursuing countercyclical policies, including the provision of fiscal stimulus and expansionary credit. They have also succeeded in preventing a significant rise in unemployment, and their incomes policies have enabled a continued growth of real wages. All this, together with public transfers in several countries, has promoted private consumption, and consequently, productive investment, even though in some countries this has not been sufficient to avoid a deceleration.

However, the developing and transition economies cannot avoid the impacts of economic troubles in the developed countries. This is already reflected in stagnating export volumes to those markets and a declining trend in commodity prices since the second quarter of 2011. Moreover, financial instability in developed countries is affecting financial flows to emerging market economies and adding to the inherent volatility of commodity prices. In several developing countries, excessive short-term capital inflows have had a negative impact on their exchange rates and competitiveness, prompting them to take measures to manage capital flows. Finally, the risk of a new major shock in global financial markets cannot be excluded, with its associated impacts on international trade volumes, asset and commodity prices, risk spreads, capital flows and exchange rates, all of which would affect developing and transition economies (Akyüz, 2012). These countries should continue to preserve their fiscal and financial room for manoeuvre, including by strengthening public revenues; capital and exchange rate management in order to avoid currency overvaluation and artificial credit booms; maintaining foreign currency reserves at an appropriate level for covering their precautionary needs; and enhancing regional monetary and financial cooperation.

2. International trade

Growth of world *merchandise trade* slowed down significantly to around 5.5 per cent in 2011, after a sharp rebound in 2010 when it grew by 14 per cent in volume (table 1.2). Moreover, available data for the first months of 2012 point to a further deceleration to around 3.5 per cent for the whole year (chart 1.2). These rates are well below the pre-crisis level of trade expansion of 8 per cent, on average, between 2003 and 2007.

The slowdown is largely the result of the weak performance of developed economies, which remain the major participants in world trade even though their aggregate share in total trade declined from 69 per cent in 1995 to 55 per cent in 2010 (UN/DESA, 2012a). Slow economic growth in these countries has dampened their imports, which grew by only 3.5 per cent (by volume) in 2011. Indeed, the recovery of trade flows from the slump of 2009 appeared to have ended by mid-2011, and the volume of imports has remained stagnant since then. Exports have performed slightly better, growing at 5.1 per cent in 2011 as a result of the rising, albeit recently decelerating, demand from the developing and transition economies. Among the developed countries, exports from the United States continued to grow at a faster rate than those from Japan, as the latter were affected by supply disruptions due to natural disasters in 2011. In the EU, intraregional trade, which accounts for a large proportion of member countries' trade has suffered as a result of the region's current economic recession. Viewed over a longer period, since 2006 the trade volume of this group of countries has almost stagnated: in the first months of 2012 compared with 2006, EU exports were only 8 per cent higher and imports were roughly at the same level (chart 1.2).

Faced with weak external demand from developed countries and heightened global uncertainties, export growth in developing countries and economies in transition also registered a deceleration in 2011, to 7 per cent and 6 per cent respectively. Sluggish demand from developed countries has primarily affected exporters of manufactures in developing countries, though increased South-South trade has partly counterbalanced this deceleration (UN/DESA, 2012a). However, the slowdown is expected to persist or even worsen in 2012 owing to the near-zero growth of imports expected in Europe, which is the largest trading partner for many developing countries. Some Asian developing countries will be the worst affected by the sluggish demand from developed countries because their exports – mostly manufactures – are highly dependent on developed-country markets. South Asia and West Asia have been the exceptions, as their exports actually accelerated in 2011, but this is somewhat misleading, as this increase was from low levels in 2010 when some large economies in these regions, such as India and Turkey, failed to bounce back above the levels they had registered in 2008. Overall, monthly data for late 2011 and early 2012 indicate a decelerating trend for exports from developing Asia, including South and West Asia: in April 2012, export levels for the whole region were only about 2 per cent higher year on year.

In the other developing regions as well as the transition economies, export volumes also slowed down significantly during the first half of 2011, but prospects seem better for 2012. Exports from Africa, Latin America and the transition economies increased well above the world average in the first months of 2012, on a year-on-year basis. This seems to reflect the higher resilience of demand for primary commodities, especially energy and food, owing to continued growth in many developing-country markets and also to the low elasticity of demand for these goods in developed countries. Imports grew significantly faster than exports in the commodity-exporting countries in these regions. These countries benefited from significant gains from the terms of trade in 2011, as the purchasing power of their exports increased well above what their volume growth would have allowed. The reverse occurred in most Asian countries, where the volume of imports grew slower than that of exports (table 1.2).

The year-on-year growth of *commercial services* (at current prices) also experienced a marked slowdown to 3 per cent for two consecutive quarters in late 2011 and early 2012, after having registered double-digit growth rates during the first three quarters of 2011 (UNCTAD/WTO, 2012). Travel and tourism services, which account for approximately a quarter of the trade in services, grew by 4.6 per cent in volume (measured by the number of arrivals), down from 6.4 per cent in 2010. Unlike overall economic activities, international tourism arrivals were particularly robust in Southern Europe, where they grew by 7.7 per cent. The prospects for tourism in 2012 also contrast with those for merchandise trade. Indeed,

Table 1.2

EXPORT AND IMPORT VOLUMES OF GOODS, SELECTED REGIONS AND COUNTRIES, 2008–2011

(Annual percentage change)

Region/country	Volume of exports				Volume of imports			
	2008	2009	2010	2011	2008	2009	2010	2011
World	**2.4**	**-13.1**	**13.9**	**5.9**	**2.5**	**-13.4**	**14.1**	**5.0**
Developed countries	**2.5**	**-15.2**	**13.2**	**5.1**	**-0.2**	**-14.5**	**11.0**	**3.5**
of which:								
Japan	2.3	-24.9	27.5	-0.4	-0.6	-12.4	10.1	1.9
United States	5.5	-14.9	15.3	7.2	-3.7	-16.4	14.8	3.8
European Union	2.4	-14.3	12.0	6.0	0.8	-14.2	10.0	3.2
Transition economies	**-0.2**	**-14.4**	**11.5**	**6.0**	**15.5**	**-28.6**	**15.5**	**17.0**
of which:								
CIS	-2.6	-11.4	13.3	2.3	22.0	-32.5	18.2	19.1
Developing countries	**3.2**	**-9.7**	**15.4**	**7.0**	**6.6**	**-9.9**	**19.2**	**6.2**
Africa	-3.1	-9.7	8.7	-5.1	10.6	-3.9	7.1	3.9
Sub-Saharan Africa	-4.1	-8.0	10.2	2.9	3.2	-4.4	8.8	7.0
Latin America and the Caribbean	-0.3	-11.0	10.3	3.4	8.5	-17.9	23.3	7.1
East Asia	7.3	-10.6	23.8	9.9	0.4	-5.3	25.0	7.5
of which:								
China	10.6	-13.9	29.0	12.8	2.3	-1.8	30.8	10.6
South Asia	6.8	-6.0	6.0	9.1	20.9	-5.6	13.9	4.1
of which:								
India	16.8	-6.6	5.9	13.7	20.7	-0.8	13.8	5.3
South-East Asia	1.6	-10.9	18.8	4.5	8.0	-16.3	21.9	6.1
West Asia	4.4	-1.1	2.6	12.7	12.5	-11.5	5.4	3.8

Source: UNCTAD secretariat calculations, based on *UNCTADstat*.

Chart 1.2

WORLD TRADE BY VOLUME, JANUARY 2000–APRIL 2012

(Index numbers, 2000 = 100)

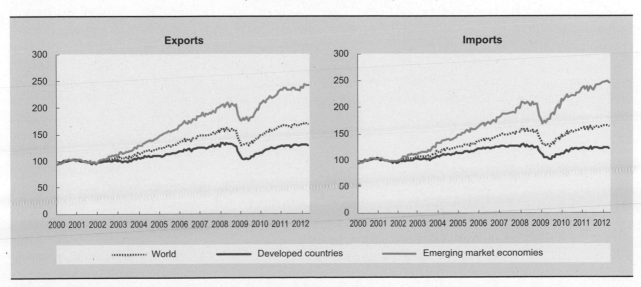

Source: UNCTAD secretariat calculations, based on the CPB Netherlands Bureau of Economic Policy Analysis, *World Trade* database.
Note: Emerging market economies excludes Central and Eastern Europe.

in the first four months of 2012, tourism grew by 5.4 per cent year on year, mainly due to accelerating tourist activities in North America, North-East Asia and Western Europe (World Tourism Organization, 2012). Thus growth of international tourism is likely to remain stable in 2012, if not slightly higher than in 2011.

Transport services, the second largest category of commercial services, also decelerated in 2011. World seaborne trade grew by about 4 per cent in 2011 compared with 7 per cent in 2010, according to preliminary estimates. Growth was mainly due to a robust increase in container and dry bulk trade, which took the total volume of goods loaded worldwide to 8.7 billion tons (UNCTAD, 2012a). By contrast, oil trade, which accounts for about one third of total seaborne trade, expanded by less than 1 per cent. The share of developing countries in world seaborne trade has also been on the rise, reflecting their growing contribution to world gross product and merchandise trade (UN/DESA, 2012a). In 2011, 57 per cent of total world seaborne trade (by volume) was delivered in developing countries while 60 per cent of this trade originated from them. Geographically, Asia maintained its lead position in seaborne trade, with its share of goods unloaded amounting to 56 per cent, and the share of goods loaded reaching 39 per cent. In addition, the surge in China's demand for imported industrial commodities since 2000 has heightened its need to diversify the sources of supply, including from distant locations such as Brazil, South Africa and the United States. The estimated average distance of global iron ore trade, for instance, increased by about 15 per cent between 1998 and 2011, and is expected to increase further as new mines in the Arctic and West Africa are exploited (UNCTAD, 2012a).

Trends in the *terms of trade* show increasing divergences across different groups of developing countries over the past few years. Since 2002, developing countries that have a high share of oil and mineral and mining products in their total merchandise exports have gained the most from higher commodity prices compared with those of manufactures (chart 1.3A). Given that most of these countries are transition economies or are located in Africa, Latin America or West Asia, they have contributed to these regions experiencing the greatest improvements in their terms of trade (chart 1.3B). In those countries where fuel exports account for the largest share of their total exports, the terms of

trade more than doubled between 2002 and 2011. By contrast, developing countries that have a large share of manufactures in their total exports, many of which are located in East or South-East Asia, experienced deteriorating terms of trade. This is partly due to the rising prices of their commodity imports, but also to the declining prices of manufactures exported by these countries relative to manufactures exported by developed countries. These divergent trends continued in 2011 as the prices of developing countries' exports of oil and mineral and mining products reached record high levels, while exporters of manufactures and net food importers experienced further deterioration in their terms of trade. Nevertheless, these trends are showing a pause or a moderate reversal in 2012, as many commodity prices have been falling since mid-2011 and might, on average, lead to levels slightly lower than those in 2011, as discussed in next section.

Turning to country-specific evidence, among the countries that have a dominant share of minerals and mining products in their exports, exporters of copper and/or gold (e.g. Chile, Peru and South Africa) have been seeing a very strong improvement in their terms of trade since 2004 (except for 2009). For these countries, the positive effect of the surge in international prices of copper and gold exceeded the combined negative effects of rising oil prices and adverse movements in the prices of manufactures.

Terms-of-trade developments have varied widely among economies where agricultural commodities have dominated their total merchandise exports, owing to a combination of three factors: differences in price movements of specific agricultural products; differences in the share of other primary commodities in total exports across countries; and differences in the share of oil in their imports. Two countries in the group of agricultural commodity exporters that witnessed increases in their terms of trade, Argentina and Uruguay, benefited from higher prices of soybeans, beef and some cereals. In Argentina, this trend has been strengthened by exports of oil (until 2010) and mining products, although the impact of higher prices of these product categories has been dampened by increases in the prices of imported manufactures.

On the other hand, some fuel-importing developing countries whose merchandise exports are dominated by manufactures, such as India and the Republic of Korea, have seen deteriorating terms

Chart 1.3

NET BARTER TERMS OF TRADE, 2000–2011

(Index numbers, 2000 = 100)

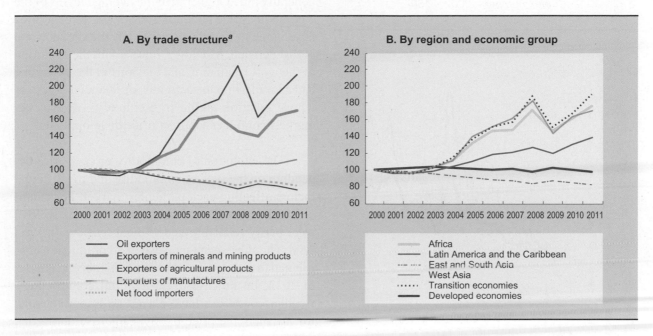

A. By trade structure[a]

- Oil exporters
- Exporters of minerals and mining products
- Exporters of agricultural products
- Exporters of manufactures
- Net food importers

B. By region and economic group

- Africa
- Latin America and the Caribbean
- East and South Asia
- West Asia
- Transition economies
- Developed economies

Source: UNCTAD secretariat calculations, based on UNCTADstat.
Note: Net food importers are low-income food-deficit countries, excluding exporters of fuels, metal and mining products.
   a Data refer to developing and transition economies.

of trade. This has been largely due to their heavy dependence on fuel and mineral imports, and sometimes to the relative decline in the prices of their exports of manufactures.

The combined effect of the lower prices of exports of labour-intensive manufactures and higher prices of commodity imports has been less pronounced in countries that have become exporters of manufactures but remain sensitive to fluctuations in the prices of specific primary commodities. This is the case, in particular, for some countries in Latin America (e.g. Brazil, Colombia and Mexico) and East Asia (e.g. Indonesia), as well as South Africa. In many of them, price movements in the different product categories neutralized each other in their impact on the terms of trade. In Mexico, the Russian Federation and Saudi Arabia, where fuels account for a sizeable share of total merchandise exports, the positive contribution of higher fuel prices largely compensated for the negative impact of the falling prices of manufacturing exports and/or rising prices of food imports on the terms of trade.

These examples illustrate the diversity of the impact of recent international price movements on the terms of trade of developing countries. The variations in the global pattern of demand and their impact on individual countries have led to a redistribution of income, not only between developing and developed countries, but also, increasingly, among different groups of developing countries.

3. Commodity markets

(a) Recent trends in commodity prices

Commodity prices have remained high and volatile in 2011 and the first half of 2012 (chart 1.4). However, they have been exhibiting a declining trend after peaking during the first months of 2011, oil being an exception to this general trend. The prices of commodities briefly rebounded at the turn of the year only to drop again in the second quarter of 2012.

Chart 1.4

MONTHLY COMMODITY PRICE INDICES
BY COMMODITY GROUP, JAN. 2002–MAY 2012

(Index numbers, 2002 = 100)

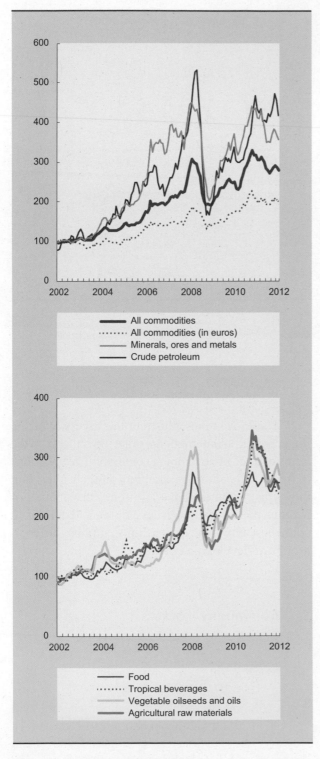

Source: UNCTAD secretariat calculations, based on UNCTAD,
Commodity Price Statistics Online database.
Note: Crude petroleum price is the average of Dubai/Brent/
Texas, equally weighted. Index numbers are based on
prices in current dollars, unless otherwise specified.

The magnitude of the price declines in the first half
of 2012 by commodity compared to their last peaks
is shown in table 1.3.[3] The last column of this table
also shows that in 2011-2012 commodity prices were
generally much higher than the average levels of the
commodity price boom of 2003-2008. Recent price
developments have been marked by the slowdown in
global demand. Moreover, news about the evolution
of the world economy and tensions in the euro zone
had an impact on the activities of financial investors
whose position-taking in commodity derivatives
markets continues to affect price developments.[4]

The evolution of commodity prices varies depending on the type of commodity and the different
factors affecting each particular market. For example, with regard to oil, price increases in early 2012
were partly related to geopolitical tensions in West
Asia. The subsequent increase in oil production contributed to a decline in oil prices in the second quarter
of 2012. In the case of agricultural commodities,
weather conditions have played an important role;
for instance, the price of soybeans rose during the
first half of 2012 due to reduced harvests associated
with dry weather conditions in South America and
more recently in the United States. Positive expectations regarding corn crop yields based on a record
planting season were reversed towards mid-2012
owing to a severe drought in the United States. As
a result, prices of corn and soybeans reached record
levels by July 2012. Similarly, the price of wheat
has been affected recently by unfavourable weather in the Black Sea area. The rapid increase in food
prices has raised fears of the possibility of a renewal of the global food crisis of 2008. However, so far
inventories of the most important commodities for
food security, rice and wheat, are not as dramatically low as they were at that time.

The fact that price movements continue to be
heavily influenced by the strong presence of financial investors in commodity markets is reflected
in an almost 40-fold increase in commodity assets
under management between 2001 and 2011. Indeed,
the price reductions in 2011 and 2012 have been
accompanied by a large decline in positions taken
by financial investors. The year 2011 was the weak-
est for commodity investment flows since 2002, and
also the most volatile (Mohammadian-Molina, 2012).
After briefly rebounding in early 2012, commodity
investments turned negative in the second quarter.
According to Barclays Capital (2012a), investors

Table 1.3

WORLD PRIMARY COMMODITY PRICES, 2006–2012
(Percentage change over previous year, unless otherwise indicated)

Commodity groups	2006	2007	2008	2009	2010	2011	2012[a]	Change from last peak[b]	2011–2012 versus 2003–2008[c]
All commodities[d]	**30.2**	**13.0**	**24.0**	**-16.9**	**18.2**	**17.4**	**-6.5**	**-15.2**	**70.8**
All commodities (in SDRs)[d]	**30.5**	**8.6**	**19.5**	**-14.5**	**19.5**	**13.5**	**-4.2**	**-13.5**	**64.1**
All food	**16.3**	**13.3**	**39.2**	**-8.5**	**7.4**	**17.8**	**-3.6**	**-9.5**	**77.9**
Food and tropical beverages	**17.8**	**8.6**	**40.4**	**-5.4**	**5.6**	**16.5**	**-3.6**	**-8.6**	**77.7**
Tropical beverages	6.7	10.4	20.2	1.9	17.5	26.8	-17.1	-26.9	97.5
Coffee	7.1	12.5	15.4	-6.9	27.3	42.9	-18.5	-31.8	124.7
Cocoa	3.5	22.6	32.2	11.9	8.5	-4.9	-22.1	-33.4	52.4
Tea	11.7	-12.3	27.2	16.5	-1.0	11.4	-1.7	-7.4	55.1
Food	19.0	8.5	42.5	-6.0	4.4	15.4	-2.1	-6.7	75.8
Sugar	49.4	-31.7	26.9	41.8	17.3	22.2	-11.3	-29.7	144.1
Beef	-2.4	1.9	2.6	-1.2	27.5	20.0	4.7	-3.8	62.8
Maize	24.4	38.2	34.0	-24.4	13.2	50.1	-5.0	-13.8	106.3
Wheat	26.6	34.3	27.5	-31.4	3.3	35.1	-12.1	-23.1	48.3
Rice	5.5	9.5	110.7	-15.8	-11.5	5.9	3.7	-0.7	61.8
Bananas	18.5	-0.9	24.6	0.7	3.7	10.8	5.0	17.0	61.5
Vegetable oilseeds and oils	**5.0**	**52.9**	**31.9**	**-28.4**	**22.7**	**27.2**	**-3.7**	**-15.4**	**78.9**
Soybeans	-2.2	43.0	36.1	-16.6	3.1	20.2	-0.1	-0.3	60.5
Agricultural raw materials	**13.3**	**12.0**	**20.5**	**-17.5**	**38.3**	**28.1**	**-15.9**	**-28.4**	**89.1**
Hides and skins	5.1	4.5	-11.3	-30.0	60.5	14.0	-2.5	-4.6	20.2
Cotton	5.9	10.2	12.8	-12.2	65.3	47.5	-36.2	-61.5	120.9
Tobacco	6.4	11.6	8.3	18.0	1.8	3.8	-2.1	-5.3	47.9
Rubber	40.6	9.5	16.9	-27.0	90.3	32.0	-20.7	-37.2	154.0
Tropical logs	-4.7	19.5	39.3	-20.6	1.8	13.8	-4.2	-10.7	32.4
Minerals, ores and metals	**60.3**	**12.8**	**6.2**	**-30.3**	**33.7**	**12.7**	**-7.7**	**-19.3**	**53.7**
Aluminium	35.4	2.7	-2.5	-35.3	30.5	10.4	-11.8	-24.9	8.3
Phosphate rock	5.3	60.5	387.2	-64.8	1.1	50.3	2.8	-13.6	92.3
Iron ore	..	77.4	26.8	-48.7	82.4	15.0	-15.4	-27.0	37.9
Tin	18.9	65.6	27.3	-26.7	50.4	28.0	-14.8	-37.3	139.4
Copper	82.7	5.9	-2.3	-26.3	47.0	17.1	-6.8	-19.7	78.1
Nickel	64.5	53.5	-43.3	-30.6	48.9	5.0	-18.0	-39.8	7.7
Lead	32.0	100.2	-19.0	-17.7	25.0	11.8	-13.9	-27.3	65.8
Zinc	137.0	-1.0	-42.2	-11.7	30.5	1.5	-8.8	-21.7	10.0
Gold	35.9	15.3	25.1	11.6	26.1	27.8	5.9	-10.5	182.5
Crude petroleum[e]	**20.4**	**10.7**	**36.4**	**-36.3**	**28.0**	**31.4**	**6.9**	**-11.6**	**80.5**
Memo item:									
Manufactures[f]	**3.4**	**7.5**	**4.9**	**-5.6**	**1.9**	**8.4**	**..**	**..**	**..**

Source: UNCTAD secretariat calculations, based on UNCTAD, *Commodity Price Statistics Online*; and United Nations Statistics Division (UNSD), *Monthly Bulletin of Statistics*, various issues.

Note: In current dollars unless otherwise specified.

  a Percentage change between the average for the period January to May 2012 and the average for 2011.
  b Percentage change between May 2012 and the last monthly peak.
  c Percentage change between the 2003–2008 average and the 2011–2012 average.
  d Excluding crude petroleum.
  e Average of Brent, Dubai and West Texas Intermediate, equally weighted.
  f Unit value of exports of manufactured goods of developed countries.

withdrew $8.2 billion from commodity investments in May 2012 in what was described as "something approaching a stampede ... evoking memories of 2008".[5] Overall, total commodity assets under management were down $28 billion from an all-time high of about $450 billion reached in April 2011 (Barclays Capital, 2012b). A recent illustration of the influence of financial investors on commodity markets is the rally in the oil markets following the agreement reached in the euro zone in late June 2012 on bank recapitalization, when the price of Brent oil rose 7 per cent in one day – an increase that could hardly be justified by fundamental supply and demand changes. The sharp increases in corn and soybean prices at the end of June 2012 would also appear to be partly related to the reaction of financial investors to the news of hot weather affecting harvests.[6]

These short-term price developments have revived the debate about long-term commodity price trends. The commodity price boom that started in the early 2000s and continued at least until 2011 – with the exception of the crisis-related break of 2008-2009 – is viewed as a new super-cycle (i.e. a trend rise in real prices of a broad range of commodities that lasts for one to two decades and is driven by urbanization and industrialization in at least one major economy). A high and growing intensity of the use of metals (i.e. the volume of metals consumed per unit of output) is often taken as an indicator of a commodity super-cycle (*TDR 2005*: 46–51).[7] However, the recent turnaround of the upward trend in commodity prices in the context of slower global economic growth may be an indication that the current commodity super-cycle is coming to an end.

Some of the factors contributing to the upward phase of the current commodity super-cycle have not disappeared, especially rapid and resilient economic growth in several major developing countries and their continuous need for investment in infrastructure and construction. In particular, China's robust demand for commodities has been a strong factor influencing the super-cycle. However, there are increasing concerns that it may be fading. There is disagreement as to whether China's high rate of fixed investment will be maintained with the same intensity of commodity demand growth per unit of output growth. There is a possibility that the expected slowdown in China's infrastructure and real estate sectors will mark an end to the commodity super-cycle (Credit Suisse, 2012). More generally, it is

widely expected that the continued sluggish growth performance of the major developed countries will cause the post-crisis slowdown in China's export growth to remain subdued for quite some time. It is uncertain whether China's investment boom in infrastructure and commercial real estate, much of it due to the Government's post-crisis stimulus package (Cai, Wang and Zhang, 2010), can continue to compensate for the associated decline in aggregate demand growth indefinitely.[8] Strong domestic private and public consumption may sustain high growth rates, although that growth may involve less intensive use of certain types of commodity inputs. This would mean that China's contribution to the favourable conditions in global non-food commodity markets, and especially in base metals markets, may decline. In addition, some investment projects initiated during the years of rising prices may now begin to generate an increase in commodity supplies, which will ease the pressure on commodity prices.

As a result, it is rather uncertain whether the combination of sustained demand growth and constraints on supply expansion on which the commodity super-cycle has been based – and whose price effects have been amplified by financial speculators on commodity markets – will last much longer. As such, this would affect, in particular, base metals and perhaps also energy. Although continuing growth in East and South Asia and in other regions of the developing world is likely to prevent a significant fall in the demand for primary commodities, it is unlikely that future commodity price developments will show a stable upward trend. Therefore, commodity producing countries should not take rising commodity prices for granted and become complacent about policies towards diversification and industrialization.

(b) Distributional implications of commodity price developments

Regardless of what the future evolution of commodity prices might be, the persistence of high and volatile prices in recent years raises a number of issues relating to inequality and distributional aspects. Commodity price movements create winners and losers between and within countries. At the country level, rising prices of certain commodities led to higher export earnings and growth rates in the countries that produced and exported those commodities in the 2000s. However, the impact on domestic inequality in those exporting countries is unclear: on the one hand, rising commodity prices improves their fiscal space enabling them to apply redistributive policies; but on the other hand it is likely that only a small number of private owners of natural resources are the main beneficiaries. By contrast, commodity-importing developing countries have been burdened with rising import bills, particularly for food and fuel. This may limit their capacity to import capital goods and inputs, which are essential for their development.[9]

In addition, this tends to impose a much heavier burden on most household budgets in developing countries than in developed countries. In the poorest countries, food can account for up to 80 per cent of household expenditure. Thus rising food prices may cause the poorest households not only to reduce their nutrient intake, but also to cut down on other basic expenditures, such as on health care or education. They may also be forced to sell assets that provide them with the means for improving both their current and future income, thereby plunging them into a poverty trap and exacerbating income inequality that will be difficult to reverse.[10]

According to World Bank estimates, the international food price spike of 2007-2008 kept or pushed 105 million people below the poverty line, and the 2010-2011 spike similarly affected 48.6 million people (World Bank, 2012). In 2011 and the first half of 2012, the most dramatic situations in this regard were the famines in the Horn of Africa and the Sahel region of West Africa. While drought was the main cause of these emergency situations, the alarming hunger problem is compounded by the high food prices in international markets and worsened by conflicts. Yet many of the concerned countries cannot afford the necessary additional social expenditure to tackle hunger and malnutrition unless they reduce spending for other purposes, including urgent infrastructure investments. This dilemma suggests the need for additional external assistance to overcome this distribution problem in the poorer countries.

Indeed, in response to the global food crisis, G-8 leaders meeting at the summit in L'Aquila in 2009 pledged to increase aid to agriculture and committed to respect country-owned plans, with priority given to public investment to benefit smallholder farmers. However, only 22 per cent of the $22 billion pledged over three years had been actually spent in the first two years. The prospects for aid to agriculture, and for development aid more generally, are grim in the context of current fiscal austerity programmes in developed countries. Moreover, the announcement of the New Alliance for Food Security and Nutrition at the G-8 summit in May 2012 offers much lower investment pledges and gives greater emphasis to private agribusiness investment. Public and private investment may be complementary, but the goals of agribusiness, which focus on profits, do not necessarily correspond with the interests of smallholder farmers in improving income and food security, and neither do they necessarily help reduce poverty (AfricaFocus, 2012).[11]

The effects of commodity price developments on growth have often been accompanied by adverse distributional impacts. Even in commodity-producing developing countries where higher commodity prices boosted growth performance, the resulting gains did not spread sufficiently to benefit the overall population. One reason is that the ownership of natural resources is typically less equally distributed than that of other assets. Commodity production and their trade are dominated by large transnational corporations (TNCs) and trading companies.[12] In this context, it is often the large TNCs – and financial investors – that capture most of the gains from the commodity price increases, and few go to the commodity producers and workers in this sector, or even to the governments of the producing countries.[13]

As a result of high food prices and global food security concerns, there has been a rush by foreign investors for large-scale land acquisitions (or leases) in developing countries in the past few years, with potentially negative effects on land distribution and food security. Different actors, such as sovereign wealth funds, investment and pension funds, food corporations and large agricultural producers and landowners, have shown an increasing interest in acquiring or leasing land. This land rush is motivated mainly by widespread expectations of robust demand for food crops on account of population growth, strong growth in emerging markets and continuing increases in demand for biofuels, in addition to seeking higher returns and diversification of investment. Some governments in food-importing countries have also been investing in land abroad with the main goal of assuring their national food security.

A comprehensive assessment of the scale of these operations is complicated by the fact that many of these deals are rather opaque. Nevertheless, available evidence suggests that there has been a very large and rapid increase in these land investment deals, particularly since the 2007-2008 food crisis, and that they are set to continue. For example, according to Oxfam (2011), as many as 227 million hectares of land have been sold or leased in developing countries since 2001. Other estimates are lower, such as that of the International Land Coalition which suggests a figure of approximately 80 million hectares since 2000 (HLPE, 2011).[14] These deals, many of which are in Africa, often take place against payment of very low fees.

The trend in large-scale land acquisitions – commonly dubbed "land grabs" – can offer opportunities for developing countries, but it also poses significant challenges. On the one hand, in theory, they could provide a push to investment in agriculture after many decades of underinvestment, potentially leading to improvements in technology and infrastructure as well as promoting job creation. On the other hand, concerns have been raised about the challenges and risks they pose, particularly for small farmers and food security in developing countries. There are indications that most of the gains from this investment in land are captured by the investors and are not fairly distributed among the population in the host developing countries. It is hard to see how alleged benefits, for example in terms of employment generation or improved food security, would materialize, as most of this investment relates to crops for export which involve highly mechanized farming. In addition, since land rights are weak in many developing countries, poor smallholder farmers are very vulnerable to the increasing pressures and competition for land. In particular, they risk being displaced from their lands without receiving appropriate compensation, if any. Therefore this investment generally leads to rising concentration of land in a few hands.[15]

There have been a number of initiatives to address these issues and guarantee that land investments respect land rights and do not harm smallholder production – which constitutes a large share of agriculture in many developing countries – or food security. In May 2012, the United Nations Committee on World Food Security adopted *Voluntary Guidelines on the Responsible Governance of Tenure of Land, Fisheries and Forests in the Context of National Food Security*. In addition, UNCTAD, together with the FAO, the International Fund for Agricultural Development (IFAD) and the World Bank, has been participating in the development of the *Principles for Responsible Agricultural Investment that Respects Rights, Livelihoods and Resources*.[16] These are examples of some initial steps that are being taken to provide governments in developing countries with an appropriate framework for ensuring that land investments are made to be truly conducive to inclusive development.

Proactive policies are also needed in order to prevent rising inequality that may result from the current high prices of mineral and fuel commodities. Indeed, there are several distributional challenges associated with the extractive industries in terms of income inequality, regional asymmetries and intergenerational distribution. As they are capital-intensive, they create relatively little direct employment. Moreover, mineral and fuel production are generally geographically concentrated and the infrastructure developed for exporting their production is usually of little use for other economic activities or for the physical integration of the country. In the absence of effective policies aimed at developing upstream and downstream productive linkages, there tends to be only modest indirect employment and income generated in the producing country. Furthermore, as these are non-renewable resources, their exploitation will not benefit future generations unless a significant share of the income generated is invested within the country.

The challenge for making resource-based activities a source of inclusive growth is therefore to pursue policies that enable all segments of the population to share the benefits derived from resource earnings. To achieve this goal, it is necessary to address the issue of the distribution of the revenues from extractive industries between TNCs, which control a large proportion of export activities in this sector, and the governments in the producing countries. Resource exploitation generates rents (i.e. the difference between the sales value and the cost of exploitation of the resources, including normal profits) which, if effectively used, can serve as a basis for structural change and increased fixed capital formation. This in turn would lead to the creation of employment opportunities. Sources of government revenues from the primary commodity sector may be royalties, taxation, joint ventures, or full public ownership of the operating firms (see also chapter V of this *Report*). In this context, and quite independently of short-term price developments, there is a fundamental need to achieve the right balance between the profitability of private investment, on the one hand, and government appropriation of a fair share of the rents accruing from the higher prices in the extractive industries on the other. Governments should avoid engaging in a "race to the bottom" in fiscal rules and environmental regulations in order to attract foreign direct investment.

Evidence indicates large variations in the distribution of the rents from extractive activities across countries and sectors, which reflect differences in the role of State-owned enterprises (SOEs) and fiscal regimes. In countries where SOEs play a major role in the extractive industries, the share of the rents captured by the governments is much higher than in countries where these companies have been privatized and where the fiscal treatment is relatively liberal (*TDR 2010*, chap. V).

A fair sharing of resource rents between the State and investors (foreign or domestic) may be best assured by country-specific agreements with room for occasional renegotiation. Otherwise, they may include flexibility to adapt to changing market conditions. Both developed and developing countries, as well as some transition economies, have recently modified their fiscal regimes governing rent sharing with a view to benefiting more from windfall profits.[17] These policies are normally easier to apply for producing countries when commodity prices rise or are

at historically high levels. Since TNCs cannot claim credit for the windfall gains, there is no economic or ethical reason for allowing them to appropriate those gains. As pointed out by the United Kingdom's Chancellor of the Exchequer, George Osborne, in justifying the Government's unilateral changing of the North Sea oil tax regime by imposing a supplementary charge on oil and gas production, "The oil companies are making unexpected profits on oil prices that are far higher than those they based their investment decisions on".[18]

By modifying their fiscal regimes to ensure more equitable rent sharing, governments can take advantage of favourable commodity price developments to achieve sustained and inclusive growth. In the long run, this goal is best achieved through policies that foster economic diversification and industrialization. The increase in government revenues can reduce income inequality and prevent deindustrialization through public investment and transfer payments that target those segments of the population that do not directly benefit from resource revenues. Policies should also aim at promoting industrial production, by encouraging exporting firms to add value locally and create a network of domestic suppliers, maintaining a competitive exchange rate and pursuing a monetary policy that stimulates private investment. Commodity-producing countries can also establish revenue stabilization funds, which could not only contribute to macroeconomic stability and intergenerational equity, but also minimize real exchange rate appreciation.

B. Economic challenges for the world economy and policy responses

1. The difficult path towards strong and balanced growth

Until the first half of 2009, governments of all the major economies responded to the economic and financial crisis by providing strong stimulus packages. The mix of policy tools varied from country to country. On the financial and monetary side, policies included the bailout of large financial institutions, the reduction of policy interest rates to historically low levels and the massive provision of liquidity in response to the freezing up of interbank credit. Some central banks interpreted their mandates broadly, providing direct support to their governments or to non-financial private agents. Many countries also relied on "automatic stabilizers" for increasing public expenditure and reducing tax collection. As all these policies were applied simultaneously in different countries, all the countries benefited from each other's stimulus measures, and the fall in GDP and international trade, albeit sharp, was relatively short-lived, especially in developing countries. This provided strong evidence of the power of economic synergies, and gave new impetus to forums for international economic cooperation such as the Group of 20 (G-20).

Leaders at the G-20 Summit in Pittsburgh in September 2009 reached a formal agreement to cooperate with a view to ensuring strong, sustainable and balanced global growth and to strengthening domestic and international financial systems. However, instead of continuing to provide general stimulus measures in order to sustain a global recovery that was still fragile, they agreed that strategies would vary across countries: those with external deficits would support private savings and undertake

fiscal consolidation, while surplus countries would strengthen domestic sources of growth. It was considered that, in principle this would be consistent with a benign rebalancing whereby stronger domestic demand in surplus countries would allow deficit countries to increase their exports. In actual fact, rebalancing has been only partial and is associated with weaker global growth. The main reason is that the policy shift towards higher public savings in developed countries with deficits took place before growth in private sector demand had a chance to recover. In addition, the stimulus packages provided by developed countries with surpluses have been meagre. At the G-20 summit in Toronto in June 2010, the developing and emerging country members with surpluses were encouraged to provide direct support to spur their domestic demand and imports, including through currency appreciation, whereas the developed-country members with surpluses were supposed to reach that goal by focusing on structural reforms that support increased domestic demand. As discussed below, such reforms cannot deliver rapid results, and, considering the nature of some of the suggested reforms, they are unlikely to boost demand.

The asymmetry in the policy approaches of the developed and developing countries is reflected in the different contributions to global rebalancing by Germany and China – the two major surplus countries in absolute terms. Germany's external surplus has shrunk only moderately since the crisis erupted, both in current prices and as a percentage of GDP (from 7.5 per cent in 2007 to an estimated 5.5 per cent in 2012). In addition, its net exports contributed to a significant share of Germany's overall growth in 2010 and 2011, while private consumption remained subdued. By contrast, China's current-account surplus declined from its peak of 10 per cent of GDP in 2007 to below 3 per cent in 2011 and 2012, and the contribution of its net exports to growth has been negligible since 2010. A fundamental rebalancing of the Chinese economy is under way, with an increasing reliance on domestic demand to spur growth (Lemoine and Ünal, 2012). However, internal rebalancing efforts remain unfinished, as private consumption has still to take on a greater role relative to investment. Rapid wage increases are supporting this internal goal while also promoting further external rebalancing.

In most developing and transition economies, the contribution of net exports to growth seems to have fallen dramatically since the start of the crisis. It was close to zero during the period 2010–2012 in developing Asia and Africa, and turned negative in Latin America and in the transition economies. By contrast, it rose significantly in the EU, where the volume of exports increased significantly more than that of imports. However, the contribution of net exports in the EU only partially compensated for the negative impact of falling domestic demand (chart 1.5).

In addition to changes in the volume of trade, price developments also had a significant impact on global imbalances. The reduction of such imbalances in 2009 had much to do with the fall in surpluses of the oil-exporting developing and transition economies, mirrored by lower deficits in the United States and Europe (excluding Germany). Due to the renewed oil price increase since mid-2009 and the sustained reduction of surpluses in China and Japan, the fuel-exporting countries were responsible in large part for the increasing global imbalances in 2010 and 2011 (chart 1.6). To some extent, rising oil prices have been dragging down global growth. This is because rising oil prices immediately affect aggregate spending in fuel-importing countries, while increased spending in fuel-exporting countries normally occurs only after a time lag. For some oil exporters, it is reasonable to maintain a certain level of surplus in the current account, as they cannot increase their imports beyond certain levels without incurring superfluous expenditure financed by a non-renewable resource, to the detriment of future generations.

Concerns about global imbalances have eased somewhat in the past year, owing to significant corrections in some major surplus countries (e.g. China and Japan) and in the largest deficit country (the United States), but related problems remain. While the euro zone as a whole is fairly balanced vis-à-vis the rest of the world, the persistent imbalances within the zone pose considerable risks (box 1.1). Additional risks stem from significant tensions related to international capital flows and exchange rates.

International capital flows have experienced wide gyrations, increasing sharply in the run-up to the financial and economic crisis and falling significantly (although with some exceptions) thereafter. International operations of banks reporting to the Bank for International Settlements (BIS) have involved mainly developed countries, as reflected in the distribution of their assets: 73 per cent of international bank claims were against debtors in developed economies in the first quarter of 2012, and this figure rises to 80 per cent if offshore centres are not taken into account.[19] However, changes in banks' assets in other regions, even if smaller in absolute terms, may have a strong macroeconomic impact in these countries given their fledgling financial and foreign exchange markets. Between the first quarter of 2002 and the first quarter of 2008, total international claims increased by 226 per cent to $28 trillion – a historical high, This rate was much higher for the new EU members[20] (630 per cent) and the transition economies (865 per cent); it was also extremely high for Greece, Ireland, Italy, Portugal and Spain (at almost 400 per cent). Between the first quarter of 2008 and that of 2012, international claims shrank globally by 16 per cent, with the strongest reductions in the developed and the transition economies (falling by 22 and 18 per cent respectively). Among the developed countries, the most severely hit were the European countries, particularly Greece, Ireland, Italy, Portugal and Spain, where international banks' assets halved. Even though part of this diminution was due to exchange rate movements,[21] sizeable credit reversals have been one of the major factors contributing to the fragility of their banking systems.

This contrasts with the continued increase in capital flows to developing countries, where the value of banks' assets had been increasing and registered a further 25 per cent rise between the first quarter of 2008 and the first quarter of 2012. In particular, in Latin America they increased by an average of 30 per cent for the whole region and by 55 per cent in Brazil. In developing Asia as a whole, they increased by an average of 21 per cent, and by as much as 80 per cent in China. A number of these countries face problems of a different kind, resulting from excessive capital inflows tending to exert appreciation pressures on

Chart 1.5

REAL GDP GROWTH AND CONTRIBUTIONS OF NET EXPORTS AND DOMESTIC DEMAND, SELECTED COUNTRY GROUPS, 2006–2012

(Per cent)

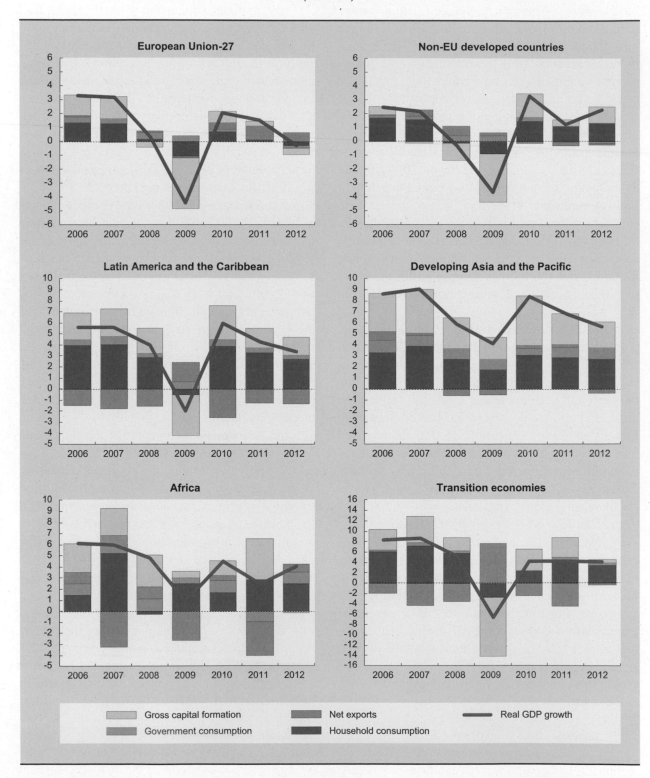

Source: UNCTAD secretariat calculations, based on table 1.1; UN/DESA, *National Accounts Main Aggregates* database; European Commission, *Annual macro-economic database* (*EC-AMECO*); ECLAC, *CEPALSTAT*; Economist Intelligence Unit (EIU) database; IMF, *World Economic Outlook*; and national sources.

Note: Data for 2011 are preliminary estimates and those for 2012 are forecasts.

their currencies. Some of these countries (most notably Brazil) contend that loose monetary policies adopted by the central banks of developed economies have had negative impacts on their macroeconomic stability and competitiveness. This implies a kind of "currency war", with developed countries seeking to recover some of their competitiveness at the expense of a number of more dynamic developing countries.

Tensions over exchange rates were exacerbated in the first half of 2011 due to tightening monetary policies in several emerging market economies. Those policies were aimed at curbing inflationary pressures stemming mainly from rising international prices of food and energy. Higher interest rates dampened domestic demand, and, as they attracted short-term capital, they also tended to put pressure on currency appreciation. This appreciation may have contributed to lowering inflation rates, but at a high cost to economic growth. As international growth decelerated and prices of commodities receded, policy goals shifted once more, from price stability to supporting growth. To this end, several countries, including Brazil, China, India and Turkey, cut their policy interest rates in 2011 and 2012, while Mexico maintained its rate at a historical low of 4.5 per cent. In addition to interest rate cuts or reduced reserve requirements, some countries have also adopted credit policies designed to support domestic demand more directly and effectively, especially investment. Development banks and other State-owned financial institutions have been playing an important role in this regard.

With lower interest rates and perhaps also greater risk aversion among financial investors owing to financial tensions in the euro zone, portfolio flows to developing countries receded somewhat in the first months of 2012. However, the negative impacts on developing and transition economies of repeated massive capital inflows followed by "sudden stops" showed the importance of adopting active capital management policies as part of macroprudential regulation. The G-20 agreement on capital flows of October 2011 explicitly acknowledges the need for the flexible use of capital-account management measures in containing the risks that may routinely arise in liberalized and integrated global financial markets. It suggests that the development and deepening of local capital and bond markets and the adoption of appropriate regulations and prudential practices will eventually enable developing countries

Chart 1.6

CURRENT-ACCOUNT BALANCES, SELECTED COUNTRIES AND COUNTRY GROUPS, 2005–2012

(Billions of current dollars)

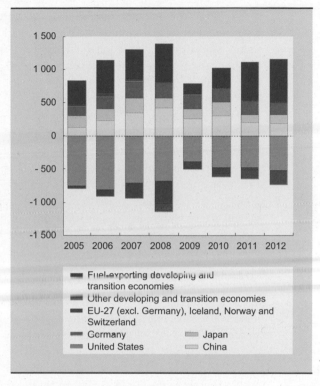

Source: UNCTAD secretariat calculations, based on UN/DESA, 2012b; IMF, *World Economic Outlook* (WEO) and *Balance of Payments Statistics* databases; and Economist Intelligence Unit (EIU) database.

Note: Data for 2012 are forecast.

to better absorb and handle volatile capital flows. But as the examples of Japan and Switzerland show, even countries with well-developed financial systems may have to intervene in foreign exchange markets in order to prevent undesired exchange rate movements and significant mispricing due to short-term capital movements. Against this background, the intention to "move towards more market-determined exchange rate systems, enhancing exchange rate flexibility to reflect underlying economic fundamentals" (G-20, 2011) seems to overlook the fact that capital movements have a much stronger influence on exchange rates than trade or current-account balances, and there is no reason to believe that they will reflect "economic fundamentals". Public intervention is needed to manage these capital flows and guide real exchange rates to sustainable levels. It seems, for instance, that the

Box 1.1

TRADE IMBALANCES AND THE EURO ZONE CRISIS

Serious intraregional divergences in competitiveness and the related build-up of regional imbalances have been the root cause of the crisis in the euro zone. Members of the currency union committed to a common low inflation rate, at "below but close to 2 percent". Members cannot stray for too long from their joint commitment to that common inflation rate without eventually undermining the union. Since wages are the most important determinant of prices, national wage trends, corrected for productivity growth (i.e. unit labour costs), must remain aligned to hold the European currency union together (Flassbeck, 2007).

In the event, lasting wage restraint in the largest member country, Germany, led to inflation differentials and had the following effects: in Germany, it caused a protracted stagnation of consumption and rising income inequality; for the union as a whole, trade imbalances built up as the low-inflation countries gained in competitiveness vis-à-vis those with high wage-price inflation. In a fiscal union, such trade imbalances can last for a long time if the surplus members finance the deficit members through fiscal transfers. In Europe's currency union, private debt flows provided the financial counterpart to rising trade imbalances, as banks in surplus countries, unable to expand business in their home markets, lent to willing borrowers and spenders in the deficit countries instead (Bibow, 2007 and 2012).

The private lending flows upon which unbalanced European growth had come to depend stopped abruptly when lenders harboured doubts about the solvency of their borrowers. The global crisis merely acted as the trigger that turned home-grown housing booms and bubbles into busts across Europe. The ending of the private debt bonanzas then resulted in a sequence of debt crises, as the original household debt overhangs turned into banking crises, which eventually morphed into sovereign debt crises. In treating the symptom of sovereign debt crises by prescribing ever higher doses of austerity, the European authorities are upping the ante: with draconian retrenchment pushing debtor countries into debt deflation, contagion across a deeply interconnected regional economy that lacks a solid fiscal backstop risks choking regional growth, with debt sustainability becoming a threat for the currency union as a whole.

Flaws in the original design of the currency union are partly to blame: demand management was not envisaged, and proactive macroeconomic policies have been generally frowned upon. Moreover, no proper policy coordination is taking place. By restricting fiscal transfers, but failing to forestall intra-area imbalances that would make such transfers indispensable, the currency union has manoeuvred itself into the current impasse. At present, by putting the burden of rebalancing disproportionately on the shoulders of deficit countries, the European authorities increase the cost of rebalancing (De Grauwe, 2012). The latter could be achieved more effectively, and at a lower cost, if surplus countries within the region agreed to an upward adjustment of their wages and prices.

The institutional measures agreed so far are inadequate, because they do not have growth recovery as their main goal. While the announcement of a €120 billion package for investment projects is a step in the right direction, it seems insufficient. Measures include the establishment of the European Financial Stability Facility and the European Stability Mechanism as the main crisis management tools ("firewall"), along with various initiatives undertaken to improve economic governance in the EU and thereby prevent future crises (ECB, 2012). In essence, all new initiatives continue to follow the old blueprint. Measures are mainly focused on strengthening the so-called Stability and Growth Pact and aligning policies with the latest version of the EU's long-standing structural reform agenda – the Europe 2020 strategy. Europe continues to ignore the vital issues of domestic demand management and proper policy coordination for internal balance.

gradual appreciation of the renminbi in real terms, which was allowed by the People's Bank of China,[22] was preferable to a combination of capital-account opening and a floating exchange rate. The latter probably would have generated financial instability and an abrupt currency appreciation, thereby posing a serious risk not only to Chinese growth but also to the global economy.

2. *The scope for monetary and fiscal policies*

The debate on the role and impact of various macroeconomic policies in the present crisis is shaped by differing views on the main problems to be addressed at any given point in time, the availability of policy tools (e.g. "fiscal space" or "monetary space"), and the results that can be expected from their use.

The first question relates to the diagnosis of the causes of the global crisis and the main economic problems that need to be overcome to surmount them. One diagnosis focuses on fiscal problems – high deficits and debt-to-GDP ratios, mainly in the developed countries. Based on this, "fiscal consolidation" is proposed as the remedy. According to this view, fiscal austerity will reassure financial investors of the solvency of sovereign debtors and thereby keep interest rates in check and restore credit supply, which in turn will lead to economic recovery. There are variations around this main position. The most optimistic observers cited the "green shoots" of 2010 as proof that the global economy was strong enough to allow retiring public stimulus without adverse consequences, since the private sector had already resumed spending on a sustainable basis (IMF, 2011). The most pessimistic argue that fiscal tightening would not restart growth, but it would buy time (i.e. prevent a financial panic) for implementing the structural reforms needed for exiting from the crisis. Adopting an intermediate position, there are those who believe that fiscal austerity must be strong enough to be credible in terms of fiscal sustainability, but loose enough for minimizing its adverse impacts on growth (IMF, 2012a).

An alternative diagnosis of the cause of the global crisis points to private overindebtedness and not fiscal profligacy – even if one of its consequences was a deterioration in the fiscal situation of developed economies. A typical feature of financial crises is that they are followed by a long process of deleveraging, as both banks and debtors try to adjust their balance sheets (Koo, 2011). In the present instance, with private demand further constrained by high unemployment, stagnating or falling wages and negative wealth effects, it was overly optimistic to assume that the private sector had already "taken the baton" and that private spending would sustain recovery. Consequently, fiscal tightening is seen as counterproductive. By further depressing growth and fiscal revenues, it probably will not even achieve "fiscal consolidation" nor regain the confidence of financial markets.[23] Confidence, especially among financial markets, is normally restored only when the economy has recovered.

For all these reasons, monetary policy cannot restart growth. The problem is not that insufficient liquidity is constraining credit supply: central banks have provided huge amounts of money to the banks. For example, since September 2008 the Federal Reserve in the United States has injected more than $2 trillion into the banking system, trebling its total assets, and in Europe the European Central Bank (ECB) has doubled its assets to around 3 trillion euros. Despite this, bank credit to the private sector stagnated in Europe and decreased by 4 per cent in the United States between the third quarter of 2008 and the end of 2011. If banks are not increasing their lending to the private sector, it is not because they lack the funds; it is either because they do not want to lend (i.e. preferring instead to consolidate their balance sheets), or because the private sector is not demanding net credit (i.e. credit in addition to roll-over of maturing debts) as it does not intend to increase its consumption or investments. Once again, credit markets are showing a tendency to procyclicality. This does not mean that monetary policy is completely ineffective – a contractionary monetary stance could considerably worsen the present situation. On the other hand, the monetary authorities could be more effective if they focused less on the global amount of money issued and more on who should receive the money and how it should be used. Nonetheless, monetary policy has revealed its limitations, which is why fiscal policy remains an indispensable tool.

There are conceptual issues underlying this policy debate. The fundamental error of fiscal orthodoxy is to treat the public finances of a country as if they function just like the private finances of an individual household. As no household can permanently live beyond its means by spending more than it earns, it is assumed that the same principle must also apply to any responsible government. This analogy is seriously misleading as a guide to sound policy-making. An isolated household may well succeed in reducing its debt by cutting back on spending, given that its revenues are unaffected by its own retrenchment. It is, however, a fundamental principle of market economies that one household's spending is another household's income. Therefore, if one big player or many households together try to reduce their debt by simultaneously cutting their spending, they will end up reducing overall income, including their own.

It was the simultaneous cutting of expenditure by the private sector (both households and firms) throughout the world that caused a slump in global revenues and growth. The world is unlikely to recover from this slump unless individual agents' attempts to reduce spending are reversed. If the tide of spending cuts is not stemmed, it will end in a downward spiral of incomes and spending. However, an individual private agent cannot expect to change the course of events by acting countercyclically; it is only governments that can counterbalance the negative impact of private retrenchment on income.

This raises the question of fiscal space. *TDR 2011* made the case for assessing the role of fiscal policy from a macroeconomic and dynamic perspective. It argued for the need to take into account the impact of fiscal policy on total income and GDP growth, and consequently on the budgetary position itself. Fiscal space and the sustainability of public finances do not depend only on the public debt-to-GDP ratio and the size of the current budget deficit; growth and interest rates must be considered as well. Hence, by its impact on GDP and the interest rate level, macroeconomic policy is a major determinant of fiscal space in an economy.

Today, several European governments are facing rising interest rates on their sovereign debt, as their borrowings are viewed by financial markets as high-risk. This has been the reason invoked for pushing towards stronger fiscal tightening. For example, EU leaders have signed off on the "golden rule", requiring legislation (or even constitutional changes) which would ban structural fiscal deficits in excess of 0.5 per cent of GDP. In the United States, there are also strong pressures for possibly large and "automatic" cuts in government spending beginning in early 2013 if a political agreement on fiscal consolidation is not reached before then.

However, what generates the solvency risk in Euro-zone countries is not their high debt-to-GDP ratios, but rather their lack of sovereign control over their monetary policy. Several euro-zone countries have debt-to-GDP ratios well below those of the United States, Japan and the United Kingdom. The difference is that the latter countries not only have sovereign control over their monetary policies, but also their central banks can act as lenders of last resort both for banks and for their governments. In the euro zone, the solution will not come from more fiscal tightening and the dismantling of the welfare State, but rather from deeper fiscal and financial integration and a cooperative approach to economic rebalancing (Aglietta, 2012).

Some of the factors determining fiscal space (most notably different GDP growth rates) explain the divergent trends of public debt-to-GDP ratios in developed, developing and transition economies (chart 1.7). Those ratios remained stable in developed economies between 1995 and 2007, and have tended to decline in the developing countries since 2002 and in the transition economies since 1999. The crisis sharply increased that ratio in developed countries, but did not reverse the declining trend in the other groups of countries, despite the sizeable fiscal stimulus packages many of them introduced. In part, this was due to the costs of the financial bailouts mainly in the developed countries. But it was also because the developing and transition economies generally returned to robust GDP growth much more rapidly, which also boosted their fiscal revenues. Indeed, developing countries generally made good use of their fiscal space, with some of them implementing sizeable fiscal stimulus packages. Several developing countries that chose proactive macroeconomic policies in response to the global crisis have fared rather well (Takats, 2012). Their stimulus programmes, which have been focusing more on boosting public spending rather than on tax cuts, have proved very effective in quickly restoring growth. As a result, their public finances have generally remained healthy and their fiscal space has also recovered.[24]

It is not only changes in the amount of public spending and taxes that can provide the needed economic stimulus, but also their composition. The aim is to improve the multiplicative impact of a given level of expenditure, or reduce the contractionary effect of taxation on private expenditure. As discussed in *TDR 2011*, what matters for stimulating the economy is not the size of the fiscal deficit or surplus per se, but rather the impact on the distribution of income of specific public revenues and expenditures. In particular, it is necessary to consider the extent to which fiscal operations generate new aggregate demand, not only directly but also indirectly through the multiplicative effect of the new demand. Indeed, a recent study by the International Monetary Fund finds that fiscal multipliers may be quite large during recessions, when "the traditional crowding-out argument is less applicable" (IMF, 2012b: 34). It also finds that increased spending provides more stimulus than cutting taxes, departing from some of its previous views (IMF, 2010). However, rather than recommending the use of those high fiscal multipliers for reversing recessionary pressures, the IMF recommends a more gradual approach to fiscal tightening. Nevertheless, it is important to note that the harm done by procyclical policies is now more widely recognized, as is also the possibility for improving economic performance through countercyclical fiscal policies.

Hence, much of the effectiveness of monetary and fiscal policies depends on their distributional effects, as they can enhance the purchasing power of agents with high propensities to consume and/or invest. This is particularly important when the main problem in an economy is the lack of demand. It is also possible to seek the same result by implementing income and employment policies that aim at increasing the share of low- and middle-income groups in primary income distribution. An incomes policy that creates expectations of a progressive rise in workers' incomes – with real wages (in the case of wage earners) growing at a similar rate as productivity – may be of critical importance in reviving growth of consumption.

In conclusion, in the context of high unemployment, ongoing deleveraging and downward pressures on real wages, an exit from recession in crisis-hit countries cannot be left to market forces alone. Public policies should aim to restore demand, instead of further depressing it with fiscal retrenchment. In order to revive aggregate demand, growth and employment, governments need to combine several instruments which may be more easily available than is frequently

Chart 1.7

PUBLIC DEBT-TO-GDP RATIO, 1980–2011

(Per cent)

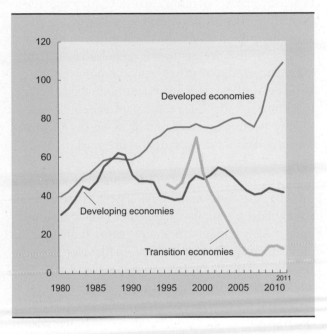

Source: UNCTAD secretariat calculations, based on IMF, *Historical Public Debt Database*, *World Economic Outlook*, April 2012, and *Country Reports 2012 for Article IV consultations*.

believed. As argued in previous *TDRs* and further discussed in chapter VI of this *Report*, incomes and labour market policies are legitimate tools that may be combined with fiscal and monetary instruments in efforts to achieve inclusive and sustainable growth.

3. Structural reforms are not a substitute for supportive macroeconomic policies

Broadly defined, structural policies are designed to establish or reshape the structure of institutions and the functioning of markets. Measures may concern both the role of government in (particular) markets and the interaction of market participants. Development and the corresponding structural transformation of economies over time require appropriate structural policies to best support and enhance economic performance in terms of efficiency, stability and growth. Reassessing the scope and form of structural policies thus constitutes a continuous challenge for governments of all countries.

As such, structural policies may cover a wide range of areas, including markets (de)regulation, education, health care, pension, tax and welfare systems, infrastructure and the public administration itself. For instance, since the global crisis of 2008-2009, financial reform has been a common priority of structural policies in many countries in their attempts to restore stability and redefine the economic role of their respective financial sectors as well as initiatives for international cooperation in this area.

There have been quite a few national and global initiatives for financial regulatory reform. However, re-regulation remains fragmented, and full implementation is unlikely for many years to come. At the global level, the "Basel III" accord (developed by the Basel Committee on Banking Supervision (BCBS) and endorsed at the G-20 Seoul Summit in November 2010) and the establishment of the Financial Stability Board (FSB, formerly the Financial Stability Forum) are among the main initiatives undertaken in the area of global financial regulation and supervision prompted by the financial crisis. The former provides international regulatory standards for transnational banks (BCBS, 2010a and b), while the latter is a conduit of information and a coordination platform for national financial authorities and international standard setting bodies charged with assessing vulnerabilities in the financial system and identifying and overseeing actions needed to address them. The Basel III requirements will be phased in gradually, with full implementation expected to be completed only by January 2019 (BCBS, 2012). Complementing the IMF's (enlarged) financial surveillance functions, the FSB is part of the new post-crisis focus on containing systemic risks through macroprudential regulation. However, macroprudential principles are undermined by pressures that favour free international capital movements, even though these have proved to be a major source of financial instability in many developing and transition economies.

Important unresolved issues relate to the threat that financial institutions and activities may once again succeed in avoiding supervision, in particular through shadow banking and offshore centres. Further, the handling of the "too-big-to-fail" banks may require cooperation between national fiscal authorities and the sharing of financial resources.

However, this issue is proving to be particularly challenging even within the EU despite its long record of deep regional integration.[25]

Much remains to be done for restructuring national and global financial systems in order to reduce the systemic risks associated with their insufficient regulation and perverse incentive systems. Equally important is the need to reorient their activities towards supporting the real economy, in particular to finance productive investment, employment generation and growth (*TDR 2011*, chap. IV). However, the focus of structural reforms has been changing over the past few years, especially in developed economies, in the direction of reform packages reminiscent of those implemented in response to an earlier financial crisis, that in Latin America in the 1980s.

Most governments of developed countries as well as the international financial institutions assume that there is very little room for manoeuvre for stimulating the economy through macroeconomic policies. There is a perception that further scope for more supportive monetary policies may be limited by the already very low policy interest rates. On the fiscal side, governments fear that a new stimulus might signal a departure from the goal of fiscal consolidation. The focus is therefore increasingly on structural reforms, which are intended to boost competitiveness and revive growth.

Accordingly, several developed countries have initiated a broad range of reforms such as reducing labour protection, shifting wage bargaining to the firm level, implementing privatization plans, liberalizing the energy and retail sectors, and cutting public employment and social expenditure. Announced privatizations have been particularly extensive in Central and Eastern European economies and in Portugal, Ireland and Greece. Other developed economies also plan to sell portions of their State-owned assets. Some tax and welfare reforms are likely to have adverse impacts on the revenues of low- and middle-income households, and consequently on inequality. For example, Greece, Ireland, Portugal and Spain have limited unemployment benefits in terms of access and amounts. In addition, several OECD countries have introduced pension reforms, raising the retirement age and/or reducing the level of pensions, and tax reforms that broaden the tax base and increase indirect taxes but reduce direct personal or corporate taxes (OECD, 2012b). On the other hand, some measures appear to aim at tempering the effects of the social crisis, such as increased resources provided for worker training and the extension of unemployment benefits.

A particular focus seems to be on labour market reform. Liberalizing what some consider to be excessively rigid labour markets is based on the general belief that more flexible markets are more efficient. Reforms that seek to lower the costs of labour and facilitate dismissal of workers are assumed to provide greater incentives to hire workers and improve overall competitiveness, which in turn will boost growth and increase employment opportunities. Chapter VI of this *Report* discusses the rationale for labour institutions and rules, and shows that so-called "rigidities" exist for good reason and do not harm growth. Furthermore, microeconomic reasoning concerning the labour market ignores the macroeconomic dimension of that market and of wage determination. Since labour income is a strong determinant of aggregate demand (especially in developed countries), extensive cuts in that remuneration subdue economic activity and therefore the demand for labour. Unlike other goods and services, lowering the price of labour also lowers its demand.

A case may be made for a policy that seeks to find a way out of the crisis through the expansion of net exports. Falling wages create scope for lowering prices, thereby improving price competitiveness, provided that changes in exchange rates do not offset inflation differentials. This seems to be the policy promoted by the European Commission and the ECB.[26] However, cutting wages in several countries of the same region at the same time is counterproductive when domestic and regional demands are quantitatively greater than exports to the rest of the world, as is the case for many crisis-hit countries in Europe.

Quite apart from the debate about the long-term effects of structural reforms, concerns are also being raised about their timeliness and their suitability for addressing the current problems. As the main problem in the present crisis is the lack of demand (Krugman, 2012), reforms aimed at improving the supply side of the economy are not the most appropriate, especially if they further weaken aggregate demand. For instance, introducing more flexibility in labour markets and increasing the participation rate (a specific goal of several governments) when there is no increase in the demand for labour will only exacerbate

the unemployment situation and further depress wages and domestic demand, which is precisely the opposite of what is needed. Even institutions that strongly support such a programme of structural reforms warn that they may be "detrimental in bad times" (OECD, 2012b: 20), and that austerity effects can be too severe in the current context of low private sector demand and persistent unemployment (IMF, 2012d). Furthermore, large privatization programmes implemented under pressure and in the midst of an economic depression will probably generate much lower revenues for governments than initially expected.

So far, economic reforms in a number of OECD countries have not been associated with a revival of economic growth. Indeed, countries that were among the most energetic in introducing these kinds of policies are failing to achieve the expected GDP growth, job creation and fiscal consolidation (OECD, 2012). This does not mean that the reforms themselves are the main cause of the current recession; it is more likely that the economic and financial crisis has been considered a justification for implementing structural reforms that were sought for other reasons, independently of the crisis context.[27]

In contrast, the structural reforms being adopted by developing countries have tended to create or reinforce social safety nets and to expand the economic role of the State. In several developing countries, welfare reforms have moved in a different direction to those in developed countries – sometimes in a kind of "counter-reform" of previous market-oriented principles. In Latin America, many countries have embarked on a major overhaul of their pension schemes, turning back the private-sector-oriented reforms of the 1980s and the 1990s, and reintroducing State involvement. For example, Chile has increased its universal coverage of non-contributory benefits paid for by the Government; Argentina has returned to the public pay-as-you-go pensions system; and related reforms are being introduced in Colombia, Mexico, Peru and Uruguay (Arza, 2012; Kritzer, 2008; Rofman, Fajnzylber and Herrera, 2010; ISSA, 2010) These structural "counter-reforms" aim to redress the perceived failures of the private pension-fund revolution of the 1980s and 1990s, which included a sharp reduction in coverage, gender inequalities, high administration and marketing costs, and low payments to beneficiaries. In some countries they also enable the government to use pension revenues or accumulated funds for public investment purposes.

In India, the Government adopted a $5 billion plan to provide free medical care to the poorest 50 per cent of the population in 2012.[28] This was coupled with a ruling that only generic drugs (and not branded ones) were to be used, which will not only improve access to health care but also give a boost to the domestic pharmaceutical industry. In South Africa, ongoing health-care reforms seek to establish some form of national insurance and improve the quality and coverage of the country's health services.

At the Los Cabos summit of the G-20 in June 2012, a number of developing economies committed to strengthening or expanding social safety nets and poverty reduction programmes. In Indonesia, for instance, Government actions have focused on family-based social assistance, community empowerment, economic opportunities for low-income households and the provision of basic needs to low-income people at an affordable price. In Argentina, the main income transfer programme, the Universal Child Allowance, which targets vulnerable children up to 18 years of age, has achieved an 85 per cent coverage rate and was extended to pregnant women in 2011. In Brazil, several schemes aimed at eradicating extreme poverty and improving opportunities for vulnerable populations were launched or strengthened. These include the Brazil Free from Extreme Poverty initiative which comprises three main pillars: (i) increasing per capita income in poor households; (ii) expanding access to public services and social welfare; and (iii) extending employment and wage-earning opportunities. Mexico has introduced measures aimed at promoting the attractiveness of formal employment for workers.

In several developing countries, structural reforms include expanding the role of public policies for supporting investment and structural change. Such measures are frequently aligned with stimulus objectives targeting both the supply and the demand side. For example, Brazil recently reduced the reserve requirements for bank lending to the automobile industry and lowered interest rates for consumer loans aimed at supporting car manufacturers and car buyers alike. This targeted measure accompanied more broad-based public investments in infrastructure on a massive scale, including transport and energy projects that can create jobs in the short-term while boosting productive capacity for the long-term. Several other governments of large developing countries have

also extended their involvement in infrastructure development to support domestic economic activities and boost job creation. In Indonesia, for instance, a significant share of public expenditure targets the information and communications technology (ICT) sector, while in Argentina and Mexico it focuses more on the energy sector. South Africa's public sector investment, which is directed principally to developing transport, electricity and water infrastructures, was 7.1 per cent of GDP in 2011, and is expected to remain above 7 per cent of GDP over the next three years at least. In parallel, the Government has strengthened its public works programmes, which guarantee work opportunities for the vulnerable and disadvantaged. Meanwhile, in Saudi Arabia, the Government's facilitation of access to credit by small and medium-sized enterprises is expected to stimulate job creation (G-20, 2012).

Most of these measures have a countercyclical purpose, as they aim to safeguard employment and support economic activity in troubled times. However, some of them are not just temporary measures that will be reversed when the international environment becomes more favourable. One important structural reform is reforming the State itself (constructing or restoring the "developmental State"), which is also the tool for implementing industrial policies and making other structural reforms. Extending social security, unemployment benefits and pension coverage also has a countercyclical component through its immediate effect on demand, but there is no reason to dismantle these social advances once growth resumes, although some associated transfers will normally decline with economic recovery and improvements in the labour market.

In conclusion, structural reforms cannot be the main tool to exit from an economic depression; that task should be left largely to supportive macroeconomic policies. These reforms should be carefully gauged against a country's long-term social objectives and development strategy. They should aim, in particular, at correcting the main dysfunctioning areas that led to the global crisis, many of which are related to global and domestic financial systems. Other factors leading to the crisis are income inequality and its determinants, which are discussed in some detail in this *Report*. Structural reforms should aim to reduce inequality, rather than amplifying it as has frequently happened in the past. ■

Notes

1 By the end of 2011, only 15 out of 35 developed economies registered GDP levels that were higher than their respective pre-crisis peaks reached between 2007 and 2008.

2 On 2 March 2012, 25 EU members signed the Treaty on Stability, Coordination and Governance which includes a fiscal compact establishing that the structural fiscal deficit must not exceed 0.5 per cent of GDP to be incorporated into national legislation.

3 These commodity price peaks generally occurred between January and April 2011, except for rice, tobacco, tropical logs and gold, which peaked in August-September 2011. The last peak for phosphate rock was in January 2012, while for oil, bananas and beef prices peaked in March 2012.

4 For a detailed discussion on the role of information and the influence of commodity investors on prices, see *TDR 2011*, chap. V.

5 Cited by *Reuters*, Barclays says $8.2 bln pulled from commodities in May, 25 June 2012.

6 See, for instance, Kemp (2012); Danske Research (2012); *Reuters*, Oil posts fourth biggest daily gain on record, 29 July 2012; and *Reuters*, Corn eases after rally, soy turns up ahead of USDA report, 10 July 2012.

7 Looking at the period 1865–2010, Erten and Ocampo (2012) identify four super-cycles. They also show that the average price of all non-oil commodity categories has significantly declined from one price cycle to the next.

8 Maintaining the post-crisis investment drive would risk creating overcapacity and non-performing loans. As noted by Akyüz (2012), China's commercial real estate sector risks heading towards a bust, and local governments appear to be facing difficulties in servicing their debt.

9 For example, the net import bill for cereals of the low-income food-deficit countries is expected to reach a record high in 2011/2012 – even higher than that of the 2008 food crisis (FAO, 2012).

10 The Food and Agriculture Organization of the United Nations (FAO, 2011) offers a detailed analysis on how food price volatility makes both smallholder farmers and poor consumers increasingly vulnerable to poverty. The International Labour Office (ILO, 2011) examines the employment and distributional impacts of increasing food prices in developing countries, and concludes that there is significant evidence of a negative poverty effect associated with higher food prices.

11 For a more detailed assessment of the progress on aid to agriculture since the L'Aquila summit, see Action Aid, 2012, and the *Guardian*, Rich nations risk breaking their pledges on farming aid, says anti-poverty group, 10 July 2011. The FAO has also highlighted the funding gap for the Sahel and Horn of Africa emergency plans. Regarding overall aid for development, the OECD (2012a) reports that aid to developing countries by major donors fell by nearly 3 per cent in 2011, after a long trend of annual increases.

12 For detailed discussions on the roles of TNCs in agriculture and in the extractive industries, see UNCTAD, 2009 and 2007 respectively.

13 According to PricewaterhouseCoopers (PWC, 2012), the world's 40 biggest mining companies posted record profits in 2011 due to high commodity prices.

14 For evidence on the global land rush, see also IIED, 2012.

15 For a discussion on how land deals have failed to provide benefits to the poor, see OXFAM, 2011.

16 The guidelines include such aspects as promoting equal rights for women in securing access to land, creating transparent record-keeping systems that are accessible to the rural poor, and help with recognizing and protecting informal and customary rights to land (Graziano da Silva, 2012). The guidelines are available at: http://www.fao.org/fileadmin/templates/cfs/Docs1112/VG/VG_Final_EN_May_2012.pdf. The principles for responsible agricultural investment refer to respecting land and resource rights, ensuring food security, transparency, good governance and a proper enabling environment, consultation and participation, responsible agro-enterprise investing, and social and environmental sustainability (UNCTAD, 2010).

17   For examples of countries that have been review-ing their mining regimes recently, see Leon, 2012; Ernst &Young, 2012; *The Economist,* 2012a; and Australian Mining, 2012.

18   See 2011 Budget statement by the Chancellor of the Exchequer at: http://www.hm-treasury.gov.uk/2011budget_speech.htm.

19   See BIS database at: http://www.bis.org/statistics/index.htm.

20   These are the 12 countries that acceded to the EU after 2004.

21   BIS statistics on international claims are stated in dollars, although some claims may be denominated in other currencies (e.g. in euros, particularly within Europe). Consequently, the appreciation of the dollar vis-à-vis the euro following the crisis tends to accentuate the reduction of banks' claims measured in dollar terms.

22   In real terms, the renmimbi appreciated since 2005 by 20 per cent vis-à-vis the dollar, and by about 30 per cent on the basis of real effective exchange rate.

23   Pleasing the markets has proved to be a difficult task, since "markets appear somewhat schizophrenic – they ask for fiscal consolidation but react badly when con-solidation leads to lower growth" (IMF, 2012a: xiv).

24   In general, the trends in low-income developing countries are less positive (IMF, 2012b; UNCTAD, 2012b). The aggregate picture masks the fact that 20 countries remain at high risk of, or are already in, debt distress (IMF, 2012c).

25   The FSB has issued recommendations on strengthen-ing oversight and regulation of shadow banks (FSB,

2011o), and has also developed a framework to address the systemic and moral hazard risks associ-ated with financial institutions that are judged "too big to fail" (FSB, 2011b; see also BCBS, 2011). The FSB and BCBS have identified an initial group of 29 global systemically important financial institu-tions (G-SIFIs), which will eventually be required to have additional loss absorption capacity.

26   According to Mario Draghi, President of the ECB, "Reforms in these areas are particularly important for countries that have suffered significant losses in cost competitiveness and need to stimulate produc-tivity and improve trade performance" (Introductory statement to the press conference, Barcelona, 3 May 2012; see also Barroso, 2012).

27   As noted by *The Economist* (2012b), "It's tempting to chalk economic failure up to profligacy, or insufficient adherence to a set of commonly accepted economic principles. Some leaders seem anxious to misdiagnose crises, intentionally or unintentionally, in order to seize the opportunity to foist preferred policies on vulnerable economies." The OECD (2012b: 25) also observed, "Overall, the crisis seems to have acted as a catalyst for structural reforms. Compared with the pre-crisis period, responsiveness rates have increased on average to *Going for Growth* recommendations for enhancing both labour productivity and labour utilization. For the latter, this partly reflects recent extensive labour market reforms undertaken in the context of the euro area debt crisis."

28   See *Financial Times*, India to give free medicine to millions, 6 July 2012.

References

Action Aid (2012). Pledges, principles and progress: Aid to Agriculture since L'Aquila. Available at: http://www.actionaid.org/usa/publications/pledges-principles-and-progress-aid-agriculture-laquila.

AfricaFocus (2012). Africa: detour on food security. *AfricaFocus Bulletin*, 24 May.

Aglietta M (2012). *Zone Euro, Eclatement ou Fédération.* Michalon Editions, Paris.

Akyüz Y (2012). The staggering rise of the South? Research Paper 44, South Centre, Geneva.

Arza C (2012). The politics of counter-reform in the Argen-tine pension system: Actors, political discourse and policy performance. *International Journal of Social Welfare*. Available at: http://onlinelibrary.wiley.com/doi/10.1111/j.1468-2397.2012.00872.x/abstract.

Australian Mining (2012). Taxing times: A look at global mining tax regimes. 5 March. Available at: http://www.miningaustralia.com.au/slider/taxing-times---a-look-at-global-mining-tax-regimes.

Barclays Capital (2012a). *Commodities Weekly*, 29 June.

Barclays Capital (2012b). *Commodities Weekly*, 1 June.

Barroso JMD (2012). State of the world economy and finance, and its impact on development in 2012. Speech to the United Nations General Assembly, 17 May. Available at: http://europa.eu/rapid/pressReleasesAction. do?reference=SPEECH/12/365.

BCBS (2010a). Basel III: A global regulatory framework for more resilient banks and banking systems. Basel, December. Available at: www.bis.org/publ/bcbs189.pdf.

BCBS (2010b). Basel III: International framework for liquidity risk measurement, standards and monitoring. Basel, December. Available at: www.bis.org/publ/bcbs188.htm.

BCBS (2011). Globally systemically important banks: Assessment methodology and the additional loss absorbency requirement. Final document, November. Available at: http://www.bis.org/publ/bcbs207.htm.

BCBS (2012). Report to G20 on Basel III implementation, June. Available at: http://www.bis.org/publ/bcbs220.pdf.

Bibow J (2007). How the Maastricht regime fosters divergence as well as instability. In: Arestis P, Hein E and Le Heron E, eds. *Monetary Policies - Modern Approaches*. Basingstoke, Palgrave Macmillan:197–222.

Bibow J (2012). The euro debt crisis and Germany's euro trilemma. Working Paper no. 721, Levy Economics Institute of Bard College, Annandale-on-Hudson, NY. Available at: http://www.levyinstitute.org/pubs/wp_721.pdf.

Cai F, Wang D and Zhang H (2010). Employment effectiveness of China's economic stimulus package. *China & World Economy*, 18(1): 33–46.

Credit Suisse (2012). China: Is the commodity super-cycle over? *Securities Research & Analytics*, 19 March.

Danske Research (2012). Commodities update: Weather premium in grains to stay elevated, 16 July.

De Grauwe P (2012). In search of symmetry in the eurozone. CEPS Policy Brief No. 268, Centre for European Policy Studies, Brussels.

ECB (2012). Policy and institutional issues. *Annual Report*. Frankfurt.

ECLAC (2012). Macroeconomic Report on Latin America and the Caribbean, Santiago de Chile, June.

Ernst & Young (2012). Business risks facing mining and metals, 2011-2012.

Erten B and Ocampo JA (2012). Super-cycles of commodity prices since the mid-nineteenth century. Working Paper No. 110, United Nations Department of Economic and Social Affairs (UN-DESA), New York, February.

FAO (2011). The State of Food Insecurity in the World: How does International Price Volatility Affect Domestic Economies and Food Security? Rome, March.

FAO (2012). Crop Prospects and Food Situation. Rome, March.

Flassbeck H (2007). Wage divergences in Euroland: Explosive in the making. In: Bibow J and Terzi A, eds. *Euroland and the World Economy: Global Player or Global Drag?* Basingstoke, Palgrave Macmillan: 43–52.

FSB (2011a), Shadow banking: Strengthening oversight and regulation. Recommendations of the Financial Stability Board. Available at: http://www.financial-stabilityboard.org/publications/r_111027a.pdf.

FSB (2011b). Policy measures to address systemically important financial institutions. Basel. Available at: http://www.financialstabilityboard.org/publications/r_111104bb.pdf.

G-20 (2011). Coherent conclusions for the management of capital flows drawing on country experiences, as endorsed by G20 Heads of State and Government, 3–4 November. Available at: http://www.g20-g8.com/g8-g20/root/bank_objects/0000005999-Coherent_Conclusions_on_CFMs_postCannes.pdf.

G-20 (2012). Policy commitments by G20 Members, Los Cabos Summit, 18–19 June. Available at: http://www.g20.org/images/stories/docs/g20/conclu/Policy_Commitments_By_G20_Members.pdf.

Graziano da Silva J (2012). Global land deal guidelines could pave the way to world without hunger. The *Guardian,* 11 May.

HLPE (High Level Panel of Experts on Food Security and Nutrition) (2011). Land tenure and international investments in agriculture. Rome.

IFS (Institute for Fiscal Studies) (2012). Public spending on education in the UK to fall at fastest rate since at least 1950s. London. Available at: http://www.ifs.org.uk/pr/bn121_pr.pdf.

IIED (International Institute for Environment and Development) (2012). The global land rush: What the evidence reveals about scale and geography. London, April.

ILO (2011). World of Work Report 2011: Making Markets Work for Jobs. Geneva, International Labour Office.

IMF (2010). *World Economic Outlook*. International Monetary Fund, Washington, DC, October.

IMF (2011). *World Economic Outlook*. Washington, DC, April.

IMF (2012a). *World Economic Outlook*. Washington, DC, April.

IMF (2012b). *Fiscal Monitor*. Washington, DC, April.

IMF (2012c). List of LIC DSAs for PRGT-eligible countries, 3 May. Available at: http://www.imf.org/external/pubs/ft/dsa/dsalist.pdf.

IMF (2012d). Concluding Statement of the 2012 Article IV Mission to The United States of America. Washington, DC, 3 July.

ISSA (International Social Security Association) (2010). Pension reform in Chile. A case of the Ministry of Finance. Geneva.

Kemp J (2012). Price jump does not mark shift in oil fundamentals. *Reuters, Inside Oil*, 4 July.

Koo R (2011). The world in balance sheet recession: Causes, cure and politics, *Real-World Economic Review*, 58(58): 19–37.

Kritzer B (2008). Chile's next generation pension reform. *Social Security Bulletin, 68*(2): 69–84.

Krugman P (2012). *End This Depression Now!* New York, W. W. Norton and Co.

Lemoine F and Ünal D (2012). China's strong domestic demand has reduced its trade surplus. VoxEU, 19 July. Available at: www.voxeu.org/article/china-s-strong-domestic-demand-has-reduced-its-trade-surplus.

Leon P (2012). Resource nationalism by taxation: A look at key African countries. Presentation at Annual Mining Seminar on Minerals Taxation and Sustainable Development. London, Centre for Energy, Petroleum and Mineral Law Policy, 26–28 June.

Maddison A (2008). World population, GDP and GDP per capita, 1-2008 AD. Available at: http://www.ggdc.net/MADDISON/oriindex.htm Maddison A (2008). World population, GDP and GDP per capita, 1-2008 AD. Available at: http://www.ggdc.net/MADDISON/oriindex.htm.

Mohammadian-Molina R (2012). Investment flows in commodities markets and the relationship with prices. Barclays Capital, London.

OECD (2012a). Development: Aid to developing countries falls because of global recession. Paris, April.

OECD (2012b). *Economic Policy Reforms 2012: Going for Growth*. Paris, OECD Publishing.

Oxfam (2011). Land and power: The growing scandal surrounding the new wave of investments in land. Oxford.

PWC (2012). *Mine 2012: The Growing Disconnect*. Available at: http://www.pwc.com/gx/en/mining/publications/mining/mine-the-growing-disconnect.jhtml.

Rofman R, Fajnzylber E and Herrera G (2010). Reforming the pension reforms: Argentina and Chile. *CEPAL Review*, No 101, August: 83–106.

Takats E (2012). Countercyclical policies in emerging markets. *BIS Quarterly Review*, June: 25–31. Basel, Bank for International Settlements.

The Economist (2012a). Resource nationalism in Africa: Wish you were mine. 11 February.

The Economist (2012b). Growth: In praise of structural reform. 27 February. Available at: http://www.economist.com/blogs/freeexchange/2012/02/growth.

UN/DESA (2012a). *World Economic Situation and Prospects 2012*. New York, United Nations.

UN/DESA (2012b). *World Economic Situation and Prospects. Update as of mid-2012*. New York, United Nations.

UNCTAD (*TDR 2005*). *Trade and Development Report, 2005. New Features of Global Interdependence*. United Nations publication, Sales No. E.05.II.D.13, New York and Geneva.

UNCTAD (*TDR 2010*). *Trade and Development Report, 2010. Employment, Globalization and Development*. United Nations publication, Sales No. E.10.II.D.3, New York and Geneva.

UNCTAD (*TDR 2011*). *Trade and Development Report, 2011. Post-crisis Policy Challenges in the World Economy*. United Nations publication, Sales No. E.11.II.D.3, New York and Geneva.

UNCTAD (2007*). World Investment Report 2007: Transnational Corporations, Extractive Industries and development*. United Nations publication, Sales No. E.07.II.D.9, New York and Geneva.

UNCTAD (2009). *World Investment Report 2009: Transnational Corporations, Agricultural Production and Development*. United Nations publication, Sales No. E.09.II.D.15, New York and Geneva.

UNCTAD (2010). Principles for Responsible Agricultural Investment that Respects Rights, Livelihoods and Resources: A discussion note prepared by FAO, IFAD, the UNCTAD Secretariat and the World Bank Group to contribute to an ongoing global dialogue. TD/B/C.II/CRP.3. Geneva, United Nations.

UNCTAD (2012a). *Review of Maritime Transport 2012*. Geneva (forthcoming).

UNCTAD (2012b). Sovereign debt crisis: From relief to resolution. Policy Brief no. 3, April. Available at: http://unctad.org/en/PublicationsLibrary/uxiiipb2012d3_en.pdf.

UNCTAD/WTO (2012). Short-term services trade statistics, 13 July. Available at: http://unctad.org/en/pages/newsdetails.aspx?OriginalVersionID=183&Sitemap_x0020_Taxonomy=Statistics;#20;#UNCTAD%20Home.

World Bank (2012). *Global Monitoring Report 2012: Food Prices, Nutrition and the Millennium Development Goals*. Washington, DC.

World Tourism Organization (2012). *UNWTO World Tourism Barometer*, 10. Madrid, July.

Chapter II

INCOME INEQUALITY: THE MAIN ISSUES

A. Inequality of incomes and market mechanisms

Economic inequality has re-emerged as a central policy concern in the wake of the global crisis, as the past three decades have witnessed rising global inequalities over periods of both growth and slump. Against this backdrop, this *Report* addresses an old question: whether rising (or high) income inequality is an inevitable outcome – or a necessary factor – of economic development; or whether it is possible, and even desirable, to reduce income inequality, in order to achieve more inclusive growth as well as to overcome the present economic challenges and create the conditions necessary for a more sustainable and rapid development process in the long run.

The issues of equality and equity have preoccupied thinkers, politicians and religions since ancient times. In contemporary debates, a distinction is often made between equality before the law (or formal equality), and equality in terms of income and wealth. The latter form of equality is affected by ownership structures as well as by market processes, social stratification and political systems which may deny true equality of opportunities to a large segment of a society. While there is broad agreement that equality before the law is desirable, there is an ongoing debate about how

> There is an ongoing debate on how much "effective inequality" can be tolerated without damaging social cohesion and the overall functioning of an economy.

much "effective inequality" can be tolerated without seriously damaging social cohesion and trust and the overall functioning of an economy. Here, equality refers primarily to what can be considered relative equality in the distribution of incomes, rather than absolute equality in terms of civil rights.

One area in which the gap between formal and real equality seems particularly strong is in market operations. On the one hand, buyers and sellers in different markets are formally equal: they are free to accept or refuse a transaction at a given price. Consequently, a market transaction theoretically takes place only if it is beneficial to both parties. In addition, market institutions assure justice through the equivalence of exchanges (Habermas, 1973). On the other hand, inequality of resources is more clearly manifested in market transactions than anywhere else, owing to asymmetries in the purchasing power of different participants. From a formal point of view, markets are the sphere of personal and legal equality whereby all participants are equally free to buy and sell to their mutual benefit. But in reality, owing to disparities in wealth and incomes, market operations reflect the lack of real (or effective) equality in starting positions.

There is nothing in the pure market mechanism that tends to rebalance an initially unequal distribution of assets and resources. Agents with more resources or greater access to credit (the two being frequently related) can invest, innovate and expand production on a larger scale than others. Thus the process of economic development is normally unbalanced, with some firms and sectors gaining market shares at the expense of others, and new products and production processes replacing older ones in a process of "creative destruction" (Schumpeter, 1942/2003). In this process, the accumulation of capital and knowledge (including that acquired through learning by doing) tends to concentrate wealth and economic power even further.

Although the principle of formal equality is the basis for social and economic interaction in most modern societies, the social consensus on how much inequality of market outcomes is acceptable, differs considerably among societies. But irrespective of cross-country differences in the level of effective inequality, the increase in inequality over time has given rise to growing concerns in many countries about its social and economic repercussions.

Accelerated economic globalization and technological progress over the past 30 years is often seen as a major factor responsible for a widening of the income gap between wage earners and earners of capital incomes, as well as between different groups within these aggregates. It is important to bear in mind, however, that trade, financial and technological factors always operate within a framework of social and economic institutions, regulations and policies. In this *Trade and Development Report* (*TDR*), it is argued that although inequality has risen in most regions since the 1980s, when globalization began to accelerate and became increasingly "finance-led", there is nothing "natural" about this development that requires society to allow or accept it. Nor does an increase in inequality improve the efficiency of market outcomes in a rapidly changing world. Even worse, a significant rise in inequality can generate economic conflicts that lead to social tensions and, in the extreme, political violence, especially when overall income growth is slow or absent. This is why economists such as Tinbergen (1956/1964) included among the objectives of economic policy the need for a better distribution of real income and expenditure among social groups and countries.

The use of certain instruments to reduce the current level of inequality is not necessarily damaging to investment and growth. On the contrary, appropriate macroeconomic, tax and labour market policies can prevent an increase in inequality or reduce it in a way that is conducive to both faster overall income growth and sustainable development.

For instance, by imposing a progressive tax on income or by taxing accumulated wealth, governments can reduce income inequality without undermining the incentive of economic agents to create and implement new ideas and projects. Taxing high incomes on the basis of progressive scales does not take away the absolute advantage of the richer individuals or the incentive for others to try out new ideas and move up the income ladder. Diamond and Saez (2011) estimate that in the United States the marginal tax rate on top incomes can be as high as 50–70 per cent without creating substantial incentive problems. Taxing wealth and inherited fortunes may even be seen as a means to providing incentives to the next generation to also engage in economic activities in a manner that maximizes outcomes for the society as a whole instead of relying on inherited fortunes. In resource-rich (mainly developing) countries, government policies aimed at capturing a significant share of the natural rents are vital for using the commodity bonanzas to improve domestic income and demand and generate a more broad-based growth of the economy, instead of allowing a few domestic and foreign actors, mainly in geographically concentrated enclaves, to take much of the windfall benefits. An incomes policy, a social safety net for unemployment and other hardships, and the provision of basic services, such as a good education for all, are instruments that simultaneously strengthen growth and reduce inequality.

These alternative views, by challenging the conventional wisdom that rising inequality is the normal result of development within market economies, may contribute to a new understanding of the functioning of a market economy, and can lead to a paradigm shift towards a pattern of economic development that is both more equitable and more efficient.

> There is nothing natural about rising inequality that requires society to allow or accept it, nor does it improve the efficiency of market outcomes.

B. Inequality and economic theory

Traditionally, economists' views on inequality have diverged. Some do not see it as a problem, arguing that, in the absence of artificial impediments to social mobility, inequality basically reflects differences in talents and choices. They believe that the most talented, thrifty and industrious prosper, even when handicapped by initially adverse social conditions. In a world in which market participants receive a compensation which is in line with their contribution to society (their marginal productivity), the prosperity of the "fittest" cannot be deemed to be unjust and should not be a policy concern. According to this view, strategies to reduce inequality would undermine the power of the market mechanism to generate the most efficient outcomes, because they would reduce incentives to engage in the economic process. This would slow down economic growth, stymieing the chance to reduce absolute poverty "by lifting all boats" (Friedman and Friedman, 1980).

According to Hayek (1960 and 1978), income distribution in a market society results from an impersonal process that nobody manages and conducts, and since justice is a human attribute, impersonal markets cannot be just or unjust. Government intervention aimed at ensuring more equality or social justice would, paradoxically, lead to an unfair result by delinking the distribution of rewards from individuals' contributions to the generation of global income. Public authorities should provide "equality of opportunities", particularly in the sense that rules should be the same for all individuals, with no barriers or advantages artificially created or distributed. Equality of opportunities would also require a universal access to elementary education, to be provided by governments, while advanced education should be left in private hands, and the public authorities should not have the power to decide who may access it for the sake of equality (Hayek 1960: 384–385). More generally, governments that try to generate "equality of results" would be discouraging more capable people and encouraging the less capable. This, according to Hayek, would not only be unfair, but it would also be costly from an economic point of view.

A long-term structural view of how economies develop has led to a different perception of the relationship between inequality and economic growth. The seminal contribution of Kuznets identified a long-term relationship between income inequality and the development process based on sectoral changes in the economic structure: during the early stages of industrialization and urbanization, inequality increases as gains in productivity and income concentrate in the cities and workers migrate from rural areas (characterized by relatively uniform low-productivity activities and income) to seek better paid occupations in urban areas. In later stages, inequality diminishes because the mechanization of agriculture and the declining proportion of the population engaged in the agricultural sector tend to close the gap between rural and urban areas, and because urban workers eventually have the social and political power to reduce income inequality (Kuznets, 1955; Galbraith, 2012). In this analysis, "the long swing in income inequality must be viewed as part of a wider process of economic growth, and interrelated with similar movements in other elements" (Kuznets, 1955: 20), without a clear causality between them; changes in the levels of income and

> Some economists believe public policies to reduce income inequality might undermine economic efficiency and growth.

inequality respond to structural changes inherent in the economic development process. Hence, at least in the first stages of development, inequality does not appear to be either a driving factor for, or an obstacle to, development.

Subsequently, this view was modified by other development economists who examined how income distribution could affect investment and growth. Kaldor (1957) presented an economic model in which GDP growth was limited by available resources and not by effective demand: capital accumulation, the flow of innovation and the growth of the population determined economic expansion. In the model, savings propensities of the community determine the rate of capital accumulation, but they are also linked to the distribution of income between profits and wages, since profit earners tend to save a higher share of their income than wage earners. Consequently, higher (functional) income inequality would be associated with higher savings and capital accumulation and higher economic growth. Kaldor did not imply that this should form the basis of any policy recommendation, since in his model income distribution was endogenous; but for many years a widespread interpretation of his model was that growth could be boosted by increasing the share of capital in income distribution (box 2.1).

Studies by the Economic Commission for Latin America and the Caribbean (ECLAC) in the 1960s followed a different approach, as they identified the highly unequal Latin American social structure as a major obstacle to development. They believed it hindered social mobility, in that it prevented the rise of the most dynamic individuals in the society, and that it weakened economic incentives for an efficient use of labour, land and machinery.[1] They also saw it as generating excessive consumption by the upper classes, contrasting with the precarious conditions of the popular masses. In their view, income inequality does not translate into stronger capital accumulation, as ostentatious consumption by the rich reduces savings. Moreover, because such consumption consists of a high proportion of imports and of goods produced by capital-intensive industries, it has little impact on domestic growth and employment, and does not provide the necessary basis for a sustainable process

of industrialization. Consequently, State-led redistribution policies must seek to reduce consumption by the upper income groups in order to increase savings and direct them to capital accumulation (Prebisch, 1963; Pinto, 1970).

Theoretical work on the macroeconomic effects of income inequality was sidelined in the mid-1970s, partly because of the dominant role of representative agent models in mainstream macroeconomics.[2] The financial turmoil and the debt crisis in developing countries in the 1980s focused attention on short-term economic management, pushing development concerns to the background. From the early 1990s, however, interest in the relationship between inequality and development resurfaced. The contrast between rapid growth in a number of Asian economies and the "lost decade" for development in Latin America raised questions about their diverging growth paths. Relatively low inequality in East Asia contrasted with historically high inequality in Latin America, which was further aggravated by the debt crisis and the policy responses. Some authors suggested that this was an important factor in explaining these regions' widely different development experiences (e.g. Fajnzylber, 1989; ECLAC, 1990).

The renewed interest in the links between growth and distribution in the early 1990s was reflected in several theoretical works, which identified four possible channels through which income inequalities can have negative impacts on economic growth. The first channel is the impact of inequality on the level and composition of aggregate demand. The second is the relationship between inequality and socio-political instability. The third concerns the political economy implications of high inequality. Finally, the fourth channel through which inequality affects the pace of output growth is related to imperfect capital markets and investment in education.

Regarding the first channel, it is argued that since entrepreneurs make their investment and hiring decisions based on their expectations of future demand for their products, higher wages (and lower inequality) can stimulate investment, employment and economic growth by increasing expected demand. Murphy, Shleifer and Vishny (1989a and b) formalize

> Development economists focus on how income inequality affects aggregate demand, investment and growth.

Box 2.1

INEQUALITY, SAVINGS AND INVESTMENT

Rising income inequality is often seen as a means to increase the investment ratio, as the higher incomes of the rich or more income appropriated by profit earners tend to augment aggregate savings at any given level of income. And it is assumed that their higher savings will quasi automatically lead to greater investments. As discussed in previous *TDRs* (see, in particular *TDR 2006*, Annex 2 to chap. I, and *TDR 2008*, chap. III), the theory of savings and investment which underlies this view (as well as the related policies to revive growth and employment creation) is highly questionable. It is even deeply flawed, because its core is a simple ex post identity.

The national product generated in an economy (plus the net capital flows) can be used either immediately (for consumption during the period of production) or at a later stage. If used at a later stage, it is counted as the savings or the investment of that economy. Hence, by simple definition, the savings (national and foreign) in any economy always equal its investments.

However, the identity is silent about causality. It is therefore highly problematic to attribute to any of its terms a specific or even a leading role in the macroeconomic process, as long as the factors that determine either of them are not taken into account. A theory is constituted only when the plans of one group of actors are analysed in conjunction with the plans of other actors. Specifically, it is necessary to identify the functional relationships which determine the consumption and investment decisions taken by the different actors in an economy. In doing so, the real income of all actors cannot be treated as an exogenous factor, but as a variable which itself is influenced by the decisions of the economic agents regarding their consumption and investment plans, as well as by policy decisions and by exogenous shocks.

Since changes in the behaviour of economic agents in an economy are subject to objective uncertainty, the determination of consumption and investment is a complex process, and the results are much less straightforward than they may appear by looking only at the ex post identity. If inequality increases, the planned savings of all households taken together will indeed rise, because the savings rates of the rich is higher than the savings rates of the poor. However, in this case producers are immediately faced with falling demand for their products and falling profits. In such a situation, they will typically react by cutting their investment in new productive capacity. On the other hand, when savings plans are based on the expectation of incomes that depend on a rise in investment but in actual fact investment falls, aggregate income will be lower than what was expected by households when they originally made their savings plans. Hence the planned rise in overall household savings may not materialize, since the total income is lower than what was expected at the time when the savings plans were made. Moreover, firms' savings (i.e. retained profits) are likely to fall. The ex post identity of savings and investments holds, but the mechanism to trigger the equalization is the unexpected fall in real income that neutralized the planned increase in savings.

The traditional theory of savings and investment ignores this latter mechanism and the fact that savings are an endogenous variable. It assumes that after an increase in the household savings rate, companies will invest more than before, despite a fall in consumption, which is the inevitable counterpart to higher savings. In the orthodox model, the economy is exclusively driven by autonomous consumer decisions. It assumes totally reactive entrepreneurs who never take into account the deterioration of actual business conditions and falling profits when making their investment plans.

Aggregate consumption and the incentive for private firms to undertake fixed investment are greater when a given national income is distributed more equally, because lower income groups spend a larger portion of their income on consumption than higher income groups. This is of particular importance in situations of high or rising unemployment. As Keynes (1936/1973: 372–373) put it: "... up to the point where full employment prevails, the growth of capital depends not at all on a low propensity to consume but is, on the contrary, held back by it ..." because "... an increase in the habitual propensity to consume will in general serve to increase at the same time the inducement to invest ..."

Rosenstein-Rodan's (1943) intuition that the simultaneous creation of many industries can be profitable even in a situation in which each industry would be individually unprofitable. They show that such a "big push" requires that the new industries pay wages that are higher than the wages in the traditional sector. With lower wages, simultaneous industrialization would not be profitable because of a lack of aggregate demand. In their model, the rich demand high-quality goods, the production of which offers little scope for increasing productivity; by contrast, the middle class demands standardized goods produced through mass manufacturing, where most productivity gains occur. Hence, a reduction of income inequality has positive effects on economic growth because it increases demand for products with growth-enhancing properties.

Another set of arguments (the second channel referred to above) emphasizes that, even if a high degree of income inequality does not have a direct adverse impact on economic growth, it has an indirect impact resulting from the social and political consequences of inequality. For example, a high level of inequality may lead to social upheaval and increase the crime rate, which create uncertainty among investors, erode property rights, raise transaction and security costs, and reduce growth (Venieris and Gupta, 1986; Benhabib and Rustichini, 1996; Grossman and Kim, 1996; Bourguignon, 1998).

The third channel is examined by different models that build a political economy link between inequality and growth. Models by Alesina and Rodrik (1994) and Persson and Tabellini (1994) suggest that high inequality in primary income distribution (i.e. distribution of incomes resulting from market outcomes alone) hampers growth. They argue that in less equal societies a majority of the population seeks more redistribution, and redistributive policies reduce growth by introducing economic distortions. In particular, taxes on capital result in lower private investment and growth. Another group of models (Bénabou, 2000, 2002; Saint-Paul and Verdier, 1996; Perotti, 1996;

> Recent theoretical work finds a negative correlation between income inequality and economic growth.

> High inequality may dampen aggregate demand, deprive many people of access to education and credit, and generate social upheavals, undermining productive investment and growth.

Dartolo, 2008) gets the same result of lower growth with higher inequality, but with opposite mechanisms. They assume a positive correlation between redistribution and growth. According to them, the pivotal voter (i.e. a voter who can change his choices in successive elections and, acting in a group, can play a decisive role) is often richer than the median voter, and therefore would not benefit from redistributive policies. Thus, in less equal societies, characterized by low participation of the poor in elections, and/or by a disproportionately greater influence of the more wealthy in elections, there is an insufficient level of growth-enhancing redistributive policies.

The fourth channel focuses on the relationship between income inequality, imperfect capital markets and investment in education. Models that emphasize the interactions between income inequality, imperfect capital markets and investment decisions suggest that risk-aversion and moral hazard are sources of capital market imperfection. They find that inequality reduces growth because it prevents some agents from investing in physical and/or human capital (Banerjee and Newman, 1991). Galor and Zeira (1993) postulate that access to education is costly, and even the poor need to pay a minimum fixed cost for it (possibly the opportunity cost of not having their children work). They show that fixed costs in education lead to persistent inequality as poor households are caught in a poverty trap.[3] Galor and Moav (2004) examine the dynamic effects of income inequality on economic growth. In their model, inequality may be good for growth when physical capital accumulation is the main driver of economic development, when such accumulation depends on savings and when high-income individuals have a higher marginal propensity to save. However, inequality may have a negative effect on economic growth when human capital is the main driver of such growth because credit constraints can limit aggregate human capital accumulation. This theory concludes that models that emphasized the positive effects of inequality on savings were an appropriate reflection of reality in the early stages of industrialization, but are no longer relevant for developed economies today. Finally, high inequality also has a direct negative impact on growth in the "capital-market imperfections" model of Aghion, Caroli and García-Peñalosa (1999). They argue that it slows down human capital formation, as the rich tend to confine their investments to relatively low-return activities, while the poor, even if they have projects with high rates of return, cannot invest more than their limited endowments permit due to their lack of access to credit arising from capital market imperfections.

This theoretical work did not always attract the attention of policymakers, especially as economic growth tended to improve during the 1990s (until 1997) in several regions, with the exception of Africa and the economies in transition. In several countries, growth seemed to be compatible with rising inequality, and the policy responses were frequently oriented towards generating safety nets for those who were marginalized from the benefits of growth. However, some international organizations that adopted a larger historical perspective were less optimistic. UNCTAD (*TDR 1997*) observed that since the early 1980s there had been rising inequalities and slow growth, which were becoming permanent features of the global economy. It also warned that this could lead to a political backlash that might undermine several of the benefits of global integration. At the same time, the Latin American Institute for Economic and Social Planning (ILPES, 1998) highlighted the shortcomings and fragility of economic growth in Latin America, owing partly to its limited social impact and its inability to reduce income inequality. It observed that compensatory social policies had not been able to contain the widening social and economic gaps, and that a reorientation of the economic policy stance was needed.

The World Bank (2006) also analysed the negative social and economic consequences of high inequality. It noted that the distribution of wealth and power affects the allocation of investment opportunities often in socially undesirable ways, because "high levels of economic and political inequality tend to lead to economic institutions and social arrangements that systematically favour the interests of those with more influence. Such inequitable institutions can generate economic costs ... [and] the inequality of opportunity that arises is wasteful and inimical to sustainable development and poverty reduction" (World Bank, 2006: 2–3).

C. Some empirical evidence on inequality, employment and growth

Most of the recent literature reviewed in section B proposes empirical tests for the relationship between inequality and growth, which, as explained in this section, generally point to a negative correlation between the two. This is consistent with some basic stylized facts that are discussed in the subsequent chapters of this *Report*. There was strong global growth during the decades immediately following the Second World War, with low or declining inequality in industrialized countries and also in many developing countries. However, over the past three decades, income inequality increased dramatically, particularly in developed countries, reaching levels not observed since the 1920s (discussed in chapter III). It coincided with slower global growth and rising imbalances within and between countries, which eventually led to the global financial crisis that erupted in late 2008.

Recent empirical work on the link between inequality and growth can be divided into three groups. The first group uses cross-country data to study the long-term relationship between inequality and growth, the second uses longitudinal panel data (still at the cross-country level) to study the medium-term relationship between the two, and the third studies this relationship by focusing on both cross-sectional and longitudinal state-level data for the United States.

Among the first group of studies, Persson and Tabellini (1994) and Alesina and Rodrik (1994) test the reduced form equations of their models, and show that there is a negative empirical relationship between income distribution and growth. Easterly (2007) uses an instrumental variable approach to show that income inequality has a negative causal effect on economic development. Perotti (1996) attempts to differentiate between the various theoretical channels discussed above. His main results can be summarized as follows: (i) there is a robust negative relationship between income inequality and growth; (ii) there is no evidence that the relationship between inequality and growth is stronger in democracies; (iii) the structural estimations support the hypothesis that inequality hinders growth by causing socio-political instability and by its impact on education and decisions relating to fertility;[4] and (iv) there is no evidence to support the political economy argument that inequality leads to higher redistribution, which in turn leads to lower growth. Indeed, Perotti finds a positive correlation between redistribution and growth.

> Excessive concentration of income was one of the factors leading to the global crisis as it was linked to perverse incentives for the top income earners and to high indebtedness in other income groups.

The second group of studies includes those by Li and Zou (1998) and Forbes (2000) who use five-year growth periods to show that regressions which control for country-specific factors yield a positive relationship between inequality and growth. These results seem to contrast with the results of the theoretical models discussed above. However, there are at least two problems with their empirical approaches. The first problem has to do with the fact that, while most theoretical models emphasize the relationship between inequality and long-term growth, these studies analyse the link between inequality and medium- or short-term growth. The second problem (which also affects the cross-country regressions discussed above) relates to the fact that the linear structure imposed in standard growth regressions may lead to biased results. In addressing these issues, Banerjee and Duflo (2003) find that changes

in inequality (in either direction) are negatively correlated with growth, and that lagged inequality is also negatively correlated with growth.

The third group of studies suggests that there is no clear relationship between different measures of income inequality and economic growth in different states of the United States. For instance, Partridge (1997) finds a negative relationship between inequality and growth when inequality is measured using the income share of the third quintile of the income distribution, and a positive relationship when inequality is measured using the Gini index. However, Panizza (2002) shows that there is a negative, but not very robust, relationship between state-level income inequality and economic growth in the United States.

Although not always conclusive, and sometimes based on opposite hypotheses, recent empirical and analytical work reviewed here mostly shows a negative correlation between inequality and growth. This growing academic consensus is consistent with the stylized fact already mentioned, that in many countries economic growth was strong in the post-war decades, when inequality was relatively low or declining, and has weakened markedly since the 1980s, when inequality has been rising. For the group of developed countries, the share of employee compensation in GDP (at factor cost) has reached its lowest level since the end of the Second World War, and yet open unemployment has reached its highest level recorded for the same period.

As the subsequent chapters of this *Report* show, in the last three decades macroeconomic policies and changes in institutional arrangements that followed the new paradigm of "labour market flexibility" played a major role in the trend of rising inequality, thereby contributing to the build-up of the global crisis. Labour market and tax policies exacerbated income inequality, as they placed the burden of adjustment to globalization and technological progress on wage earners and on the middle and lower income groups. In the United States, for example, tax cuts have favoured the wealthy, who are paying some of the lowest tax rates in the history of the country. There is evidence that the reduction in the progressive tax in the 2000s did not result in higher growth and employment generation than in the previous decade, although tax rates on top incomes were increased in the early 1990s (Krueger, 2012).

In addition, several recent analyses suggest that some of the main causes of the global financial crisis – including private overindebtedness and the dominance of an unregulated financial sector over the real sector of the economy – are linked to growing income inequality.[5] In particular, rising private debt-to-income ratios in some developed countries – most notably the United States – were partly attributed to stagnating real wages, which reduced the purchasing power of households. With stagnating wages, households could increase their expenditure, or even just maintain it, only by incurring debt. The increase in such debt, in turn, boosted the activities and profits of the financial sector, resulting in a further concentration of wealth and income. The credit bubble thus created eventually burst with the subprime crisis that triggered the global economic crisis.

The predominance of the financial sector in the economy is reflected in the compensation paid to corporate executives, managers and financial agents. Extremely high wages in this sector are mainly responsible for the huge differences between the top income earners and the rest. Compensation packages often include stock or stock options, which create perverse incentives and lead to excessive risk taking. In this context, the changes in corporate behaviour that have accompanied finance-led globalization have given strong emphasis to short-term profits and shareholder dividends, while wage earners have borne the greatest burden of adjustment to economic shocks.

If increasing inequality has been one of the factors leading to the financial crisis, the subsequent global recession and the policies devised to handle it are also having a significant impact on income inequality (UNCTAD, 2012). The social consequences of the economic and financial crisis have been record levels of unemployment in many countries, as well as increased poverty

> Developing countries must increasingly rely on domestic markets and South-South trade …

> … but the size and composition of domestic and regional markets depend largely on income distribution.

and higher inequality. In developed countries, particularly in Europe, most proposals to overcome the current crisis, such as cutting wages and downsizing social services, would tend to increase inequality. Cuts in public spending are largely focused on reducing social expenditure on education, health, pensions, and social services and transfers, as well as on cutting public sector salaries and employment. They also include reductions in public investment, which have a negative impact on employment and on private investment. When fiscal tightening takes the form of higher tax rates, this typically involves an increase of – regressive – indirect taxes rather than progressive taxes on wealth and on higher income groups. Hence, fiscal austerity typically has negative distributional effects, as it results in a reduction of the disposable income of lower income groups, and, since these are precisely the groups with a higher propensity to consume, this exerts further downward pressure on aggregate demand.

The crisis has taken a heavy toll on society in terms of employment losses, particularly among the youth. In order to restore pre-crisis employment and absorb the new labour entrants, an employment deficit, estimated at 48 million jobs in 2011, would need to be eliminated (UN/DESA, 2012).[6] Apart from the immediate loss of wage income, long-term high unemployment tends to weaken the bargaining power of workers, with severe impacts on wages and labour conditions. It also leads to a loss of qualifications and reduced employability. In addition, the poorest and middle segments of the population are most likely to suffer a significant loss of assets, such as housing and savings, while their access to basic social services is further impaired. The ILO (2012b) provides compelling evidence on how the crisis has deepened inequalities in Europe.

Contrary to what happened in most developed countries and transition economies, over the last decade a number of developing countries have recorded significant improvements in income distribution. To a large extent, these improvements have been the result of redistributive fiscal policies and incomes policies which have linked wage increases to productivity increases. The record of declining inequality in Latin America during the 2000s provides proof of the effectiveness of these policies in improving income distribution. However, in absolute terms inequality tends to be considerably higher in developing countries than in developed countries.

Restrictive policies and increased inequality in developed countries not only harm domestic economic activity, but also generate negative spillovers to other countries. In the current context of slow growth in developed countries, it has become evident that developing countries will not be able to depend on exports for growth as much as in the past, and must increasingly rely on domestic markets and South-South trade (*TDR 2010*). But the size and composition of such markets depend to a large extent on income distribution. Therefore, these countries will need to progress further in reducing income inequality and find the appropriate balance between external and domestic demand.

D. Looking ahead

The gap between formal and real equality of opportunities has deep economic roots and far-reaching economic consequences. Inequality that begins in the cradle is not easily redressed through social mobility. It tends to pass from one generation to the next and is generally compounded, in particular by unequal access to education and health services, and inertia on the part of existing power structures in different groups of society. Effective equality of opportunities requires more than just ridding a system of legal impediments to social mobility, such as those that existed in feudal times. It requires providing all social groups with access to an acceptable minimum level of living standards and to adequate public services, including education and health; otherwise, formal equality is little more than an empty shell. It is, in the words of Anatole France (1894/2007: 75), the "majestic equality of the laws, which forbid rich and poor alike to sleep under the bridges, to beg in the streets, and to steal their bread". The absence of equal opportunities in practice implies an enormous waste of development potential, since a large segment of the population is excluded from modern productive activities and consumption, which negatively affects the potential for the creation of value added and the development of strong domestic markets.

The greater the inequality, the less possible it becomes to separate outcomes and opportunities. Outcome determines opportunity through access to health, education and influence. This relates not only to opportunity among the lower income groups; it also concerns the distribution of profits (e.g. between rents and entrepreneurial profits, and between profits of innovative and declining sectors and firms). The extent to which profits feed back into investment and the overall dynamics of the economy has implications for the generation of employment.

Inequality, growth and structural change interact in different ways, as discussed in subsequent chapters. It is therefore necessary to examine if – and how – reducing inequality and increasing degrees of inclusiveness can lead to a process of strong and sustained growth. Revising the policy approach to inequality is all the more urgent in the light of the continuing impact of the global financial crises and the negative distributional effects of the fiscal and wage policy responses experienced in many developed countries today. In developing countries, a greater participation of workers of all occupations in overall productivity growth and more social protection for the poor are essential not only for alleviating poverty, but also for strengthening the dynamics of domestic markets.

The analysis of the relationship between inequality and growth and development is a complex task because inequality involves many dimensions. It is compounded by the difficulties in measuring inequality and problems of data availability. This *Report* focuses mainly on income inequality within countries. However, it must be emphasized that inequality between countries also remains a major concern, as global inequality results from both intra- and inter-country inequality. Indeed, it is income differences between countries that is the major determinant of global income inequality. Assuming a stable income distribution within a country, narrowing the gap in per capita GDP among countries will reduce global income inequality, and vice versa. Thus continuing efforts at the national and international levels aimed at increasing the per capita GDP in developing countries and helping them catch up with the more advanced countries therefore remain crucial.

Chapter III of this *Trade and Development Report* presents some empirical evidence of the magnitude and evolution of inequality. It focuses on income inequality within countries, although it also examines how inequality has evolved at the global level. It suggests that policymakers need to target inequality within their countries with policies aimed at reducing the income gap, which in turn will influence overall economic and social outcomes. The chapter also briefly examines some other aspects of inequality, such as gender, access to education and the distribution of wealth. All of these are also relevant for income distribution and require specific policy actions.

Chapter IV discusses what are widely perceived to be the main structural causes of recent changes in income distribution, including trade, technological change and finance-led globalization. It argues that the impacts of globalization and technological change on domestic income distribution are not necessarily uniform. Rather, they depend on initial conditions as well as on how macroeconomic, financial and labour market policies interact with the forces of globalization and technological development. Structural changes do not necessarily lead to greater inequality if appropriate employment, wage and income distribution policies are in place. This issue is further elaborated in chapters V and VI of this *Report*.

> Revising the policy approach to inequality is all the more urgent in the light of the continuing impact of the global financial crisis and the negative distributional effects of the policy responses.

Chapter V discusses how income distribution has been and may be modified by proactive public policies, including the use of fiscal instruments aimed at redistribution. It argues that the use of such instruments does not necessarily reduce incentives to invest in fixed capital, innovation and skills acquisition. On the contrary, the reduction of inequality that can be achieved with such instruments is more likely to accelerate growth and employment creation than the past trend towards less progressive taxation and lower social transfers, which aimed at eliminating distortions in market outcomes.

Finally, chapter VI examines how labour market institutions and policies, together with an appropriate macroeconomic framework, can respond to the present challenges and lead to both sustained growth and more inclusive development. The chapter starts with the proposition that slow growth has a strong impact on inequality due to rising and high unemployment. The latter increases inequality both as a result of income losses incurred by the unemployed, and, more fundamentally, by weakening the bargaining power of labour. It argues that the paradigm of labour market flexibility has not just failed to reduce unemployment, but has even tended to exacerbate it, because the unemployed are prone to accept lower wages. It asserts that the economic model underlying this paradigm is fundamentally flawed, and suggests an alternative approach based on the recognition that wage growth in line with productivity growth prevents a rise in inequality and supports the process of economic growth and employment creation in a dynamic economy. ∎

Notes

1   For instance, Prebisch (1963) believed that extreme inequality in the ownership of agricultural land hampered the use of modern techniques of intensive production because large properties obtain huge rents even without having to resort to such production, and very small units, owing to extreme poverty, cannot afford to use the modern techniques.

2   These models are based on the assumption that the economy as a whole behaves like an individual economic unit – the "representative agent". Due to the way in which they are constructed, they exclude consideration of distributive issues among several agents or groups of agents.

3   However, this model does not always arrive at the conclusion that inequality is bad for growth. There is a set of parameters and initial conditions under which inequality allows some agents to invest in education, while under fully egalitarian distribution, where average income per capita is lower than the fixed cost of education, nobody would invest in education.

4   Alesina and Perotti (1996) also find evidence of a negative correlation between inequality and growth owing to the socio-political instability caused by high inequality.

5   See, for instance, Attali, 2009; *TDR 2010*, chap. II; Kumhof and Rancière, 2010; and Galbraith, 2012.

6   The International Labour Office also estimated a deficit of 50 million jobs as a result of the crisis (ILO, 2012a).

References

Aghion P, Caroli E and García-Peñalosa C (1999). Inequality and economic growth: The perspective of the new growth theories. *Journal of Economic Literature*, 37(4): 1615–1660.

Alesina A and Perotti R (1996). Income distribution, political instability and investment. *European Economic Review*, 40(6): 1203–1228.

Alesina A and Rodrik D (1994). Distributive politics and economic growth. *Quarterly Journal of Economics*, 109(2): 465–490.

Attali J (2009). *La Crise, et Après?* Paris, Fayard.

Banerjee AV and Duflo E (2003). Inequality and growth: What can the data say? *Journal of Economic Growth*, 8(3): 267–299.

Banerjee AV and Newman AF (1991). Risk-bearing and the theory of income distribution. *Review of Economic Studies*, 58(2): 211–235.

Bartels L (2008). Unequal Democracy: *The Political Economy of the New Gilded Age*. Princeton, NJ, Princeton University Press.

Bénabou R (2000). Unequal societies: Income distribution and the social contract. *American Economic Review*, 90(1): 96–129.

Bénabou R (2002). Tax and education policy in a heterogeneous-agent economy: What levels of redistribution maximize growth and efficiency? *Econometrica*, 70(2): 481–517.

Benhabib J and Rustichini A (1996). Social conflict and growth. *Journal of Economic Growth*, 1(1): 125–142.

Bourguignon F (1998). Équité et croissance économique: une nouvelle analyse? *Revue Française d'Économie*, XIII(3): 25–84.

Diamond P and Saez E (2011). The Case for a Progressive Tax: From Basic Research to Policy Recommendations. *Journal of Economic Perspectives*, 25(4): 165–190.

Easterly W (2007). Inequality does cause underdevelopment: Insights from a new instrument. *Journal of Development Economics*, 84(2): 755–776.

ECLAC (1990). Transformación productiva con equidad. (LC/G.1601-P). Santiago, Chile, March.

Fajnzylber F (1989). Industrialización en América Latina: de la 'caja negra' al 'casillero vacío': comparación de patrones contemporáneos de industrialización. *Cuadernos de la CEPAL*, No. 60 (LC/G.1534/Rev.1-P), Santiago, Chile, ECLAC.

Forbes JK (2000). A reassessment of the relationship between inequality and growth. *American Economic Review*, 90(4): 869–887.

France A (1894, reprinted in 2007). *The Red Lily*, Wildside Press LLC.

Friedman M and Friedman R (1980). *Free to Choose*. London, Secker & Warbur.

Galbraith J (2012). *Inequality and Instability*. Oxford and New York, Oxford University Press.

Galor O and Moav O (2004). From physical to human capital accumulation: Inequality and the process of development. *Review of Economic Studies*, 71(4): 1001–1026.

Galor O and Zeira J (1993). Income distribution and macroeconomics. *Review of Economic Studies*, 60(1): 35–52.

Grossman HI and Kim M (1996). Predation and accumulation. *Journal of Economic Growth*, 1(3): 333–350.

Habermas J (1973). *La technique et la science comme idéologie*. Paris, Gallimard.

Hayek F (1960). *The Constitution of Liberty*. London, Routledge and Kegan.

Hayek F (1978). *Temas de la Hora Actual*. Buenos Aires, Ediciones de la Bolsa de Comercio de Buenos Aires.

ILO (2012a). *World of Work Report 2012: Better Jobs for a Better Economy*. Geneva.

ILO (2012b). *Work Inequalities in the Crisis: Evidence from Europe*. Geneva.

ILPES (1998). Reflexiones sobre el desarrollo y la responsabilidad del Estado. Instituto Latinoamericano y del Caribe de Planificación Económica y Social (ILPES), United Nations, Santiago de Chile.

Kaldor N (1957). A model of economic growth. *The Economic Journal*, 67(268): 591–624.

Keynes JM (1936/1973). The general theory of employment, interest and money. In: *The Collected Writings of John Maynard Keynes*, Vol. VII. London, Macmillan and St. Martin's Press for the Royal Economic Society.

Krueger AB (2012). The rise and consequences of inequality in the United States. Speech delivered at the Center for American Progress in Washington, DC.

Council of Economic Advisers, 12 January. Available at: http://www.whitehouse.gov/blog/2012/01/12/chairman-alan-krueger-discusses-rise-and-consequences-inequality-center-american-pro.

Kumhof M and Rancière R (2010). Inequality, leverage and crises. IMF Working Paper, WP/10/268, Washington, DC.

Kuznets S (1955). Economic growth and income inequality. *American Economic Review*, 45(1): 1–28.

Li H and Zou HF (1998). Income inequality is not harmful for growth: Theory and evidence. *Review of Development Economics*, 2: 318–334.

Murphy KM, Shleifer A and Vishny RW (1989a). Industrialization and the Big Push. *Journal of Political Economy*, 97(5): 1003–1026.

Murphy KM, Shleifer A and Vishny RW (1989b). Income distribution, market size, and industrialization. *Quarterly Journal of Economics*, 104(3): 537–564.

Panizza U (2002). Income inequality and economic growth: evidence from American data. *Journal of Economic Growth*, 7(1): 25–41.

Partridge M (1997). Is inequality harmful for growth? Comment. *American Economic Review*, 87(5): 1019–1032.

Perotti R (1996). Democracy, income distribution and growth: What the data says. *Journal of Economic Growth*, 1(2): 149–187.

Persson T and Tabellini G (1994). Is inequality harmful for growth? *American Economic Review*, 84(3): 600–621.

Pinto A (1970). Naturaleza e implicaciones de la 'heterogeneidad estructural' de la América Latina. *El Trimestre Económico*, 37(1), No. 145, January–March, Mexico City.

Prebisch R (1963). *Hacia una Dinámica del Desarrollo Latinoamericano*. México City, Fondo de Cultura Económica.

Rosenstein-Rodan PN (1943). Problems of industrialization of Eastern and South-Eastern Europe. *Economic Journal*, 53(210/211): 202–211.

Saint-Paul G and Verdier T (1996). Inequality, redistribution and growth: A challenge to the conventional political economy approach. *European Economic Review*, 40(3–5): 719–728.

Schumpeter JA (1942/2003). *Capitalism, Socialism and Democracy*, Routledge, London and New York. First published in 1942.

Tinbergen J (1956, reprinted in 1964). *Economic Policy, Principles and Design*. North Holland.

UNCTAD (*TDR 1997*). *Trade and Development Report, 1997. Globalization, Distribution and Growth*. United Nations publication, Sales No. E.97.II.D.8, New York and Geneva.

UNCTAD (*TDR 2006*). *Trade and Development Report, 2006. Global Partnership and National Policies for Development*. United Nations publication, Sales No. E.06.II.D.6, New York and Geneva.

UNCTAD (*TDR 2008*). *Trade and Development Report, 2008. Commodity Prices, Capital Flows and the Financing of Investment*. United Nations publication, Sales No. E.08.II.D.21, New York and Geneva.

UNCTAD (*TDR 2010*). *Trade and Development Report, 2010. Employment, globalization and development*. United Nations publication, Sales No. E.10.II.D.3, New York and Geneva.

UNCTAD (2012). Breaking the cycle of exclusion and crisis. UNCTAD Policy Brief No. 5, June, Geneva.

UN/DESA (2012). *World Economic Situation and Prospects 2012. Update as of mid-2012*. New York, NY, United Nations.

Venieris Y and Gupta D (1986). Income distribution and sociopolitical instability as determinants of savings: A cross-sectional model. *Journal of Political Economy*, 94(4): 873–883.

World Bank (2006). *World Development Report: Equity and Development*. Washington, DC.

Chapter III

EVOLUTION OF INCOME INEQUALITY: DIFFERENT TIME PERSPECTIVES AND DIMENSIONS

A. Introduction

The world economy has experienced profound changes over the past few decades. Many countries have adopted different development strategies and even changed their economic systems. At the same time, trade and financial globalization have deepened, and technological advances and sectoral shifts are transforming the patterns of production and consumption. Successive financial and economic crises have had varying negative impacts on different regions. And the rapid growth rates of GDP in a number of large developing countries are altering the relative weight of different regions in the international economy. These developments were bound to have an effect on income distribution both within and between countries.

There are two major measures of income distribution. One measure is the *functional distribution of income*, which examines the distribution between the main factors of production (labour and capital). It shows the respective shares in national income of wages and salaries on the one hand, and profits, interests and rents on the other. It follows the tradition in political economy of looking at the determinants and evolution of income distribution among social classes based on their insertion in the production system (workers and owners of capital and land). This measure highlights the sources of primary income earned through participation in economic activity.

The second measure is that of *personal distribution of income*, which refers to its distribution among households or individuals, irrespective of the source of the income. A given household or individual may receive income from both labour activity and capital revenues, as well as from pensions and other transfers from the public sector. The most comprehensive data are normally gathered from household surveys. After obtaining the total amount of their different types of incomes, households are sorted by per capita income – from the poorer to the richer – and inequality is assessed through inter-quantile ratios or synthetic statistical indicators which measure concentration. The most frequently used indicators for this purpose are the Gini and Theil coefficients.[1]

The different degrees of inequality in the distribution of primary revenues partly determine inequality in household incomes. Since capital is generally concentrated in relatively few hands, a rising share of returns on capital in total income tends to increase personal inequality, and vice versa. However, the relationship between functional and personal income distribution is not straightforward, for a number of reasons. First, not all returns on capital are distributed among households: some remain within the firm as undistributed profits. Second, household revenues may come from different sources: capital income, wage income and mixed income (in the case of self-employed workers). And third, households pay taxes on their primary revenues, and some of them receive public transfers, including pensions, family allocations and unemployment benefits. Hence, the distribution of gross income may differ significantly from that of net disposable income, after redistribution by the public sector.

Statistical evidence on income distribution is highly incomplete and heterogeneous. It also suffers from methodological breaks, which makes it difficult to present a comprehensive picture of how inequality – in its various definitions – has evolved, especially in the long run. In addition, definitions and methodologies frequently differ in developed and developing economies. Thus extreme caution is needed when making comparisons of inequality among countries and regions.[2] For instance, in most countries of Africa, West Asia and South Asia, statistics present the distribution of households' expenditure rather than that of their income. Although both variables are correlated, concentration of income is significantly higher than that of expenditure, since the share of income saved rises with the level of income. Moreover, functional income distribution also depends on the social structure. In developed countries and economies in transition, wage earners represent more than 80 per cent of the active population, which makes it easy to identify the income distribution between labour and capital. In many developing countries, on the other hand, the largest proportion of the active population does not consist of wage earners, but rather of the self-employed in low-productivity activities (agriculture or retail commerce). It is therefore misleading to consider all their revenues as a share of "capital" incomes. In some developing countries, this income is presented separately as "mixed income", but in others it is included in capital revenues. By contrast, in statistics of the Organisation of Economic Co-operation and Development (OECD), self-employed revenues are distributed between salaries (applying a representative wage to the work of this population) and capital. Finally, the distinction between wage incomes and profit incomes has also become blurred at the upper end of the income scale where remuneration of those at the top of the wage hierarchy often follows more closely the logic of capital income (e.g. bonuses or stock options).

Bearing these caveats in mind, it is nonetheless possible to extract some stylized facts from the available data. One is that income inequality has changed significantly over time in all regions as a result of major crises or changes in development strategies and in the international economic framework. The 1980s (or in some countries the late 1970s or the early 1990s) appears to be one of the turning points, when there was a sizeable increase in income inequality in virtually all regions. However, it is difficult to generalize: this simultaneous rise in inequality happened in very different situations and resulted from diverse mechanisms. In some countries it was linked to rapid economic growth, as in some major Asian countries; whereas in others, it took place in a context of economic stagnation or depression, as in Latin America in the 1980s and 1990s, and in Africa and the transition economies in the 1990s. More recently, with Latin America recovering its economic dynamism, inequality has declined. A similar positive correlation between rapid growth and falling inequality was observed in the industrialized countries in the decades following the Second World War. All this indicates that the relationship between growth and inequality is complex, and can be altered by proactive economic and social policies.

Another stylized fact is the rising inequality in developed countries – with a growing share of the very rich in total income – in the run-up to the two major financial crises of 1929 and 2008. That inequality probably was one of the factors leading to the crises, as it was related to perverse incentives for the top income earners and led to a high level of indebtedness in other income groups. The way income inequality and excessive indebtedness are addressed is of particular importance in the face of the still unresolved global financial crisis. In the past, many industrialized countries were able to generate sustained and inclusive growth with more equal income distribution as a result of governments playing a more active role. However this happened after an extensive destruction of capital and debts, in particular through hyperinflation, massive bankruptcies and wars. In the current situation, a strategy of "growing out of debt" (*TDR 2011*: 82–83) would need progressive income redistribution and debt restructuring in order to restore domestic demand and growth. However, it appears that in many crisis-hit countries – particularly in the European Union – the policy responses are most likely to lead to further increases in inequality. Proposals for achieving macroeconomic balance are relying strongly on labour market flexibilization and wage restraint, as well as on fiscal austerity with a focus on spending cuts, particularly on cuts in social expenditures, public wages and employment. This kind of adjustment, with regressive distributional effects, is likely to hamper economic growth in the short and medium run and to generate a less inclusive society for the next generation.

This chapter describes the main changes in income distribution in different regions over time. Section B traces the evolution of income inequality within countries, thereby providing a historical context for the analysis of more recent changes, particularly those that have occurred since the early 1980s, which are analysed in section C. Section D shows how income inequality evolved between countries and among the world's individuals, and provides an estimate of global income inequality. Finally, section E discusses some dimensions of inequality – distribution of wealth, gender inequality and differing access to education – which, while distinct from income inequality, are closely related to it and frequently tend to reinforce it.

B. Long-term trends in inequality within countries

1. *Functional income distribution*

Economists have often defended the notion that functional income distribution is to some extent empirically stable, although they offer very different explanations of the causes of stability (Krämer, 2010). This long-run stability was among Kaldor's famous "stylized facts", as reasonable "starting points for the construction of theoretical models" (Kaldor, 1961: 178). However, according to modern Keynesian/Kaleckian theories,[3] which posit that functional income distribution strongly depends on political factors, the occurrence of periods of stability should be considered the result of a pause or balance in the "class conflict", arising from a combination of political and economic factors. In particular, the post-war social consensus in the North, in which workers' compensation roughly followed gains in productivity led to relative stability in the income shares of capital and labour. The neoclassical approach, on the other hand, has treated the stability of functional income distribution both as an empirical fact and as a prediction based on a strictly techno-economic explanation with substitutable factors of production: the nature of available technology (as represented, for instance, by the Cobb-Douglas aggregate production function)

would be such that, in the case of a wage rise, labour would be replaced by capital, thereby keeping their relative shares stable (Piketty, 2008: 45).[4]

Long-term statistics on functional distribution without major methodological breaks are available for only a handful of developed countries. Piketty (2008) observed that between 1920 and 1995, income distribution between wages and profits in France, the United Kingdom and the United States was fairly stable: functional income distribution in these three countries has been around two thirds of wages and one third of profits, and no systematic trend altering this distribution has been visible in the long run (although this seems to have changed since 1980, as discussed below; see table 3.1). This stability may seem inconsistent with the significant socio-economic changes that have taken place during the twentieth century, including a reduction in the number of self-employed (e.g. peasants and small shop owners) and a concomitant increase in the share of wage earners in the workforce. This is not fully reflected in the rising share of wages in total income, as reported by the OECD, whose statistical conventions allocate a proportion of self-employed revenues to wages and the residual to capital income (as noted earlier).

Table 3.1

SHARE OF WAGES IN GDP IN SELECTED COUNTRIES, 1920–2010

(Per cent)

	1920	1925	1930	1935	1940	1945	1950	1955	1960	1965	1970	1975	1980	1985	1990	1995	2000	2005	2010
France	66.3	65.1	67.5	69.5	68.7	..	62.2	65.9	65.6	67.6	66.4	70.3	71.7	68.0	62.4	60.3	60.5	61.0	61.4
United Kingdom	61.9	61.9	61.9	64.2	63.7	..	66.8	67.5	68.8	67.5	67.6	70.6	67.1	61.9	62.9	60.3	62.8	61.4	62.6
United States	..	..	55.4	56.7	57.2	60.1	57.5	59.3	61.3	60.5	65.3	63.7	64.6	62.0	62.6	61.4	61.5	59.7	59.0
Japan	..	..	..	..	..	..	..	40.9	39.4	43.7	43.0	55.0	54.6	55.0	54.1	57.3	57.0	54.8	55.0
Republic of Korea	..	..	..	..	..	..	..	..	..	..	37.1	35.3	44.3	45.2	50.5	52.7	48.6	51.6	50.6
Argentina	..	..	..	..	..	..	47.5	46.2	36.4	38.1	44.1	47.6	40.5	39.5	38.6	41.9	39.4	31.6	41.5
Chile	..	..	..	..	..	..	..	..	44.6	43.0	47.8	45.3	43.3	42.4	38.7	40.9	46.5	42.5	44.1

Source: UNCTAD secretariat calculations, based on *OECD.StatExtracts* database; ECLAC, *CEPALSTAT* database; United States, *Bureau of Economic Analysis* database; United Kingdom, *Office for National Statistics* database; Lindenboim, Kennedy and Graña, 2011; and Piketty, 2008.

Note: Data refer to total compensation of employees as a per cent of GDP at factor costs.

The relative stability in the respective shares of wages and capital in France, the United Kingdom and the United States was not replicated in other countries, and it tended to vanish even in these three countries after 1980. Indeed, after 1980 there was a significant reduction in the share of wages in most developed countries (discussed further in section C). Data for the other OECD countries do not corroborate the hypothesis of a stable distribution between labour and capital in the long run. In Japan, the very rapid growth rates of GDP between 1960 and 1975 were accompanied by substantial increases in the share of wages in total income (from 39 per cent to 55 per cent), which remained fairly stable thereafter. The share of wages in the Republic of Korea has also shown an upward trend since the late 1970s owing to a significant increase of real wages in manufacturing, in parallel with industrial upgrading, possibly related to changes in both labour markets and political conditions.

In the Latin American countries for which relatively long statistical time series are available, there have also been significant changes in functional income distribution. In particular, the share of wages in total income has been very unstable, owing to rapid changes in real wages and employment, which in turn mirrored unstable political and economic conditions. Real wages and the share of wages in GDP generally increased under progressive governments and/or during periods of economic growth, and plummeted during economic crises or after military coups (e.g. in 1955 and 1976 in Argentina, and in 1973 in Chile). For instance, the share of wages in GDP fell between 10 and 20 percentage points during episodes of economic recession and an acceleration of inflation in Argentina (1975–1976, 1981–1982, 1989 and 2002), Brazil (1981–1983 and 1992), Chile (1973–1975 and 1982–1983) and Mexico (1982–1987 and 1994–1995). Hence, in these countries, labour has absorbed much of the economic shocks over the past few decades, and the wage share has recovered at least partially during economic upturns. This pattern contrasts with that more frequently observed in developed economies, where profits adjust faster to short-run changes in growth, and consequently, the share of profits rises in an upswing and falls during a downswing. In Latin America, it has been easier for profit earners to transfer most of the cost of recessions to wage earners. As a result, the share of wages in total income tends to be positively correlated with economic growth in that region. Thus, with low and unstable growth in the 1980s and 1990s, the position of wage earners deteriorated over a long period, resulting in a larger incidence of informality and self-employment. This made the recovery of their previous share in income distribution more difficult; when it eventually occurred, it was due not only to economic growth, but also to proactive public policies in support of employment and real wages.

2. The share of top incomes in total income

Historical tax statistics can also provide an indication of how income inequality evolved over the long term. Based on the income declared by the richest tax payers and on estimations of national income, the share of "top incomes" (e.g. those received by the 1st or 5th upper percentiles in the income distribution) in total income has been estimated for more than 20 countries, for many of them since the first decades of the twentieth century (Atkinson and Piketty, 2007 and 2010).[5] However, these statistics should be treated with some caution as they are likely to be underestimations, since taxable revenues are often understated, especially by wealthy people who have strong incentives, more opportunity and better skills to do so. There may also be time breaks due to changes in the tax system, particularly with regard to taxation of capital revenues. Indeed, the share of capital income that is reportable on income tax (and that consequently features in tax statistics) has decreased over time in a number of countries. Since such excluded capital income relates, disproportionately, to the top income groups, this may lead to an underestimation of their shares of income. In addition, estimation of total national income over a long period is a complex exercise in itself (Atkinson, Piketty and Saez, 2011). Notwithstanding these limitations, the analysis of the evolution of the share of top incomes over the past century provides valuable insights for explaining the concentration of personal income.

Regarding the evolution of the share of income of the top 1 per cent, a general feature is the relatively high concentration of income around 1920–1930 in countries of different regions and development levels (chart 3.1). At that time, the "top 1 per cent" accounted for between 15 and 20 per cent of national income in developed countries such as Canada, Finland, France, Germany, Ireland, Japan, the Netherlands, Sweden, the United Kingdom and the United States, but also in developing countries such as Argentina, India and Indonesia. Subsequently, their share declined sharply in almost all the countries. Hyperinflation in Germany and the 1929 crisis in France and the United States eroded rent revenues which are concentrated in the upper income strata. Top income shares were even more dramatically affected by the Second World War, due to the destruction of physical capital, inflation and wartime regulations or confiscations, and, in

Chart 3.1

SHARE OF INCOME OF THE TOP 1 PER CENT IN TOTAL INCOME IN SELECTED COUNTRIES, 1915–2010

(Per cent)

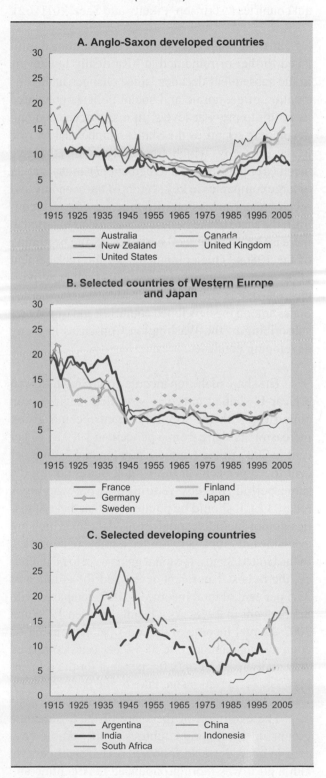

Source: Paris School of Economics and Institute for New Economic Thinking, *The World Top Income Database*.

some cases, the loss of revenues from the colonies. A significant reduction of top shares occurred in 13 out of 14 countries for which data are available. The exception was a non-combatant country, Argentina, where the top income shares benefited from high food prices and increasing food exports to combatant countries (Atkinson, Piketty and Saez, 2011: 62).

In most countries, income concentration diminished further or remained at historically low levels in the subsequent decades, since changes in the orientation of economic and social policies prevented its return to pre-war levels. In many developed and developing countries the State assumed a larger role in the economy, which frequently involved active incomes policies, financial regulation, nationalization of large companies in key sectors of the economy and much greater provision of public services. By contrast, the share of the richest in total income started to increase again in several countries by the beginning of the 1980s. This coincided with the replacement of the post-war social consensus by neoliberal policies, starting in the United Kingdom and the United States among the developed countries, and by policies subscribing to the Washington Consensus in many developing countries.

The share of the top income groups has followed a clear U-shaped curve in so-called Anglo-Saxon countries, with the top 1 per cent income group increasing its share from 6 per cent in 1979 to 16 per cent in 2007 in the United Kingdom and from 8 per cent to 18 per cent in the United States during the same period, thereby returning to pre-war highs (chart 3.1). It should be pointed out that these statistics do not include capital gains, data for which are available only for a very limited number of countries. In the United States, if capital gains were to be included, the richest 1 per cent accounted for as much as 23.5 per cent of total income in 2007, compared with 8.5 per cent in 1978. As a result, between 1976 and 2007 the real income of the top 1 per cent increased at an average annual rate of 4.4 per cent, compared with an increase of only 0.6 per cent for the remaining 99 per cent (Atkinson, Piketty and Saez, 2011: 9).

The evolution of the share of the top income groups in developing countries in the sample covered in chart 3.1 also followed a U-shaped pattern, although it was more pronounced in Argentina and South Africa than in India and Indonesia. In all these countries, the upward trend started between the mid-1970s and the mid-1980s. China (with a much shorter time series) has also shown an increase in income concentration since the mid-1980s, although concentration in its top 1 per cent (at around 6 per cent of total income) remains low by international standards. By contrast, the share of the top 1 per cent has been fairly stable in continental Europe and Japan since about 1950 – at below 10 per cent. The relatively low level of inequality in these countries is most likely related to relatively high progressive taxation. Nevertheless, even in these countries the share of the top 1 per cent has increased somewhat since the mid-1980s (the exceptions being Denmark, the Netherlands and Switzerland), and most notably in Finland, Ireland, Italy, Norway and Portugal.

Regarding the composition of the highest revenues, this has changed since the first half of the last century, especially in the so-called Anglo-Saxon countries. Earlier, the income of the very rich consisted overwhelmingly of revenues from capital, whereas at present, a significant share consists of wage incomes. Both the new "working rich" and the rentiers may have benefited from financial deregulation, the latter through high interest rates in the 1980s and 1990s and capital gains from rising asset prices, and the former from bonuses and other emoluments gained during financial booms, which are not returned in case of financial losses. Bakija, Cole and Heim (2012) find that in the United States employees in executive positions and top management, together with financial professionals, have accounted for about 60 per cent of the top 0.1 per cent of income earners in recent years.

The very high revenues of corporate executives, managers and financial dealers are indicative of new forms of corporate governance (as discussed further in chapter IV). Since part of their pay is in the form of stocks and stock options, the distinction between wages and capital incomes has become blurred. Apart from ethical considerations, extremely high compensation for senior managers also raises the question of its economic rationale. It would be difficult to explain this by highly concentrated skills, since the education and training of the top 1 or 0.1 per cent of income earners does not differ from that of the top 10 per cent, whose income is significantly lower. Interestingly, Krugman (2012) notes that there are very few true entrepreneurs in this small group: for the most part, they are executives at firms they did not themselves create, but they receive stocks or stock options of their companies as part of their pay packages, which are decided in a collusive way by compensation committees. As for the top earners in the financial industry, their earnings have often been disproportionately high compared with their actual achievements owing to their highly risky "heads-I-win-tails-you-lose" compensation structure which has nothing to do with their contribution to economic growth; on the contrary, such a structure has led to excessive risk taking, which was one of the reasons behind the global financial crisis.

3. Personal income distribution

In several countries, changes in the share of the top income earners have been large enough to affect overall personal income inequality quite significantly. For instance, rising income concentration in the top 1 per cent in the United States between the second half of the 1970s and 2007 explains in large part, if not entirely, the increase in the Gini coefficient during that period.[6]

The disproportionate rise in top incomes is only part of the picture. However, a more comprehensive assessment of income distribution among all the social strata over a long period is more difficult to produce. New estimates for household income inequality between 1820 and 2000 in a large number of countries (chart 3.2; see also van Zanden et al., 2011) confirm the evidence already presented on top income shares.[7] The main results of these estimates are generally in line with the evidence already presented. Income inequality fell markedly in most developed countries between 1929 and 1950, and continued its decline in some of them until approximately 1980. Between the 1980s and 2000, Gini coefficients increased in most countries of this group, sometimes significantly. Inequality also diminished in Eastern Europe after 1929, and was particularly low during the period 1980–1990, before increasing fairly sharply during the 1990s.

During most of the twentieth century, the experiences in these countries, most of which have mature industrial sectors, seem to corroborate Kuznets' hypothesis: there was increasing inequality during the first decades and a marked decline thereafter, when further increases of income over a long period

Chart 3.2

GINI COEFFICIENT BY REGION, 1890–2000

(Unweighted average)

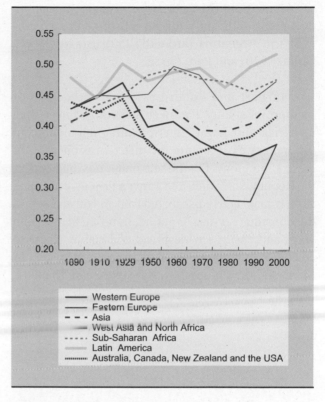

Source: van Zanden et al., 2011.
Note: Regional compositions follow those of the source.

were associated with falling inequality. This is also consistent with Kuznets' view that poor countries tend to be more unequal than rich ones. It is true that more recently, in many developed and transition economies, further growth has been associated with rising inequality. However, it must be emphasized that higher inequality is largely due to changes in the capital-labour income distribution. As Galbraith (2012) notes, for most countries in the past half century, the relationship between pay inequalities and per capita income has been downward sloping. The recent exceptions to this rule lie at the top rather than at the bottom of the per capita income scale.

In developing countries, the pattern of evolution of income inequality was less clear during the last century. Inequality tended to increase in Africa until 1950, and remained at relatively high levels in the subsequent decades. Indeed, it has been the region with the highest inequality, together with Latin America. The unweighted average Gini coefficient was fairly stable in Latin America, although individual countries in the region experienced significant (but temporary) changes in inequality owing to specific political factors; for instance, inequality declined significantly during left-of-centre governments in Argentina (around 1950), Brazil (1950), Chile (1970) and Peru (1985).

In East and South-East Asia, the degree of income inequality has been generally lower than in Africa and Latin America, although significant differences exist among the different economies of these subregions. On the one hand, governments in the Republic of Korea and Taiwan Province of China expropriated and redistributed land and other assets in the immediate post-war period, imposed high wealth taxes and ensured widespread and stable access to education. On the other hand, in countries such as Malaysia, the Philippines, Singapore and Thailand,

the Gini coefficients have tended to be higher (Cornia, Addison and Kiiski, 2003). China is a unique case, as its Gini coefficient rose significantly during the first half of the twentieth century, reaching a peak in 1950, and then fell steeply (i.e. showing a decline in inequality) in subsequent decades following a change in its economic system. However, since the 1990s, personal income inequality has again increased, as discussed in the next section. In India (where a decrease in inequality during the 1970s reversed the increase in the previous decades) and Pakistan in South Asia, there was no clear trend in income inequality between 1950 and 1980.

To sum up, there seems to have been a general increase in income inequality in all the regions of the world between 1980 (or 1990 for some regions) and 2000 (the last year for which data were available in the van Zandenn long-term database). However, inequality evolved less uniformly among the different regions during the 2000s, as discussed next.

C. A closer look at trends in income inequality since 1980

There was a significant change in the economic paradigm in all the major economies and regions between the late 1970s and early 1990s. After three decades of rapid growth with falling inequality in industrialized economies and fairly stable inequality in other economies, decisive steps were taken towards finance-led globalization. In addition, many countries opted for a smaller role of the State in the economy (UNCTAD, 2011; see also chapters V and VI of this *Report*). These changes had a strong impact on income inequality within countries.

1. Functional income distribution

Since 1980, functional distribution has shown a significant decline in the share of wages in many countries, both developed and developing (chart 3.3).

In developed countries, the share of labour income declined, falling by 5 percentage points or more between 1980 and 2006–2007 – just before the global financial crisis – in Australia, Belgium, Finland, France, the Netherland, Norway, Sweden, the United Kingdom and the United States, and by 10 points or more in Austria, Germany, Ireland, New Zealand and Portugal. In several major economies (including France, Germany, Italy and the United States), a significant proportion of the decline in the share of wages had already occurred between 1980 and 1995. This appears to have been linked to a departure from the post-war social consensus, when wage increases closely followed productivity gains. In some countries – most notably Germany – this trend continued into the 2000s, owing to a deliberate policy of wage restraint and efforts to improve competitiveness. Its effects on domestic demand and imbalances within the euro area are discussed in chapter VI. Another

Chart 3.3

FUNCTIONAL INCOME DISTRIBUTION IN SELECTED COUNTRIES, 1980–2010

(Percentage share of wages in GDP at factor costs)

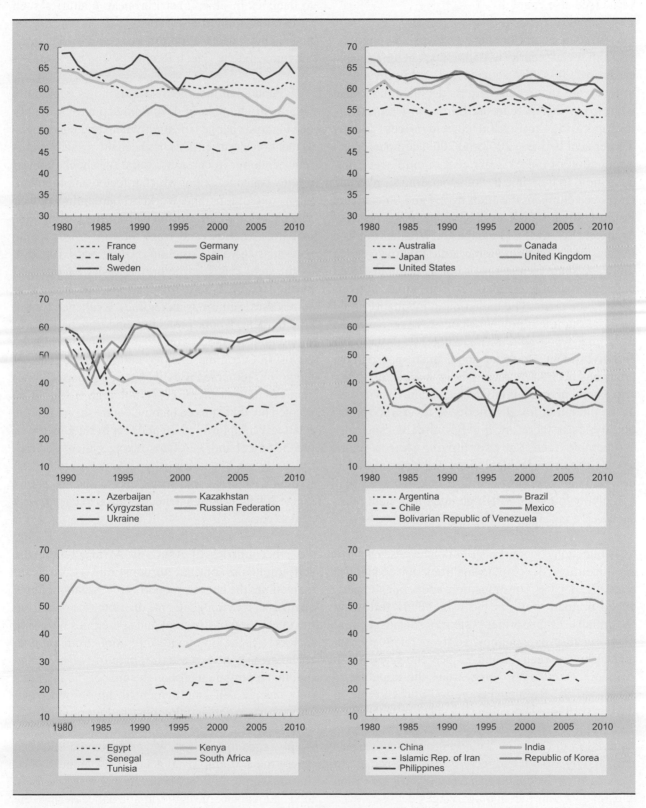

Source: UNCTAD secretariat calculations, based on *OECD.StatExtracts* database; United Nations Statistics Division (UNSD), *Main Aggregates and Detailed Tables* database; ECLAC, *CEPALSTAT* database; and United Kingdom, *Office for National Statistics* database.

major cause of the rising share of capital has been the growing dominance of the financial sector over the real sector of the economy and changes in corporate governance which aimed at maximizing shareholder value (see also chapter IV).

In some countries with advanced labour protection and social security nets, the shock of the financial crisis in 2008–2009 actually led to improvements in the wage share, since profits declined more than wages. For instance, in the European Union (EU), the operating surplus (at current prices) fell by 8.5 per cent between 2007 and 2009, compared with a reduction of only 1.2 per cent in employee compensation. In the same period, operating surplus and employee compensation fell by 2.4 and 0.6 per cent in the United States, and by 11.4 and 4.5 per cent in Japan (EC-AMECO database). Whether this is a turning point heralding a more durable recovery of the wage share or just a pause in its declining trend depends to a large extent on policies aimed at overcoming the crisis. The reduction in inequality could be more durable if policy responses were to include fiscal and wage policies that support consumption and investment. However, so far the response to the crisis has been to promote labour market flexibility and extend precarious employment contracts as well as the pursuit of fiscal austerity. A reversal of previous trends is therefore highly unlikely, especially as unemployment rates are proving slow to return to their pre-crisis levels. Indeed, the share of labour declined again in most countries in 2010 and 2011, notably in countries with high unemployment rates, such as Estonia, Greece, Hungary, Ireland and Spain.[8]

Functional income distribution has also changed significantly in developing and transition economies since the 1980s. The transition economies experienced dramatic falls in the wage share following the collapse of the former system of socialist central planning: this share plummeted (from relatively high levels) by between 15 and 23 percentage points in Armenia, Azerbaijan, Kyrgyzstan, the Republic of Moldova, the Russian Federation and Ukraine in the early 1990s. Thereafter, the share of wages was quite volatile in the Republic of Moldova, the Russian Federation and Ukraine, following a procyclical pattern, and by 2010 it had recovered to levels close to those of 1990. By contrast, in Azerbaijan, Kazakhstan and Kyrgyzstan, the share of wages declined even further as revenues derived from extractive industries boosted the share of capital (or "operating surplus").

There were also significant declines in the share of wages in countries of South-East Europe (e.g. Croatia, the former Yugoslav Republic of Macedonia and Serbia) during the 1990s and 2000s, similar to declines in other East European countries such as Estonia, Poland and Slovakia. It is noteworthy that such a deterioration did not occur in Hungary, Slovenia and the Czech Republic.

Functional income distribution has been quite volatile in a number of developing countries, mainly due to rapid changes in employment and real wages, as mentioned earlier. This has been the result of recurrent economic recessions, inflation shocks and/or political changes, all of which affected employment, labour conditions and workers' bargaining power. The share of wages declined from the early 1980s in Latin America (and from the mid-1970s in the particular cases of Argentina, Chile and Uruguay), as the debt crisis, structural reforms encouraged by the Bretton Woods financial institutions and, in some cases, authoritarian regimes, weakened formal employment, labour protection and trade unions. In some countries the downward trend persisted into the 2000s: in Colombia, Mexico and Peru, the share of labour has remained roughly between 25 and 35 per cent of GDP (at factor cost), although it should be pointed out that "mixed income" in these countries is relatively high (around 20 per cent of total income). On the other hand, the share of wages increased significantly in Chile (during the 1990s), the Bolivarian Republic of Venezuela (since 1997) and Argentina (since 2003), although it did not return to its previous peaks (chart 3.3).

In countries of Asia and Africa, where the self-employed continue to constitute a significant (sometimes the largest) proportion of the labour force, changes in functional income distribution result from the interaction of different and sometimes opposing factors. On the one hand, migration from rural to urban areas can increase the share of wage earners in total employment, although some of the migrants only change self-employment in low-productivity agriculture to self-employment in low-productivity urban services. On the other hand, an excess of labour supply tends to keep real wages depressed. In India, where the self-employed account for about half of the workforce, evidence suggests that wage shares in total national income in the organized sector since the early 1990s have been falling in parallel with shares of informal sector income in total national income.

Indeed, the movement of factor incomes illustrates the tendency towards greater inequality: the share of wages in national income fell from 40 per cent at the start of the 1990s to only 34 per cent by 2009-2010, while in the organized sector that share fell from 69 per cent to 51 per cent over the same period. Meanwhile, even though the unorganized sector continues to account for the overwhelming majority of workers in the country, including the self-employed, its share in national income fell from 64 per cent to 57 per cent (Ghosh, 2012).

2. Personal income distribution

How these trends in functional income distribution impact on households' disposable income depends to a large extent on redistributive measures taken by governments, which are traditionally fairly large in developed countries. In fact, a particular feature of these countries is the significant difference between the inequality indices of their gross and net income, compared with those of other countries (chart 3.4). This difference was 13 percentage points on average in developed countries in the 2000s, compared with 4 points in the transition economies and around 2 points in developing countries. This highlights the important role of public policies in influencing income distribution in developed countries. Indeed, it is mainly because of public sector involvement that income inequalities are lower in developed countries than in the rest of the world. With a Gini coefficient close to 0.45 (on average), inequality of gross incomes in developed countries does not differ significantly from that of the transition and developing economies. However, net income inequality is clearly lower.

Over the last three decades, income inequality increased significantly in developed countries and the transition economies, as well as in Asian developing countries. It also increased in Latin America and Africa in the 1980s and 1990s from already high levels, but during the 2000s it experienced a not negligible decline of 4–5 points in the Gini coefficient. The transition economies recorded the sharpest increase, of 20 points in the Gini coefficient, between the mid-1980s and the mid-1990s. Income inequality also increased significantly in developed countries – mainly between 1981 and 2000. However,

inequality of gross incomes increased substantially more (almost 8 points) than inequality of net income (half as much), which shows the compensatory – although partial – role of public policies.

These aggregate figures provide a general overview of recent trends, but as they are based on weighted averages, they are mainly determined by changes in populated countries. They need to be complemented by an examination of individual country experiences. Table 3.2 summarizes the changes in inequality of per capita household income in selected countries during the 1980s and 1990s, and throughout the 2000s. The first period was characterized by the widespread adoption of neoliberal policies as well as by a series of financial, banking and currency crises. Inequality increased in 73 out of the 104 countries in the sample, and fell in only 24. It rose in almost all regions during that period, with the exception of Africa, and West and South Asia, where the number of countries with rising inequality was offset by the number where inequality declined.

Inequality increased in most developed countries between 1980 and 2000. As mentioned above, capital income increased vis-à-vis labour income, benefiting a small number of capital owners. In addition, there was growing inequality in the distribution of wages and salaries, as the wages of the best paid workers rose more than those of the lowest paid, with few exceptions. Finally, income taxes and cash transfers became less effective in reducing high levels of inequality of gross incomes (or market inequality) (OECD, 2011a: 23, 37). In the transition economies, the economic meltdown of the early 1990s affected wage earners disproportionately, and the crisis in government finances caused a reduction in social transfers. In addition, hasty privatizations led to the concentration of wealth in several countries, resulting in enduring new levels of inequality. Finally, most developing countries also experienced rising inequalities during this period, mainly related to economic reforms and the impacts of financial crises.

By contrast, during most of the 2000s there was an improvement in the global economic environment (at least until 2008), with several developing regions adopting pragmatic macroeconomic and social policies. Practically all developing and transition economies experienced rapid GDP growth and benefited from the rapid expansion of world trade, easier access to global finance and rising migrant

Chart 3.4

GINI COEFFICIENTS FOR GROSS AND NET INCOME, SELECTED REGIONS, 1980–2010

(Population-weighted average)

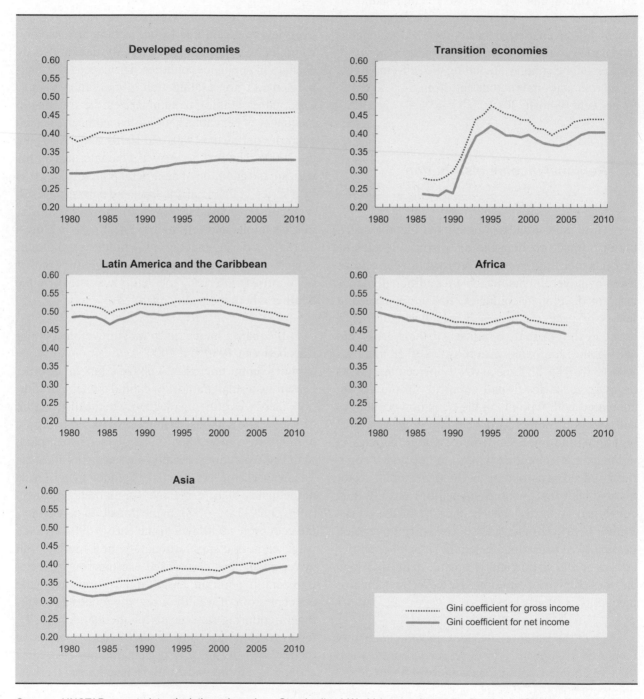

Source: UNCTAD secretariat calculations, based on *Standardized World Income Inequality Database* (*SWIID*); ECLAC, *Social Panorama* database; and national sources.

Note: *Developed countries* comprises: Australia, Austria, Belgium, Canada, Denmark, Finland, France, Germany, Greece, Ireland, Israel, Italy, Japan, Luxembourg, the Netherlands, New Zealand, Norway, Portugal, Spain, Sweden, Switzerland, the United Kingdom and the United States. *Transition economies* comprises: Armenia, Belarus, Croatia, Kyrgyzstan, Republic of Moldova, Russian Federation, the former Yugoslav Republic of Macedonia, and Ukraine. *Africa* comprises: Côte d'Ivoire, Egypt, Kenya, Malawi, Mauritius, Morocco, Sierra Leone, South Africa, Tunisia and Zambia. *Asia* comprises: Bangladesh, China, China, Hong Kong SAR, China, Taiwan Province of India, Indonesia, Islamic Republic of Iran, Jordan, Republic of Korea, Malaysia, Nepal, Pakistan, the Philippines, Singapore, Thailand and Turkey. *Latin America and the Caribbean* comprises: Argentina, Bahamas, the Bolivarian Republic of Venezuela, Brazil, Chile, Colombia, Costa Rica, El Salvador, Guatemala, Mexico, Panama, Peru, Puerto Rico, Trinidad and Tobago, and Uruguay.

Table 3.2

CHANGES IN INEQUALITY BY REGION, 1980–2010
(Number of countries)

	Developed countries 1980–2000	Eastern Europe and CIS 1990–1998	Africa 1980–1995	Latin America and the Caribbean 1980–2002	South and West Asia 1980–2000	South-East and East Asia 1980–1995
Rising inequality	15	24	10	14	3	7
No change	1	0	3	1	2	0
Falling inequality	6	0	10	3	3	2
Total	22	24	23	18	8	9
	Developed countries 2000–2010	Eastern Europe and CIS 1998–2010	Africa 1995–2007	Latin America and the Caribbean 2002–2010	South and West Asia 2000–2010	South-East and East Asia 1995–2010
Rising inequality	9	13	9	2	3	5
No change	5	5	1	1	2	1
Falling inequality	8	6	15	15	3	4
Total	22	24	25	18	8	10

Source: Cornia and Martorano, 2012; and *SWIID*.
Note: Changes are based on variations of Gini coefficient.

remittances over the last decade. However, only some experienced a drop in income differentials. Over this period, there was a divergence in inequality trends: there was a marked and unanticipated decline in income inequality in most Latin American countries and in parts of Africa and South-East Asia, whereas in most of the developed countries, the transition economies and East Asia inequality continued to rise, albeit at a slower pace. These contrasting experiences may help to identify the sources of inequality decline in some regions and its increase in others.

There appears to be no obvious reason why recent economic improvements should directly reduce income inequality. In the countries that experienced gains in the terms of trade, rising commodity prices may have benefited only a small minority, since they occurred in a general context of high concentration of ownership of land and mineral resource. Likewise, the direct effect of an increase in workers' remittances on inequality is uncertain, depending on whom they benefited the most – middle class or unskilled working class households.[9] The sizeable inflow of foreign capital at declining interest rates mainly benefited large companies and

banks, but did not ease the problems of access to credit for labour-intensive, small and medium-sized enterprises (SMEs). Meanwhile, it simultaneously caused an appreciation of the real exchange rate in most countries, which may lead to a deterioration in competitiveness and employment and potentially increase inequality. On the other hand, there is evidence that in some countries improvements in the terms of trade and higher remittances and capital inflows helped to alleviate the balance-of-payments constraint on growth and increase employment and public revenues (Thirlwall, 2011). These conditions can favour improvements in income distribution, both through their direct impact on revenues from additional employment and their indirect impact on public transfers. This suggests that several factors have an impact (sometimes contradictory) on the evolution of inequality, and the eventual relationship between inequality and growth can vary considerably by region and at different times.

In **Latin America**, the rise in inequality in the 1980s and 1990s was not driven by a massive migration from low productivity activities in rural areas to industrial and modern services jobs in urban areas in the context of rapid growth — as would be expected in a Kuznets' type development process. On the contrary, it resulted from the reduction of formal and relatively well-paid jobs in industry and in the public sector in countries that were already largely urban and had achieved a significant level of industrialization. Moreover, it took place during more than two decades of slow growth and declining investment rates. Between 1990 and 1999, two thirds of job creation was in the informal sector, comprising microenterprises, domestic employees and the unskilled self-employed (ECLAC, 2004). In this context, higher inequality was not the price the region had to pay for accelerating development; rather, it was closely associated with economic stagnation.

By contrast, the income gap has narrowed in Latin America since the early 2000s, in parallel with a significant economic recovery. Between 2002 and 2010, the average regional Gini coefficient declined by 4 percentage points, and by even more in several countries in South America (Argentina, the Bolivarian Republic of Venezuela, Bolivia, Brazil, Paraguay and Peru). Together with significant improvements in external conditions, the general policy reorientation played a central role in achieving growth with better income distribution. On the macroeconomic side, many of the successful countries followed countercyclical fiscal policies, achieving fiscal balances through an increase in public revenues (including commodity rents) rather than by expenditure cuts. In addition, there was an increase in the progressivity of tax systems (Cornia, Gomez Sabaini and Martorano, 2011). These countries also adopted managed exchange rate systems with the aim of preventing currency overvaluation. Moreover, they shifted economic activity towards labour-intensive, trade-oriented production in both manufacturing and agriculture that had favourable effects on income distribution, exports and growth. Finally, they managed to reduce their foreign public debt and sharply increase their foreign currency reserves. This not only lowered the amount of interest payments on their fiscal and external balances, but also provided substantially more room for manoeuvre in policy-making.

The new policy model also introduced perceptible changes in labour and social policies. These included labour policies that explicitly sought to resolve the problems inherited from the previous two decades, such as unemployment, job informalization, falling minimum wages, reduced social security coverage and weakened institutions for wage negotiations. In this respect, a number of countries enacted incomes policies that included public works, which extended the coverage of formal employment, and they reintroduced tripartite wage bargaining and sizeable hikes in minimum wages, which generated equalizing effects. The policies also included, almost universally, an acceleration of the upward trend in public expenditures on social security and education, which was made possible by the rise in tax-to-GDP ratios. In addition, many countries introduced social assistance programmes, such as conditional and non-conditional cash transfers, which appear to have contributed significantly to reducing income inequality (Cornia, 2012).

As a result, between 2003 and 2010 the fall in inequality in Latin America almost entirely offset the increase recorded between 1980 and 2002. Thus much of the improvement in the 2000s resulted from a reversal of the unequalizing effects of Washington Consensus-type policies and their negative impact on industrialization and formal employment.

Africa is the world's most inequitable region together with Latin America (chart 3.4).[10] In 2010, 6 of the 10 countries with the most unequal income distribution in the world were in sub-Saharan Africa, specifically in Southern Africa (African Development Bank, 2012). One reason is that in several natural-resource-rich countries, local elites, together with international capital, have been able to appropriate most of the rents from natural resources. The dispersion of income varies dramatically across countries. For example, the ratio of the income of the top decile to that of the bottom decile ranges from 10.5 times in the United Republic of Tanzania to 44.2 times in South Africa (Africa Progress Panel, 2012: 23). The greatest income inequalities are generally in non-agricultural occupations, where education is one of the determining elements in the wage scale. While the income benefits from education are high in Africa, educational inequalities are also the highest of all the world's regions (Cogneau et al., 2006).

The pattern of change of inequality has also differed among the subregions of Africa. Inequality increased in all the subregions except North Africa between the 1980s and the 1990s, particularly in Central, East and West Africa. In the 2000s, it decreased in Southern Africa and to a lesser extent in West Africa, but showed little change (or even increased) in the other subregions, where the pattern of economic growth has reinforced inequalities (African Development Bank, 2012). Despite conditions specific to Africa, the macroeconomic mechanisms have been similar to those evident in other parts of the world resulting in falling shares of wage incomes and the incomes of petty self-employed workers in the gross national product, and inadequate generation of productive employment opportunities.

The case of South Africa is particularly interesting, because neither the end of the apartheid regime nor income growth appear to have resulted in any decline in South Africa's historically high levels of inequality. Income inequality has been very high and has been increasing since the early 1990s – the Gini coefficient on gross income grew from 0.63 in 1993 to 0.70 in 2005. While race-based inequalities still dominate, inequality within racial/ethnic groups has also been on the increase. Indeed, by 2008, inequality among Africans (who account for 80 per cent of the population) was the highest of all the racial groups. Increasingly, this reflects spatial inequalities (particularly rural-urban income differences) as well as access to education, as better educated Africans have benefited disproportionately from the recent growth process (Finn, Leibbrandt and Wegner, 2011).

Inequality trends in **Asia** are less clear-cut trends, with inequality rising in some countries and falling in others. However, considering that the countries where the income gap has widened are the most highly populated, overall regional inequality has increased significantly since the 1980s. In the **South Asian** region, the processes of globalization have been associated with greater inequalities of income and consumption. This is particularly evident in India, which shows an increase in the national Gini coefficient for consumption from 0.31 in 1993/94 to 0.36 in 2009/10, while the urban-to-rural consumption ratio rose from 1.62 to 1.96. Vanneman and Dubey (2010) estimated a Gini coefficient for expenditure of 0.35 in 2005, and a much higher Gini coefficient for income of 0.48.[11] Thus the gains from growth in India have been concentrated among the surplus-takers (which include profits, rents and financial incomes). A major reason for this is that growth in the modern sectors (e.g. manufacturing and high productivity services like the software industry) has not been sufficiently employment generating. Therefore about half of the workforce continues to languish in low-productivity

agriculture (even though that sector now accounts for less than 15 per cent of the country's GDP) and in low remuneration services.

In Bangladesh, the share of farm incomes in total income dwindled over time. Increasing wage differentials in non-agricultural activities (between relatively less skilled wage workers and relatively greater skilled salaried workers) added to the inequality. As a result, the Gini coefficient for income increased from a relatively low 0.28 in 1991/92 to 0.40 in 2005 (Khan, 2005). Inequality also increased in Sri Lanka, which was the first country in South Asia to engage systematically in greater global integration through economic liberalization and market-oriented reforms in 1978. Initially, in the 1980s income inequality remained relatively low, but by the mid-2000s, it exceeded that of it neighbours, with a Gini index for income of 0.50 (Vidanapathirana, 2007). Rising inequality reflects two components: first, growing inequality within the fast growing modern industrial sector, driven by a concentrated ownership of assets and differences in skill levels, and second, growing inequality between the modern industrial fast-growing sectors and regions and the traditional lagging agricultural sectors and regions (Gunawardena, 2008). In Pakistan, by contrast, inequality has remained relatively stable. Consumer surveys indicate that inequality of consumption decreased in the first half of the 1990s and then increased over the next decade (Asad and Ahmad, 2011; Shahbaz and Islam, 2011).

In **East and South-East Asia,** prior to the financial crisis several countries experienced structural transformations that increased inequality, as the acceleration of technological change generated new employment opportunities for better skilled workers in the higher income groups. Moreover, the labour market functioned in such a way that wages in these occupations grew faster than average wages, as insufficient public spending on education caused the supply of better skilled workers to fall short of demand. In addition, economic and financial liberalization reduced the scope for redistributive policies and spurred incomes from financial activities. Following the 1997-1998 crisis, the Gini coefficient fell in Malaysia, the Philippines, Thailand and the Republic of Korea, while it continued to rise in Indonesia, Taiwan Province of China and Singapore. Some common policy-related factors help to explain the distributive gains recorded in the first group of countries in the post-crisis era. These included pragmatic macroeconomic policies which assured stability and boosted growth (especially in Malaysia[12] and Thailand). In addition, large investments in public education extended the number of years of schooling and improved the distribution of human capital by upgrading the skills of the labour force in line with new technical advances, while avoiding a further rise of the wage skill premium. There was also a strengthening of redistributive policies with a focus on social protection (in the Republic of Korea), a reduction of the rural-urban gap (in Thailand), and a narrowing of income differentials among ethnic groups (in Malaysia) (see also chapter V).

Economic transformations in **China** since the 1980s have had a strong impact on inequality. The first wave of reforms during the period 1978–1984 was centred on the "household responsibility system" in agriculture: rural communes were replaced by egalitarian, family-based farms and higher food procurement prices were paid to farmers. The resulting acceleration of agricultural and overall growth led to a rapid rise in rural incomes, which helped reduce overall inequality. By contrast, income concentration increased rapidly during the second phase of the reforms which began in 1985. This was due to a widening urban–rural income gap, driven by a faster expansion of urban activities, a 30 per cent decline in agricultural prices and a tripling of agricultural taxes levied by the central and local authorities (Ping, 1997). At the same time, a rise in corporate profits and growing earnings disparities as the result of a surge in the skills premium led to greater intra-rural and intra-urban income inequality (Luo and Zhu, 2008). In addition, owing to fiscal decentralization in 1978 the national tax-to-GDP ratio fell to 10.2 per cent by 1996, which substantially reduced the ability of the central Government to control regional inequality by means of transfers to poorer provinces. During the third phase of reforms in the 2000s, the Gini coefficient continued to rise, and was estimated at close to 0.47 in 2009 (compared with 0.27 in 1984; see Chen et al., 2010). Although infrastructure in the western and central provinces was improved, trade and industrial policy continued to promote the creation of special economic zones in coastal areas, export-oriented firms, and the capital-intensive sector over the small-scale one. Despite rapid growth in the average real wage, the share of labour in total income declined as private, corporate and public savings increased in line with rapid accumulation of

capital. Disparities among wage earners contributed to overall inequality, with the distribution of wages shifting in favour of skilled workers in the high-tech, financial and services sectors, and migrants from rural areas receiving lower wages and social benefits than urban workers with formal residence status (Luo and Zhu, 2008). A number of measures have been taken aimed at redressing the rising inequality and "constructing a harmonious society" in what may be the beginning of a new phase. The contract labour law of 2008 improved workers' conditions, as further discussed in chapter IV of this *Report*; and an increase in the tax-to-GDP ratio from 10.2 per cent of GDP in 1996 to 18.4 per cent in 2010 provided resources to augment public spending on health, education, pensions and other social areas.

3. Inequality and poverty

Personal inequality and poverty are closely related, as they both depend on household income. Poverty is defined as the lack of sufficient income for covering basic needs. It is measured by estimating a "poverty line" – which is the per capita cost of satisfying basic needs – and comparing it with the actual per capita income of households. Households whose current income is below the poverty line are considered poor. Therefore, the magnitude of poverty depends on the cost of covering basic needs (in particular, the price of food), the average level of income in a country and the distribution of that income. Different combinations of these factors may lead to a reduction or to an increase in poverty. Clearly, an increase in real per capita income and a more equitable income distribution – with low incomes growing faster than the average income – are the most favourable conditions for reducing poverty. Other combinations would deliver less clear outcomes: per capita GDP and inequality may grow (or fall) at the same time, and lower food prices may pull urban households out of poverty but reduce the earnings of low-income peasants.

The question of how to reduce poverty has been the subject of considerable analytical work and policy debate. These have focused mainly on the links between growth, income distribution and poverty. For several years, an influential view that growth was the main, if not the only, factor for reducing

Table 3.3

PROPORTION OF PEOPLE LIVING BELOW THE POVERTY LINE, SELECTED COUNTRY GROUPS, 1981–2008

(Per cent)

	1981	1984	1987	1990	1993	1996	1999	2002	2005	2008
Africa	43.5	46.1	45.4	46.8	49.3	48.3	48.5	46.7	43.9	40.0
of which:										
North Africa	18.2	17.3	16.0	14.8	13.6	12.6	12.0	9.5	8.2	5.8
Latin America and the Caribbean	11.9	13.6	12.0	12.2	11.4	11.1	11.9	11.9	8.7	6.5
Asia	41.2	39.7	37.8	37.5	34.4	31.5	26.9	25.7	20.2	17.1
of which:										
China	84.0	69.4	54.0	60.2	53.7	36.4	35.6	28.4	16.3	..
South Asia	57.5	53.9	52.0	50.6	48.6	46.0	42.7	41.8	37.1	33.8
South-East Asia	45.2	43.5	42.6	37.7	32.7	27.4	25.4	22.2	16.9	12.9
West Asia	6.6	6.4	4.2	4.7	4.9	6.0	5.8	5.4	4.6	3.2
Transition economies	2.4	2.0	2.1	2.5	3.0	5.1	4.9	2.6	1.3	0.5

Source: UNCTAD secretariat calculations, based on World Bank online tool for poverty measurement, *PovcalNet*.

poverty prevailed. According to this view, structural reforms, including greater openness to international trade, low government consumption and financial development, would favour growth, and therefore would also be "good for the poor". It was assumed that the earnings of the bottom fifth of the income distribution tended to evolve at a similar rate as a country's average income, and would improve proportionately with GDP growth without the need for redistributive policies. What is more, it was argued that "pro-poor" policies, including public expenditure on health and education, would be ineffective for boosting economic growth and the incomes of the poor (Dollar and Kraay, 2000).

Both the empirical evidence supporting this view and the ensuing policy recommendations have been challenged. Indeed, it has been shown that the share of the low-income groups in total income tended to decline during economic recessions, and. did not recover rapidly during upturns (La Fuente and Sainz, 2001). Moreover, there is significant evidence of the positive impact of government expenditures and transfers on the incomes of the poorest, and consequently on poverty reduction (see chapter V). Finally, redistributive policies tend to encourage growth, especially in situations of insufficient domestic demand.

Significant progress has been made in tackling poverty over the last three decades. Yet progress in reducing the rate of extreme poverty – defined by the World Bank as earnings below $1.25 a day at 2005 PPP prices, and which corresponds to the mean of the consumption per capita in the 15 poorest countries – has been very mixed across countries and regions (table 3.3). On the one hand, in the fast-growing countries in Asia, the proportion of people living on less than $1.25 a day, which was initially very high, has fallen enormously. In China, for example, it fell from 84 per cent in 1981 to 16.3 per cent in 2005. In absolute terms, this means that more than 600 million people in China moved out of extreme poverty during this period, despite its population increasing by more than 300 million.

On the other hand, in Africa, Latin America and West Asia poverty reduction was very slow during the 1980s and 1990s. In some of the most populous countries in Africa and Latin America the proportion of people living in extreme poverty even increased during these two decades. In Nigeria, for example, that proportion rose from 53.9 per cent in 1985 to 68.5 per cent in 1996, and has averaged 65.5 per cent in the 2000s. In absolute terms, an additional 59 million people moved into extreme poverty between 1985 and 2009, which corresponds to 86 per cent of the increase of Nigeria's population during this period. In Brazil, the pattern was similar at first, albeit at a lower level, but improved subsequently. From 13.6 per cent in 1981, the extreme poverty rate peaked to 17.9 per cent in 1992 and stabilized at 11.6 in the second half of the 1990s. It started to decline from the early 2000s, to reach 6.1 per cent in 2009, as a result of Brazil's policies aimed at more inclusive growth. In absolute terms, this means that more than 5 million people moved out of extreme poverty between 1981 and 2009, despite a population increase of about 70 million. In the transition economies, the evolution of the extreme poverty ratio followed an inverted U-shaped curve: having increased in most of these economies after the collapse of the Union of Soviet Socialist Republics, this ratio has been falling rapidly since the early 2000s owing to the recovery of economic growth and employment.

These varying performances in terms of poverty reduction largely mirror the rate at which the different economies have grown since the early 1980s. However, the kinds of policies contributing to economic growth also matter. Some countries have been more successful than others in tackling poverty with higher growth, by increasing public spending, including through social transfers and employment creation programmes (discussed in more detail in chapter V). This partly explains why the growth elasticity of poverty differs among countries. Another reason for different elasticities is related to the initial conditions. A country with an average per capita income well above the poverty line will have a relatively low elasticity, as it needs more growth to achieve the same percentage of poverty reduction as a country with an average level of income closer to (or below) the poverty threshold. This illustrates the limitation of using the same absolute poverty line for very different countries: if the poverty line is very far from the average (or median) per capita income, changes in the latter, even if significant, may be reflected only marginally in changes in the poverty ratio.

D. Global income inequality

This *Report* focuses mainly on income inequality within countries. Most economic and social policies that affect income distribution and redistribution are applied within countries, and, in turn, the evolution of inequality within their boundaries has a direct impact on their economic performance and political debates. However, inequality at a global level – be it among countries or among individuals of all countries – is also a matter of serious concern. Indeed, several multilateral and regional institutions and agencies have the mandate to reduce inequality between countries and regions.[13] More generally, developing countries' well-established goal of catching up with developed countries entails lowering inequalities between the two groups whereby their respective per capita GDPs will tend to converge. That goal cannot be delinked from income distribution within countries. In other words, progress towards meeting development goals will not be achieved if the rise of per capita GDP in a developing country results from an increase in incomes of its small social elite alone. Hence, global inequality springs from income inequality both between and within countries. Therefore policies aimed at improving global income distribution must address both of these aspects.

There are different definitions of global inequality.[14] One of these definitions corresponds to "international" inequality, or inequality between countries of different average income. It uses the GDP per capita of each country measured in the same currency – in this case the United States dollar at purchasing power parity (PPP) – for all the countries in the world, and ranks them from the poorest to the richest in order to compute a measure of inequality, such as the Gini coefficient. By this definition, global inequality first declined between mid-1960s and the late 1970s, since the GDP of a significant number of developing countries grew at faster rates than it did in developed countries (chart 3.5); it then increased between 1980 and 2000, as growth rates in many Latin American, African and transition economies either stagnated or declined, while those of developed countries continued to increase, although at a slower pace than in the immediate post-war decades.[15] Finally, global inequality narrowed again in the 2000s as a result of a significant recovery of GDP growth in most developing and transition economies and a slowdown in developed countries.

A major shortcoming of this approach to measuring global inequality is that it does not take into account the number of people living in different countries: a very small country has the same "weight" as a very populous one. Therefore, this estimate of inequality may not reflect the living conditions of the majority of the world's population. The picture changes significantly if different weights are allocated to different countries according to their population. This shows that, first, population-weighted global income inequality until the early 1990s was significantly higher than in the previous definition, as indicated by a Gini coefficient at around 0.65, compared with 0.55 (chart 3.5). Much of this difference is due to the fact that the most populous countries (China and India) were low-income countries at that time. Second, the evolution of population-weighted income inequality reflects more accurately the growth performance of these large countries: global inequality barely changed until the early 1980s, when growth rates in China and India were in line with global growth rates, and declined significantly thereafter, as China and India began to grow much faster than most other countries. Inequality declined even more rapidly in the 2000s, as more developing and transition economies began or resumed the catching up process.

Although this second method is a more accurate approach to analysing global inequality, it is still based on inter-country inequality, and assumes implicitly that all individuals in each country receive the same income. It is relatively easy to calculate, since it is based only on per capita GDP, which is available from national accounts and demographic sources, and is only complicated by the need to estimate PPP.[16] However, for assessing inequality among

Chart 3.5

INCOME INEQUALITY BETWEEN COUNTRIES AND INDIVIDUALS, 1963–2009

(Gini coefficient)

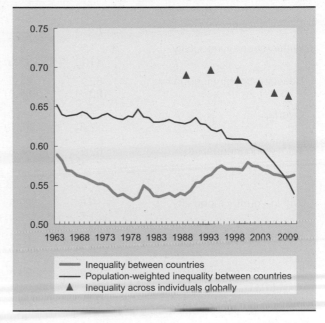

Source: UNCTAD secretariat calculations, based on Milanovic, 2005; Eurostat; World Bank online tool for poverty measurement, *PovcalNet*; and UNSD databases.
Note: Inequality between countries is based on per capita GDP.

the world's individuals, data on income distribution within countries for a large set of countries are also needed. It was only in the early 2000s that researchers were able to take advantage of numerous national household surveys conducted worldwide since the late 1980s to present new empirical evidence for the world as a whole, ignoring national boundaries and considering income distribution throughout the world (see, in particular, Milanovic, 2005; 2006).

The level of global inequality calculated using this method is significantly higher than the alternative measures, because it reflects income inequality not only among countries but also within them. It is also higher than inequality in any individual country in the database. This illustrates how the measurement of income inequality may change with geographical coverage. For instance, within a given country, some rural areas or urban slums may be uniformly poor and some neighbourhoods may be uniformly rich; measuring inequality in each of these areas separately would show very low Gini coefficients, even if such

Tablo ? 4

DECOMPOSITION OF WORLD INCOME INEQUALITY, 1988–2008

(Per cent)

	1988	1993	1998	2002	2005	2008
Gini coefficient						
Within-country inequality	1.1 (1.5)	1.1 (1.5)	1.1 (1.6)	1.2 (1.7)	1.3 (1.9)	1.3 (2.0)
Between-country inequality	62.7 (90.7)	62.5 (89.8)	61.0 (89.3)	60.8 (89.5)	59.0 (88.4)	58.4 (88.1)
Overlap	5.4 (7.8)	6.0 (8.6)	6.2 (9.1)	6.0 (8.8)	6.5 (9.7)	6.5 (9.9)
Total world inequality	69.2	69.6	68.4	67.9	66.7	66.3
Theil coefficient						
Within-country inequality	19.6 (21.7)	22.9 (24.5)	23.0 (25.4)	22.7 (25.4)	23.1 (27.1)	23.0 (27.4)
Between-country inequality	70.7 (78.3)	70.4 (75.5)	67.7 (74.6)	66.9 (74.6)	62.0 (72.9)	61.0 (72.6)
Total world inequality	90.2	93.3	90.7	89.6	85.1	84.0
Number of countries	*93*	*116*	*121*	*121*	*120*	*110*

Source: UNCTAD secretariat calculations, based on Milanovic, 2005; Eurostat; World Bank online tool for poverty measurement, *PovcalNet*; and United Nations Statistics Division (UNSD) databases.
Note: The figures in brackets represent the percentage share of each component in the total.

coefficients were very high at the national level. Similarly, according to the average of national Gini coefficients, the EU appears to be a more egalitarian region than indicated by the coefficient for the region as a whole.[17]

Global inequality is, by definition, determined by (population-weighted) differences in income levels between countries and within countries. To what extent do each of these (i.e. intra- and inter-country income disparities) affect global inequality? A decomposition of inequality between and within countries[18] shows that, in 2008, 73 per cent and 88 per cent (according to the Theil and the Gini coefficients, respectively) of total inequality is due to differences between countries, while the rest is due to differences within countries (table 3.4). The higher impact of inter-country inequality in global inequality seems to be a relatively recent development if viewed from a historical perspective. Long-term studies on countries' GDP estimate that by the middle of the nineteenth century, the ratio between the per capita

income in the richest countries (the Netherlands and the United Kingdom) and the poorest countries (formerly Ceylon – now Sri Lanka – and China) was around 4 to 1. This ratio rose to more than 100 to 1 in 2007 (Maddison, 2004; Milanovic, 2011a). Hence, at the beginning of the industrial revolution, global inequality could be explained by inequalities within countries at least as much as by inequalities between countries (Bourguignon and Morrison, 2002). At present, the average income of the lower 10 per cent or even 5 per cent of the population in a developed country is higher than the average real income of the 10 per cent or 5 per cent richest in low-income countries. A comparison of the per capita income of the richest 15 countries with that of the poorest 15 countries over the past few decades confirms this widening gap: the incomes of the richest countries were 44 times those of the poorest in the 1980s, 52 times in the 1990s and 60 times in the 2000s. However, there was a change in the trend during the last decade, with the ratio declining from 62.3 in 2000 to 55.8 in 2009.

Consequently, it could be expected that declining inequality between countries would immediately translate into declining inequality among individuals all around the world. This does indeed seem to be happening, but with a significant lag. Between 1988 and 2002, the Gini coefficient measuring income inequality among individuals remained at between 0.68 and 0.70, while population-weighted inequality among countries was already on the decline due to the fast growth of China and India, which, together, account

for more than one third of the world's population. It seems that for most of that period higher intra-country inequality largely offset the reduction of inter-country inequality (Milanovic, 2011b). It is only since the 2000s that all measures of global inequality have been showing a clear and simultaneous decline. It is worth emphasizing that the reduction of global inequality (among individuals) that seems to have been taking place since the mid-1990s is the first decline in global inequality since the mid-nineteenth century.

E. Other dimensions of inequality

Inequality has several interrelated dimensions, of which the most prominent is income inequality, since it directly determines the level of access to goods and services, either for consumption or investment. Differences in income do not depend only on individuals' differences in talent and effort; they are also the result of an uneven distribution of wealth and of varying access to education and basic services, which in turn are frequently determined by social, racial and gender factors. As discussed in chapter II, this set of factors may significantly undermine equality of opportunities and social mobility, with severe economic, social and political consequences. Moreover, a high level of income inequality tends to be perpetuated – or even widens – through increasing wealth concentration that generates a dual society: only one segment of the population is able to afford access to good-quality private education, health and basic services, while the rest have to settle for low-quality services because their public provision is inadequate. This section briefly presents some other aspects of inequality to show that policies for reducing income inequality need to go beyond measures that only alter primary income (e.g. wages policies) or secondary income (e.g. taxation and social transfers); such policies also need to address some of the fundamental social determinants of inequality.

1. Wealth distribution

Income and wealth distribution are closely interrelated. Some primary income can be obtained from asset ownership in the form of interests, dividends and other revenues from capital. Indeed, revenues from property may represent a large share in the total income of the higher income groups.[19] Some of that income is then saved and used for capital accumulation to generate more wealth. Generally, this interrelationship applies to high-income groups who are able to save a significant proportion of their revenues, so that most of the wealth is concentrated in these groups. As a matter of fact, countries with a high concentration of wealth also tend to have a high concentration of income, and vice versa. Furthermore, wealth concentration tends to be higher than income concentration (chart 3.6). This higher concentration is not surprising, since wealth represents a stock of financial and real assets accumulated over several years and transmitted through generations. The concentration of wealth also reflects the fact that savings of the upper-income groups accumulate faster than those of the lower income groups; the former can regularly save a larger proportion and a much greater absolute amount of their income than the latter.

Chart 3.6

WEALTH AND INCOME GINI COEFFICIENTS IN SELECTED COUNTRIES

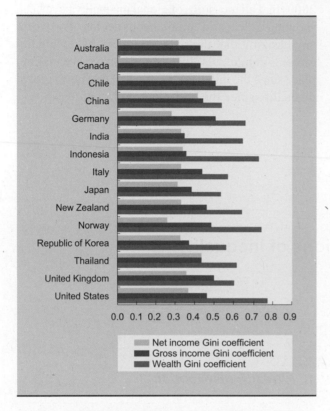

Net income Gini coefficient
Gross income Gini coefficient
Wealth Gini coefficient

Source: UNCTAD secretariat calculations, based on *Credit Suisse Global Wealth Databook*, 2011; and *SWIID*.
Note: Wealth data for the most recent year differ by country: Australia (2006), Canada (2005), Chile (2007), China (2002), Germany (2003), India (2002–2003), Indonesia (1997), Italy (2008), Japan (1999), New Zealand (2001), Norway (2004), Republic of Korea (1988), Thailand (2006), the United Kingdom (2008) and the United States (2007).

Indeed, in some countries the lower income groups barely earn enough to cover their basic needs.

Far more than income, a large proportion of the total wealth of households is generally concentrated in the richest percentile. In most countries for which reasonably comparable data are available, the top 1 per cent hold a much larger share of the total wealth of the economy than the bottom 50 per cent (for example, 33.8 compared with 2.5 per cent in the United States, 28.7 compared with 5.1 per cent in Indonesia, and 24 per cent compared with 4 per cent in France), and their share of wealth is significantly higher than their share of income (table 3.5).

A greater concentration of wealth implies that newly created wealth from annual income is

concentrated in already wealthy households. This phenomenon can contribute significantly to the persistence of inequality within a society. For instance, richer parents can afford to provide their offspring with a better education, which in turn increases their chances of earning a high income. Moreover, the offspring of wealthy people often benefit from a substantial inheritance, thus supporting the process of wealth concentration for the next generation. In some cases, this reflects a plutocratic regime in which the rich have a disproportionate influence on the government so that it operates in their favour, enabling them to continue to increase their wealth.

However, the degree of wealth concentration has not always increased. Historical statistics relating to the share of wealth of the top echelons in some developed countries during the twentieth century show that there was a drop in both income and wealth concentration – primarily due to a fall in their capital incomes – mainly during the world wars and the Great Depression. Subsequently, the introduction of a progressive income tax and real estate taxes

Table 3.5

WEALTH AND INCOME CONCENTRATION IN SELECTED COUNTRIES

(Per cent)

		Share of wealth		Share of income
	Year	Lowest 50%	Top 1%	Top 1%
Canada	2005	5.4	15.5	13.1
France	2010	4.0	24.0	9.0
India	2002-03	8.1	15.7	9.0
Indonesia	1997	5.1	28.7	11.0
Ireland	2001	5.0	23.0	9.7
Italy	2008	11.5	12.2	10.0
Rep. of Korea	1988	12.3	14.0	..
Sweden	2007	..	29.0	6.9
Switzerland	1997	..	34.8	8.0
United Kingdom	2005	9.2	12.5	14.3
United States	2007	2.5	33.8	13.8

Source: *Credit Suisse Global Wealth Databook, 2011*, table 1-4; and Paris School of Economics and Institute for New Economic Thinking, *The World Top Incomes Database*.

made it difficult for the wealthiest capital holders to recover fully to pre-war concentration levels (Piketty, 2003). In France, the United Kingdom and the United States (countries for which long-term series are available), household wealth declined significantly more than disposable income, pushing down the wealth-to-income ratio from 6–7 (at different times between 1900 and 1940) to close to 4 in the 1970s. It was only around 1980 that wealth started to grow rapidly again in all the G-7 countries, driving up the wealth-to-income ratio from 4.6 (on average) in 1980 to 7.4 in 2007. Despite the losses of financial wealth during the financial crisis, the ratio fell only slightly to around 7 in 2008-2009 (Credit Suisse, 2011). The long-run increase reflected a strong rise in asset prices, particularly in stock markets and real estate and it was only partially reversed with the bursting of the financial and real estate bubbles in several developed countries in the present crisis.

The net wealth-to-income ratio in a sample of developing and emerging countries is significantly smaller (roughly half), on average, than that in developed countries. A notable exception is China, where this ratio is close to 7, similar to those of France, Japan and Sweden, resulting mainly from high household savings rates which have exceeded 20 per cent of GDP during the last two decades.[20] The composition of wealth is also different in developed and developing countries. In developing countries, the share of non-financial assets in total wealth is significantly higher than it is in developed countries, as land and housing are more important and financial markets less developed. In developed countries, on the other hand, financial and non-financial assets, as a proportion of total wealth, are generally of similar importance. The share of financial assets actually exceeds that of real assets in Canada, the Netherlands, Switzerland and the United States, while the converse is the case in France, Germany, Italy and Spain as well as in Australia, a country with considerable land and natural resource endowments.

In developed countries, the strong increase in wealth assets, which have grown faster than disposable income, and their significant concentration in the top income groups have contributed to rising income inequality since the 1980s. According to Galbraith (2008: 99), rising inequality in some developed economies seems to be "a phenomenon of financial markets, of the distribution of wealth, of the valuation of capital assets, and fundamentally

of the distribution of power". While in developed countries the increasing concentration of wealth is largely linked to financial and real estate markets, in a number of developing and transition economies it is partly attributable to large-scale privatizations in the 1980s and the 1990s. As noted by Stiglitz (2012: 42), "It's easy to get rich by taking a state asset at great discount". And once a dominant position is acquired, monopoly rents can be obtained, thereby further widening income and wealth inequality.

Of particular importance in many developing countries is the distribution of land ownership. A comprehensive estimate of the distribution of operational land holdings in more than 100 countries by the Food and Agriculture Organization of the United Nations (FAO) suggests land concentration to be the highest in Latin America, with a median Gini coefficient of 0.81, followed by West Asia and North Africa (0.66), Eastern Europe (0.62) and South Asia (0.59). The Gini coefficient is lower in OECD countries, at 0.56, and is the lowest in East Asia (0.51) and sub-Saharan Africa (0.49) – two regions that still have a very high proportion of rural population (Vollrath, 2007). However, these statistics on land *holdings* do not exactly reflect the distribution of land *ownership*, because the same agent may own several land holdings, some of which may be worked on by landless peasants. Thus, the above-mentioned values are underestimates for actual ownership concentration. In any case, it is evident that land concentration is higher than income concentration.

There are significant social and economic implications of high land concentration. Land ownership provides not only a means of livelihood, but also facilitates access to credit, and it is associated with greater social and political participation (World Bank, 2006). High land concentration has been identified as a major source of economic inefficiency, as small tenants frequently lack the resources and the access to credit to invest and improve productivity, while big owners may lack the incentive to do so (Vollrath, 2007; Prebisch, 1963). From a historical point of view, the landed aristocracy who owned most of the land also had considerable political influence, and were less interested than the owners of industries in having a well-educated labour force. It is suggested that this may explain the lower priority given to universal schooling and improved access to public health care. All this in turn affected the pace and the nature of the transition from an agricultural to an industrial economy (Galor, Moav and Vollrath, 2009). Thus it is important to examine potential benefits of land reforms that generate a more equitable distribution of land. Experiences of land reforms in East Asia, for example, suggest that they can indeed improve both social cohesion and economic efficiency. However, they need to be accompanied by technical support and access to inputs and training within a broader strategy for rural development (World Bank, 2006).

2. Gender inequality

An important aspect of social and economic inequality relates to gender. Gender-related differences in incomes and opportunities (within and across households) are determined by a wide range of factors, such as employment and wage conditions, differences in access to education and health, as well as other social and cultural factors. With regard to employment, inequality does not refer only to paid work, since unpaid work within households tends to be disproportionately undertaken by female household members in most societies.

Given that most women perform a considerable amount of unpaid work, the evidence on their participation in paid or recognized work can be misleading. However, it has been found that a higher participation of women in paid and recognized work is associated with a decline in gender inequality over time. This is because it leads to greater social recognition of women's economic role, and to an improvement in the bargaining power of women workers. However, there are wide variations in the participation rates of women in work across countries and regions. The past two decades have witnessed an increase in their participation rate in the adult labour force, from 52.8 per cent in 1991 to 54.3 per cent in 2010. Over the same period, the growth rate of women's labour force was higher than that of men (50.4 and 43.2 per cent, respectively). In developed and transition economies, the participation rates of women were close to 55 per cent in 2010. In developing countries this rate was the highest in East Asia and sub-Saharan Africa (about 70 per cent), followed by South-East Asia and Latin America (around 60 per cent). By contrast, they were the lowest in West Asia, North Africa and South Asia (between 20 and 35 per cent), where women face a range of educational, social and cultural barriers to entering the labour market (ILO, KILM database).

While involvement in paid work matters for women, what also matter are their working conditions and remuneration levels. Further, without social provision for the unpaid work performed by women who also engage in paid work, their increasing involvement in paid work can impose a double burden on them. In addition, macroeconomic policies, and especially fiscal spending on public services, can have particular implications for women by reducing or adding to their burden of unpaid work.

The relatively low proportion of women who own firms, work in top management or are engaged in full-time employment also provides an indication of the inferior position of most women workers in labour markets (table 3.6).

Women workers tend to be underrepresented in the top echelons (legislators, senior officials and managers). By contrast, they are overrepresented in the bottom echelons (elementary occupations, which include domestic cleaners, labourers and street sales) (table 3.7). A significant proportion of women are employed as professionals and technicians in developed and transition economies. To a lesser extent this is also the case in Latin America, probably as a result of their having better access to education than in the past. However, these are rather heterogeneous groups, which include medical doctors and medical secretaries, university professors and primary school teachers. Activities requiring lower qualifications, such as clerks, services and sales workers, are typically "women's" occupations, as they provide employment to 46 per cent of women in paid work in developed countries and between one third and one quarter in Latin America, Asia (excluding China) and the transition economies (more than twice as much as for men in all these regions). Conversely, it is generally men who work in most crafts and manufacturing occupations. In Africa and Asia, women workers remain heavily involved in agricultural occupations, including unpaid family workers in subsistence agriculture. Moreover, women workers are concentrated in the production of certain types of non-traditional agricultural goods (e.g. cut flowers and vegetables) in sub-Saharan Africa and Central America, in low-grade manufacturing activities, such as in garments and leather goods as well as some electronics in several Asian countries, and in

Table 3.6

PERCENTAGE OF WOMEN IN OWNERSHIP OF FIRMS, TOP MANAGEMENT AND FULL-TIME EMPLOYMENT, BY REGION

	Ownership of firms	Top management	Full-time employment
Eastern Europe and Central Asia	36.7	19.0	38.4
East Asia and the Pacific	54.3	27.1	39.1
South Asia	17.1	6.0	12.5
Middle East and North Africa	17.2	13.6	14.5
Sub-Saharan Africa	33.0	15.2	24.5
Latin America and the Caribbean	40.4	20.8	37.9
High-income OECD	31.9	17.3	34.6
World	35.3	18.4	30.9

Source: World Bank Enterprise Surveys available at: http://www.enterprisesurveys.org/CustomQuery#Economies.
Note: The survey data refer to different years between 2002 and 2011, depending on the country. Country groups are as listed by the source.

Table 3.7

DISTRIBUTION OF EMPLOYMENT BY GENDER AND OCCUPATION GROUPS, 2008

(Percentage share)

	Developed countries		Transition economies		Africa		Asia		Latin America and the Caribbean	
	Male	Female	Male	Female	Male	Female	Male	Female	Male	Female
Legislators, senior officials, managers	11.2	8.0	8.2	6.0	4.8	1.7	4.0	1.4	3.8	2.9
Professionals and technicians	22.1	29.8	19.9	37.6	10.3	10.4	6.3	7.8	13.2	18.0
Clerks	7.1	20.0	1.9	6.5	3.5	5.0	4.0	3.3	5.4	11.2
Services and sales workers	15.2	25.7	9.4	19.6	10.2	9.7	9.8	12.6	12.2	23.1
Agricultural and fishery workers	3.5	2.4	7.7	5.8	39.4	53.6	48.1	58.9	17.7	9.7
Craft workers, plant and machine operators and assemblers	35.4	7.9	39.2	9.3	21.6	6.2	21.1	11.5	30.4	10.4
Elementary	4.8	5.8	12.9	14.8	9.9	13.3	6.4	4.4	15.9	24.2
Armed forces and non-classified	0.8	0.3	0.8	0.6	0.3	0.2	0.2	0.0	1.4	0.5

Source: UNCTAD secretariat calculations, based on ILO, *KILM* and *Laborsta* databases; UNECE, *Gender Statistics.*
Note: Craft workers, plant and machine operators and assemblers include "Elementary" for China and Japan in the respective regional aggregates (Asia and developed countries). Data refer to 2008 or latest available year. *Developed countries* comprises: Australia, Austria, Belgium, Bulgaria, Canada, Cyprus, Czech Republic, Denmark, Estonia, Finland, France, Germany, Greece, Hungary, Iceland, Ireland, Israel, Italy, Japan, Latvia, Lithuania, Luxembourg, Malta, the Netherlands, New Zealand, Norway, Poland, Portugal, Romania, San Marino, Slovakia, Slovenia, Spain, Sweden, Switzerland, the United Kingdom and the United States. *Transition economies* comprises: Albania, Armenia, Azerbaijan, Belarus, Bosnia and Herzegovina, Croatia, Georgia, Kazakhstan, Kyrgyzstan, the Republic of Moldova, the Russian Federation, the former Yugoslav Republic of Macedonia, Serbia and Ukraine. *Africa* comprises: Botswana, Burkina Faso, Egypt, Ethiopia, Madagascar, Mauritius, Morocco, South Africa and the United Republic of Tanzania. *Asia* comprises: Bhutan, Cambodia, China, China Hong Kong SAR, China Macao SAR, Indonesia, Islamic Republic of Iran, Lebanon, Maldives, Mongolia, Pakistan, the Occupied Palestinian Territory, the Philippines, Qatar, the Republic of Korea, Saudi Arabia, Singapore, Sri Lanka, the Syrian Arab Republic, Thailand, Turkey and the United Arab Emirates. *Latin America and the Caribbean* comprises: Argentina, Aruba, Bahamas, Bolivia, Brazil, Cayman Islands, Costa Rica, Dominican Republic, Ecuador, El Salvador, Jamaica, Mexico, Netherlands Antilles, Nicaragua, Panama, Paraguay, Peru and Uruguay.

Chart 3.7

WAGE GAP BETWEEN MEN
AND WOMEN, 1985–2010

(Percentage of male earnings)

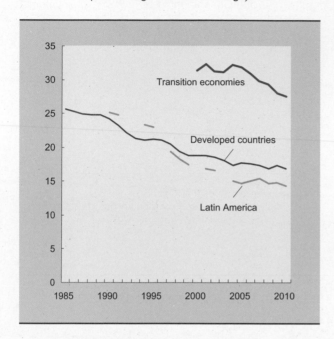

Source: UNCTAD secretariat calculations, based on UNECE, *Statistical Database*; ECLAC, *CEPALSTAT* database; and OECD, *Employment* database.

Note: For *developed countries,* data refer to the simple average of the gender wage gap in median earnings of full-time employees for Australia, Finland, France, Germany, Italy, Japan, the Netherlands, New Zealand, Sweden, the United Kingdom and the United States. For *transition economies*, data refer to the simple average of the gender gap in monthly earnings for Armenia, Azerbaijan, Belarus, Croatia, Georgia, Kazakhstan, Kyrgyzstan, the Republic of Moldova, the Russian Federation, Tajikistan and Ukraine. For *Latin America*, data refer to the simple average of the gender gap in urban salaries for Argentina, the Bolivarian Republic of Venezuela, Bolivia, Brazil, Chile, Colombia, Costa Rica, Ecuador, Guatemala, Mexico, Panama, Paraguay and Uruguay.

"traditionally feminine" aspects of the services trade, such as tourism, data entry and call centres (Dejardin, 2009; Seguino and Grown, 2006).

Regarding the quality of women insertion in employment, this depends on whether their work is formal or informal, full-time or part-time. More qualitative studies show that women are more likely to be working in precarious, low-paid or unpaid jobs (ILO, 2012) and on smaller farm plots, producing less profitable crops than men (World Bank, 2012). In addition, they tend to be concentrated in the lower

paid sectors of the formal labour market so that, "as a result, women everywhere tend to earn less than men" (World Bank 2012: xxi). Even in regions where young women workers have contributed significantly to export-oriented production, they have been concentrated in the relatively lower paid and less skilled segments of production processes.

The gap between formal, regular employment on the one hand, and informal employment – whether as wage earners or self-employed – on the other, is one of the most significant characteristics in the overall structure of employment today. This increasingly translates into income inequalities in developing countries and, more recently, in high-income industrialized countries as well. This fundamental dichotomy tends to be reinforced by gender-based income gaps that are evident across occupations, despite similar educational levels. Gender gaps in wages have been extremely high in Asia; employers in trade-oriented activities have preferred to hire women workers, not only because they usually accept lower pay than men for a given job, but also because events such as marriage or childbirth may be used as an excuse to replace them in production line activities associated with high worker burnout (Seguino, 2000). As gender gaps have narrowed, employers have begun to find such workers less attractive. Indeed, the phase of rapid increase of women's involvement in export-oriented activities appears to have passed, as recent trends show both relative and absolute declines in the number of women in manufacturing employment even in the most export-driven economies (Ghosh, 2009). Instead, much more of such work is now concentrated in even lower paid locations, such as home-based work and small cottage industries, within larger production chains.

In developed countries, there has been a long-running tendency towards reducing gender-based gaps in remuneration (chart 3.7). However, this decline has been less marked in the last decade, and in some countries the decline has even been reversed. The earnings gap between men and women is larger in the transition economies, at 28 per cent, compared with 17 per cent in developed countries, though it shows a declining trend. In Latin America, policies in some countries have played a role in reducing gender-based wage gaps. In Argentina, Brazil, Costa Rica and Ecuador, for example, an increase in the legal minimum wage and better protection for domestic workers have contributed to reducing wage gaps and improving working conditions for women workers. In the region as a whole, the gap between the urban salaries received by men and women fell from 25 per cent in 1990 to 15 per cent in 2010. However, a comparison between the earnings of men and women with the same educational level shows a larger gap: 38 per cent in 1990 and 30 per cent in 2005 (ECLAC, CEPALSTAT). This suggests that women not only get lower pay for a similar activity as men, but they also obtain less well-paid jobs with comparable qualifications.

Gender-based inequalities in employment are reflected in and related to other kinds of important gender-related inequalities. Women's participation in the paid labour force can help to reduce poverty, as it increases household income, but this is not the same as equity within the household, or equity between men and women. Women are more likely to be poor than men and this trend is perpetuated from one generation to the next. Households headed by women have lower incomes than those headed by men. Women are less likely than men to hold or inherit income-generating assets such as land, capital and equity, or to own houses (Agarwal, 1994; World Bank, 2006, 2012). Women are also less likely to have income-buffering stocks such as savings or other transfers. Furthermore, they are more likely to be financially precarious in old age because they participate less in public and private pension schemes. All this also makes households in gender-unequal societies less likely to invest in women and girls.

In conclusion, one major structural change that is taking place in labour markets in many parts of the world – although at different paces – is the increasing participation of women. In this process, women frequently obtain jobs that tend to be of lower quality than those of men in terms of formality, decision-making positions and working hours (i.e. full-time or part-time). In addition, women's pay is consistently lower than that of men for a similar job or a similar skill or educational qualification. It could be expected that the increasing participation of a group which is paid below the average income would increase overall income inequality. This is not shown, however, in income distribution statistics, which are based on household surveys, as they conceal the gender dimension. Indeed, data from those surveys could even show a reduction of inequality, because a supplementary source of income actually increases the per capita income of low-income households, where

employment density tends to be smaller. As a result, although gender-related income inequality is one of the most widespread forms of income inequality, it is one that is the least visible in aggregate statistics. Just as for other inequalities, there are strong arguments for reducing gender inequality at different levels. Improving women's conditions of employment would strengthen the bargaining power of workers in general, and would thereby help correct the downward trend in the share of wages that has been taking place in many countries.

3. Unequal access to education

Access to education is a key factor in generating equality of opportunities. Widespread access to education can facilitate social mobility, whereas access limited to the elite or upper income groups will perpetuate existing social stratification and income inequalities. Inequalities of education and income inequalities are mutually linked: good education leads to better remunerated occupations, and, in many countries, a higher income can buy a better education. Moreover, education impacts on other important forms of inequality, including infant mortality and longevity, health and nutrition, employability and income levels, gender parity and participation in social, civil and political life (Sen, 1980).

Today more people have access to education, including at higher levels, than ever before. One of the most basic indicators of this progress can be seen in rising levels of literacy, the ability to read or write being a minimum threshold towards equalizing access to knowledge. The youth literacy rate exceeds 95 per cent in 63 of the 104 countries for which data are available, and is 99 per cent in 35 developing countries (UNDP, 2010). People who are illiterate today tend to be older, reflecting highly unequal levels of education in the past. Worldwide, only 7 per cent of 15–24 year-olds have never attended school compared with more than one third of people over the age of 65 years.

Primary school enrolment ratios are now virtually universal in both developed and developing regions, although there are still large gaps in some individual developing countries.[21] Not only are more children attending school, more are also finishing it: primary school completion rates reached 95 per cent

Table 3.8

GROSS SECONDARY EDUCATION ENROLMENT RATIO, 1971–2010
(Population-weighted averages, per cent)

	1971	1976	1981	1986	1991	1996	2001	2006	2010
Developed countries	78.6	83.5	87.2	92.0	94.5	101.7	101.7	101.9	102.6
Transition economies	..	..	97.7	99.4	94.7	89.9	91.4	88.2	91.8
Africa	14.6	18.3	24.2	29.5	31.7	32.9	37.2	43.1	48.8
Asia	29.7	41.6	35.9	36.3	41.4	51.3	55.5	63.5	70.7
Latin America and the Caribbean	30.2	41.5	50.6	58.4	59.3	64.0	74.2	81.5	86.2

Source: UNCTAD secretariat calculations, based on UNESCO Institute for Statistics database.
Note: Enrolment may exceed 100 per cent owing to students repeating the year. The regional aggregates are averages weighted by population. *Developed countries* excludes Australia, Cyprus, Estonia, Germany, Latvia, Lithuania, Romania, Slovakia, Slovenia and Switzerland for 1971–1986. *Transition economies* excludes Armenia, Croatia, the Republic of Moldova, Tajikistan and the Former Yugoslav Republic of Macedonia for 1981–1986 and Serbia for 1981–1996. *Latin America and the Caribbean* excludes Brazil.

in 2010, and expected years of schooling rose from 9 years in 1980 to 11 years by 2010. Even in countries which rank lowest in the Human Development Index of the United Nations Development Programme (UNDP), expected years of schooling rose from 5 years to 8 years. Secondary school enrolment has also increased appreciably since 1970 (table 3.8); by 2010 it covered more than 80 per cent of this age group not only in developed economies, but also in the transition economies of Europe and Central Asia, and in Latin America and East Asia. This coverage was comparatively low in South Asia (around 60 per cent) and in the sub-Saharan African countries (close to 40 per cent), with some exceptions.[22] Tertiary education has followed a similar evolution, with enrolment ratios increasing notably during the 2000s, in particular in Europe (both Western and Eastern), Latin America and East Asia.

The UNDP, which measures inequality of education by average years of schooling, has found that since 1970 this inequality has declined sharply in Central and Eastern Europe and in Central Asia, followed by East Asia and the Pacific, and Latin America and the Caribbean (UNDP, 2011). However, this measure does not take into consideration differences in educational quality, in which important gaps remain. In addition to universal schooling, it is important to improve the quality of public schooling through more spending and other measures so as to ensure more equal educational opportunities.

For example, pre-school attendance is especially important in reducing learning inequalities that reflect family background and income rather than a child's intrinsic abilities. Yet such access is still highly unequal: only 17.5 per cent of eligible children are enrolled in pre-school in sub-Saharan Africa compared with 85 per cent in high-income countries (UNESCO, 2012).[23] Moreover, a reduction in education inequality through better pre-school coverage and a longer school day would reduce the hours that adults, especially women, have to devote to child care. It would also facilitate women's access to paid employment, with positive effects on both income and gender equality.

Low income remains a major barrier at all levels of education, despite the fact that in many countries, educational policies directly support education for the lowest income quintiles (Cornia and Martorano, 2012). For instance, in Latin America, only one in five children from the lowest quintile complete secondary school, compared with four out of five from the highest quintile. According to ECLAC (2010: 209), "these contrasts show that education in its current form reinforces the intergenerational transmission of inequality instead of reversing it".

Inequality of access, and in particular the barriers associated with low-income, is also a concern in many developed countries. Socio-economic status is a strong predictor of educational success in many

OECD countries (OECD, 2011b). In the United States, for example, only 8 per cent of young adults from poor (bottom quartile) households gained a college degree by the age of 24 years, compared with 82 per cent from the top quartile (Educational Trust, 2011). Moreover, students who performed the best in standardized mathematics tests at 8th grade but coming from low-income households were less likely to complete their college education than the lowest-ability students coming from high-income households (Roy, 2005). High and rising college fees are one of the reasons for the stark inequality of access to the top universities: in the United States, only 9 per cent of students in the top universities come from the bottom half of the population, while 74 per cent come from the top quartile (Stiglitz, 2012: 19). Tuition fees are also relatively high in other OECD countries, such as Australia, Chile, Japan, New Zealand, Poland and the Republic of Korea (Oliveira Martins et al., 2009). In general, the higher the direct costs of access to education, the more likely this will deter or pose a heavy burden on poorer households.[24] The growing privatization of higher education across the developing world is also cause for concern, as it directly and adversely affects access by lower income groups.

Public spending on education is a major tool for improving equality of opportunities. It is particularly beneficial to the poorest households, who might otherwise not be able to afford an education. Enhancing skills in the entire population, rather than disproportionately among the rich, will create a much greater dispersion of skills and income-earning opportunities, apart from the wider social benefits of equity. The ILO (2008: 132) notes that countries that spent more on education in the early 1990s tended to have lower income inequality in the 2000s.

Educational inequalities are closely linked to the question of who pays for education. The wider coverage of schooling noted globally in recent years is associated with significantly increased public funding in much of the world, especially in developing countries. Public spending on education averaged around 5 per cent of GDP in 2009, up from around 4 per cent in the 1970s and only around 1 per cent a century ago (which was a time when only the wealthy, and usually only boys, received an education). Even the LDCs spend around 4 per cent of GDP on education today, which has helped to increase enrolment of children from poor households, and particularly girls. However, there are still many disparities in expenditure between regions and countries.

Public spending on education has changed the most in middle-income countries in recent years. It was affected by economic crises in several Latin American and transition economies, leading to a reduction of enrolments in some countries, particularly the transition economies. However, it recovered rapidly in most of these countries during the 2000s and reached new highs, particularly in Argentina, Brazil, Cuba, Mexico, Armenia, Kyrgyzstan, the Russian Federation, Tajikistan and Ukraine. Case studies indicate that the strong increase in public expenditure on education in many countries in Latin America and Asia, particularly Malaysia and the Republic of Korea, has generated a more egalitarian distribution of human capital and wages (Cornia, 2012; Ragayah, 2011; di Gropello and Sakellariou, 2010; Kwack, 2010). It appears that a better educated workforce has a strong impact on the distribution of wages, as it increases the supply of skilled and semi-skilled workers (the "quantity effect") and avoids or reduces a rise of the skill premium (the "price effect"). For many middle-income countries, this requires increasing enrolment and completion rates in secondary education and broadening access to subsidized tertiary education. The resulting impact on inequality may lag by 5–10 years but it tends to be very effective. Higher spending for education may contribute to better income distribution, particularly in the poorest countries. But this would require the provision of additional job opportunities for those that have received such education. This depends on overall growth dynamics and especially those of the formal manufacturing and services sectors. ∎

Notes

1   The Gini index or coefficient is the most commonly used measure of income distribution. It is a summary statistic of the Lorenz curve: whereas the Lorenz curve maps the proportion of the total income of a population that is cumulatively earned by different segments of the population, the Gini coefficient represents the area of concentration between the Lorenz curve and the 45-degree line of perfect equality. A Gini coefficient of 0 signifies perfect equality of income, and a coefficient of 1 signifies perfect inequality, i.e. one person earns all the income and the others none. Thus, the closer the coefficient is to 1, the more unequal is the income distribution. The Theil coefficient also provides information about income inequality in a country or region. It varies between 0 (perfect equality), and the log of the number of individuals or countries (perfect inequality). The advantage of this index is that it can decompose inequality into that between countries and within countries without any overlap.

2   For a discussion of the data problems in measuring and comparing inequality across countries, see Galbraith, 2012, chap. 2.

3   For a survey, see Blecker, 2002.

4   As stated by Gollin (2002: 458), "Many widely used economic models implicitly assume that income shares should be identical across time and space".

5   See: World Top Incomes Database at: http://g-mond. parisschoolofeconomics.eu/topincomes/#.

6   Atkinson, Piketty and Saez (2011: 10) calculated that the totality of the increase of the Gini coefficient of about 8 points can be explained by the rise in the share of the top 1 per cent alone. According to other estimates, the larger share of the income of the top 1 per cent accounts for approximately half of the increase in the Gini coefficient during that period (Krugman, 2012: 77).

7   These estimates cover between 41 and 71 countries for the nineteenth century, and between 85 and 108 countries for the twentieth century. From 1985 onwards, the Gini coefficients on households' gross income from the Standardized World Income Inequality Database (SWIID) are used. For previous years (especially before 1945), as these coefficients

are not available (or they are available for only a few countries), they are estimated using different statistics related to income inequality. When some segments of the income distribution are known (typically top incomes), the Gini coefficient is inferred by assuming a statistical distribution for the whole population. Another proxy used for estimating the Gini coefficient is the ratio of average family income to the annual wage earnings of unskilled workers. Finally, extensive use is made of the distribution of heights in a population as a proxy for income inequality. Since nutritional status, health care and shelter in the first years of life, which are essential factors determining individuals' height, are closely linked to household income, a significant and positive correlation between height variation and income Gini coefficients was found (van Zanden et al., 2011: 5–13). For alternative long-term income estimates, see Bourguignon and Morrison, 2002.

8   From a medium-term perspective, higher inequality seems to be a handicap rather than an advantage in handling the crisis. Galbraith (2012) uses wage inequality data to show that more egalitarian societies have lower unemployment and higher rates of technological progress and productivity growth.

9   For example, there is evidence that remittances were equalizing in El Salvador and Mexico (Acevedo and Cabrera, 2012), but the evidence from India (where the export of skilled labour has only recently become significant) is more mixed.

10 The average estimated Gini index in the mid-2000s was 0.46 for the region as a whole (Cogneau et al., 2006), similar to that of Latin America in 2010. However, it should be pointed out that in Latin America inequality measures normally refer to income distribution, while in Africa, most of the available surveys relate to expenditure, and tend to show lower inequality.

11 Other authors found income inequality levels largely exceeding previous estimates based on inequality of expenditure. Using the first detailed income distribution estimates for India, Desai et al. (2010) calculated a Gini coefficient of 0.54 which exceeded that of Brazil in the late 2000s. Estimates based on

village surveys show even higher Gini coefficients: on average 0.64 among households and 0.59 among individuals, even within villages (Swaminathan and Rawal, 2011).

12   As noted by Wee and Jomo (2006: 194), "Malaysian macroeconomic policy has been summarized as optimizing growth subject to restraint on prices and the balance of payments." The Government increased public investment in a way that complemented market forces.

13   The European Union and the Common Market of the South (Mercosur), for example, have established financial mechanisms for rebalancing development levels within their respective regions.

14   For a discussion on the alternative concepts on global inequality, see Milanovic, 2005.

15   This comparison between per capita GDP among countries has occasionally been altered by the increase in their number, particularly in the early 1960s with the decolonization process, and then again in the 1990s with the disintegration of previously federal States, particularly in transition economies.

16   The use of PPP exchange rates may be problematic since they are based on dated and often questionable price surveys of a fixed basket of goods across countries. These shortcomings are not always adequately taken into account when making inter country income comparisons.

17   On the basis of this alternative calculation, Galbraith (2008) challenges the widespread belief that Europe is more egalitarian than the United States.

18   For methodological details on this decomposition, see Pyatt (1976). It must be noted that, unlike the Theil coefficient, the Gini coefficient is not totally decomposable, and therefore the exercise calculates an "overlapping" component that refers to the fact that somebody in a richer country may have a lower income than somebody in a poorer country (and the converse). Milanovic (2005) argues that it is acceptable to ascribe the entire "overlap" term in the Gini coefficient to the intra-country component.

19   In developed countries, revenue from property tends to account for between 20 per cent (in Japan) and more than 50 per cent (in France) of the total income of the highest income group (i.e. the top 1 per cent of the population).

20   The simple average of the net wealth-to-income ratio for Chile, China, Colombia, the Czech Republic, India, Slovakia, Slovenia, South Africa and Ukraine is estimated at 3.25, compared with 6.35 for 16 developed countries (Credit Suisse, 2011).

21   According to UNESCO (2012), enrolment in primary school was below 70 per cent in Djibouti, Eritrea, Niger, Papua New Guinea and Somalia around 2010.

22   For instance, enrolment in secondary school exceeded 85 per cent in Cape Verde, the Islamic Republic of Iran, Mauritius, the Seychelles, South Africa and Sri Lanka.

23   In Latin America, pre-school enrolments rose sharply, from 9 per cent in 1970 to 71 per cent in 2008. However there are still significant differences among countries in the region, with relatively high enrolment rates in Argentina, the Bolivarian Republic of Venezuela, Brazil, Chile, the Dominican Republic and Uruguay, and relatively low enrolment rates in several Central American countries. In addition, "preschool attendance by children from 3 to 5 years is highly stratified, with access proportional to household income: participation is lowest among children from poor households and those vulnerable to poverty" (ECLAC, 2010: 207–208) – precisely the social groups most in need of such services, which in many countries are not free. Pre-school enrolment rates remain comparatively low in Central, South and West Asia and in Africa – regions in which women's participation in formal labour markets tends to be low.

24   The cumulated debt from education credits may reach significant levels not only for household budgets, but also from a macroeconomic perspective. The Consumer Financial Protection Bureau in the United States notes that the outstanding debt on student loans rose to more than $1 trillion (Chopra, 2012) – an amount that exceeds auto or credit-card debt and is second only to mortgage debt (Evans, 2012).

References

Acevedo C and Cabrera M (2012). Social Policies or Private Solidarity? The Equalizing Role of Migration and Remittances in El Salvador. UNU-WIDER Working Paper 2012/13, United Nations University, World Institute for Development Economics Research, Helsinki.

Africa Progress Panel (2012). Africa Progress Report 2012, Jobs, Justice and Equity: Seizing opportunities in times of global change. May.

African Development Bank (2012). Inequality in Africa. Briefing Note No. 5, Abidjan, March.

Agarwal B (1994). *A Field of One's Own: Gender and Land Rights in South Asia*. Cambridge, Cambridge University Press.

Asad MA and Ahmad M (2011). Growth and consumption inequality in Pakistan. *Pakistan Economic and Social Review*, 49(1): 69–89.

Atkinson AB and Piketty T (eds.) (2007). *Top Incomes over the Twentieth Century – A Contrast between Continental European and English-Speaking Countries*. Oxford, Oxford University Press.

Atkinson AB and Piketty T (eds.) (2010). *Top Incomes: A Global Perspective*. Oxford and New York, Oxford University Press.

Atkinson AB, Piketty T and Saez E (2011). Top Incomes in the Long Run of History. *Journal of Economic Literature*, 49(1): 3–71.

Bakija J, Cole A and Heim BT (2012). Jobs and income growth of top earners and the causes of changing income inequality: Evidence from U.S. tax return data. Williams College Working Paper, Williamstown, MA. Available at: http://web.williams.edu/Economics/wp/BakijaColeHeimJobsIncomeGrowthTopEarners.pdf.

Blecker R (2002). Distribution, demand and growth in neo-Kaleckian models. In: Setterfield M, ed. *The Economics of Demand-led Growth*. Cheltenham, Elgar.

Bourguignon F and Morrison C (2002). The size and distribution of income among world citizens, 1820-1990. *American Economic Review*: 727–744.

Chen J, Dai D, Pu M, Hou W and Feng Q (2010). The trend of the Gini coefficient of China. Working Paper 109, Brooks World Poverty Institute, University of Manchester, Manchester.

Chopra R (2012). Too big to fail: student debt hits a trillion. Washington, DC, Consumer Financial Protection Bureau. Available at: http://www.consumerfinance.gov/blog/too-big-to-fail-student-debt-hits-a-trillion/.

Cogneau D, Bossuroy T, De Vreyer P, Guenard C, Hiller V, Leite P, Mesple-Somps S, Pasquier-Doumier L and Torelli C (2006). *Inequalities and Equity in Africa*. Working paper Institut pour la Recherche de Développement, INSEE, DIAL, Paris.

Cornia GA (2012). Inequality trends and their determinants: Latin America over 1990-2010. UNU/WIDER Working Paper 2012/09, Helsinki.

Cornia GA, Addison T and Kiiski S (2003). Income distribution changes and their impact in the post-world war II period. UNU-WIDER Discussion Paper No. 2003/28, UNU-WIDER, Helsinki.

Cornia GA and Martorano B (2012). Development policies and income inequality in selected developing regions, 1980-2010. Background paper for *TDR 2012*. Geneva, UNCTAD.

Cornia GA, Gomez Sabaini JC and Martorano B (2011). A new fiscal pact, tax policy changes and income inequality: Latin America during the last decade. UNU/WIDER Working Paper 2011/70, Helsinki.

Credit Suisse (2011). *Global Wealth Databook 2011*, October.

Dejardin A (2009). Gender (in) equality, globalization and governance, Working Paper No. 92, Policy. Integration and Statistics Department, International Labour Organisation, Geneva.

Desai SB, Dubey A, Joshi BL, Sen M, Shariff A and Vanneman R (2010). *Human Development in India: Challenges for a Society in Transition*. New Delhi: Oxford University Press.

di Gropello E and Sakellariou C (2010). Industry and skill wage premiums in East Asia. The World Bank, Policy Research Working Paper Series 5379.

Dollar D and Kraay A (2000). Growth is good for the poor. World Bank, Policy Research Working Paper 2587, World Bank, Washington, DC.

ECLAC (2004). *A Decade of Social Development in Latin America*. Economic Commission for Latin America and the Caribbean, Santiago, Chile.

ECLAC (2010*). Time for equality, closing gaps, opening trails*. Economic Commission for Latin America and the Caribbean, Santiago, Chile, May.

ECLAC (2012). *Social Panorama of Latin America 2011*. Economic Commission for Latin America and the Caribbean, Santiago, Chile, March.

Education Trust (2011). The condition of education, 2011. The Education Trust, Washington, DC.

Elson D (1993). Gender-aware analysis and development economics. *Journal of International Development*, 5: 237–247.

Evans K (2012). Student loans: the next bailout? CNBC, 25 April. Available at: http://www.cnbc.com/id/47171658/Student_Loans_The_Next_Bailout.

Finn A, Leibbrandt M and Wegner E (2011). Policies for reducing income inequality and poverty in South Africa. *Transformation Audit: From Inequality to Inclusive Growth*. Institute for Justice and Reconciliation, Cape Town.

Galbraith J (2008). *The Predator State*. Free Press, New York.

Galbraith J (2012). *Inequality and Instability*. Oxford and New York, Oxford University Press.

Galor O, Moav O and Vollrath D (2009). Inequality in Landownership, the Emergence of Human-Capital Promoting Institutions, and the Great Divergence. *Review of Economic Studies*, Wiley Blackwell, 76(1): 143–179.

Ghosh J (2009). *Never Done and Poorly Paid: Women's Work in Globalizing India*. New Delhi, Women Unlimited Press.

Ghosh J (2012). Trends in inequality in South Asia. Background paper for *TDR 2012*. Geneva, UNCTAD.

Goldsmith RW (1986). *Comparative National Balance Sheets, A Study of Twenty Countries, 1688-1978*. Chicago, University of Chicago Press.

Gollin D (2002). Getting income shares right. *Journal of Political Economy*, 110(2): 458–474.

Gunawardena D (2008). Inequality in Sri Lanka: Key trends and policy responses. In: *Inequality in Social Justice in South Asia*. UNDP and Macmillan India: Delhi: 241–286. Available at: http://hdru.aprc.undp.org/areas of work/pdf/Sri_Lanka.pdf.

ILO (2008). *World of Work Report 2008: Income Inequalities in the Age of Financial Globalization*. Geneva, International Labour Office.

ILO (2012). Global Employment Trends 2012: Preventing a deeper jobs crisis. International Labour Organisation, Geneva.

Kaldor N (1961). Capital accumulation and economic growth. In: Lutz FA and Hague DC, eds. *The Theory of Capital: Proceedings of a Conference Held by the International Economic Association*. London, Macmillan.

Khan AR (2005). Measuring inequality and poverty in Bangladesh: An assessment of the survey data. *Bangladesh Development Studies*. Dhaka, Bangladesh

Institute of Development Studies. Volume XXXI (3-4): 1–34.

Krämer H (2010). The alleged stability of the labour share of income in macroeconomic theories of income distribution. Macroeconomic Policy Institute (IMK), Working Paper 11/2010, August.

Krugman P (2012). *End this Depression Now!* New York, W.W. Norton & Company.

Kwack SY (2010). Wage Inequality and the Efficiency of Workers in Korea, 1965–2007. The Bank of Korea, Institute for Monetary and Economic Research, Working Paper No. 437.

Kwon H (2005). Transforming the developmental welfare state in East Asia. *Development and Change*, 36: 477–497.

Kwon H, Dong G and Moon H (2010). The future challenges of the developmental welfare State: The case of Korea. Paper presented at the Conference on Social Policy in Times of Change of the Social Policy Association at University of Lincoln, 5–7 July.

La Fuente M and Sainz P (2001). Participation by the poor in the fruits of growth. *CEPAL Review*, No. 75, December: 153–162.

Lindenboim J, Kennedy D and Graña J (2011). Distribución funcional y demanda agregada en Argentina: Sesenta años en perspectiva internacional. Working paper no. 16, Centro de Estudios sobre Población Empleo y Desarrollo (CEPED), Buenos Aires, August.

Luo Z and Zhu N (2008). Rising income inequality in China: A race to the top. Policy Research Working Paper no. 4700, World Bank, East Asian and Pacific Region, Washington, DC.

Maddison A (2004). World population, GDP and GDP per capita, 1-2000 AD. Available at: http://www.eco.rug.nl/~Maddison/.

Milanovic B (2005). *Worlds Apart: Measuring International and Global Inequality*. Princeton, NJ, Princeton University Press.

Milanovic B (2006). Global Income Inequality: What it is and why it Matters? Working Paper No. 26, United Nations Department of Economic and Social Affairs, New York.

Milanovic B (2011a). Global inequality: From class to location, from proletarians to migrants. Policy Research Working Paper WPS5820, World Bank Development Research Group, Washington, DC, September.

Milanovic B (2011b). More of less. *Finance and Development*, September.

Ocampo JA (2009). Latin America and the global financial crisis. *Cambridge Journal of Economics*, 33(4): 703–724.

OECD (2011a). *Divided We Stand. Why Inequality Keeps Rising*. Paris, December.

OECD (2011b). *Equity and quality in education: Supporting disadvantaged students and schools*. OECD: Paris.

Olivera Martins J, Boarini R, Strauss H and de la Maisonneuve C (2009). The policy determinants of investment in tertiary education. *OECD Journal: Economic Studies.* OECD: Paris.

Piketty T (2003). Income Inequality in France, 1901–1998, *Journal of Political Economy*, 111(5): 1004–1042.

Piketty T (2008). *L'Economie des Inegalités*. Paris, La Découverte.

Ping Z (1997). Income distribution during the transition in China. UNU/WIDER Working Paper 138, Helsinki.

Prebisch R (1963). *Hacia una Dinámica del Desarrollo Latinoamericano*. México City, Fondo de Cultura Económica.

Pyatt G (1976). On the interpretation and disaggregation of Gini coefficients. *Economics Journal*, 86: 243–255.

Ragayah HMZ (2011). Malaysia's new economic model: An assessment of its strategies for inclusive growth. Paper presented at the Asian regional workshop on Social Inclusiveness in Asia's Emerging Middle Income Countries, 13 September 2011, Jakarta, Indonesia, Organized by The Asian Development Bank, the International Labour Organization Regional Office for Asia and the Pacific and the International Poverty Reduction Center in China.

Razavi S (2011). *World development report 2012: gender quality and development - an opportunity both welcome and missed*. UNRISD, United Nations, Geneva.

Roy J (2005). Low income hinders college attendance for even the highest achieving students. Economic Policy Institute. Economic snapshot/Jobs Wages and Living Standards, Washington, DC.

Seguino S (2000). Gender inequality and economic growth: a cross country analysis. *World Development*, 28(7): 1211–1230.

Seguino S and Grown C (2006). Gender equity and globalisation: macroeconomic policies for developing countries. MPRA paper 6540. University library of Munich.

Sen A (1980). Equality of what. Tanner Lectures in Sen A (1982). Choice, Welfare and Measurement, Blackwell, Oxford. Reprinted: Harvard University Press, Cambridge 1997.

Sen A (1992). Inequality Re-examined. Clarendon Press, Oxford. Harvard University Press, Cambridge.

Shahbaz M and Islam F (2011). Financial development and income inequality in Pakistan. *Journal of Economic Development*, 6(1): 35–58.

Solt F (2009). Standardizing the World Income Inequality Database. *Social Science Quarterly*, 90(2): 231–242.

Stiglitz J (2012). *The Price of Inequality*. W. W. Northon and Company Ltd., New York.

Swaminathan M and Rawal V (2011). Is India really a country of low income-inequality? Observations from eight villages. *Review of Agrarian Studies,* 1(2): July-December. Available at: http://www.ras.org.in/index.php?Abstract=income_inequality_and caste_in_village_india.

Thirlwall P (2011). Balance of payments constrained growth models: History and overview. Studies in Economics no. 1111. Kent School of Economics, University of Kent, Canterbury, May.

UNCTAD (*TDR 2010*). *Trade and Development Report, 2010. Employment, globalization and development.* United Nations publication, Sales No. E.10.II.D.3, New York and Geneva.

UNCTAD (*TDR 2011*). *Trade and Development Report, 2011. Post-crisis policy challenges in the world economy.* United Nations publication, Sales No. E.11.II.D.3, New York and Geneva.

UNCTAD (2011). Report of the Secretary-General of UNCTAD to UNCTAD XIII. Development-led globalization: Towards sustainable and inclusive development paths. New York and Geneva.

UNDP (2010). *Human Development Report 2010: The Real Wealth of Nations: Pathways to Human Development.* United Nations publication, New York and Geneva.

UNDP (2011). *Human Development Report 2011: Sustainability and equity: a better future for all.* United Nations publication, New York and Geneva.

UNESCO (2012). Institute for Statistics (UIS) online database. Available at: www.uis.unesco.org.

Vanneman R and Dubey A (2010). Horizontal and vertical inequalities in India. Paper presented at the conference on Inequality and the Status of the Middle Class: Lessons from the Luxembourg Income Study, Luxembourg, 28–30 June.

van Zanden JL, Baten J, Földvari P and van Leeuwen B (2011). The changing shape of global inequality 1820-2000: Exploring a new dataset. CGEH Working Paper Series, Centre for Global Economic History, Utrecht University.

Venieris Y and Gupta D (1986). Income distribution and sociopolitical instability as determinants of savings: A cross-sectional model. *Journal of Political Economy*, 94(4): 873–883.

Vidanapathirana U (2007). Emerging income inequality and the widening economic divide: The case of Sri Lanka. Paper presented at IDEAs Conference on Policy Perspectives on Growth, Economic Structures and Poverty Reduction at Tsinghua University, Beijing, 7–9 June.

Vollrath D (2007). Land distribution and international agricultural productivity. *American Journal of Agricultural Economy*, 89(1): 202–216.

Wee CH and Jomo KS (2006). Macroeconomic policy, growth, redistribution and poverty reduction: The case of Malaysia. In: Cornia GA, ed. *Pro Poor Macroeconomics: Potential and Limitations*. London, Palgrave.

World Bank (2006). *Word Development Report. Equity and Development*. Washington, DC.

World Bank (2012). *World Development Report 2012. Gender equality and development*. World Bank, Washington, DC.

Chapter IV

CHANGES IN GLOBALIZATION AND TECHNOLOGY AND THEIR IMPACTS ON NATIONAL INCOME INEQUALITY

A. Introduction

The evidence presented in the preceding chapter suggests that a multitude of factors influence income distribution through their effects on various categories of income at different points in time and at different phases of a country's economic development. The objective of this chapter is to examine the pressures that technological advances and globalization of trade and finance have exerted on the evolution of national income inequality over the past two decades.

Many observers who subscribe to traditional theoretical approaches believe that the negative effects of globalization and technological change on income distribution are inevitable. Thus, as far as they are concerned, the main question is which one of these two forces has been the stronger. However, this *TDR* challenges that position: chapters IV and V aim to show that the rise of income inequality observed in many countries could have been mitigated, if not prevented, by more appropriate macroeconomic and labour market policies that would have had a positive effect on countries' trade and technological progress.

Technological change and the progressive globalization of trade and finance can affect income distribution through various channels. However, it is not clear, *a priori*, which direction this influence takes. Different channels unleash forces that may well pull in opposite directions, and the strength of these forces is likely to depend on country-specific and time-bound factors. Among the country-specific factors, macroeconomic and financial policies, especially exchange-rate management, as well as the organization of labour markets play a decisive role.

Another country-specific factor is the level of industrial and technological development, as discussed in general terms in chapter III. This is because the level of a country's economic and industrial development and how close it has come to the global technological frontier determine whether integration spurs its industrialization process, or whether its greater exposure to globalization causes deindustrialization. Accordingly, the way in which globalization affects income distribution is often seen to depend to a large extent on how economic integration changes the structural composition of a country's economic activities.

Against this background, this chapter addresses the impact of globalization and technological developments on income distribution within countries. Its main objectives are to: (i) identify the channels through which globalization and technological developments have exerted pressure on national income distribution; (ii) examine differences among countries in their exposure to such channels; and (iii) highlight the economic forces that make such cross-country differences mutually interdependent.

Recommendations for policies designed to ensure a level of income equality that is socially acceptable and conducive to sustained economic growth and development are addressed in the subsequent chapters.

Given that many country-specific factors affect changes in income distribution, this chapter cannot cover all countries in the same way. Rather, the distributional impacts of technology and globalization are illustrated through evidence for specific countries and country groups for which the identified channels have been of major importance.

The chapter argues that the ways in which globalization and technological change influence income distribution are closely interrelated, and that the combined effects of these two factors have increased significantly over the past two decades. But whether these combined effects reduce or accentuate income inequality also depends on a country's initial conditions and its level of industrial development. It also depends crucially on its macroeconomic policies, especially exchange-rate management, and arrangements and institutions relating to the labour market and wage determination, as well as on policies that influence the nature and speed of economic integration.

The evidence presented in the chapter indicates that, in developed countries, the effect of the forces of globalization on income inequality since the early 2000s is also largely due to behavioural changes in the corporate sector in response to greater international competition. Companies have given less attention to upgrading production technology and the product composition of output through productivity-enhancing investment with a long-term perspective; instead, they have increasingly relied on offshoring production activities to low-wage locations, and on

> The distributional effects of globalization and technological change are closely interrelated …

> … and their combined impacts have increased significantly over the past two decades.

seeking to reduce domestic unit labour costs by wage compression. This trend has been associated with a polarization of incomes in developed countries. For the United States, evidence suggests that a new mode of corporate governance aimed at the maximization of shareholder value is pushing corporations to maintain external competitiveness through wage repression and offshoring, and to increase profits through, often speculative, financial investments, rather than by boosting productive capacity.

Finally, the chapter shows that the expansion of global trade and the related increase in developed countries' manufactured imports from developing countries have been associated with growing income inequality in some of the large, rapidly industrializing developing countries, especially in Asia. Distributional changes in these countries are likely to reflect the unequal rate of growth of living standards between rural and urban areas, as well as between interior and coastal regions, as was anticipated by Kuznets (1955) for countries at early stages of industrial development. The evidence for emerging economies, especially economies in transition but also some developing economies, suggests that economic instability related to rapid financial integration has had adverse effects on income distribution. By contrast, several countries with rich natural-resource endowments, both the more and less advanced ones, have seen an improvement in their terms of trade over the past decade. Under certain circumstances, this improvement has facilitated the adoption of policies designed to reduce income inequality.

The next section revisits the literature focusing on the channels through which trade globalization and technological changes have affected income distribution. It starts with a brief account of the trade-inequality debate of the early 1990s, which emphasized the rise in wage inequality between skilled and unskilled labour in developed countries. It then focuses on the more recent trade-inequality debate, which has brought to the fore a number of new facets of the distributional effects of technology and trade globalization. It examines: (i) employment concerns; (ii) the polarization of wages by considering medium-skilled workers in addition to the traditional high- versus low-skilled dichotomy; (iii) a wider range of countries that covers developing and transition economies in addition to developed countries; and (iv) shifts in employment away from manufacturing towards the primary and services sectors, in addition to employment shifts within manufacturing. Section C discusses the channels through which financial globalization has affected income distribution over and above technology and trade globalization. Section D concludes.

B. Trade, technology and shifts in production structure

In the early 1990s, there was a lively debate on the relationship between trade, technology and income distribution (see also the contribution of *TDR 1997* to this debate). About a decade later, this debate has been revived, mainly for two reasons: the first is the recent increase in income inequality in many countries around the world, and the second arises from theoretical advances (discussed, for example, in Harrison, McLaren and McMillan, 2011) and the availability of more comprehensive data that allow a better understanding of the relationship between changes in income distribution, on the one hand, and technological developments and countries' increasing trade integration on the other. The theoretical advances allow a broadening of the analysis so as to assess the joint influences of trade, technology and foreign direct investment (FDI) on income distribution.

For a full understanding of the rise of inequality in many countries that has accompanied the acceleration of globalization and technical progress, account has to be taken of macroeconomic and labour market policies that have led to persistently higher unemployment and a weakening of labour in the wage bargaining process. These policies are analysed in chapter VI of this *Report*. This section concentrates on the specific channels through which, with given macroeconomic and labour market policies, trade globalization and technological change have exerted pressure on income distribution. It starts with a brief review of the trade-inequality debate of the early 1990s. It then focuses on the main changes in the character of both inequality and countries' exposure to global trade that have prompted the more recent trade-inequality debate.

1. The trade-inequality debate of the early 1990s

Standard international trade theory in the tradition of Heckscher and Ohlin assumes that trade is driven by international differences in factor endowments. In its simplest form, it predicts an increase in real income of a country's abundant factor when that country engages in trade. More precisely, it suggests that the price of unskilled labour-intensive goods falls in more advanced countries that are assumed to have abundant skilled labour, when these engage in trade with developing countries that are assumed to have abundant unskilled labour. In the more advanced countries, this decline in the price of unskilled labour-intensive goods causes a shift in production towards more skill-intensive goods and a decline in the real wages of less educated workers, both in absolute terms and relative to better skilled workers. The latter effect is usually described as an increase in the so-called "skill premium", which represents a growing gap in wages between skilled and unskilled workers and a worsening of wage disparities. The inverse is predicted to hold in developing countries: the movement in prices causes a shift in production towards unskilled labour-intensive sectors, which boosts the demand for unskilled workers and thus their real wages, both in absolute terms and relative to skilled workers. Given that in developing countries the proportion of unskilled labour in the total labour force is much higher than that of skilled labour, income gaps among wage earners in these countries are expected to decline.

In the 1990s, there was a heated debate as to whether such trade-related effects could explain the increasing income inequality that had been observed in many developed countries over the 1980s and early 1990s (see also *TDR 1997*).[1] Eventually, there was a wide consensus that trade had played a relatively modest role in depressing the relative wages of less-skilled workers in those countries, and that therefore it was not the dominant – or even an important – factor for explaining the increase in income inequality. Rather, this increase in inequality was attributed mainly to skill-biased technological progress (for reviews, see, Anderson, 2005; Goldberg and Pavcnik, 2007; and Harrison, McLaren and McMillan, 2011).

> The trade-inequality debate of the 1990s attributed the increase in income inequality mainly to skill-biased technological progress.

The debate discounted international trade as an explanation for two main reasons.[2] First, empirical studies of developed countries (e.g. Lawrence and Slaughter, 1993; Berman, Bound and Griliches, 1994) found that the bulk of the changes in the prices of goods and increases in the skill premiums resulted from shifts *within* industrial sectors, rather than *between* sectors, contrary to what is predicted by standard trade theory. Second, empirical studies for developing countries (e.g. Berman, Bound and Machin, 1998; Desjonqueres, Machin and van Reenen, 1999) noted that the shift towards higher pay for skilled workers that had been observed for developed countries also occurred in developing countries; yet according to standard trade theory, wages in developing countries should have moved in the opposite direction to those in developed countries.[3]

Part of the explanation for the latter finding may be that trade theory assumes free movement of goods, while in the 1980s and 1990s developing-country exports of labour-intensive manufactures faced significant barriers to accessing developed-country markets

(*TDR 1997*, Part Two). The major barriers were tariff peaks, which often affected labour-intensive goods, and the Multi-Fibre Arrangement (MFA), which comprised a complex set of quantitative restrictions that allowed the expansion of developing-country exports of textiles and clothing only insofar as it would not entail sizeable short- and medium-term adjustment costs, in particular unemployment, in the importing (i.e. developed) countries.

Attributing the rise in income inequality during the 1970s and 1980s to skill-biased technological change alone has been challenged on the grounds that such a skill bias was not a new phenomenon during that period (Card and DiNardo, 2002). Within the framework of traditional economic theory this issue may be resolved by examining the long-term trend of skill-biased technological change in combination with developments in the availability of skilled workers. Regarding the evolution of the skill premium, there may well be a race between technological progress, on the one hand, which tends to increase the demand for skilled labour, and educational attainment on the other, which increases the supply of skilled labour (Tinbergen, 1975; Goldin and Katz, 2008). Many observers argue that, following a long period of relatively stable technological progress, rapid progress in information technology and the widespread use of computers in the workplace accelerated the rate of technological change in the 1980s and 1990s. They suggest that the resulting increase in the demand for skilled labour outpaced educational advances in developed and developing countries alike, which caused the increase in wage inequality.[4]

Neither conventional trade theory based on simple Stolper-Samuelson relationships nor technological progress alone can fully explain the increase in the relative demand for skilled labour that was observed across countries during the 1980s and early 1990s. An empirical analysis for the United States found the combination of offshoring and technological change to be an important additional explanation (Feenstra and Hanson, 1999).[5] The general rise in unemployment during that period was not considered to be of particular importance, as a rise of unemployment in all skill groups would depress all wages but not relative wages. However, in times of general high and persistent unemployment, employers may choose to hire relatively well-qualified people even for rather low-skill jobs. This tends to prolong unemployment and the pressure on wages of the low-skilled. Moreover, when unemployment persists, more and more governments put pressure on low-skilled workers, in particular, to accept jobs from which they cannot even earn a decent living.

2. The "new" trade-inequality debate

In the past few years there has been a revival of concerns about trade-related distributional effects. This section addresses this new debate. It first looks at developed countries, where the main reason for this new interest is the significant worsening of income inequality, combined with persistently high unemployment and a change in the character of both income inequality and countries' trade exposure. The section then turns to the many other countries, especially developing countries in Africa and Latin America and a number of economies in transition, where distributional concerns have arisen because of perceptions that the forces of globalization may be causing deindustrialization and an associated worsening of employment and wage-earning opportunities. The section also discusses distributional concerns in some Asian developing countries, which have arisen from the observation that globalization may have spurred rapid industrialization and buoyed up economic growth, but at the same time also caused an increase in income inequality.

(a) New features of the trade and inequality relationship in developed countries

The new aspect of income inequality in developed countries – also termed "polarization" (Autor, Katz and Kearney, 2006) – concerns employment in addition to wages. The trade-inequality debate in the early 1990s focused on the divergence between the wages of high-skilled and low-skilled workers. However, the more recent period has been characterized by a very different pattern of labour demand that benefits those in both the highest-skill and the lowest-skill occupations, but not workers in moderately skilled occupations (i.e. those involved in routine operations). The moderately skilled workers have

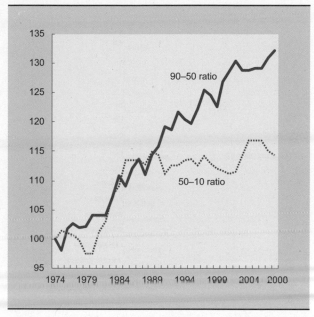

Chart 4.1

RATIOS OF AVERAGE HOURLY WAGES AT VARIOUS PERCENTILES OF THE DISTRIBUTION IN THE UNITED STATES, 1974–2008

(Index numbers, 1974 = 100)

Source: UNCTAD secretariat calculations, based on United States National Bureau of Economic Research, *Current Population Survey Merged Outgoing Rotation Groups* database.

Note: The 50–10 ratio refers to the ratio of the average hourly wage at the 50th percentile of the distribution to that at the 10th percentile, and the 90–50 ratio refers to the ratio of the average hourly wage at the 90th percentile of the distribution to that at the 50th percentile.

been experiencing a decline in wages and employment relative to other workers.

To examine the polarization of wages, it is useful to set aside the wages of the top-level income earners, which were addressed in chapter III, as well as those of the bottom-level earners. Decomposing wage developments of earners between the 90th (top) and the 10th (bottom) percentiles allows a comparison of the ratio of wages at the 90th percentile with that of the 50th percentile (the 90–50 ratio) and the ratio of wages at the 50th percentile with that of the 10th percentile (the 50–10 ratio). Evidence for the United States indicates that both these ratios (90–50 and 50–10) were fairly stable in the 1970s and grew rapidly in the 1980s, but also that their evolution diverged sharply after the 1980s (chart 4.1).[6] The 90–50 ratio has been growing steadily, and is now

Chart 4.2

CHANGE IN EMPLOYMENT SHARES BY OCCUPATION LEVEL IN THE UNITED STATES AND SELECTED COUNTRIES IN THE EU, 1993–2006

(Per cent)

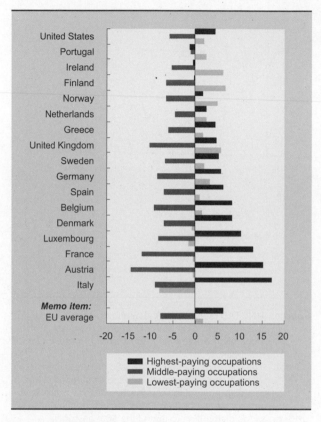

Source: Goos, Manning and Salomons, 2011; and Acemoglu and Autor, 2012.
Note: Occupations are grouped by wage terciles. Data points for members of the EU are ordered by changes in the share of highest-paying occupations.

Polarization of employment has also occurred in virtually every developed country (chart 4.2).[7] In the vast majority of the countries shown in chart 4.2 the employment shares of the highest-paying occupations (such as lawyers, bankers, management consultants, professors and doctors) have risen significantly, and in most of these countries, the employment shares of the lowest-paying occupations (such as hairdressers, cleaners, drivers, waiters and supermarket workers) have also grown. By contrast, the shares of middle-paying occupations (such as office clerks, workers in crafts and related trades, and plant and machine operators and assemblers) have declined in all the countries. This hollowing out of middle-income occupations may be due to automation (i.e. related to technological advances). The greater use of computers in the workplace may have wiped out the jobs of moderately skilled workers and pushed them into lower-paying jobs in services that computers cannot perform (Autor and Dorn, 2012). However, it may also be related to the offshoring of manufacturing activities and services.

Indeed, countries' exposure to trade has assumed a new character with respect to two factors. First, the share of developing countries in global exports crossed 30 per cent in 2000 and reached 40 per cent in 2010, which reflects a significant growth from the average level of 25 per cent during the 1970s and 1980s – the period that was the focus of the earlier trade-inequality debate.[8] Second, the growth of developing countries' exports of manufactures has been concentrated in only a few countries, especially China. China's per capita income and wages are considerably lower than in those economies which accounted for the bulk of manufactured exports from developing to developed countries in the 1970s and 1980s, such as the Republic of Korea and Taiwan Province of China, as well as other countries that had experienced rapid economic catch-up after the Second World War, such as Japan and Germany. Even though data that allow precise cross-country comparisons are available only for the period since 1975, a comparison of the wage levels in manufacturing of countries experiencing rapid economic catch-up relative to United States levels broadly shows that there are still substantial wage differences between some of the main developing-country exporters of manufactures and their developed-country partners (chart 4.3). Indeed, with China's opening up to global trade, this difference has most likely increased, even when adjusted for the higher productivity of

about 35 per cent higher than in 1973. By contrast, the 50–10 ratio has remained fairly stable at a level of about 15 per cent above its level of the early 1970s. More detailed evidence indicates that the gap between the 10th percentile and the median has substantially contracted over the past few years (Acemoglu and Autor, 2012: 13). Further evidence, which includes a gender dimension, indicates that the 50–10 ratio has stagnated for women but has actually declined for men (Lemieux, 2007; Acemoglu and Autor, 2012). Taken together, this evidence indicates that income gains have been concentrated in the higher and lower echelons at the expense of the middle layers of the income distribution.

United States workers (Ceglowski and Golub, 2011). This contrasts with the debate of the early 1990s, when the rise in the average wage of the newly industrializing economies (NIEs) relative to that of the United States was used to allay fears about the effect of trade on income inequality.

In line with earlier experiences of rapid economic catch-up in Asia, as well as in Germany, China may now have reached the stage in the catch-up process when wages in manufacturing are beginning to rise substantially (chart 4.3). This may be partly due to a declining growth in labour supply and restrictions on geographical labour mobility (*TDR 2010*, chap. II, sect. C). Moreover, the new labour contract law, which came into effect in 2008, stipulates minimum wage requirements and allows a strengthening of the bargaining power of employees.[9] Finally, labour compensation has also increased because of rapidly rising labour productivity. According to Banister and Cook (2011), labour productivity in China's industrial sector (including manufacturing, as well as construction, mining and utilities) increased at an average annual rate of about 10 per cent between 1991 and 2008. The reason for this rapid productivity growth is a combination of sizeable and growing capital investment and improved education and skill levels of Chinese workers, along with the use of advanced technologies by transnational corporations (TNCs) engaged in international production sharing, as discussed below. Labour compensation in Chinese manufacturing has increased at a faster rate in dollar terms than in renminbi because of the appreciation of the Chinese currency by about 25 per cent between 2005 and 2012.[10]

To illustrate the increase in manufactured exports from developing countries, it is useful to focus on a group of "low-wage economies". Following Bernard, Jensen and Schott (2006), this group can be defined as countries with a per capita income lower than 5 per cent of that of the United States before 2007 (i.e. prior to the onset of the current economic crisis). The resulting group of 82 developing and transition economies (see the text at the end of the Notes to this chapter for the full list) includes many small economies but also some of the large economies in Asia, especially China, as well as countries such as India, Indonesia, and the Philippines.

Indeed, much of the debate on the new pattern of countries' exposure to global trade relates to

Chart 4.3

WAGES IN MANUFACTURING OF SELECTED COUNTRIES DURING ECONOMIC CATCH-UP RELATIVE TO THE UNITED STATES

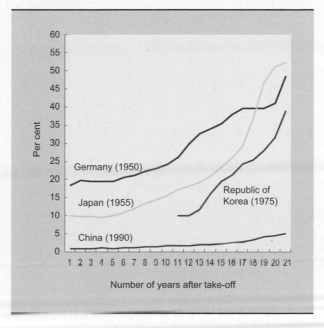

Source: UNCTAD secretariat calculations, based on *United States Bureau of Labor Statistics* database.

Note: The years in brackets indicate when economic take-off began. The dates used to determine the beginning of economic take-off are the result of a breakpoint analysis of productivity growth series, measured by growth rates of GDP per worker.

the rapid expansion of China's exports, especially exports of labour-intensive goods and electronics to the United States, following China's accession to the World Trade Organization (WTO) in December 2001. This event symbolized China's formal entry into the global economic arena. It included, in particular, the granting of Permanent Normal Trade Relations status with the United States – its largest single trading partner. This normalization removed the uncertainties in bilateral trade relations between these two large economics, and played a key role in the rapid increase of FDI to China, which accelerated production-sharing across East Asia.[11] China's accession to the WTO also implied the eventual elimination of discriminatory, WTO-inconsistent measures against its exports within an agreed time frame. For example, China would be covered by the phasing out of the Agreement on Textiles and Clothing, which represented an end to the quota regulations that, through the MFA, had governed international trade in apparel since the mid-1960s.

Empirical evidence points to significant differences across countries in terms of the share of low-wage economies in total imports, the increase of imports from low-wage economies since 1995, and the share of imports originating from China in total imports from low-wage economies (chart 4.4). The share of low-wage economies in the total imports of Japan exceeds 30 per cent, closely followed by their respective shares in the United States and in the group of relatively advanced developing countries in Asia. In the United States, the European Union (EU) and Latin America, China accounts for the bulk of the increase, while the increase in the share of low-wage economies in imports in Africa and the group of Asian countries is more evenly distributed between China and other low-wage economies. Moreover, in all countries, electronic goods have accounted for a major share of the imports from China.[12]

> The increase in the distributional effects from trade, especially in developed countries, may have been triggered by deeper, non-trade factors such as international wage competition and changes in corporate behaviour.

Taken together, this evidence on the increase of imports from developing countries, combined with an increase in the wage differentials between the main importers and the main exporters of these goods, suggests that the pressure from globalization of trade on wages and income distribution is greater today than it was 20 years ago, especially in developed countries. However, these trade-related distributional effects may well be triggered by deeper, non-trade factors, such as international wage competition (see chapter VI), as well as changes in corporate behaviour, as discussed in the following section.

(b) Channels of trade-related distributional effects in developed countries

The change in the character of national income inequality and countries' exposure to global trade, discussed in the preceding section, has provoked a new trade-inequality debate. Similar to the earlier one, the recent debate concerns the distributional impact of skill-biased technological change and international trade. There are those who argue that skill-biased technological change has been the cause of changes in wages and employment of different categories of workers because, "information technology complements highly educated workers engaged in abstract tasks, substitutes for moderately educated workers performing routine tasks, and has less impact on low-skilled workers performing manual tasks" (Autor, Katz and Kearney, 2008: 301). The reason is that computers can replace routine tasks such as assembly-line or clerical work, while non-routine tasks are more difficult to digitize, and computers facilitate large-scale data analysis, which complements the tasks of skilled workers.

These technology-related changes are considered to be responsible for the evolution in the relative wage and employment positions of different worker categories over the past two decades, as discussed earlier (and shown in charts 4.1 and 4.2). However, these developments can also be explained by trade-related arguments that emphasize the rapid increase of trade in intermediate products, such as parts and components – a key feature in electronics industries – and the offshoring of service activities. Trade in intermediate products and offshoring have often figured prominently in the trade-inequality debate in developed countries.

In addition to the decline in policy-related barriers to trade, there has been a decline in transportation costs and, especially, in communication costs related to information and communication technologies (ICTs). Less costly and more sophisticated ICTs have enabled firms to profitably manage multifaceted procedures and undertake different stages of production in different geographical locations. As a result, some of the production of intermediate goods has moved from developed to developing countries, thereby spurring international trade in those goods. Trade of this type not only has an impact on the relative wages of skilled and unskilled workers, but also affects labour demand in the industries that undertake offshoring. As a result, the impact of trade in parts and components on wages and employment can vastly exceed that of trade in final goods. Moreover, in developed countries, trade in intermediate goods has much the same impact on labour demand and the skill premium as skill-biased technological change: both of them shift demand away from low-skilled activities and increase the relative demand for and the wages of those with higher skills.

Chart 4.4

MERCHANDISE IMPORTS OF SELECTED COUNTRIES AND COUNTRY GROUPS FROM LOW-WAGE ECONOMIES, BY PRODUCT CATEGORY, 1995–2010

(Percentage share in total merchandise imports)

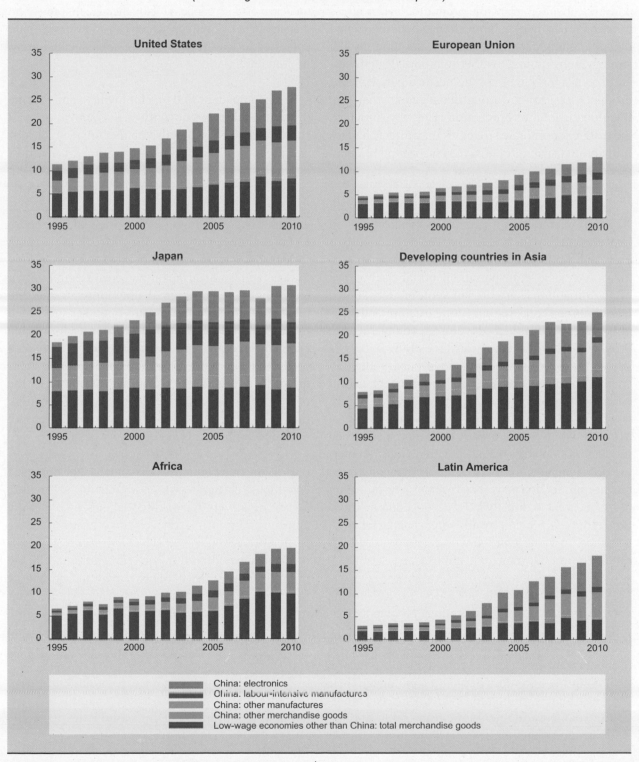

Legend:
- China: electronics
- China: labour-intensive manufactures
- China: other manufactures
- China: other merchandise goods
- Low-wage economies other than China: total merchandise goods

Source: UNCTAD secretariat calculations, based on *UNCTADstat*.

Note: Low-wage countries are defined as countries whose per capita income was lower than 5 per cent of United States per capita income before 2007 (i.e. prior to the onset of the current economic crisis). For the composition of country groups, see the text at the end of the Notes to this chapter. The category "labour-intensive manufactures" includes leather, textiles, clothing and footwear.

This explains why fragmentation and trade in intermediate goods spurs labour productivity, and is therefore akin to technological progress in final goods production. However, the two sources of productivity growth result from substantially different corporate behaviour: while technological progress relies on investment in innovation and the associated dynamic gains in an enterprise's long-term growth strategy, substituting lower-cost imported intermediate products for higher-cost domestic inputs achieves productivity growth through cost reductions from the globalization of production. The ways in which the different corporate strategies may affect changes in income distribution are addressed in more detail below.

The geographical dispersion of the different stages of manufacturing and the associated trade in intermediate products is costly. The manufacture of parts and final goods in different countries entails not only costs of transportation and tariffs, but also of coordination. Therefore, an appropriately skilled labour force, good trading infrastructure and geographical proximity to developed countries have proved to be advantages for developing countries whose firms participate in international production chains. This participation takes the form of inter-firm agreements, networks and alliances of various kinds. But most often it involves hosting affiliates of TNCs, as coordination costs are likely to be minimized when production chains are managed within the same enterprise. Independent of the specific form employed to manage production networks, the internationalization of production has directly influenced income distribution at the top echelon by allowing specific talent to be used everywhere in the world against very high remuneration (Gordon and Dew-Becker, 2007).

The important role played by TNCs in this context relates to their integrating the output from production stages outsourced to a specific country seamlessly into the continuously evolving total production process. TNCs typically achieve this by deploying specific slices of their technology in their foreign affiliates, combining their advanced technology developed at home with cheap labour abroad. This arrangement implies that "the multinational 'lends' a narrow range of technology to a producer located in the developing nation with the aim of getting the offshoring part produced at the lowest possible cost for the requisite quality" (Baldwin, 2011: 21). Such a strategy of "technology lending"

implies that TNCs aim at minimizing the transfer of technology and know-how to the host country. This is very different from the paradigm that has usually governed policies designed to attract as much FDI as possible. It views FDI as a bundle of assets, including, most importantly, access to advanced technology and management techniques, which can allow developing countries to leapfrog into more sophisticated areas of production.[13]

The impact of FDI on employment and income distribution depends not only on the motivations and strategies of TNCs, but also on the initial conditions and policies of the host country. Some of the most rapidly growing developing countries have, in recent years, successfully linked their development efforts to these international production networks. China, for example, began to attract large-scale FDI in the context of regional networks in the early 1990s. Hosting foreign enterprises was part of the country's strategy to accelerate industrialization, create employment and support technological upgrading. A specific regulatory structure and proactive policies succeeded in attracting FDI in the manufacturing sector, which added to existing productive capacity, increased productivity and supported the technological upgrading of local productive capacities, even though the country's exports continued to have a relatively high import content, particularly of technology-intensive parts and components (*TDR 2006*: 186–189).

Many other countries have not had the domestic conditions, particularly a good trade infrastructure, a large, relatively well-skilled labour force and the appropriate administrative capacity, to exercise sufficient leverage over TNCs to secure technology transfer and allow wage earners to participate in productivity growth. This is why the growth of manufactured exports that has accompanied their participation in these networks has not always been matched by comparable increases in value added and employment.

Available evidence for the period 1995–2010 suggests that outward FDI has generally led to a decline of employment in manufacturing in the largest developed countries (chart 4.5A).[14] Whereas FDI inflows have been accompanied by a decline of employment in manufacturing in a number of countries in Eastern Europe, evidence for developing countries indicates that such inflows have most often been associated with expanding employment

FOREIGN DIRECT INVESTMENT, EMPLOYMENT IN MANUFACTURING AND INCOME INEQUALITY, SELECTED COUNTRIES, 1995–2010

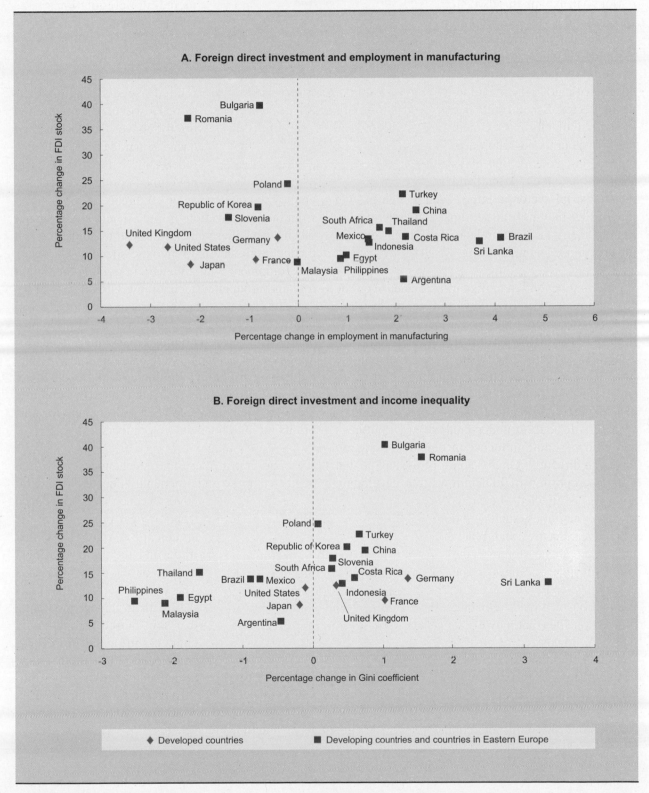

Source: UNCTAD secretariat calculations, based on *Lane and Milesi-Ferretti External Wealth of Nations* database; *Standardized World Income Inequality Database* (*SWIID*); ILO, *Laborsta* and *KILM* databases; OECD, Eurostat, UNIDO and ECLAC databases.
Note: FDI data refer to outflows for developed countries and to inflows for developing countries and countries in Eastern Europe. Data for China refer to 2000–2010.

in manufacturing.[15] However, this evidence also shows that the same volume of FDI inflows can have very different effects on the magnitude of changes in employment in manufacturing. Several reasons can explain this diversity. First, not all the inward FDI is in fixed capital formation that expands productive capacity and employment, and neither does all of it go to the manufacturing sector. Second, the size of the manufacturing sector in the host country in relation to the existing stock of FDI plays a role: if that stock is small and the industrial sector is large, even a high growth rate of FDI may have little impact on employment. Finally, many factors unrelated to FDI may explain job creation in manufacturing.

Going beyond manufacturing, evidence on the correlation between FDI flows and income distribution is mixed (chart 4.5B). For the period 1995–2010, higher FDI outflows from developed countries generally coincided with an increase in income inequality in these countries. But many host countries, especially those that had large FDI inflows, also experienced an increase in income inequality.[16] It is difficult to understand why FDI outflows and inflows should influence income distribution in the same direction. One reason for this may be that a large proportion of FDI inflows into developing countries is directed to capital-intensive activities, such as the extractive industries, and creates little employment. Moreover, the employment effects may even be negative when FDI involves the acquisition of already existing production sites that may eventually be downsized or closed. Another important reason may be a similar policy response with regard to labour market regulation and wage setting: home countries may attempt to slow the trend towards relocation of production abroad by deregulating the labour market, while host countries may believe that more flexible labour markets will attract additional FDI.

Openness to FDI is just one element of economic policies, and changes in employment and income

> Both FDI outflows from developed countries and inflows to developing countries are associated with a widening income gap …

> … probably due to production sharing and related labour market deregulation and wage restraints in both groups of countries.

distribution can result from other, concomitant factors. For instance (as discussed in chapter III), rising inequality in transition economies was driven by comprehensive market-oriented economic reforms, including deregulation of the labour market.

All of the issues discussed so far concern narrow, trade-related aspects of globalization. However, as mentioned briefly above, the documented changes in trade flows may also reflect shifts in the strategies that developed-country enterprises employ to counter perceived threats of competition from the globalization of trade. There are two main mechanisms these enterprises use to adjust to such competition. One is to increase spending on plants and equipment with a view to upgrading the output mix and production technology. The other is to try to reduce labour costs. Whereas the first mechanism relies on investment in innovation to increase productivity, the second builds on asymmetric negotiating power to impose wage restraint, applying pay reductions or holding pay increases at levels lower than productivity growth, in addition to outsourcing. These are sometimes combined with attempts to boost profits through financial investments.[17]

The first of these two mechanisms was often neglected in the trade-inequality debate of the early 1990s. It concerns trade-induced technological progress, i.e. the argument by Wood (1994) that trade and technology effects cannot be easily separated.[18] Thoenig and Verdier (2003) formalize this argument, predicting that skill-biased technological change should be more pronounced in industries that have been liberalized more. They provide evidence for this from case studies that focused on the automobile and clothing industries in Europe, Japan and the United States.[19]

However, these empirical findings may be sensitive to the specific time period under consideration. Evidence for the United States suggests that the source of productivity growth in this country changed from the 1990s to the 2000s. During the 1990s, output expansion was achieved through innovations, which were largely related to the microelectronics revolution, and spurred productivity and the upgrading of product quality. In the 2000s, the focus turned to efficiency gains by reducing input costs for given levels of output.

Sector-specific evidence for the United States for the period 1990–2000 indicates that all of the four sectors with the largest growth in productivity (computers and electronic products, wholesale trade, retail trade and manufacturing, excluding computers and electronic products) experienced positive average employment growth, adding a total of nearly 2 million new jobs (chart 4.6A). By contrast, the sectors with the largest productivity gains during the 2000s experienced a substantial decline in employment (chart 4.6B). Computers and electronic products, information, and manufacturing (excluding computers and electronic products), accounted for a sizeable share of overall productivity growth, but employment fell, with a loss of more than 6.6 million jobs, about 60 per cent of which occurred before the onset of the Great Recession of 2008.[20] Moreover, most of the sectors with the largest employment growth were among those with the lowest productivity growth, notably services (chart 4.6B).

> The source of productivity growth in the United States changed between the 1990s and the 2000s, from investment in innovation to reducing input costs, including through offshoring.

These developments in productivity and employment may well be associated with the ascendancy of "shareholder value maximization" as a mode of corporate governance.[21] This concept implies evaluating the performance of a company in terms of its financial value per share, rather than by the goods and services it produces, the number of people it employs or its long-term earnings potential as reflected by the company's investment in innovation. This has a direct impact on income distribution, as the compensation of top executives often takes the form of stock options whose market price can rise if the company's share value goes up. More importantly, striving for short-term increases in the market price of a company's stock is inimical to investment in innovation because innovation typically is an uncertain activity that in the short term involves sunk costs, and its long-term return depends on many factors, including some that

are beyond the control of a company's executives. By contrast, shareholder value can be influenced directly by a company repurchasing its own shares and granting higher dividends on its shares. This implies that a larger proportion of company profits that could have been reinvested for innovation tends to be distributed through dividend payments or injected in the stock market to buy back shares. The resulting drain on labour demand and, more generally, the threat to move production abroad may well have been used by companies to erode the bargaining power of unions and workers.[22]

Empirical evidence shows that stock repurchases by the 419 companies in the Standard and Poor's S&P 500 index that were publicly listed between 1997 and 2010 oscillated around a fairly stable level of $300–$350 million throughout the period 1997–2003. Over the subsequent four years, the value of such purchases almost quadrupled. Some of this increase was due to an increase in the value of the underlying stocks. However, the S&P 500 index itself rose by only about 80 per cent over this four-year period, so that the bulk of the fourfold increase in stock repurchases reflects a genuine increase in such repurchases. Perhaps most importantly, the ratio of these companies' stock repurchases to their net income was fairly stable, at a level of about 0.45 between 1997 and 2000, before increasing sharply to 0.6 following the bursting of the dot-com stock market bubble in 2001, and then collapsing to about 0.3 in 2003. Over the period 2003–2008, this ratio continuously increased to reach about 0.8 in 2007, and spiked to more than 1.0 in 2008 before declining to about 0.35 in 2009–2010. Dividend payments evolved in a similar way: they almost doubled, from about $320 million in 2003 to almost $600 million in 2008, before slightly declining in 2009–2010 (Lazonick, 2012).[23]

Offshoring of manufacturing activities has been a major development in global economic relations over the past two decades. However, the tide seems to be turning, at least for the United States. With growing domestic demand in rapidly industrializing developing countries, less of the production capacity in these countries, including in affiliates owned

Chart 4.6

GROWTH IN EMPLOYMENT, VALUE ADDED AND PRODUCTIVITY, BY SECTOR IN THE UNITED STATES

(Per cent)

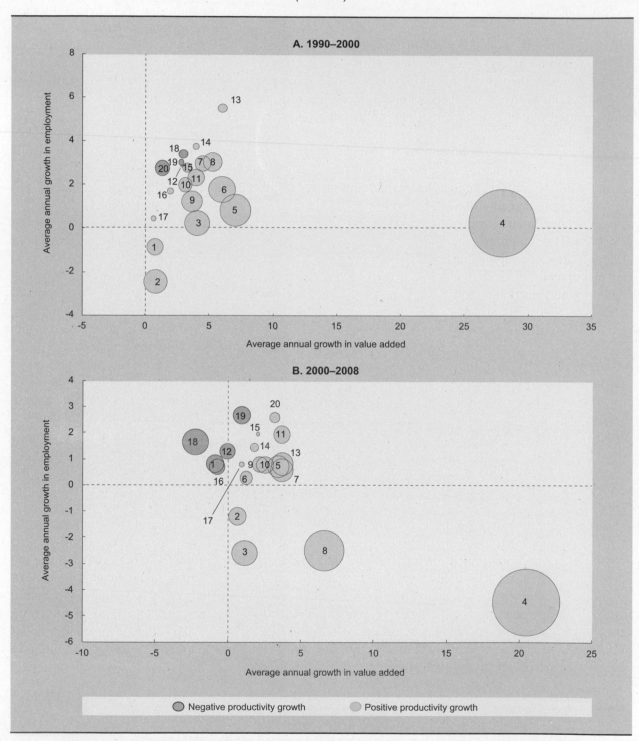

Source: UNCTAD secretariat calculations, based on data from United States Bureau of Economic Analysis.
  Note: The size of each bubble reflects productivity growth in the respective sector. 1: Agriculture and mining; 2: Utilities; 3: Manu-
         facturing (excl. computer and electronic products); 4: Computer and electronic products; 5: Wholesale trade; 6: Retail trade;
         7: Transportation and warehousing; 8: Information; 9: Finance and insurance; 10: Real estate, and rental and leasing; 11: Pro-
         fessional, scientific and technical services; 12: Management of companies and enterprises; 13: Administrative and waste
         management services; 14: Arts, entertainment, and recreation; 15: Accommodation and food services; 16: Other services,
         except government; 17: Government; 18: Construction; 19: Educational services; 20: Health care and social assistance.

by TNCs, will be utilized for exports. Moreover, in China, the recent rapid wage growth, discussed above, and sizeable currency appreciation have considerably reduced its low-cost labour advantage. And it is unlikely that offshoring to China will be replaced by offshoring to other developing countries in Asia. This is because, since these countries have mainly produced intermediate products for final processing and sale in China, they may find that continuing with this option is easier than retooling their production processes to manufacture finished goods for export to the United States. Finally, the strong increase in oil prices has sharply driven up logistic and transportation costs, and a reassessment of supply chain risks and management costs may lead corporations to reconsider manufacturing goods in the United States. On the other hand, returning production ("reshoring") to the United States, or to other developed countries for that matter, could prove difficult because local suppliers no longer exist and the local labour force may no longer possess the requisite skills.

Nevertheless, any reshoring of production will undoubtedly have positive employment effects in developed countries.[24] The implication for income distribution is less clear. According to media reports, reshored production appears to be located predominantly in jurisdictions with a low degree of unionization, where it is easily possible to rapidly adapt working hours and move to a two-tier wage regime, with new employees being paid barely half the wage of workers that had been employed before reshoring started.[25]

(c) Distributional effects in developing and transition economies

The increase in developing countries' exposure to globalized trade has changed the character of the trade-inequality relationship in two ways. First, rising concerns that some developing countries, mainly in Africa and Latin America, which possessed some industrial production capacity relatively early may also have been adversely affected by imports of manufactured goods, including from low-wage economies (as shown in chart 4.4). Second, countries,

especially China, that started rapid industrialization more recently and have become the main source of South-South trade in manufactures, have also experienced more unequal income distribution. An additional change in the nature of the trade-inequality relationship relates to the greater tendency to complement trade with financial integration. Financial integration may have a substantial effect on the exchange rate, which in turn can have an impact on a country's trade performance. This aspect has been ignored by both the old and the new trade-inequality debates (see also section C).

Concerns about trade-related inequality in developing and transition economies often focus on distributional effects stemming from changing production structures. Such effects are likely to be larger in developing than in developed countries because productivity gaps between different economic sectors, as well as among enterprises within the same sector, tend to be much larger in developing countries.

> The recent evolution of productivity and employment in developed countries may be associated with the ascendancy of "shareholder value maximization" as a mode of corporate governance.

In addition to the impact of trade on changes in the total number of jobs, trade-related effects on inequality also depend on whether labour moves towards more productive or less productive activities, or even away from formal employment towards informality or unemployment. Assessments of the consequences of trade liberalization have shown that in developing countries in Asia taken as a group, and most notably in China, labour has moved from low-productivity jobs, often rural, towards higher productivity jobs, especially in manufacturing, while in Latin America and sub-Saharan Africa labour has moved in the opposite direction (i.e. from high-productivity jobs in manufacturing towards lower productivity jobs), such as in informal services and the production of primary commodities (Sainz and Calcagno, 1992; McMillan and Rodrik, 2011). Distinct from the earlier trade-inequality debate, these considerations refer to the economy as a whole, and not just to the manufacturing sector. Taking this broader perspective enables the capturing of structural transformations that give rise to both intersectoral factor movements and sector-specific productivity shifts. Other factors that need to be taken into account are external shocks and macroeconomic and exchange-rate policies.

Looking at the trade inequality relationship from this broader perspective suggests that the pressures on income distribution arising from trade globalization can vary considerably across countries, depending on macroeconomic shocks and on different effects from trade integration on the process of structural change. One explanation given for the varying distributional effects of trade globalization is that each country has different endowments and has attained a different degree of industrialization when it becomes exposed to the forces of globalization. According to this reasoning, in countries with poor natural resource endowments, many of which are in South and East Asia, integration into the global economy will initially result in greater inequality, because it tends to increase the incentives for expanding manufacturing and other modern sector activities. When such economies are at an early stage of industrialization, such as China two decades ago, their income inequality tends to widen. On the other hand, when such economies already have a well-skilled labour force and reach a relatively advanced stage of industrialization, such as the Republic of Korea in the 1990s, their income distribution tends to narrow, as incentives from trade globalization, often helped by supportive policies, allow labour to move towards more productive and more technology-intensive activities.

The same reasoning, emphasizing structural factors, leads to the perception that countries that have rich natural resource endowments and have achieved a certain degree of initial industrialization will find it very difficult to sustain a dynamic process of structural change after opening up to global competition. The reason is that these countries – unlike developed countries – have not yet acquired the capabilities for technological innovation that would allow them to benefit from globalization-related incentives to progress to capital- and technology-intensive activities. Moreover, unlike low-income countries at the initial stage of industrialization, they do not, or no longer, possess abundant cheap labour to benefit from offshoring of labour-intensive activities by developed-country firms. Rather, their opening up to global trade will tend to cause a decline in their manufacturing employment and output (i.e. a

process of deindustrialization). Indeed, in many countries in sub-Saharan Africa, Latin America and Central and West Asia, as well as some countries in South-East Asia, greater integration into globalized trade may well have reduced incentives to expand manufacturing activities and reinforced traditional specialization patterns in primary commodities and natural-resource-intensive manufactures.

However, independently of factor and technological endowments and the level of industrialization already reached, macroeconomic shocks stemming from the international monetary system and, in particular, from currency overvaluation can seriously compromise or even halt the process of structural change derived from a country's integration into the global economy. The way in which a country manages its integration into the global economy, not only through its trade and FDI policies, but also through its financial and exchange-rate policies, eventually determines globalization-related effects.[26] The inability of a number of countries to sustain a dynamic process of structural change has sometimes been called a "middle-income trap". This is when certain countries find it difficult to increase the share of domestic value added in their manufactured exports and sustain the movement of labour towards more productive and technologically more demanding manufacturing activities (UNCTAD, 2011: 40). Reversing the process of structural change is likely to have adverse distributional effects, because the labour displaced from the manufacturing sector will tend to move into low-productivity activities, and often to informal services or unemployment.

Looking first at countries that faced the forces of trade globalization at an initial stage of industrialization, China clearly shows how structural change affected the pattern of income distribution in the country. Rising income inequality in China over the past two decades has been characterized by a strong increase in spatial inequality (with high incomes concentrated in some locations and low incomes in others). Rapid income growth has been concentrated in coastal areas which benefited from deep trade integration as a result of policies promoting openness pursued since the mid-1980s. These have included

> Concerns about trade-related inequality in developing and transition economies often focus on distributional effects stemming from changing production structures.

the provision of good infrastructure and rapid logistical access to world markets. However, it has led to growing inequality relative to the internal provinces, although even the latter have seen rapid income growth compared with their earlier levels.[27] Furthermore, sustained investment in the biggest cities, where administrative, financial and export-oriented manufacturing activities are concentrated, has also contributed to increasing urban-rural inequalities (Asian Development Bank, 2012; Galbraith, 2012).[28] According to one estimate, the rural-urban gap, combined with inequality between urban areas, accounts for over two thirds of national income inequality in China (Zhu and Wan, 2012: 98).[29]

Sectoral employment shifts combined with inter-industry wage differentials are an important channel through which structural transformation affects income distribution. These effects are magnified when structural change occurs in economies that undergo significant ownership changes, such as land ownership reform and the dismantling of State-owned enterprises (SOEs). In China, for example, the acceleration of land ownership and labour-market reforms in the late 1990s was followed by a decline of employment in manufacturing in most provinces. However, this decline was overcompensated by sharply rising employment in manufacturing in those coastal provinces that spearheaded China's involvement in global trade and attracted significant FDI, particularly after the country's accession to the WTO in 2001. A favourable exchange rate was a key factor in this process. The wages paid in the labour-intensive activities, which constitute the bulk of manufacturing activities in these coastal provinces, are, by necessity, higher than in the internal provinces in order to attract migrant workers, and especially the better-skilled amongst them. The reason why such export-oriented sectors can afford to pay higher wages may well be that most of those activities are undertaken by TNC affiliates that are more profitable because they combine state-of-the-art technologies with very low

absolute wages. These specific distributional impacts of trade and FDI may also explain why intersectoral wage patterns in China have become increasingly similar to those of developed countries (Kwon, Chang and Fleisher, 2011).[30]

The growing wage differentials within the private sector are likely to be a major factor contributing to the increase in overall wage inequality in China, in addition to the declining importance of SOEs. However, the geographical concentration of the largely State-controlled banking and finance sector in China and the high remuneration in that sector have also contributed significantly to the increase in income inequality (Chen, Lu and Wan, 2010; Galbraith, 2012).[31]

China's opening up to global trade was supported by a monetary regime of fixing the exchange rate at a competitive level. This allowed a sustained dynamic process of structural change to unfold and employment in high-productivity activities to expand. In much of Latin America and sub-Saharan Africa, however, trade liberalization seems to have resulted in labour moving towards lower-productivity activities, including informality and unemployment (McMillan and Rodrik, 2011). This gives rise to the question whether competition from manufactured imports from low-wage economies is responsible for this pattern, in particular in Latin America which has a much higher level of industrialization than sub-Saharan Africa.

One recent study on how China's opening up to global trade may have affected changes in other developing countries' composition of output and exports points to three broad conclusions (Wood and Mayer, 2011). First, China's impact has been greatest on other East Asian economies that are open to trade and produce goods similar to those made in China. Second, the "China effect" on other developing countries has depended on other, region-specific factors. For example, the rise in manufactured imports in Latin America during the 1980s

> The way in which a country manages its integration into the global economy, through its trade and FDI policies as well as its financial and exchange-rate policies, eventually determines globalization-related effects.

> The common view that China's emergence is a threat to economic progress and equity in the rest of the developing world is exaggerated.

was the result of the region's own trade liberalization at a time when China exported very little to that region. Subsequent adverse effects of China's export expansion are likely to have been compensated in part by regional integration schemes and industrial policies designed to improve the competitiveness of Latin America's manufactured exports. Third, overall, it seems that the "common view of China's emergence as a threat to economic progress and equity in the rest of the developing world is exaggerated" (Wood and Mayer, 2011: 346).[32]

> An improvement in the terms of trade and related incentives for labour to shift from manufacturing to primary activities are not necessarily detrimental to income distribution …

It should also be emphasized that much of the effect of trade liberalization on structural transformation in Latin America is due to premature, or badly managed, integration into the international financial system. In many cases, this is associated with currency appreciations as a result of surging capital inflows that did not translate into higher domestic fixed investment. The weakening or phasing out of supportive industrial policies and a general retreat of the State from the economy has also played an important role (*TDR 2003*, Part Two, chap. VI). China's favourable monetary regime, on the one hand, and frequent currency overvaluation in Latin America, on the other, has had a major influence on the composition of output and exports in other developing countries.

Another question that arises from structural change in Latin America and sub-Saharan Africa is related to the distributional impact of terms-of-trade developments. This is very likely to depend on country- and time-specific circumstances. A change in a country's terms of trade (i.e. prices of its exports compared with those of its imports), is a crucial country-specific factor that affects the distributional impact of the globalization of trade. In this regard, it is important to look at both the rapid expansion of manufactured exports from low-wage economies, especially from China-centred production networks in East Asia, and the strong growth in the latters'

> … much depends on the pace of capital accumulation and the building of domestic productive capacities, supported by government policies, including the prevention of external macroeconomic and financial shocks.

demand for primary commodities. The reason is that the enormous magnitude, breadth and duration of the upswing in commodity prices since the early 2000s has boosted the export earnings and improved the terms of trade of resource-rich countries, many of which are in Latin America and sub-Saharan Africa.

It may be argued that terms-of-trade effects favouring natural resource sectors cause adverse distributional outcomes. One reason is that ownership of natural resources is typically less equally distributed than other assets. Another reason is that, unlike manufacturing industries and services, natural-resource-related activities do not generate much employment (*TDR 2010*, chap. IV). This may contribute to widening the disparities in income distribution when the terms-of-trade effect makes manufacturing less competitive, so that workers may be pushed from manufacturing into lower wage jobs or even into informality and unemployment. An increase in inequality can be avoided if good-quality jobs are created elsewhere in the economy. This depends on the linkages that can be established between the export-oriented activities in the primary sector, on the one hand, and modern services (public and private) and manufacturing on the other. Such linkages rarely emerge from market forces alone; they normally require supportive macroeconomic and wage policies as well as targeted fiscal and industrial policies aimed at ensuring that most of the income generated by natural-resource-related activities is used within the country. In particular, to the extent that an improvement in the terms of trade leads to increases in a government's fiscal revenues, this would enable greater public spending to create jobs directly in the public and services sectors, and indirectly in jobs related to infrastructure development, as well as in manufacturing if macroeconomic conditions are favourable.[33]

Most Latin American countries have succeeded in combining an improvement in their terms of trade since 2000 with an improvement in income

Chart 4.7

TERMS OF TRADE AND INCOME INEQUALITY, SELECTED COUNTRIES, 2000–2010

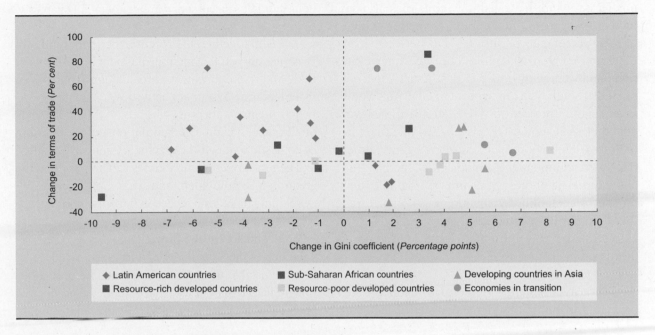

Source: UNCTAD secretariat calculations, based on *SWIID, UNCTADstat*; and IMF, *World Economic Outlook* database.

Note: For some countries the end of the period is the last year for which data were available. Period for Azerbaijan starts in 2001. *Latin America:* Argentina, the Bolivarian Republic of Venezuela, Bolivia, Brazil, Chile, Colombia, Costa Rica, Ecuador, Honduras, Mexico, Paraguay, Peru, Uruguay. *Sub-Saharan Africa:* Ghana, Mauritius, South Africa. *Asia:* China, India, Indonesia, the Philippines, the Republic of Korea, Thailand, Turkey. *Resource-rich developed countries:* Australia, Canada, New Zealand, Norway, the United States. *Resource-poor developed countries:* Austria, Belgium, Denmark, France, Germany, Italy, Japan, the United Kingdom. *Economies in transition:* Azerbaijan, Kazakhstan, Kyrgyzstan, the Russian Federation, Uzbekistan.

distribution. However, this has generally not been the case in most other resource-rich economies (chart 4.7). Drawing conclusions from such a comparison is difficult because of incomplete data coverage, especially for sub-Saharan Africa and West Asia. Nonetheless, available evidence indicates that all the Latin American countries shown in the chart which experienced an improvement in their terms of trade also saw a reduction in income inequality, and in countries where the terms of trade deteriorated (Costa Rica, Honduras and Uruguay), there was an increase in income inequality. By contrast, the income gap widened in the only two sub-Saharan African countries in the chart in which the terms of trade improved (Ghana and South Africa), while it narrowed in Mauritius where the terms of trade deteriorated slightly. Income inequality also increased in all the economies in transition in the chart, even though their terms of trade improved, while there is mixed evidence for developing countries in Asia and for developed countries.

An improvement in the terms of trade resulting from increases in the prices of commodity exports usually has positive fiscal effects, because direct and indirect revenues from commodity export earnings often constitute an important source of fiscal revenues. The groups of countries that benefited most from improved terms of trade over the last decade (Africa, Latin America, West Asia and the transition economies) were also those that had faced slow growth and low investment rates over the 1980s and 1990s. The rise in commodity prices helped these countries to increase their fiscal revenues significantly (see chapter V, section C) and enabled them to increase their current and capital public expenditures, even while reducing their fiscal deficits; in some cases, they even generated a fiscal surplus.

The increase in public investment, which is often necessary for private investment to follow or to rise in parallel, contributed to a rise in the total fixed investment rate in Latin America by an average of 6 percentage points of GDP between 2003 and 2011 (i.e. from 16.8 per cent of GDP to 22.9 per cent) (ECLAC, 2011). Africa, West Asia (excluding Turkey) and the transition economies also saw increases in gross fixed capital formation (GFCF) of 4–6 percentage points of GDP between 1999-2000 and 2009-2010. While these investment rates remained well below those in East Asia (42 per cent of GDP), South Asia (28 per cent of GDP) and South-East Asia (27 per cent of GDP) in 2010, they were nonetheless the highest levels reached since the early or mid-1980s. Moreover, these rising investment rates were complemented by macroeconomic, trade and industrial policies which improved employment prospects, including by encouraging regional trade that tends to have a higher share of manufactures, as well as by new minimum-wage legislation, as discussed in chapter VI.[34]

Improved fiscal revenue also enabled better provision of public goods, and widened the scope for public redistributive policies, including the introduction of cash transfer programmes, which in some countries, such as Brazil, cover millions of households, as discussed in greater detail in chapter V.

Taken together, the recent experiences in Latin America suggest that an improvement in the terms of trade and related incentives for labour to shift from manufacturing to primary activities are not necessarily detrimental to income distribution. Much depends on the pace of capital accumulation and the building of domestic productive capacities. Public expenditure and general government policies can help support the creation of employment and wage opportunities by developing linkages between export-oriented primary sectors and the rest of the economy. However, unless external shocks can be prevented, such as a real revaluation of the Brazilian *real* during the past decade, it is impossible to implement reasonable redistribution policies and policies that promote the productive potential of the economy, especially in manufacturing.

C. Financial integration of developing and transition economies

The previous section has argued that Kuznets' basic insight that the structural composition of an economy is a major determinant of income distribution most likely remains valid. However, the increasing complexity of economies, owing partly to globalization processes, has made it difficult to find inverted U-curves in inequality data for countries for the period since 1980. This difficulty may be partly due to methodological issues,[35] but certainly also to the greater importance of non-labour incomes (whereas Kuznets referred only to pay inequality) and of post-industrial economic sectors, such as services and, especially, finance. This is because rapid and sizeable changes in asset prices and the associated substantial capital gains, or losses, may sometimes have greater effects on income distribution than the slower moving processes of economic structural change (i.e. changes in the relative shares in employment and GDP of individual sectors emphasized by Kuznets).

However, the greater financial integration of developing and transition economies over the past three decades has probably had an even more significant impact on the macroeconomic variables that shape structural change and the attendant distributional effects. Against this background, this section briefly outlines the benefits these economies sought through financial integration. It then concentrates on the macroeconomic effects of volatile international capital flows, outlining the attendant adverse distributional outcomes in terms of the creation of employment and wage opportunities in high-productivity activities, especially in the traded goods sector.

International financial integration has been a particularly important feature of emerging market economies in recent years. Financial integration[36] can bring significant income and distributional benefits, such as through FDI inflows which can create employment and wage opportunities and help broaden technology transfer, as discussed in the previous section. Financial integration confers additional benefits when it helps to finance imports of capital goods for the creation of new productive capacities. Theoretically, it may also reduce the pressure for macroeconomic adjustment to temporary shocks by bolstering a country's capacity to pursue countercyclical policies through the provision of access to external financing, thereby smoothing or avoiding recessions and job losses. This will be the case, in particular, when shocks have domestic origins and a country's economic cycles have little correlation with global economic developments.

However, the adverse macroeconomic and distributional effects that have often been seen to accompany financial integration, especially in developing and transition economies, tend to outweigh these potential benefits. There are four main adverse effects of increased cross-border private capital flows resulting from international financial integration: (i) due to their volatility and pro-cyclicality they create or exacerbate macroeconomic instability; (ii) they often respond perversely to changes in macroeconomic fundamentals; (iii) they tend to destabilize domestic financial systems; and (iv) they tend to generate asset price bubbles.[37] As a result of these effects, the gains from such cross-border capital movements are primarily, if not entirely, appropriated by the owners of financial assets, whereas the losses are mostly borne by those who earn wages or profits from productive activities in the real sector of the economy.

Regarding the first of these channels, it is notable that financial flows to developing and transition economies generally occur in waves (i.e. simultaneously across these countries), and are driven by push factors emanating from macroeconomic conditions in the major developed countries. Such push factors include growing interest rate differentials between the latter economies and emerging economies, as

well as greater global "risk appetite" (Ghosh et al., 2012).[38] Empirical evidence indicates that private capital flows to emerging market economies are significantly more volatile than those to developed countries (Broner and Rigobon, 2006), and that a surge of inflows is a good predictor of their sudden stop and reversal (Agosin and Huaita, 2012). Moreover, since they tend to behave in a procyclical manner, they do not smooth the impact of external shocks on the current account; on the contrary, they tend to reinforce those shocks or may act as an external shock themselves. As a result, financial integration is often characterized by boom-bust cycles of financial inflows. The benefits reaped during boom times are mostly limited, since surges of capital inflows generally do not lead to higher fixed investments, or to increased imports of capital goods and technology transfer that would strengthen the process of growth, structural change and sustained employment creation. On the contrary, they exert upward pressure on the exchange rate, which reduces the international competitiveness of domestic producers. And, rapid capital exit during the bust phases cause financial turmoil and economic contraction with attendant adverse effects on employment. Thus the net distributional effects of financial integration may well be negative.

Second, capital inflows often occur in the form of surges, which indicates that they tend to be subject to herd behaviour. This causes them to go beyond or even against what would be determined by macroeconomic fundamentals, such as the current-account balance or inflation differentials.[39] This implies that capital inflows, which are often very large compared with the size of receiving countries' financial sectors, may overwhelm those countries' regulatory and policy frameworks, such as prudential regulations or foreign-exchange market interventions. Financial inflows can therefore cause macroeconomic instability and sharp appreciations of the real exchange rate. As a result, the private sector becomes less willing to invest and investments in tradables sectors become less profitable. Again, this has adverse effects on the creation of employment and wage opportunities.

The evolution of private capital inflows is closely associated with real exchange rate movements

> Financial integration affects the macroeconomic variables that shape structural change and the attendant distributional outcomes.

Chart 4.8

**REAL NET PRIVATE CAPITAL INFLOWS AND REAL EFFECTIVE EXCHANGE RATE
IN EMERGING ECONOMIES, 1995–2010**

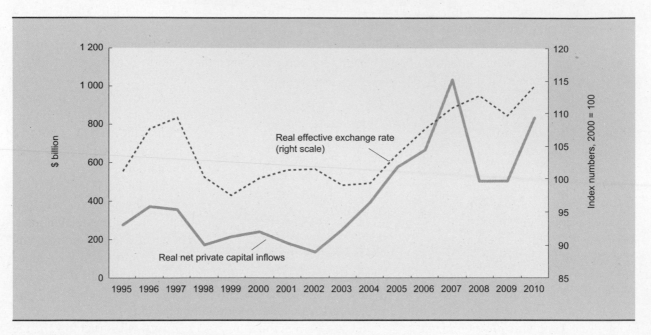

Source: UNCTAD secretariat calculations, based on Institute of International Finance (IIF), *Capital Flows to Emerging Market Economies*, September 2011.

Note: Nominal net private capital flows are deflated by the United States GDP deflator index (2008 = 100). IIF defines the following countries as "emerging economies": Argentina, the Bolivarian Republic of Venezuela, Brazil, Bulgaria, Chile, China, Colombia, the Czech Republic, Ecuador, Egypt, Hungary, India, Indonesia, Lebanon, Malaysia, Mexico, Morocco, Nigeria, Peru, the Philippines, Poland, the Republic of Korea, Romania, the Russian Federation, Saudi Arabia, South Africa, Thailand, Turkey, Ukraine and United Arab Emirates.

in receiving countries (chart 4.8). However, there are differences in the degree of this association across countries, as revealed by more disaggregated evidence for the period since the early 1990s. It also shows that many emerging market economies, especially in Latin America and Eastern Europe, received sizeable capital inflows but saw little increase in private investment. This has been the case even in countries with current-account deficits, such as Brazil, India, South Africa and Turkey, whose currencies should have depreciated in order to compensate for relatively high inflation and move towards a balanced current account (*TDRs 2008* and *2011*). By contrast, emerging economies in Asia, as well as Chile, which successfully used systematic intervention and capital controls to prevent real exchange rate appreciation for a sustained period of time, saw private investment grow rapidly and employment and wage opportunities in their manufacturing sectors expand (*TDR 2003*; see also Akyüz, 2011). This suggests that differences in government policies relating to financial integration and its management

could partly explain the differences in labour movements between high- and low-productivity sectors, and therefore how globalization affects structural change and income distribution, as discussed in the previous section.

Third, financial integration has often caused an excessive rise in bank credit to the private non-bank sector and a progressive currency and maturity mismatch in the balance sheets of firms, households and banks that borrow in foreign currency at lower interest rates than those charged for domestic credit. Once the financial inflows dry up or reverse, the host country's currency sharply depreciates and the currency mismatches in balance sheets tend to result in increased debt servicing difficulties and default (*TDR 2008*, chap. VI).

However, in the aftermath of the Asian crisis in 1997–1998, emerging economies began to accumulate sizeable foreign-exchange reserves as a form of self-insurance against sudden stops and reversals

Chart 4.9

COMPOSITION OF EXTERNAL ASSETS AND LIABILITIES IN EMERGING ECONOMIES, 1980–2010

(Per cent)

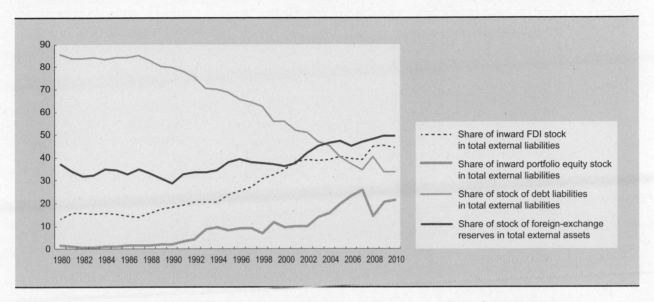

Source: UNCTAD secretariat calculations, based on *Lane and Milesi-Ferretti External Wealth of Nations* database.
Note: The numbers shown reflect GDP-weighted averages. The following emerging market economies are covered in the chart: Argentina, the Bolivarian Republic of Venezuela, Brazil, Bulgaria, Chile, China, Colombia, the Czech Republic, Ecuador, Egypt, Hong Kong Special Administrative Region of China, Hungary, India, Indonesia, Lebanon, Malaysia, Mexico, Morocco, Nigeria, Peru, the Philippines, Poland, the Republic of Korea, the Russian Federation, Taiwan Province of China, Saudi Arabia, South Africa, Thailand, Turkey, Ukraine and United Arab Emirates.

of capital inflows. The average share of foreign-exchange reserves in total foreign assets increased from about 36 per cent in 2000 to almost 50 per cent in 2010 (chart 4.9). Moreover, emerging market economies' external liabilities are no longer dominated by foreign-currency-denominated debt, having shifted towards FDI and portfolio equity instead. Indeed, the share of foreign-currency-denominated debt in total external liabilities declined from almost 90 per cent in 1980 to slightly over 30 per cent in 2010. This was made possible by a favourable external economic environment prior to the onset of the economic crisis, which allowed these economies to improve their debt position more generally. Hence they are increasingly able to issue debt denominated in local currency. One observer notes that this shift towards the issuance of local currency debt "has been facilitated by increasing demand from foreign investors for higher-yielding local currency assets" (Leijonhufvud, 2007: 1839).

This growing preference on the part of foreign financial investors for assets in local currency is reflected in the increase in portfolio equity flows to emerging market economies: the share of portfolio equity holdings in total foreign liabilities almost tripled between 2000 and 2007, when it reached about 26 per cent, although it declined sharply with the onset of the current crisis. This increase is also likely to have been supported by attempts in emerging market economies to strengthen their stock markets by opening them to foreign investors.

This increase in the relative importance of portfolio equity inflows could be indicative of the rising importance of financial activities relative to activities in the real economy (namely investment and consumption). Indeed, a fourth source of possible adverse macroeconomic and distributional effects accompanying financial integration is the potential of capital surges to produce asset price or real estate bubbles. Empirical evidence indicates that movements in the stock market indices of emerging markets, especially those in Eastern Europe but also in parts of Africa, Asia and Latin America, have now become closely correlated with portfolio equity inflows (chart 4.10). This close correlation presents a potential risk of capital flow reversals easily creating

Chart 4.10

STOCK OF PORTFOLIO EQUITY LIABILITIES AND EQUITY MARKET
INDICES, SELECTED EMERGING ECONOMIES, 1990–2010

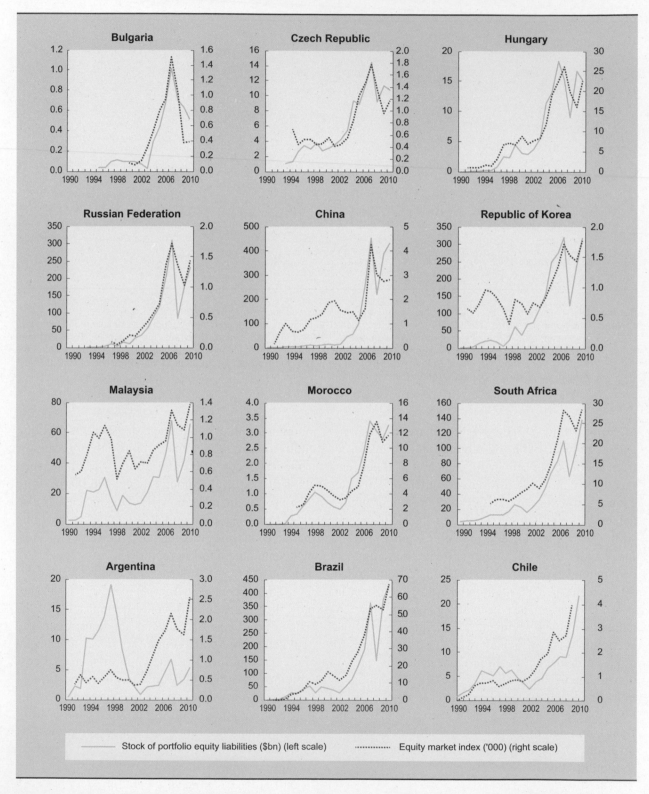

Source: UNCTAD secretariat calculations, based on *Lane and Milesi-Ferretti External Wealth of Nations* database; and Bloomberg.
  Note: The following equity market indices were used: Bulgaria: SOFIX; Czech Republic: PX; Hungary: BUX; Russian Federation:
       INDEXCF; China: SHCOMP; Republic of Korea: KOSPI; Malaysia: FBMKLCI; Morocco: MOSENEW; South Africa: JALSH;
       Argentina: MERVAL; Brazil: IBOV; and Chile: IPSA.

an asset price bust, or even a credit crunch, with severe macroeconomic consequences and attendant adverse distributional effects.

In 2008, following the onset of the global financial and economic crisis, a reversal of capital flows to emerging market economies, caused a downward pressure on their currencies and their equity markets dropped sharply (charts 4.8–4.10). Most countries were able to smoothen much of the related adverse macroeconomic and distributional effects through countercyclical policies made possible by significantly improved fiscal positions and price stability achieved during the previous boom years. But capital inflows have recovered remarkably quickly since 2009.

In the hope of spurring their development process, and encouraged by recommendations of the international financial institutions, many developing and emerging countries have attempted to integrate rapidly into the international financial system, a number of them prematurely. Like earlier episodes analysed in various *TDRs* over the past three decades[40] (see, in particular, *TDR 1998*, chap. III; *TDR 1999*, chap III and *TDR 2003*, chap. II), the boom-bust cycle over the past five years shows that countries that have undertaken deep financial integration are highly vulnerable to adverse impacts from a potential worsening of the global economic environment, such as a worsening of the euro-zone crisis, and instability of international financial markets. Particularly exposed are countries that have a current-account deficit (or a declining surplus) and finance their deficit through capital inflows that do not translate into the creation of new productive capacity, but instead stimulate the demand for existing assets, such as stocks and real estate.[41] This implies that the counterparts of current-account deficits are liquid portfolio flows or one-time foreign investment flows into real estate, both of which are exposed to investors losing their appetite for risk, and neither of which contributes to the resilience of the productive sector. The damage to growth and income distribution resulting from a drying up of such financial inflows could be more severe at the present juncture than in 2008. This is because the reversal of capital inflows may last much longer and there is considerably less room for countercyclical fiscal measures to avert renewed macroeconomic instability and recession, as discussed in chapter I.

D. Conclusions

The analysis in this chapter suggests that the extent to which globalization and technological change affect income distribution depends on how trade and financial integration are managed. Policies that influence the nature and speed of economic integration affect the process of structural change and the related creation of employment and wage opportunities in high productivity activities. From this perspective, it is possible to distinguish five broad categories of economies, described below.

- The first group comprises developed countries, notably the United States, which experienced polarization of their employment and wage structures, resulting in a decline in wages and employment of moderately skilled workers relative to the highest-skilled and the lowest-skilled workers. These countries also saw a strong increase in their manufactured imports from developing countries, especially from low-wage economies. Under the macroeconomic and labour market policies that were pursued, the rapid rise of such imports since the mid-1990s probably stems from offshoring, which is closely associated with FDI and international production sharing. However, these new features in the trade and inequality relationship also appear to be closely related to a change in strategy chosen by developed-country enterprises to adjust to competition resulting from increasing globalization. During the 1990s, these enterprises achieved productivity growth and output expansion through investment in innovation. By contrast, during the 2000s, they placed greater emphasis on becoming more competitive internationally through wage restraints and reduced employment opportunities, combined with attempts to boost profits through financial investments. This latter strategy was facilitated by the deregulation of financial markets and greater flexibility of the labour market, which strengthened the power of profit earners vis-à-vis wage earners.

- The second group consists of countries that are industrializing rapidly. These include several countries in Asia, especially China. The defining characteristic of this group is the creation of numerous employment and wage opportunities in high-productivity activities, mainly in manufacturing. These are the result of macroeconomic policies supportive of productive investment and exchange-rate management which has preserved the international competitiveness of domestic firms. As a result of these processes there has been rapid growth in average per capita incomes. But the structural transition of their economies from low-productivity to high-productivity activities has also led to rising income gaps and spatial inequalities. It is likely that these countries can maintain high average incomes while gradually closing their income gaps over time through the fuller absorption into high-productivity activities of the workers who now remain employed in disadvantaged areas and activities. A less benign distributional outcome will probably result if a shift from export-oriented production, emphasizing manufacturing, to production oriented more towards domestic markets leads increasingly to employment and wage opportunities in service activities, which tend to be less well remunerated than jobs in manufacturing. Such an outcome could slow down the increase in wages observed over the past few years and result in greater equality, though at lower levels of average income. However, this could be avoided by an incomes policy that links wage

adjustments in all sectors of the economy to average productivity growth, as discussed in chapter VI of this Report.

- The third group comprises countries that have reached a certain level of industrialization, but have been unable to sustain a dynamic process of industrial deepening. Instead, their economic integration has been accompanied by a process of deindustrialization. These include natural-resource-rich countries in Latin America, sub-Saharan Africa and parts of Asia. Their macroeconomic, trade and exchange-rate policies during their integration into the world economy have undoubtedly contributed – in particular during the 1980s and 1990s – to increasing income gaps in conjunction with generally declining average per capita incomes. However, the substantial increase in commodity prices and the associated strong improvements in these countries' terms of trade have facilitated their attempts to improve their macroeconomic policy stances and fiscal accounts. By creating good-quality jobs elsewhere in their economies, some of these countries, especially in Latin America, have successfully averted adverse distributional effects of deindustrialization. Especially important in this context have been supportive macroeconomic and wage policies, as well as targeted fiscal and industrial policies aimed at ensuring that most of the income generated in the commodities sector is used within the country.

However, some of these countries are likely to face substantial challenges in sustaining their moves towards more equal income distribution. The reason is that the benign distributional outcomes have, at least in part, depended on higher fiscal revenues resulting from soaring commodity prices. Not all countries can assume that such favourable developments in their export revenues will last much longer. While net food exporting countries are likely to continue to benefit from a favourable external environment, a prolonged global economic slowdown could well have less favourable outcomes for exporters of energy commodities and base metals, many of which are in Africa and Central and West Asia, and where recent distributional changes have already been less favourable than those in many Latin American countries.

• A fourth category consists of countries in South-East Asia and parts of Africa that have attained a certain level of industrialization through integration into international production networks. However, most of their activities have focused on simple labour-intensive activities, and they have been unable to ignite or sustain a dynamic process of industrial deepening. Over the past two decades, these countries have experienced rapid growth, while distributional outcomes have changed little (such as in Malaysia, the Philippines and Thailand) or worsened (Indonesia) for reasons similar to those for countries in the second category described above. Over the next few years, there is a risk that these countries' employment and wage opportunities will be adversely affected by a probable prolonged decline in global aggregate demand, and that the workers displaced from the manufacturing sector will move to low-productivity activities, or even to informal services or unemployment. Such distributional effects could be compounded by adverse impacts stemming from financial openness if a decline in earnings from manufactured exports leads to a deterioration of these countries' current accounts, and if the resulting deficits are then financed through increased international portfolio inflows. For these countries, it will be particularly important to strengthen domestic demand-growth-employment dynamics by adopting macroeconomic policies that promote domestic mass incomes. This could be achieved through well-designed incomes policies, while a higher level of fixed investment could be encouraged through measures that improve domestic financing conditions.

• A final category consists of countries (mostly in Central and Eastern Europe, as well as Central Asia) that have fully embraced liberal policy agendas and whose processes of structural change and related distributional effects have been strongly affected by financial integration, as well as by changes in the ownership structure of enterprises. The further evolution of distributional outcomes in these countries will depend largely on how they manage their financial integration, and whether their macroeconomic and labour market policies will be reoriented towards reversing the trend of increasing inequality.

The examination of the distributional impacts of technological change and globalization in this chapter has focused on the process of structural change and the related shifts in employment and wage opportunities. However, this emphasis on structural factors does not imply a deterministic view of income distribution. On the contrary, policies are the key determinant of distributional outcomes. Nevertheless, in order to design policies so that the desired distributional outcomes are achieved as far as possible, it is important to understand how the forces of globalization and technological developments affect income distribution and what kinds of policies can maximize the distributional benefits of globalization and technological change. ∎

Notes

1 Aghion, Caroli and Garcia-Penalosa (1999) observed that wage inequality rose sharply in the United Kingdom and the United States, but only moderately in countries like Australia, Austria, Belgium, Canada, Japan, New Zealand and Sweden, remained stable in Finland and France, and declined in Germany and Italy.

2 As an additional reason, some economists (e.g. Krugman, 1995) argued that the increase in magnitude of developed countries' imports of manufactures from developing countries was too small to make a qualitative difference. However, as suggested by Feenstra and Hanson (2003), given the structural change in developed countries during the twentieth century, the correct comparator is not the share of manufactured imports in GDP, but rather the share of value added in manufacturing. On that measure, between 1913 and 1990 "merchandise trade has indeed grown substantially relative to the production of these commodities in many advanced countries" (Feenstra and Hanson, 2003: 149).

3 This prediction is based on the so-called "factor price equalization theorem", which is one of the major theoretical results of Heckscher-Ohlin trade models. In its simplest form, it postulates that free and frictionless trade will cause factor prices in different countries to converge, provided they have identical linearly homogeneous technologies and their factor endowments are sufficiently similar to be in the same diversification cone.

4 See, for example, Berman, Bound and Griliches, 1994; Berman, Bound and Machin, 1998; and Aghion, Caroli and Garcia-Penalosa, 1999. Focusing on the United States, others have argued that the increase in the wage premium was caused by a decline in the rate of growth of supply of skilled labour after the 1970s (Card and Lemieux, 2001; Goldin and Katz, 2008; Rajan, 2010). Still others argue that the sharply rising supply of skilled workers from the baby-boom generation in the late 1960s made it more profitable to develop skill-biased technologies such as those produced by the information technology revolution of the 1980s and 1990s (Acemoglu, 1998).

5 Feenstra and Hanson (1999) also show that the relative contributions of the two measures are sensitive

to how the greater use of high-tech equipment is measured. Trade and technology explain income inequality equally well if high-tech equipment is measured as a share of the total capital equipment used in each industry, while trade is of only marginal importance if high-tech equipment is measured as a fraction of new investments in computers and other high-tech devices.

6 Van Reenen (2011) shows similar evidence for the United Kingdom.

7 Goos, Manning and Salomons (2011) rank occupations by their average wages in 1979 with a view to examining how the proportion of total employment in each type of occupation has changed over time. Similar evidence for developing countries is not available.

8 Data from UNCTADstat.

9 The labour contract law, enacted on 1 January 2008, requires employers to issue written contracts, which limit probationary periods to two years, give permanent status to workers who have been with the same firm for at least 10 years, restrict workers' dismissal and increase severance pay. The new legislation also includes a rise in minimum wages, allows trade unions to become genuine representatives of workers, and improves the dispute resolution system. Surveys of migrant workers in the Pearl River Delta before and after the law took effect suggest that the law has been effective in improving working conditions (Li, 2011).

10 According to Banister and Cook (2011), there are no official nationwide statistics on employment and labour compensation in Chinese manufacturing. Rather, data for formal urban enterprises from the Ministry of Human Resources and Social Security are combined with data for other manufacturing units (i.e. town and village enterprise (TVE)) from the Ministry of Agriculture. This evidence shows that although workers in manufacturing are earning more than ever before, the average hourly compensation was only $1.36 in 2008. Although it is difficult to make cross-country comparisons, this is far below those of many of China's East Asian neighbours in 2010, such as Japan ($32), the Republic of Korea ($16.6) and Taiwan Province of China ($8.36). The hourly compensation costs in China are roughly on par with those of other countries in the region,

such as the Philippines ($1.90), but lag significantly behind those of developing countries with higher per capita incomes such as Argentina ($12.7), Brazil ($10.1) and Mexico ($6.2) (United States Bureau of Labor Statistics, 2011). For qualitatively similar estimates, see Ceglowski and Golub, 2011.

11 Despite large inflows of FDI, the share of FDI in China's gross capital formation has actually declined.

12 While, *a priori*, electronics may be considered skill-intensive manufactures, it is well known that data reporting electronics as part of developing countries' skill-intensive exports are mostly a statistical mirage. The reason is that these exports contain little of the exporting country's own technology and production factors, apart from low-skilled labour. Evidence suggests that some developing countries, especially China, have succeeded in increasing domestic value added in their electronics exports over the past decade or so, while "most exporters in Mexico and Central America remain in the assembly stage" (Hanson, 2012: 47). Other evidence suggests that China's exports, nonetheless, occupy low-price – though not necessarily low-quality – niches within certain product categories on the United States market (Schott, 2008).

13 The perception that FDI does not carry debt obligations to the host country and is devoid of speculative mentalities has reinforced its appeal as an instrument for promoting development. However, as profit remittances accumulate over time, the actual impact on the balance of payments may eventually become negative.

14 Some studies concentrating on earlier periods have led to different findings. One study on manufacturing firms in the United States, examining the period 1982–2004, found a strong positive correlation between the domestic and foreign activity levels of TNCs (Desai, Foley and Hines, 2009). However, this result may be sensitive to both the level of aggregation and the period under review. Indeed, a more disaggregated analysis focusing on specific sectors in the United States and China – two countries tightly linked through TNC activities – indicates significant labour substitution between them (Ebenstein et al., 2012). Moreover, other evidence suggests that United States firms have recently shifted to a business mode where expanding employment abroad is associated with downsizing employment at home, as discussed in the main text.

15 Evidence for the United States and China indicates that this kind of labour substitution may exist even at the sectoral level. One recent study finds that employment growth in China has been largest in those industrial sectors which, in the United States, have experienced a decline in employment (Ebenstein et al., 2012). However, the sample period on which this evidence is based ends in 2005, and therefore does not cover the past few years when

wages in China have strongly increased and renminbi appreciation has further increased unit labour costs measured in dollars. It is therefore not clear whether the observation of this study still holds, and even less so, whether it can be expected to be sustained.

16 For example, the OECD (2011: 113) finds a "strong and statistically [highly] significant" effect indicating that "relaxing FDI regulation (to attract more external investment) is associated with higher wage inequality." IMF (2007a) also finds inward FDI in developing countries and outward FDI in developed countries to exacerbate income inequality and attributes this finding to an increase in the relative demand for skilled workers in both advanced and developing countries.

17 According to Milberg and Winkler (2010: 276), "the expansion of global production networks has served a dual purpose in the evolving corporate strategy. Cost reductions from the globalisation of production have supported the financialisation of the non-financial corporate sector, both by raising profits and by reducing the need for domestic reinvestment of those profits, freeing earnings for the purchase of financial assets and raising shareholder returns." These authors have also reviewed studies indicating that an inverse relationship between shareholder maximization and innovation applies in several developed countries.

18 The link between trade and technology may be particularly close in global production sharing, as "offshoring would be unthinkable without low-cost information technology, and information technology would not be as low cost if not for the effective extension of global supply chains into low-wage countries" (Milberg and Winkler, 2009: 3).

19 Concentrating on firms in European countries and imports from China, Bloom, Draca and van Reenen (2011) find a strong and positive correlation between European industries that were more exposed to competition from Chinese imports (e.g. furniture, textiles, clothing and toys) and technological change. The evidence indicates that increased trade with China accounted for about 15 per cent of the technological upgrading in Europe during the period 2000–2007. Half of this effect was due to genuinely faster technological change, reflected in a larger number of patents and resulting from greater spending on research and development (R&D), while industry downsizing accounted for the other half of the 15 per cent.

20 If the data for the period 2000–2010 were to be included, it would have no material impact on the results, except for indicating negative employment growth for construction (for similar evidence, see McKinsey Global Institute, 2011).

21 The rationale for this concept comes from agency theory that argues that there may be tension between

the interests of principals (i.e. shareholders) and their agents (i.e. corporate managers) if the latter are not subject to market discipline. Corporate takeovers would be a way to discipline managers, and the rate of return on corporate stock could be used as a measure of corporate performance (Jensen and Meckling, 1976).

22   Milberg and Winkler (2009) review studies that point to a role of offshoring in the decline of the labour share in GDP.

23   For an eloquent account of the deleterious effects on productivity-increasing innovation of corporate behaviour that concentrates on shareholder value maximization, see Mintzberg, 2007, especially pages 9–10.

24   Reshoring manufacturing from China to the United States would also contribute to a smooth unwinding of global imbalances.

25   Ed Crooks, "GE takes $1bn risk in bringing jobs home", *Financial Times* 3 April 2012; Sylvain Cypel, "La Caroline du Sud devient un pôle automobile", *Le Monde*, 8 May 2012.

26   In particular, policies fostering capital accumulation and technology upgrading can stem adverse pressures from globalization.

27   Distributional developments in China differ considerably from the "growth with equity" model pursued by the NIEs earlier. As shown in *TDR 2003* (chap. V), rapid industrialization and growth of manufactured exports in the Republic of Korea and Taiwan Province of China were based on significant increases in labour productivity. Thus, manufacturers in these economies could maintain international competitiveness, while at the same time allowing rapid increases in wages. Wage growth in the Republic of Korea during its rapid economic catch-up in the period 1975–2000 was broad-based, as reflected by a continuous decline in wage inequality (i.e. wage earnings of skilled workers relative to those of unskilled workers) over this period (Kwack, 2012).

28   The household registration, or *hukou*, system has been a major factor in the evolution of rural-urban inequalities. While this legal barrier to mobility between rural and urban areas has helped prevent the problem of large slums, it has also meant that migrants from rural areas receive lower wages and social benefits than urban workers. Selden and Wu (2011) observe that until the early 1980s the *hukou* system bound villagers to their local communities. However, more recently it has channelled labour towards manufacturing activities and urban areas, but preserved highly differentiated wages and pay structures that permit firms and public entities to realize large savings and investments.

29   The Chinese Government has launched a series of initiatives to address spatial inequality, including the "campaign of 'western development'". This campaign, launched in 1999 is targeting the east-central-west divide. The movement of "constructing a socialist new countryside", formally initiated in 2005, aims at bridging the urban-rural gap. With the declaration, of "building a harmonious society" of October 2006, the Government launched a comprehensive attack on inequality. It envisaged measures to encourage rural-urban migration, increased funding for education and health services for the poor, and shifting demand away from investment and exports toward domestic consumption and public services (Zhu and Wan, 2012: 85).

30   A positive relationship between the share of FDI in aggregate output and inter-industry wage differentials has also been found in Mexico (Lopez Noria, 2011).

31   Integration into the world economy, combined with privatization and the ensuing substantial shifts in sectoral employment and wage structure, also affected income distribution in the Russian Federation. In this case, however, wages in SOEs increased less than in private companies (Gimpelson and Lukyanova, 2009). Moreover, growing spatial inequality stems from rising incomes in finance, especially in Moscow and St. Petersburg, and from major income gains in geographically highly concentrated construction and industrial production (Galbraith, Krytynskaia and Wang, 2004).

32   These findings are supported by McMillan and Rodrik (2011: 75) who argue that "whatever contribution globalization has made, it must depend heavily on local circumstances, choices made by domestic policymakers and domestic growth strategies." Indeed, much of the effects of trade liberalization on structural transformation in Latin America are due to countries' premature, or unregulated, financial integration and the often associated currency appreciations, as well as the weakening, or phasing out, of supportive industrial policies and a general retreat of the State from the economy, as discussed in detail in *TDR 2003*.

33   The experience of Chile between 1987 and 1992 is a case in point. During this period, the Chilean economy saw a cumulative GDP growth of 40 per cent and employment growth of 27 per cent (equivalent to one million jobs). This expansion was largely export-driven. Exports contributed to more than 30 per cent of aggregate demand growth, and, taking into account investment in export-oriented sectors plus the effect of higher consumption resulting from the new income generated, it was calculated that the "exports conglomerate" accounted for 70 per cent of GDP growth and 66 per cent of employment creation (ECLAC, 1994). However, only a few jobs were created in the main export sectors themselves: mining and fisheries contributed less than 2 per cent

to overall employment growth. The bulk of new jobs were created in non-tradable sectors (retail trade, construction) and in manufacturing, which was almost exclusively oriented to the domestic market. A highly favourable real exchange rate was important at that time for generating a strong multiplier effect of export-related income. In particular, the State-owned copper company was a supplementary vehicle for channelling revenues from exports to higher domestic demand.

34   See Peres (2011) for a review of the sectoral policy programmes launched over the past decade in several countries in Latin America (including Argentina, Brazil, Chile, Costa Rica, Mexico, Peru and Uruguay).

35   Regarding the methodological dispute about the empirical validity of the Kuznets hypothesis, see, for example, Anand and Kanbur, 1993.

36   Financial globalization refers to the increase in cross-border financial holdings and in the sum of countries' gross external assets (such as private financial assets denominated in foreign exchange and outward FDI stocks) and liabilities (such as private debt owed to foreign creditors, portfolio investment by non-residents, and inward FDI stocks); see also IMF, 2007b.

37   For a similar argument, though along somewhat different lines, see Akyüz (2011). Others have argued that countries can benefit from financial globalization only when excessive borrowing and debt accumulation can be avoided and when the domestic financial market is well developed (IMF, 2007b). However, a less developed financial market is precisely one of the main distinctions between developed and other countries, so that this argument is of little operational use to developing and emerging market economies.

38   While the occurrence of these waves depends on global push factors, country-specific pull factors determine the magnitude of the financial flows to that economy. These pull factors include economic performance and capital account openness, as well as institutional factors such as the exchange rate, given that expected changes in the exchange rate affect expected returns on financial investment.

39   Leijonhufvud (2007) discusses how risk-management practices in developed-country financial institutions give rise to excessive risk taking and "short-termism" in their investment strategies for emerging markets.

40   For a survey, see UNCTAD (2012), in particular section 5.2.

41   Price-to-income ratios in the real estate markets seem relatively high in a number of Asian countries (Balakrishnan et al., 2012). But prices in such markets are likely to have been inflated by financial inflows also in offshore financial centres, such as Mauritius, where comprehensive data are not available.

Country coverage of chart 4.4:

The country groups covered are as follows:

Latin America (10): Argentina, the Bolivarian Republic of Venezuela, Brazil, Chile, Colombia, Costa Rica, Ecuador, Mexico, Paraguay and Peru.

Developing countries in Asia (7): Malaysia, Nepal, Pakistan, the Republic of Korea, Singapore, Thailand and Turkey.

Africa (5): Ghana, Mauritius, Morocco, South Africa, Tunisia.

The following are the 82 low-wage economies covered:

Developed countries (1): Bulgaria.

Transition economies (13): Albania, Armenia, Azerbaijan, Belarus, Bosnia and Herzegovina, Georgia, Kazakhstan, Kyrgyzstan, the Republic of Moldova, Tajikistan, Turkmenistan, Ukraine and Uzbekistan.

Latin America (6): Bolivia, Guatemala, Guyana, Haiti, Honduras and Nicaragua.

Developing countries in Asia (23): Afghanistan, Bangladesh, Bhutan, Cambodia, China, India, Indonesia, Iraq, Kiribati, the People's Democratic Republic of Korea, Lao People's Democratic Republic, Mongolia, Myanmar, Papua New Guinea, the Philippines, Samoa, Solomon Islands, Sri Lanka, the Syrian Arab Republic, Tuvalu, Vanuatu, Viet Nam and Yemen.

Africa (39): Angola, Benin, Burkina Faso, Burundi, Cameroon, Cape Verde, Central African Republic, Chad, Comoros, Côte d'Ivoire, the Democratic Republic of the Congo, Djibouti, Egypt, Eritrea, Ethiopia, Gambia, Guinea, Guinea-Bissau, Kenya, Lesotho, Liberia, Madagascar, Malawi, Mali, Mauritania, Mozambique, Niger, Nigeria, Rwanda, Sao Tome and Principe, Senegal, Sierra Leone, Somalia, Sudan, Togo, Uganda, the United Republic of Tanzania, Zambia and Zimbabwe.

References

Acemoglu D (1998). Why do new technologies complement skills? Directed technical changes and wage inequality. *Quarterly Journal of Economics*, 113(4): 1055–1089.

Acemoglu D and Autor D (2012). What Does Human Capital Do? A Review of Goldin and Katz's The Race between Education and Technology. Working Paper No. 17820, National Bureau of Economic Research. Cambridge, MA, February.

Aghion P, Caroli E and Garcia-Penalosa E (1999). Inequality and economic growth: The perspective of the new growth theories. *Journal of Economic Literature*, 37(4): 1615–1660.

Agosin MR and Huaita F (2012). Overreaction in capital flows to emerging markets: Booms and sudden stops. *Journal of International Money and Finance*, 31(5): 1140–1155.

Akyüz Y (2011). Capital flows to developing countries in a historical perspective: Will the current boom end with a bust? Research Paper 37, South Centre, Geneva, March.

Anand S and Kanbur SMR (1993). Inequality and development. A critique. *Journal of Development Economics*, 41(1): 19–43.

Anderson E (2005). Openness and inequality in developing countries: A review of theory and recent evidence. *World Development*, 33(7): 1045–1063.

Asian Development Bank (2012). Confronting rising inequality in Asia. In: *Asian Development Outlook 2012*. Manila: 35–95.

Autor DH and Dorn D (2012). The growth of low skill service jobs and the polarization of the U.S. labor market. Cambridge, MA, Massachusetts Institute of Technology. Available at: http://economics.mit.edu/files/1474.

Autor DH, Katz LF and Kearney MS (2006). The polarization of the US labor market. *American Economic Review*, 96(2): 189–194.

Autor DH, Katz LF and Kearney MS (2008). Trends in U.S. wage inequality: Revising the revisionists. *Review of Economics and Statistics*, 90(2): 300–323.

Balakrishnan R, Nowak S, Panth S and Wu Y (2012). Surging capital flows to emerging Asia: Facts, impacts, and responses. Working Paper 12/130, International Monetary Fund, Washington, DC.

Baldwin R (2011). Trade and globalization after globalization's 2nd unbundling: How building and joining a supply chain are different and why it matters. Working Paper No. 17716, National Bureau of Economic Research, Cambridge, MA, December.

Banister J and Cook G (2011). China's employment and compensation costs in manufacturing through 2008. *Bureau of Labor Statistics Monthly Labor Review*, March: 39–52.

Berman E, Bound J and Griliches Z (1994). Changes in the demand for skilled labor within U.S. manufacturing: Evidence from the annual survey of manufactures. *Quarterly Journal of Economics*, 104(2): 367–398.

Berman E, Bound J and Machin S (1998). Implications of skill-biased technological change: international evidence. *Quarterly Journal of Economics*, 113(4): 1245–1280.

Bernard AB, Jensen JB and Schott PK (2006). Survival of the best fit: Exposure to low-wage countries and the (uneven) growth of US manufacturing establishments. *Journal of International Economics*, 68(1): 219–237.

Bloom N, Draca M and van Reenen J (2011). Trade induced technical change? The impact of Chinese imports on innovation, IT and productivity. Working Paper No. 16717, National Bureau of Economic Research, January.

Broner FA and Rigobon R (2006). Why are capital flows so much more volatile in emerging than in developed countries? In: Caballero RJ, Calderon C and Cespedes LS, eds., *External Vulnerability and Preventive Policies*. Santiago, Chile: Central Bank of Chile: 15–39.

Card D and DiNardo JE (2002). Skill-biased technological change and rising wage inequality: Some problems and puzzles. *Journal of Labor Economics*, 20(4): 733–783.

Card D and Lemieux T (2001). Can falling supply explain the rising return to college for younger men? A cohort-based analysis. *Quarterly Journal of Economics*, 116(2): 705–746.

Ceglowski J and Golub S (2011). Does China still have a labor cost advantage? CESifo Working Paper 1579, September. Available at: http://www.swarthmore.edu/Documents/academics/economics/cesifo1_wp3579.pdf.

Chen Z, Lu M and Wan G (2010). Inter-industry wage differentials: An increasingly important contributor to urban China income inequality. Hi-Stat Discussion Paper 130, Hitotsubashi University. Available at: http://gcoe.ier.hit-u.ac.jp/research/discussion/2008/pdf/gd09-130.pdf.

Desai MA, Foley FC and Hines JR (2009). Domestic effects of the foreign activities of US multinationals. *American Economic Journal: Economic Policy*, 1(1): 181–203.

Desjonqueres T, Machin S and Van Reenen J (1999). Another nail in the coffin? Or can the trade based explanation of changing skill structures be resurrected? *Scandinavian Journal of Economics*, 101(4): 533–554.

Ebenstein A, McMillan M, Zhao Y and Zhang C (2012). Understanding the role of China in the "decline" of US manufacturing. Jerusalem, Hebrew University of Jerusalem. March. Available at: http://pluto.huji.ac.il/~ebenstein/Ebenstein_McMillan_Zhao_Zhang_March_2012.pdf.

ECLAC (1994). El crecimiento económico y su difusión social: El caso de Chile de 1987 a 1992. LC/R.1483. Santiago, Chile, 27 December.

ECLAC (2011). Preliminary overview of the economies of Latin America and the Caribbean. Santiago, Chile. Available at: http://www.eclac.cl/publicaciones/xml/2/45452/2011-882-BPI-LANZAMIENTO-WEB.pdf.

Feenstra RC and Hanson GH (1999). Productivity measurement and the impact of trade and technology on wages: Estimates for the U.S., 1972–1990. *Quarterly Journal of Economics*, 114(3): 907–940.

Feenstra RC and Hanson GH (2003). Global production sharing and rising inequality: A survey of trade and wages. In: Choi EK and Harrigan J, eds., *Handbook of International Trade*. Malden, MA, Blackwell.

Galbraith JK (2012). *Inequality and Instability. A Study of the World Economy just before the Great Crisis*. Oxford, Oxford University Press.

Galbraith JK, Krytynskaia L and Wang Q (2004). The experience of rising inequality in Russia and China during the transition. *European Journal of Comparative Economics*, 1(1): 87–106.

Ghosh A, Kim J, Qureshi MS and Zalduendo I (2012). Surges. Working Paper 12/22, International Monetary Fund, Washington, DC.

Gimpelson V and Lukyanova A (2009). Are public sector workers underpaid in Russia? Estimating the public-private wage gap. Discussion Paper 3941, Institute for the Study of Labour (IZA), Bonn. Available at: http://ftp.iza.org/dp3941.pdf.

Goldberg PK and Pavcnik N (2007). Distributional effects of globalization in developing countries. *Journal of Economic Literature*, 65(1): 39–82.

Goldin C and Katz LF (2008). *The Race between Education and Technology*. Cambridge, MA, Belknap Press of Harvard University Press.

Goos M, Manning A and Salomons A (2011). Explaining job polarization: The roles of technology, offshoring and institutions. Discussion Paper Series 11.34, University of Leuven, Center for Economic Studies, Leuven.

Gordon RJ and Dew-Becker I (2007). Selected issues in the rise of income inequality. *Brookings Papers on Economic Activity*, 2: 169–190. Washington, DC, Brookings Institution.

Hanson GH (2012). The rise of middle kingdoms: Emerging economies in global trade. *Journal of Economic Perspectives*, 26(2): 41–64.

Harrison A, McLaren J and McMillan M (2011). Recent perspectives on trade and inequality. *Annual Review of Economics*, 3: 261–289.

IMF (2007a). *World Economic Outlook*. Washington, DC, April.

IMF (2007b). Reaping the Benefits of Financial Globalization. Washington, DC.

Jensen MC and Meckling WH (1976). Theory of the firm: Managerial behavior, agency costs and ownership structure. *Journal of Financial Economics*, 3(4): 305–360.

Krugman PR (1995). Growing world trade: Causes and consequences. *Brookings Papers on Economic Activity*. (1): 327–377. Washington, DC, Brookings Institution.

Kuznets S (1955). Economic growth and income inequality. *American Economic Review*, 45(1): 1–28.

Kwack SY (2012). Wage inequality and the contribution of capital, differential labor quality and efficiency to economic growth in Korea, 1965–2007. *Seoul Journal of Economics*, 25(1): 1–23.

Kwon OH, Chang S and Fleisher BM (2011). Evolution of the industrial wage structure in China since 1980. Columbus, Ohio, Ohio State University. Available at: http://www.econ.ohio-state.edu/Fleisher/working_papers/IWS%2012_22_11.pdf.

Lawrence RZ and Slaughter MJ (1993). International trade and American wages in the 1980s: Giant sucking sound or small hiccup? *Brookings Papers on Economic Activity, Microeconomics*, (2): 161–226. Washington, DC, Brookings Institution.

Lazonick W (2012). The fragility of the US economy: The financialized corporation and the disappearing middle class. In: Breznitz D and Zysman J, eds., *National Adjustments to a Changing Global Economy*. Oxford, Oxford University Press (forthcoming).

Leijonhufvud C (2007). Financial globalisation and emerging market volatility. *World Economy*, 30(12): 1817–1842.

Lemieux T (2007). The changing nature of wage inequality. *Journal of Population Economics*, 21(1): 21–48.

Li X (2011). How does China's new labor contract law affect floating workers? Cambridge, MA, Harvard University. Available at: http://www.law.harvard. edu/programs/lwp/papers/How%20Does%20 China's%20New%20Labour%20Contract%20 Law%20Affect%20Floating%20Workers%20in%20 China%20_Xiaoying%20Li_.pdf.

Lopez Noria G (2011). The effect of trade and FDI on inter-industry wage differentials: The case of Mexico. Working Paper 2011-10, Bank of Mexico, DF Mexico. Available at: http://www.banxico.org. mx/publicaciones-y-discursos/publicaciones/docu-mentos-de-investigacion/banxico/%7B0392ACC7-E257-6DB2-5AE3-BF1DFADD4C77%7D.pdf.

McKinsey Global Institute (2011). Growth and Renewal in the United States: Retooling America's Economic Engine. Available at: http://www.mckinsey.com/Insights/MGI/ Research/Productivity_Competitiveness_and_Growth/ Growth_and_renewal_in_the_US.

McMillan M and Rodrik D (2011). Globalization, structural change and productivity growth. In: Bacchetta M and Jansen M, eds., *Making Globalisation Socially Sustainable*. Geneva, World Trade Organization and International Labour Office: 49–84.

Milberg W and Winkler D (2009). Globalization, off-shoring and economic insecurity in industrialized countries. Working Paper No. 87, United Nations Department of Economic and Social Affairs, New York, November.

Milberg W and Winkler D (2010). Financialisation and the dynamics of offshoring in the USA. *Cambridge Journal of Economics*, 34(2): 275–293.

Mintzberg H (2007). How productivity killed American enterprise. Montreal, McGill University. Available at: http://www.mintzberg.org/sites/default/files/ productivity2008.pdf.

OECD (2011). *Divided We Stand: Why Inequality Keeps Rising*. Paris.

Peres W (2011). Industrial policies in Latin America. Discussion Paper 2011/48, World Institute for Development Economics Research, Helsinki.

Rajan RG (2010). *Fault Lines: How Hidden Fractures Still Threaten the World Economy*. Princeton and Oxford, Princeton University Press.

Sainz P and Calcagno A (1992). In search of another form of development, *CEPAL Review*, No. 48, ECLAC, Santiago, Chile, December.

Schott PK (2008). The relative sophistication of Chinese exports. *Economic Policy*, 23(issue 53): 5–49.

Selden M and Wu JM (2011). The Chinese State, incomplete proletarianization and structures of inequality in two epochs. *The Asia-Pacific Journal*. Available at: http://japanfocus.org/-Mark-Selden/3480.

Tinbergen J (1975). *Income Distribution: Analysis and Policies*. Amsterdam, North Holland.

Thoenig M and Verdier T (2003). A theory of defensive skill biased innovation and globalization. *American Economic Review*, 93(3): 709–728.

UNCTAD (*TDR 1997*). *Trade and Development Report, 1997. Globalization, distribution and growth*. United Nations publication, Sales No. E.97.II.D.8, New York and Geneva.

UNCTAD (*TDR 1998*). *Trade and Development Report, 1998. Financial instability. Growth in Africa*. United Nations publication, Sales No. E.98.II.D.6, New York and Geneva.

UNCTAD (*TDR 1999*). *Trade and Development Report, 1999. Fragile recovery and risks: Trade, finance and growth*. United Nations publication, Sales No. E.99. II.D.1, New York and Geneva.

UNCTAD (*TDR 2003*). *Trade and Development Report, 2003. Capital accumulation, growth and structural change*. United Nations publication, Sales No. E.03. II.D.7, New York and Geneva.

UNCTAD (*TDR 2006*). *Trade and Development Report, 2006. Global partnership and national policies for development*. United Nations publication, Sales No. E.06.II.D.6, New York and Geneva.

UNCTAD (*TDR 2008*). *Trade and Development Report, 2008. Commodity prices, capital flows and the financing of investment*. United Nations publication, Sales No. E.08.II.D.21, New York and Geneva.

UNCTAD (*TDR 2010*). *Trade and Development Report, 2010. Employment, globalization and development*. United Nations publication, Sales No. E.10.II.D.3, New York and Geneva.

UNCTAD (*TDR 2011*). *Trade and Development Report, 2011. Post-crisis policy challenges in the world economy*. United Nations publication, Sales No. E.11.II.D.3, New York and Geneva.

UNCTAD (2011). *Report of the Secretary-General of UNCTAD to UNCTAD XIII. Development-led globalization: Towards Sustainable and Inclusive Development Paths*. Document UNCTAD (XIII)/1. New York and Geneva, United Nations.

UNCTAD (2012). *Trade and Development Report, 1981–2011: Three decades of Thinking Development*. New York and Geneva: United Nations publication, Sales No. E.12.II.D.5.

United States Bureau of Labor Statistics (2011). International comparison of hourly compensation costs in manufacturing, 2010. News Release USDL-11-1778, 21 December. Available at: http://www.bls.gov/news. release/pdf/ichcc.pdf.

Van Reenen J (2011). Wage inequality, technology and trade: 21st century evidence. *Labour Economics*, 18(6): 730–741.

Wood A (1994). *North–South Trade, Employment and Inequality*. Oxford, Clarendon Press.

Wood A and Mayer J (2011). Has China de-industrialised other developing countries? *Review of World Economics*, 147(2): 325–350.

Zhu C and Wan G (2012). Rising inequality in China and the move to a balanced economy. *China & World Economy*, 20(1): 83–104.

Chapter V

THE ROLE OF FISCAL POLICY IN INCOME DISTRIBUTION

A. Introduction

Achieving a pattern of income distribution that policymakers deem desirable and that is acceptable to society as a whole has been an objective of fiscal policy in its own right. This is because it favours social cohesion and political stability and enables the entire society to participate in the overall growth process of the economy, even if the contribution of different groups of the population varies. But achieving a pattern of income distribution that boosts growth and employment creation should also be considered an intermediate objective. For both reasons, it is essential for developing countries to carefully consider the way in which fiscal policies influence income distribution as part of their development strategies.

There are two perspectives on what sort of income distribution fiscal policy should aim to achieve and why. One perspective, from the supply side, believes a more unequal income distribution that favours profit-making and higher income groups, which have a greater propensity to save, will enhance growth. This is because it is expected to lead to greater investment as a result of increasing net profits and aggregate savings. Another perspective, from the demand side, expects that a more equal distribution in favour of middle- and lower income groups, which have a lower propensity to save, will strengthen

domestic consumption and lead to greater investment and employment by firms on the expectation of higher demand. In both cases, investment in real productive capacity is understood to be the driving force for economic progress.

In the first three decades of the post-war era, this latter approach dominated the thinking about the link between income distribution, investment, growth and economic policies, especially in most developed countries. These policies reduced inequality and led to relatively fast growth and relatively low unemployment. However, the policy orientation from the late 1970s onwards shifted towards the former approach, resulting in greater inequality, higher unemployment and slower growth.

In addition to labour market policies, which are discussed in chapter VI of this *Report*, fiscal policy provides the main instruments for influencing income distribution. These instruments include taxation, social transfers and the provision of public services. All of these have played a central role in governments' attempts not only to influence income distribution, but also to support the growth process in both developed and developing countries. Therefore, an assessment of the causes of the rise of inequality in most countries since the early 1980 must include an enquiry into the role that fiscal policy has played in this context.

To be sure, influencing income distribution is only one of several objectives of fiscal policy. But even when decisions regarding the ways in which public revenue should be raised and public expenditure allocated are not taken with the specific intention of influencing income distribution, they inevitably influence this distribution in one direction or the other. Therefore, the conduct of fiscal policies over the past three decades has to be seen in the context of a broader reorientation of macroeconomic policies and structural reforms that have rarely helped to reduce inequality; indeed, they have often increased it.

From the mid-1970s onwards, fiscal policies in developed countries gradually changed their focus to the elimination of "market distortions" resulting from taxation. At the same time, policy decisions tended to place a greater emphasis on achieving fiscal balance, and much less than in the past on other macroeconomic or development needs. The general tendency to reduce the role of the State in the economy meant that whenever budgetary adjustment was considered necessary, it was sought through spending cuts rather than by raising additional revenue.

In many countries, market-friendly tax reforms reduced the tax-to-GDP ratio, lowered marginal tax rates and served to strengthen those elements of the public revenue system that had regressive effects on income distribution (i.e. elements which tended to increase income inequality). This new orientation also shaped fiscal policies in developing countries, where policy reforms in the 1980s and 1990s were strongly influenced by the conditionalities and recommendations of the international financial institutions. These institutions also emphasized the need to strengthen the financial position of the public sector and reduce government interference in the allocation of resources (*TDR 2006*, chap. II).

This chapter discusses how fiscal policy on both the revenue and expenditure sides has affected income distribution across different social and income groups, and how it can be modified to narrow the income gap. It argues that more progressive taxation can help to reduce inequality in the distribution of income and wealth without curtailing incentives to undertake investment in fixed capital, innovation and skills acquisition. On the public expenditure side, social transfers and the provision of social services can alleviate the effects of socially undesirable distributive outcomes arising from market forces and from unequal initial endowments. The precise mix of the instruments that have been used or that can be recommended varies according to the specific conditions prevailing in each country, in particular its stage of development, administrative capacities and social preferences.

This chapter is organized as follows. Section B reviews some major changes in the design of revenue systems and the pattern of public expenditure that appear to have contributed to greater inequality over the past 30 years. It also describes more recent fiscal policy measures taken in developing and transition economies with a view to reducing inequality. Section C draws on these experiences and on further theoretical considerations to offer some recommendations for fiscal measures that would reduce inequality while at the same time strengthening the dynamics of growth and development.

> It is essential for developing countries to consider the way in which fiscal policies influence income distribution as part of their development strategies.

B. Fiscal policies and inequality

1. Public finances and income distribution

From the mid-1970s onwards, there was an increasing convergence of views among influential economists and policymakers that tax systems generally needed to be modified to achieve greater "neutrality" of taxation (Tanzi, 1987). This was part of a broader shift in the economic paradigm, based on the perception that the stagflation (i.e. high unemployment combined with high inflation) experienced by developed and some developing countries in the 1970s was partly due to the distorting effects of State intervention (for a more detailed discussion, see *TDR 2010*, chap. 5, sect. B). As a result, monetary policy began to give priority to fighting inflation at the expense of efforts to check rising unemployment. It was believed that the unemployment problem could be solved by introducing greater flexibility in "hiring and firing" conditions and in wage determination, and by shifting the distribution of income in favour of profit-making. The perception of what makes a "good tax system" shifted from one that explicitly introduces distortions into the functioning of capitalist market economies to one that minimizes such distortions (Steinmo, 2003). It was based on a revival of the belief in the efficiency of markets. According to this view, the tax burden and government expenditure should be kept to a minimum, and the distribution of the tax burden and allocation of public expenditure should be determined primarily by efficiency criteria (McLure, 1984; Musgrave, 1990). Distributional considerations should only come into play to avoid extreme income inequality, which should be reduced mainly through expenditures (e.g. Engel, Galetovic and Raddatz, 1999). High taxation of corporate profits and high marginal income tax rates for those at the top of the income scale were seen as slowing down economic activity, but also as being ineffective in redistributing income and wealth (Bird and Zolt, 2005).

In the context of slow growth and rising unemployment, the change in economic thinking also influenced broad public opinion about what is "socially acceptable". Although it was clear that the reduction of progressive taxation would increase inequality, there was little popular opposition to it in the developed countries, because the tax reforms, similar to labour market reforms, were widely believed to be the only way to restore growth and keep companies from relocating production abroad. Similarly, in developing countries, policies that provided extensive tax privileges to owners of capital, in particular to TNCs, were considered "socially acceptable" or "desirable" because they promoted foreign capital inflows.

2. Tax reforms in developed countries

In developed countries, tax reforms typically included: scaling back the progressive tax rates on personal income, particularly marginal rates at the top end of the income scale; reducing the number of income tax brackets; cutting back corporate tax rates; broadening the income tax base by eliminating loopholes and exemptions; and increasing rates of indirect taxes – in particular the value-added tax (VAT) – and social security contributions (Sandford, 1993: 10–20).

Table 5.1

FISCAL REVENUE INDICATORS, DEVELOPED COUNTRIES, 1981–2010

(Per cent of current GDP)

	1981–1985	1986–1990	1991–1995	1996–2000	2001–2005	2006–2010
Total revenue and grants *of which:*	41.6	42.5	42.8	42.2	41.5	41.8
Tax revenue *of which:*	26.6	27.8	26.9	26.3	25.9	26.0
VAT	5.5	6.1	6.3	6.7	7.0	7.1
Border tax	0.9	0.8	1.1	1.1	0.8	0.6
Income tax *of which:*	13.3	13.9	12.8	12.3	12.0	12.1
Corporate income tax	2.5	2.7	2.7	3.1	3.2	3.5
Other tax revenue	6.9	7.0	6.7	6.2	6.1	6.1
Social contributions	9.5	9.7	10.9	10.3	10.1	10.0
Other revenues[a]	7.3	3.3	5.1	6.1	5.4	5.3
Memo item:						
Ratio of income tax to VAT	2.42	2.28	2.03	1.84	1.71	1.70

Source: UNCTAD secretariat calculations, based on Eurostat, *Statistics Database*; *OECD.StatExtracts* database.
  Note: Data refer to the five-year average of the mean observation of general government revenue.
     a Includes capital revenues.

The changes in the tax structure, allegedly aimed at making the tax system more "neutral", favoured some interests over others. The elimination of loopholes and exemptions in most cases reduced certain privileges of taxpayers in the higher income groups. At the same time, cuts in income and capital taxation, together with increases in consumption taxes, led to a redistribution of the tax burden which fell more heavily on lower income groups. The overall effect of these changes in the tax structure made taxation more regressive. Indeed, a review of tax reforms in OECD countries did not find a single country where the tax system became more progressive (Steinmo, 2003: 223).

The redistributive effects of the tax system depend to a large extent on the share of income tax in total revenues and the progressivity of the personal income tax schedule. In developed countries, but also in a number of developing countries in Asia, income tax is the largest source of public revenues (tables 5.1 and 5.2). During the period 2006–2010, income tax in developed countries, including corporate income tax, accounted for 46.5 per cent, on average, of total tax revenues, compared with a regressive VAT of

27.3 per cent, on average. Since the early 1980s, the share of income tax has fallen and that of VAT has risen continuously. The ratio of income tax to VAT, which may be taken as an approximate measure for the progressivity of the tax system, fell from 2.42 in the first half of the 1980s to 2.03 per cent in the first half of the 1990s and to 1.70 per cent in the 2006–2010 period. In addition, it is also important to consider the scale of income tax. In particular, marginal tax rates at the top of the income scale are an important element in overall progressivity, even though the top earners constitute a small segment of the population, because they often account for a large share of aggregate income and the total income tax yield. Yet marginal personal income tax rates at the top of the income scale in OECD countries fell from an average of 71 per cent in the late 1970s to around 57 per cent in the late 2000s (chart 5.1).

Although these rates fell in a majority of OECD countries, the change in the degree of progressivity of the tax system as a whole differed among these countries. One reason for this was divergent patterns in the taxation of wealth (Piketty, 2010). The evolution of estate and wealth taxes in France, for

Table 5.2

FISCAL REVENUE INDICATORS, SELECTED REGIONS, 1991–2010

(Per cent of current GDP)

	1991–1995	1996–2000	2001–2005	2006–2010
Africa				
Total revenue and grants	22.1	21.0	23.8	28.2
of which:				
Tax revenue	14.4	14.0	15.0	16.4
of which:				
VAT	4.4	4.4	4.9	5.4
Border tax	5.3	5.0	4.2	4.2
Income tax	4.0	4.2	5.1	6.2
of which:				
Corporate income tax	2.5	2.4	2.3	3.4
Other tax revenue	0.7	0.4	0.8	0.6
Social contributions	2.0	1.8	2.3	2.7
Other revenues[a]	5.6	5.3	6.5	9.1
Memo item:				
Ratio of income tax to VAT	0.91	0.95	1.04	1.15
Latin America				
Total revenue and grants	21.3	22.7	23.9	27.3
of which:				
Tax revenue	12.5	13.8	14.8	16.7
of which:				
VAT	4.7	5.4	6.4	7.3
Border tax	1.8	1.6	1.3	1.2
Income tax	2.8	3.3	3.6	4.7
of which:				
Corporate income tax	2.0	2.2	2.2	3.0
Other tax revenue	3.2	3.5	3.5	3.4
Social contributions	2.9	2.8	2.8	3.1
Other revenues[a]	5.9	6.1	6.3	7.5
Memo item:				
Ratio of income tax to VAT	0.60	0.61	0.56	0.64
East, South and South-East Asia				
Total revenue and grants	20.9	19.6	19.2	20.7
of which:				
Tax revenue	14.4	13.8	13.7	14.9
of which:				
VAT	4.5	4.5	5.2	5.6
Border tax	2.4	1.7	1.5	1.4
Income tax	4.8	5.4	5.4	6.2
of which:				
Corporate income tax	3.0	3.1	3.5	4.3
Other tax revenue	2.7	2.2	1.6	1.7
Social contributions	0.7	1.2	2.2	3.0
Other revenues[a]	5.8	4.6	3.3	2.8
Memo item:				
Ratio of income tax to VAT	1.07	1.20	1.04	1.11
West Asia				
Total revenue and grants	28.5	30.3	34.6	35.8
of which:				
Tax revenues	5.5	5.9	6.5	6.9
Social contributions	1.0	2.1	1.8	3.8
Other revenues[a]	22.0	22.2	26.3	25.1
Transition economies				
Total revenue and grants	..	28.0	29.9	34.2
of which:				
Tax revenue	..	18.7	18.3	20.6
of which:				
VAT	..	8.8	10.1	12.2
Border tax	..	2.1	1.9	1.9
Income tax	..	4.9	5.1	5.9
of which:				
Corporate income tax	..	2.7	3.3	3.3
Other tax revenue	..	2.9	1.2	0.6
Social contributions	..	8.5	8.6	9.2
Other revenues[a]	..	0.8	3.0	4.4
Memo item:				
Ratio of income tax to VAT	..	0.56	0.50	0.48

Source: UNCTAD secretariat calculations, based on ECLAC, *CEPALSTAT*; IMF, *World Economic Outlook* and *Government Finance Statistics* databases; and national sources.

Note: Data refer to the five-year average of the mean observation of general government revenue, except for Argentina, Bolivia, the Bolivarian Republic of Venezuela, Colombia, Costa Rica, Ecuador, El Salvador, Mexico, Nicaragua, Panama, Paraguay and Uruguay, for which data refer to the non-financial public sector. For the composition of developing country groups, see table 5.3.

a Includes capital revenues.

Chart 5.1

TOP MARGINAL INCOME TAX RATES IN SELECTED OECD COUNTRIES, 1975–1979 AND 2004–2008
(Per cent)

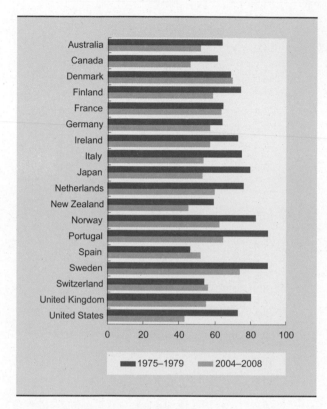

Source: Piketty, Saez and Stantcheva, 2011.
Note: Data are averages for each period. They refer to personal income tax at both central and local government levels. Whenever data for those periods are not available, the first five-year period after 1975 and the most recent five years were used (for details, see Piketty, Saez and Stantcheva, 2011, appendix C).

instance, contrasted sharply with that in the United Kingdom and the United States during the period 1970–2005 (Piketty and Saez, 2007). The progressivity of the overall tax system clearly declined in the United Kingdom and the United States. In these countries since the early 1980s, there has been a drop in average individual income tax rates, payroll taxes, estate, gift and wealth taxes, and corporate tax (only in the United States) for those at the very top of the income distribution, who also hold a large share of the capital. By contrast, progressivity in the overall French tax system has remained almost unchanged, as the introduction of a wealth tax and an increase in the inheritance tax in the early 1980s more than offset the reduction of the personal income tax rate.

At the same time, inequality in the distribution of disposable incomes increased much less in France than in the United Kingdom and the United States.

The proponents of neoliberal tax reforms justified the reduction of progressive taxation on the grounds that this would reduce distortions in factor allocation and thereby improve the efficiency of the economy, with positive effects on gross incomes for all. The OECD endorsed this approach: "The pursuit of greater neutrality has been based on the growing acceptance of the fact that a proportional tax system is more likely to be optimal from an efficiency point of view than one which is graduated and selective" (OECD, 1989: 184–185). However, the idea that tax "neutrality" increases economic efficiency derives from an economic model that does not take account of the numerous cases of market failures and unequal initial endowments that occur in the real world, and which discriminatory taxation seeks to correct (see, for example, Aiyagari, 1995; Koskela and Vilmunen, 1996; Pissarides, 1998). It also neglects the role of income distribution in determining the level of domestic demand.

Lower taxation of high-income groups and profits was expected to lead to greater investment in two ways. First, it was believed that higher net profits would increase the incentives and financial resources for reinvestment by companies. Second, higher net incomes at the upper end of the income scale were expected to boost aggregate savings, since these income groups have a higher-than-average propensity to save. This, in turn, would also – quasi automatically – lead to higher investment. As globalization advanced in the 1990s, it was also argued that reducing the tax burden, especially on profits, was necessary because high corporate taxes had an adverse impact on the international competitiveness of companies. Moreover, lower corporate taxes would prevent a relocation of production to low-tax countries (which, mostly, were also low-wage countries).

However, it is unlikely that investment will grow in an economy when the propensity to consume falls and expectations of a growth of demand worsen, especially in a situation when both labour and existing productive capacities are not fully employed. Indeed, policies that aim at increasing aggregate savings and result in lowering mass consumption are more likely to lead to reduced investment and further weaken output growth.

It is therefore not surprising that tax reforms which lowered the progressivity of the tax structure did not result in higher overall efficiency and faster growth in OECD countries (Piketty, Saez and Stantcheva, 2011; see also chart 5.2A). However, the magnitude of the decline of top tax rates was a good predictor of the increases in pre-tax income concentration in these countries (chart 5.2B).[1] Reduced top marginal tax rates also encourage a greater distribution of corporate profits among shareholders – who are mainly to be found in the top income groups – rather than reinvestment of such profits. Such income, in turn, is more likely to be saved in the form of acquisitions of existing assets, rather than being spent for consumption (Bakija, Cole and Heim, 2012).

In sum, tax reforms in many developed economies at the end of the last century mainly benefited the highest income households, except when the decline of top marginal rates was counterbalanced by increases in other taxes with a progressive incidence. But despite the reduction in progressivity of the tax systems and lower corporate taxes, growth remained slow and unemployment relatively high.

3. Public revenues in developing countries and transition economies

(a) Structure of public revenues

The structures and levels of government revenue collection differ considerably between developing and developed countries (tables 5.1 and 5.2). In developing countries, especially in Latin America, as well as in the transition economies, the share of income taxes in total public revenues is much lower than in developed countries. On the other hand, the shares of regressive VAT as well as other revenues, such as royalties and State property taxes, are considerably higher in developing countries.

The lower share of the income tax yield and the higher share of VAT in total tax revenues indicate that the tax system overall is more regressive in developing and transition economies than in developed countries. In the 2006–2010 period, the share of income tax (including corporate income tax) in total tax revenue was the lowest in Latin America (28 per

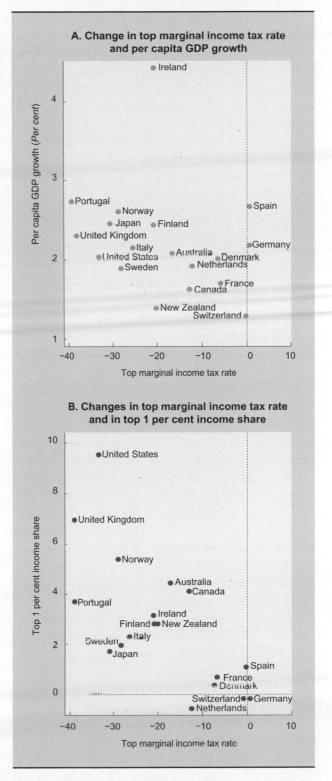

Chart 5.2

CHANGE IN TOP MARGINAL INCOME TAX RATE, PER CAPITA GDP GROWTH AND CHANGE IN TOP 1 PER CENT INCOME SHARE IN SELECTED OECD COUNTRIES FROM 1975–1979 TO 2004–2008

A. Change in top marginal income tax rate and per capita GDP growth

B. Changes in top marginal income tax rate and in top 1 per cent income share

Source: Piketty, Saez and Stantcheva, 2011.
Note: Data refer to changes in the average for each period. They are in percentage points unless otherwise specified.

cent) and the highest in East, South and South-East Asia (42 per cent). The share of VAT was the lowest in Africa (33 per cent) and the highest in the transition economies (59 per cent).

To some extent, the impact on income distribution that results from the lower progressivity of the tax system in developing countries is mitigated by a high share in public revenue from royalties and State property, especially from the extractive industries. This higher share results mainly from exports of oil and minerals, and thus does not represent a charge on domestic taxpayers. However, its share in total public revenues varies by region. In 2006–2010, these revenues accounted for 9.1 per cent of GDP in Africa and 7.5 per cent in Latin America; it was especially high in West Asia (25.1 per cent) but very low in East, South and South-East Asia (2.8 per cent). Nevertheless, the redistributive effects of the tax systems in developing countries are relatively limited, not only because of their overall structure but also because of the generally smaller share of public revenue in GDP.

> Revenue collection structures are more regressive in developing and transition economies than in developed countries.

Particularly at early stages of economic development, owing to a large informal sector and limited government capacities, direct and progressive taxes are difficult to collect.[2] Moreover, in most of those developing countries where income distribution is highly unequal, taxation is also regressive, and tax evasion by earners of non-wage incomes is widespread. This contributes to even greater inequality because richer people have greater opportunities and skills for evading taxes. According to estimates from Tax Justice Network (2011), tax evasion or avoidance reduces tax revenues by $3.1 trillion worldwide every year. Similarly, transfer pricing – which refers to the setting of prices in international transactions between associated enterprises within a TNC – enables the shifting of TNCs' profits to low- or no-tax jurisdictions, and thus unfairly deprives a country of tax revenues (Jomo, 2012).

There have been significant changes in the structure of tax revenues in developing countries and the transition economies over the past three decades, owing partly to recommendations of the international financial institutions and the conditionalities attached to their lending, especially in the 1980s and 1990s.

About 50 per cent of all adjustment loans provided by the IMF and the World Bank between 1979 and 1989 included conditions relating to fiscal reforms, and more than 50 per cent included conditions relating to both trade reforms and the rationalization of government finances which had tax reform elements (Webb and Shariff, 1992: 71).

The emphasis of the reforms of the 1980s and 1990s was primarily on two of the three classic functions of fiscal policy (Musgrave, 1959): ensuring macroeconomic stability and efficient resource allocation. The third function, that of influencing income distribution, was considered to be of minor importance. Especially at the beginning, advice by the international financial institutions focused on generating greater revenue to enable countries to keep up with their debt repayments and to reduce fiscal deficits. From the early 1990s onwards, they paid greater attention than before to encouraging what was considered to be a more efficient allocation of revenues to private production and investment, but also to equity and tax administration (World Bank, 1991: 9–10). Like other market-friendly reforms undertaken in many developing countries, changes in the structure of public finances generally presupposed a trade-off between efficiency (to be optimized by relying on market forces as much as possible) and equity (requiring government intervention).

The fall of public revenue as a result of reduced trade taxes and tariffs owing to greater trade liberalization was replaced in part by higher revenue from income tax, and partly by more broad-based consumption taxes, particularly VAT. In the 1990s (and probably also in the 1980s, though no comprehensive data are available for that period), such tax reforms appear to have led to a more regressive tax system if the ratio of income tax revenue to VAT revenue is taken as a rough indicator. In the 1980s, this ratio fell in 10 out of 14 countries in Latin America and the Caribbean for which data are available (Sáinz and Calcagno, 1992). Subsequently, this ratio fell again, from an already very low average level of 0.60 in the first half of the 1990s to 0.56 in the period 2001–2005, before increasing to reach 0.64 in 2006–2010. In East, South and South-East Asia, it first rose from 1.07 in the first half of the 1990s to 1.20

in the late 1990s, and then fell to 1.11 in 2006–2010. Distinct from these two regions, in Africa the ratio of income tax revenue to VAT revenue has been rising continuously over the past 20 years, from 0.91 in the first half of the 1990s to 1.15 in 2006–2010. By contrast, the transition economies have seen, on average, a decline in this ratio, from an already low level of 0.56 in the second half of the 1990s to 0.48 in 2006–2010. While this rough indicator does not take into account possible shifts in the income tax scale or possible variations in the rates of the VAT for different types of goods and services that are consumed in different quantities by the various income groups, it suggests that the evolution of the tax system has become more regressive.

(b) Level of public revenues

The fact that in many developing countries tax systems are more regressive also explains to a large extent why the share of total public revenue in GDP is, on average, much lower in developing than in developed countries. Regressive structures of revenue collection make the system dependent on the purchasing power of the lower and middle-income groups, but since this tax base is relatively small, the yield from this source is also limited.

During the period 2006–2010, the share of total public revenue and grants in GDP in developed countries ranged from 30 per cent to almost 60 per cent, with a mean of 41.8 per cent (table 5.1). This was much higher than in developing countries, where that share was, on average, only 28.2 per cent in Africa, 20.7 per cent in East, South and South-East Asia, 27.3 per cent in Latin America, 34.2 per cent in the transition economies, and 35.8 per cent in West Asia (table 5.2). As a result, developing countries, on average, have had less scope to influence income distribution through fiscal measures.

The effects of changes in the tax structure on total public revenue have differed across countries. Several studies have found that many low-income and least developed countries experienced a decline in their public revenue in the 1980s and 1990s, mostly as result of falling income and trade taxes (Heady, 2001; Khattry and Mohan Rao, 2002; Gemmell and Morrissey, 2003). Moreover, the expected efficiency gains from trade liberalization did not materialize

partly due to the absence of fiscal schemes that could have compensated for the loss of revenue from trade taxes (Rodrik, 2006).

Available data for countries in sub-Saharan Africa and Latin America suggest that there were seldom any increases in government revenues in the 1980s and early 1990s. In the 1980s the fiscal-revenue-to-GDP ratio declined in 7 out of 14 countries in Latin America and the Caribbean (Sáinz and Calcagno, 1992). On average, Latin American countries saw a slight increase in this ratio after 1995 and especially after 2005, on account of a rise in both tax and non-tax revenues.

In Africa, the share of total public revenue in GDP fell until the second half of the 1990s, but then recovered, particularly after 2005, when rising earnings from commodity exports boosted non-tax revenues. In East, South and South-East Asia, the share of public revenue in GDP fell between 1995 and 2005, but subsequently recovered to reach almost the same level as in the first half of the 1990s. The budgets of countries in West Asia and those of the transition economies benefited from a continuous increase, on average, in public revenue as a share of GDP.

Where public revenues fell in the 1980s and 1990s, this reduced the scope for governments to enhance the development process and improve income distribution, especially as slow growth prevented an expansion of the income and consumption tax base in African and Latin American countries. These countries also experienced difficulties in borrowing on international capital markets during these years, while a large proportion of their public revenue was absorbed by high interest rates on their foreign debt and debt repayments. Thus, even where public revenue rose, it was insufficient to finance the large amounts required for investment in infrastructure to enhance growth (given the complementarity of public and private investment) and to increase social spending aimed at reducing income inequality.

Alternative sources of revenue could have been the surpluses of State-owned enterprises (SOEs), particularly in countries with rich natural resource endowments. However, from the mid-1980s onwards, in most countries many SOEs, including in the extractive industries, were privatized and the proceeds were used in large part to repay external debt.

In order to obtain the necessary foreign exchange, the privatization operations were often promoted by offering tax incentives to foreign investors, and the distribution of the rents from the exploitation of natural resources (i.e. the difference between the sales value and the cost of exploitation of natural resources) was often strongly biased in favour of the TNCs. This also led to considerably reduced gains of government revenues (*TDR 2005*, chap. III). It is only in recent years that a number of governments started to renegotiate their contracts with TNCs in the extractive sector (see *TDR 2010*, chap. V sect. 5), as reflected partly in the figures for "other revenues" in table 5.2.

In order to adjust public budgets to this shortage of revenues, many countries reduced the provision of public services, or could not expand them in line with the needs of their growing populations. Following recommendations by the international financial institutions, many of them introduced user fees for public services such as education, health care and highways, which previously had been provided without charge. While the positive effects of these measures on fiscal balances appear to have been limited, they adversely affected disposable incomes in various ways, depending on the income profiles of the different users. The imposition of user fees for highways, for instance, tends to affect mainly the richer households in developing countries who are the main consumers of such services. By contrast, school fees, especially for primary education, and medical fees are more regressive, and have often led to the exclusion of the poor and vulnerable segments of society from the use of such services.[3] This, in turn, has adverse consequences for economic growth and the future distribution of primary income, as it perpetuates low skill levels among the members of the poorest households.

In lower income countries an increase in official development assistance (ODA), especially in the form of budgetary support for countries undertaking fiscal reforms, could have compensated for the

> Market-friendly tax reforms of the 1980s and 1990s presupposed a trade-off between efficiency and equity ...

> ... However, recent experiences in Latin America and elsewhere suggest that progressive taxation can improve the fiscal balance, income distribution and economic growth.

decline in public revenues from domestic sources. However, during the 1980s ODA flows per capita stagnated, and in the first half of the 1990s they even fell dramatically, not only in per capita terms but also in absolute terms (*TDR 2008*, chap. V).

From the mid-1990s onwards, ODA disbursements recovered from a historically low level. However, much of this increase was directed at a few countries emerging from several years of conflict, or was provided in the form of debt relief, so that it had a limited effect on current budgets. Despite the increase in ODA, a large gap – in the order of $50–$60 billion per year – remained between actual ODA flows and the aid estimated to be necessary for implementing measures to achieve the Millennium Development Goals (MDGs), in particular the goal to reduce poverty by half between 2000 and 2015. On the other hand, an increasing proportion of ODA targeted health, education and other social activities, with positive effects on income distribution in the recipient countries. But since the increasing share of ODA for these purposes meant a decline in the share of ODA allocated to growth-enhancing investment in economic infrastructure and productive capacities, its effects on structural change and the creation of new employment and wage opportunities were limited (*TDR 2008*, chap. V).

Various factors contributed to the general increase in public revenues as a percentage of GDP in developing and transition economies after 2000. In some countries, especially in Africa, the increase in ODA flows was a major factor, but in general it was the result of higher tax revenues, and in countries where the primary sector accounts for a large share of GDP, it was due to higher commodity prices.

In all regions, the rise in public revenues in the 2006–2010 period was on account of higher indirect taxes and income taxes. But equally important was the rise in non-tax income in commodity-exporting countries. The rise in commodity prices helped these countries to increase their fiscal revenues significantly, in some cases by 8 to 12 percentage points of GDP between the late 1990s and 2010 (*TDR 2011*, table 2.1).[4]

For Latin America there is evidence that a growing share of commodity rents has been captured by the State in recent years (Cornia, Gómez-Sabaini and Martorano, 2011). But tax reforms introducing a more progressive tax system also drove the rise in public revenues in some Latin American countries. For example, in Uruguay a new progressive labour income tax and a flat capital income tax were introduced, while some indirect taxes were reduced, with the objective of improving the fiscal balance, income distribution and economic growth. It is estimated that this reform helped to reduce the Gini coefficient, and thus inequality in personal income distribution, by 2 percentage points, without having any discernible disincentive effect (Martorano, 2012).

4. Fiscal space and public expenditure

The design of a national revenue system and the pattern of public expenditure can influence income distribution, but the effects vary. A progressive tax system affects all income groups and their relative incomes, including the income gap between the middle-class and top income earners. On the expenditure side, social transfers and the free or subsidized provision of public services are often directed at specific groups, such as the poorest, families with many children, the elderly and the unemployed. From this perspective, social expenditure is better suited to preventing or reducing poverty and to protecting social groups that are particularly disadvantaged or vulnerable. However, to what extent public expenditure aimed at reducing inequality should be targeted to specific social groups, and how, has been subject to debate (UN/DESA, 2008).

Targeting specific groups most in need, as opposed to providing more generalized coverage, has often been suggested by the multilateral financial institution and bilateral donors as a way to achieve social objectives, especially poverty reduction, without a rise in total social spending (Besley and Kanbur, 1990; Gelbach and Pritchett, 1995). This may mean greater support to certain groups at the expense of

others who may also be in need of social support for other reasons, or it may be at the expense of public spending for purposes that are important for enhancing the development process more generally. It has also been argued that targeting requires administrative capacities and involves transaction costs, and that the selection of the groups to be targeted may often be influenced by political interests (Mkandawire, 2007). Targeting can also lead to social segmentation and differentiation that can have negative effects on social cohesion (UN/DESA, 2008).

In practice, the rationale for social spending in most countries is mixed: while certain types of spending aim to benefit society as a whole, others are targeted to specific groups that are in need of economic support and social protection. Both types of social spending in different combinations may be justified, depending on each country's specific situation. In general, the public provision of health care and education is of particular importance for overall economic development, while transfers in cash and in kind to specific segments of the population may be necessary for the eradication of extreme poverty. The main challenge, therefore, appears to be not so much to decide whether social spending should be targeted or provided universally when budgetary resources are limited, but to raise additional public revenues and, when necessary, to seek additional financial resources from international donors.

It appears that the scope for increasing public revenues through fiscal measures such as progressive taxation of high incomes may well be underestimated in many developing countries, including the poorer ones. As seen in chapter III, comparisons between the distribution of market income (gross income) and disposable income show that redistributive fiscal measures, although weakening (OECD, 2011), have been more effective in reducing inequality of disposable income in developed countries than in developing countries (Chu, Davoodi, and Gupta, 2000).[5] This is largely explained by the fact that in developing countries tax collection represents a smaller share of GDP and is less progressive (or even regressive). However governments in developed countries also tend to be more successful than those in most developing countries in influencing income distribution through greater social transfers and better public provision of social services. Most developing countries have fewer public financial resources for these purposes.

Policy reforms under structural adjustment programmes of the 1980s and 1990s failed to provide adequate protection and services to a majority of the population. The provision of health services, to be financed through cost recovery or pre-payment schemes, became "less accessible and less affordable and worse" in many African countries (Narayan et al., 2000: 87; UNCTAD, 2002). In Latin America, the quality of education provision varies, with the lower income groups having access to lower quality educational services (ECLAC, 2010). With respect to Latin America's pension systems, coverage declined across the board after the reforms that privatized the public pay-as-you-go systems (Mesa-Lago, 2004). Owing to falling or insufficiently growing government revenues – in particular in a period of growing debt service – the level of social transfers and provision of public goods necessary to tackle growing inequality were inadequate. In addition, overall GDP growth remained subdued despite greater income inequality.

Since the late 1990s, and especially after 2002, a rise in public revenues has enabled governments in some developing and transition economies to enlarge their fiscal space, including for taking measures aimed at reducing inequality. In addition to an increase in government revenues as a share of GDP, a reduction of the interest burden on the public debt since the late 1990s has also contributed to the enlargement of fiscal space in many countries. The lower interest burden was partly the result of lower international interest rates in countries that are primarily indebted to private creditors, and partly due to debt relief in countries primarily indebted to official creditors. Indeed, the unprecedented amount of official debt relief that has been granted to developing countries since the mid-1990s reduced the share of public finances that had to be allocated to debt repayment in a number of low- and middle-income countries. However, the impact of international debt relief on developing countries has varied considerably, especially between those that benefited from the Heavily Indebted Poor Countries initiative (and later the Multilateral Debt Relief Initiative) and others that did not. Moreover,

> Structural adjustment programmes of the 1980s and 1990s failed to provide adequate protection and services to a majority of the population.

there is no clear evidence that debt relief has been additional to other forms of aid (*TDR 2008*, chap. VI; UNCTAD, 2008). In many instances the debt relief provided has been insufficient to allow the redirecting of significant funds for enhancing infrastructure development and for reducing inequality. In some countries this has meant that governments have had to incur new debt, including domestically.

To the extent that a greater amount of public revenues have become available over the past decade, governments in several countries have been able to increase their current and capital expenditures, especially in Latin America, and to a lesser degree in Africa and East, South-East and South Asia more recently (table 5.3). At the same time many of them have been able to reduce their fiscal deficits, in some cases even generating a fiscal surplus. In Latin America, the mean total public expenditure rose by 5.3 percentage points of GDP and the mean total current expenditure by 4.9 percentage points between the early 1990s and late 2000s. In Africa, they increased by 3.8 percentage points and 1.5 percentage points, respectively, between the late 1990s and late 2000s.[6]

One important effect that higher fiscal revenues can have on income distribution is that it increases the potential for redistributive effects by lowering the tax burden for low-income groups. In the short run, enlarged fiscal space also allows an increase in public expenditures for infrastructure investment, improving the provision of public goods and expanding cash transfer programmes.

Public investment increased in Africa, Latin America and West Asia, and at the same time public debt and interest payments declined as a percentage of GDP. The increase in public investment is a key factor for enabling structural change and employment generation, not only because of its direct demand effects, but also because it is often necessary for inducing private fixed investment to follow or to take place in parallel.

Table 5.3

FISCAL EXPENDITURE, SELECTED REGIONS AND COUNTRY GROUPS, 1991–2010

(Per cent of current GDP)

	1991–1995	1996–2000	2001–2005	2006–2010
Developed countries				
Total expenditure	47.4	44.1	43.1	44.5
of which:				
Capital expenditure	5.0	4.6	4.3	4.7
Current expenditure	42.5	39.6	38.8	39.7
of which:				
Interest payments	5.2	3.9	2.7	2.3
Africa				
Total expenditure	26.6	23.8	26.2	27.6
of which:				
Capital expenditure	5.5	5.5	6.6	7.8
Current expenditure	21.1	18.3	19.6	19.8
of which:				
Interest payments	2.7	2.4	2.5	1.7
Latin America				
Total expenditure	24.5	26.6	27.7	29.8
of which:				
Capital expenditure	5.2	5.3	4.6	5.7
Current expenditure	19.3	21.3	23.1	24.2
of which:				
Interest payments	2.8	2.8	3.3	2.3
East, South and South-East Asia				
Total expenditure	22.0	20.7	21.5	22.1
of which:				
Capital expenditure	5.7	5.1	4.8	4.8
Current expenditure	16.3	15.5	16.7	17.3
of which:				
Interest payments	4.4	2.5	2.5	2.1
West Asia				
Total expenditure	37.7	33.6	32.0	30.0
of which:				
Capital expenditure	4.9	5.0	5.7	6.5
Current expenditure	32.8	28.5	26.3	23.6
of which:				
Interest payments	2.7	4.7	4.1	2.2
Transition economies				
Total expenditure	..	36.1	30.7	33.1
of which:				
Capital expenditure	..	5.9	4.6	5.1
Current expenditure	..	30.2	26.1	28.1
of which:				
Interest payments	..	1.9	1.1	0.6

Source: UNCTAD secretariat calculations, based on Eurostat, *Statistics Database*; OECD.StatExtracts database; ECLAC, *CEPALSTAT*; IMF, *World Economic Outlook* and *Government Finance Statistics* databases; and national sources.

Note: Data refer to the five-year average of the mean observation. East, South and South-East Asia comprises: China, China, Hong Kong SAR, Taiwan Province of China, India, Indonesia, the Islamic Republic of Iran, the Republic of Korea, Malaysia, Nepal, the Philippines, Singapore, Sri Lanka, Thailand and Viet Nam. (Data for China refer to budget revenue and expenditure; they do not include extra-budgetary funds or social security funds.) Latin America comprises: Argentina, Bolivia, the Bolivarian Republic of Venezuela, Brazil, Chile, Colombia, Costa Rica, Cuba (only for revenue indicators), Dominican Republic, Ecuador, El Salvador, Guatemala, Haiti, Honduras, Mexico, Nicaragua, Panama, Paraguay, Peru and Uruguay. Africa excludes: Botswana, Burkina Faso, Equatorial Guinea, Lesotho, Liberia, Madagascar, Mauritania, Mayotte, Saint Helena, Seychelles, Somalia, Western Sahara and Zimbabwe. West Asia excludes: Iraq, Jordan, Occupied Palestinian Territory and Yemen. Transition economies excludes Montenegro.

J. Influencing income distribution through public spending

Improved fiscal accounts have also enabled governments to influence income distribution through the better provision of public goods, including education. In Latin America, for example, public expenditure on education increased from 4.1 per cent to 5.2 per cent of GDP between 2000 and 2010.[7] It was accompanied by an increase in secondary school enrolment rates, from 72 per cent to 86 per cent, and an increase in the number of years of education of the workforce from 7.4 years to 8.2 years.[8]

An enlarged fiscal space can have a more immediate effect on income distribution to the extent that it is used for increasing social transfers. Indeed, parallel with enlarging their fiscal space, many developing and transition economies have undertaken reforms in the area of social protection. In particular, there has been a fairly sizeable expansion of social protection in Latin America and in some South-East Asian countries over the past decade.

A review of recent experiences suggests that social transfers and the public provision of social services can be powerful tools for reducing inequality of disposable incomes. Detailed international data on social expenditure spanning the past two decades are rather scarce, but data on current public expenditure suggest that public spending aimed at reducing inequality may have risen. In Latin America, in 7 countries out of 10 for which ECLAC provides data, public spending on subsidies and other current transfers increased significantly, though in some cases from relatively low levels. The increases ranged between 50 per cent and more than 200 per cent. In Argentina, for instance, these expenditures increased from a 3-year average of 8.2 per cent of GDP in 1990–1992 to 14.8 per cent in 2007–2009, and in the Bolivarian Republic of Venezuela they rose from 7 per cent to 13.9 per cent of GDP during the same period.

Since 2002, the widespread introduction of targeted social assistance in the form of conditional and non-conditional cash transfers appears to have had a sizeable impact on income inequality in Latin America (Cornia, 2012). In the transition economies, both total and current government expenditure as percentage of GDP rose by more than 2 percentage points or more between 2001–2005 and 2006–2010.

In East, South and South-East Asia, although the share of government social expenditures in GDP rose less, in absolute terms it increased significantly. By contrast in West Asia, the share of such expenditure in GDP fell, though it remained higher than in Africa and other parts of Asia.

Some examples of social expenditure programmes that have recently been introduced in developing and transition economies following an enlargement of their fiscal space are presented below.

In Latin America, the failure of the earlier market-friendly policy reforms prompted a fundamental rethinking of the approach to social policy (Huber, 2009). The new approach aims at providing broad social protection against significant risks, improving access to social transfers for those in need, and greater provision of public services and goods with the same quality standards for all groups of society. Entitlements are based on citizenship and are conferred as rights, with a minimum of discretionary authority on the part of the agencies concerned, but the entitlements are also linked to corresponding obligations (Filgueira et al., 2006). This principle has shaped a number of new initiatives, such as a universal child allowance in Argentina, a universal old-age pension in Bolivia, and an old-age pension, and disability, sickness and maternity benefits in Brazil (ILO, 2010 and 2012).

In parallel, key instruments of social policy for poverty alleviation and redistribution, including conditional cash transfers (CCTs), have been introduced in a number of countries.[9] Non-contributory expenditures on social assistance in general, and CCTs in particular, appear to have been quite effective in protecting the poorest segments of society (Lindert, Skoufias and Shapiro, 2006; Cornia 2012), making the overall effects of the public finance system more progressive. There is also evidence that democratization and the abandonment of clientelism have improved the incidence of social expenditure (Lopez-Calva and Lustig, 2010). Such tax-financed programmes can have a stronger inequality reducing effect than social insurance schemes, even if unit transfers are relatively small (Skoufias, Lindert and Shapiro, 2010; Goñi, López and Servén, 2011). Significant fiscal redistribution in Latin America has also been achieved through in-kind transfers, such as the provision of health and education services provided cost-free or at a low cost.

In sub-Saharan Africa, only a few countries, mainly in Eastern and Southern Africa have expanded their social protection programmes so far. Social protection in this region differs from other developing regions in terms of coverage, quality and level of assistance. Until the late 1990s, formal social protection schemes covered, on average, less than 5 per cent of the workforce (Palacios and Pallarés-Millares, 2000). More recently, two types of social assistance schemes have been introduced. One, applied in some countries of Southern Africa, aims at old-age protection; the other targets extreme poverty, and is applied mostly in low-income countries in Central, East and West Africa (Niño-Zarazúa et al., 2012: 163–164).

In many Southern African countries, non-contributory social pension schemes that formerly targeted only certain groups of elderly poor have been extended to provide almost universal coverage, without discrimination by ethnic origin, and they are largely tax-funded. In many Southern African countries, the provision of non-contributory social pension schemes that targeted the elderly poor of certain ethnic groups have been extended as domestic initiatives no longer based on racial discrimination. This scheme is largely tax-funded, and the transfer payments to the elderly are almost universal. In Lesotho, Namibia, South Africa and Swaziland, the pension schemes reach between 80 and 100 per cent of the elderly at an estimated cost of 1–3 per cent of GDP (Barrientos, Niño-Zarazúa, and Maitrot, 2010; Devereux, 2007; Niño-Zarazúa et al., 2012). In Southern Africa, family structures have enhanced the effectiveness of income transfers since old-age grants are, in practice, income transfers to poor households with older people. This is because they tend to be deployed by recipient families for children's schooling, for improved health care and for reallocating productive resources within households (Barrientos, 2008; Møller and Sotshangaye, 1996).

Several of the new transfer programmes in Central, East and West Africa are financed largely by ODA. And in many cases their design reflects the influence of international organizations and changing donor priorities as they attempt to shift their support from emergency and humanitarian aid to social protection.[10] These programmes have also benefited the recipient countries in terms of improving their fiscal space. The latter is a result of both debt relief and increased public revenues from faster growth and from natural resource exploitation in several countries. These recent experiences suggest that even in poor countries it is politically, fiscally and administratively feasible to implement social protection programmes (Giovannetti and Sanfilippo, 2011). However, they also show that in countries with a small fiscal base, increases in ODA remain crucial for institution-building.

In Asia, reforms of social protection systems vary considerably, reflecting a host of historical and other factors, including the level of economic development and the structure of the different economies. Several developing Asian countries, such as Bangladesh, Cambodia, Pakistan, and, more recently, Indonesia and the Philippines, have implemented CCT programmes over the past decade (ADB, 2012: 78). In the Republic of Korea, the expansion of the welfare system has strengthened the redistributive capacity of fiscal policies (Sung, 2009), with the largest contribution originating from direct taxation and cash transfers.[11] Redistributive policies in Thailand focus on poor rural areas,[12] while reform of the social protection system includes the provision of monetary transfers to the elderly poor, universal health coverage and 15 years of free education. In Malaysia, social objectives have traditionally been an integral part of the country's development strategy and constituted an important element of the National Development Policy (1991–2000) and the National Vision Policy (2001–2010) (Ragayah, 2011: 2).[13] In addition, the country's regional development strategy seeks to achieve balanced growth between the different regions of the country, regulate migration to urban areas and promote agricultural development. In all these efforts, State investments in infrastructure (transport, water and electricity, health and education) have been of paramount importance. However, in many developing Asian countries social protection usually has limited coverage. Moreover, the possibility to shield the poor against negative shocks remains constrained by the insufficient amount of resources allocated to social protection (ADB, 2008).

> Recent experiences suggest that social transfers and the public provision of social services can be powerful tools for reducing inequality of disposable incomes.

In China, the transition from a planned to a market economy has been accompanied by reform of the social security system. Work-related social insurance programmes, in particular for urban residents, were redesigned. In response to the emergence of urban poverty since the mid-1990s, the Government has shifted its emphasis to means-tested social assistance programmes as a major tool for combating poverty and maintaining social stability. As a result, the coverage of the Minimum Living Standard Guarantee System has been growing since the late 1990s, particularly in the coastal areas. In the western and central provinces, however, a significant proportion of the eligible population remains uncovered owing to insufficient funds at the disposal of local governments (Tang, Sha and Ren, 2003). Meanwhile, there is some support for housing, health care, education, employment and social services, but some argue that it needs to be further institutionalized (Leung, 2006). It has also been suggested that strengthening social policies and institutions that protect people against the many hazards associated with the rapid structural change China has been undergoing would help ensure that the benefits from fast growth are distributed to a larger proportion of the population (Xiulan and Yuebin, 2010).

In India, since the initiation of economic planning in 1951, there has been a long tradition of social transfers by both the central and state governments through a range of measures aimed at improving socio-economic security.[14] However, the large, centrally administered national programmes for poverty reduction had only limited success. Therefore in the 1980s more flexible schemes were implemented at a lower level of government with greater participatory and political oversight. A range of programmes aimed at reinforcing education and skills acquisition have also been initiated gradually since the 1990s by both the central and state governments,[15] but their effects have not yet fully materialized. Consequently, so far they have not prevented a significant rise of income inequality, especially in urban areas, since the beginning of the 1990s.

In several transition economies of Central Asia, recent social transfer schemes have not been particularly effective in addressing the needs of poor households owing to their limited coverage and funding (Gassmann, 2011). The social welfare policies of universal entitlement to State subsidies, inherited from the former Soviet Union, often means that meagre resources for social pensions are spread thinly over a large population. In addition, in many countries the design of transfer programmes appears to be inadequate. In Tajikistan, for instance, only 43 per cent of poor households receive transfers from the Government, while 33 per cent of non-poor households receive transfers (Son, 2012). Moreover, owing to decentralized budgets, poor localities that are the most in need tend to receive the least financial support. Hence, spending on social protection measures may need to be given greater priority as an item in the central government budget to ensure sustained and predictable funding (Gassmann, 2011). In the region's poorest countries, opportunities for rapid reforms seem to be more limited in the absence of increased domestic revenues. These countries therefore require additional external support for this purpose.

C. Policy recommendations

1. *Learning from experience*

Despite growing awareness of the social problems associated with increasing inequality, the design of fiscal policy in a large number of countries continues to be based on the belief that it is by minimizing State intervention not only in the economy in general, but also in favour of a more equal income distribution in particular, that maximum welfare for a society can be achieved. However, the market-friendly tax reforms that were undertaken over the past three decades based on this belief did not achieve their objective. When the redistributive elements in tax systems were weakened, thereby reinforcing the tendency towards greater inequality, the increase in the share of capital in GDP was not accompanied by the expected rise of fixed investment.

This shows that looking primarily, or exclusively, at the formal incidence of taxes and other public charges (i.e. the apparent income reduction for those who have to pay a higher tax) often leads to wrong assessment of the overall effects of a fiscal measure. Such a view fails to consider the benefits for the economy as a whole from a more equitable distribution of income and wealth resulting from fiscal measures – both on the revenue and expenditure side. First, there is a social return for taxpayers, even though it may not be proportional to each income group's tax burden. This return consists of direct benefits, in the form of overall government services and the provision of improved infrastructure, as well as indirect benefits for all in the form of greater social peace and cohesion when revenues are spent in a way that helps to reduce inequality and poverty and the likelihood of corruption and crime.

Second, and probably even more important, are the effects of the budgetary spending on aggregate demand and real income. Government expenditure, no matter how this is financed, has direct effects on income. Government revenues feed back into the economy as public spending which supplements private demand. It is often forgotten that the net demand effect of raising the average tax rate and, in parallel, overall government expenditure, is positive, since some of the additional tax payments are at the expense of the savings of taxpayers, while spending of the tax revenue will cause aggregate demand to rise by the full amount of the tax yield (Haavelmo, 1945).

The design of fiscal policy should also take into account the tax structure's indirect effects on demand, since it influences the pattern of net disposable incomes across different social groups. Aggregate consumption and the incentive for private firms to undertake fixed investments is greater when a given national income is distributed more equally, because lower income groups spend a larger share of their income on consumption than higher income groups. This is of particular importance in situations of high or rising unemployment.

Redistribution through fiscal measures may therefore be in the interest of society as a whole, especially where inequality is particularly pronounced as in many developing countries. This is supported by the experience in developed countries,

> The scope for using progressive taxation and government spending for reducing inequality and supporting economic growth is greater than is commonly assumed.

as investment rates were not lower – but indeed often higher – in the first three decades of the post-war era, even though taxes on profits and top incomes were higher than after the widespread fiscal reforms implemented subsequently. There are strong reasons to believe that the willingness of entrepreneurs to invest in new productive capacity does not depend primarily on net profits at a given point in time, but on their expectations regarding future demand for the goods and services they can produce with additional capacity. This is of particular importance when considering the overall effect of an increase in corporate taxes. Provided that higher tax revenues are used for additional government expenditures, companies' expectations of a growth in demand will improve. This demand effect is independent of whether the additional government expenditures take the form of government consumption, public investment or social transfers. When the level of fixed investment is maintained as a result of favourable demand expectations, gross profits will rise – and generally so will net profits, notwithstanding the initial tax increase. In the process, additional income and employment will be created for the economy as a whole.

Based on these considerations, the role of fiscal measures as instruments for simultaneously stimulating economic activity and improving income distribution can be viewed in a different light. Indeed, the scope for using taxation and government spending for reducing inequality without compromising economic growth is likely to be much greater than is commonly assumed. Taxing high incomes at higher rates by using progressive scales does not remove the absolute advantage of richer individuals and does not take away the incentive for entrepreneurs to innovate and move up the income ladder. Taxing wealth and inherited fortunes may even be considered a means to providing incentives to the next generation to engage in economic activities in a manner that maximizes outcomes for society as a whole instead of relying on inherited fortunes.

2. Taxation, distribution and growth

As shown in chapter III, the share of income accruing to the highest percentiles has recently become larger in several developed countries. This means that in these countries there is greater potential

for boosting government tax revenues, or for alleviating the tax burden of middle- and lower income groups, by increasing the top marginal rate. Clearly, there are upper and lower limits to the level of taxation. The lower limits are determined by the need to finance a minimum amount of public investment and services. The upper limits are difficult to determine due to the endogeneity of tax revenue (discussed in the next subsection), but also due to uncertainty about how the economic behaviour of taxpayers will respond to changes in tax rates. If tax rates are raised above a certain threshold, which is, however, impossible to determine precisely, the behavioural response of those who have to bear the greatest share of the tax burden may cause the tax base to shrink along with the economic activity that determines the tax base.

However, even on this count, the scope for higher marginal tax rates imposed on top incomes or on corporate profits is likely to be larger than is often assumed. One recent study has found that current top income tax rates in most OECD countries are well below those at which the total tax yield would be maximized (Piketty, Saez and Stantcheva, 2011). According to this study, revenue-maximizing top marginal income tax rates range between 57 per cent and 83 per cent. The lower bound rate refers to the taxation of top incomes from "productive" work, while the upper bound rate refers to the taxation of top incomes resulting from both rent-seeking activities (i.e. personal enrichment from capturing a larger slice of existing production rather than by increasing it) and productive work. In any case, these figures contrast sharply with the actual average of the top marginal income tax rate of 43 per cent in the 18 OECD countries during the 2004–2008 period. During this period, only three of these countries had average top marginal tax rates slightly above the lower bound of this range (57 per cent). To the extent that the income of the highest percentiles arises from rent-seeking activities, the impact of rising top income marginal tax rates on economic growth may even be beneficial because it will discourage rent-grabbing behaviour and increase others' revenues.

It is also worth noting that fiscal policy pursues multiple objectives. From the point of view of development, fiscal measures that provide direct support to private fixed investment are essential. But the issue here is not to keep taxation of profits at a minimum; indeed, the gradual decline of the statutory corporate income tax rates did not lead to a rise in gross fixed capital formation (GFCF) in developed countries from the 1990s onwards (chart 5.3). Rather, what is needed is a differentiation in taxation of profits based on the origin of the profits and how they are used. For example, profits from productive entrepreneurial activity may be taxed at a lower rate than profits from purely financial activity, especially speculation and "unearned" capital gains that provide no benefits for the overall economy.

This is of particular concern in light of the immense expansion of the financial sector. Taxation of transactions in equity, bond, currency and derivatives markets, applied internationally or nationally, may help check a further expansion of destabilizing speculative activity that is conducted at the expense of financing real investment, while also having a progressive incidence (see also UN/DESA, 2012). Similarly, taxing bonuses in the financial sector at a higher rate than regular wage incomes may reduce the incentive for excessive risk taking.[16] In a financial-ized economy, taxation of capital gains – which so far has typically been lower than taxation of income from productive activities – and its differentiation between short-term and long-term changes in the value of financial and real assets, may also be worth considering in many countries. Again, it is justified on the grounds of reducing the incentives for short-term speculative investments and having the effect of increasing the progressive incidence of the tax system (Dodd, 2007; Toder and Banemann, 2012).

Additionally, in developed and developing countries alike, reinvested profits in the non-financial sector may be taxed at a lower rate than distributed profits. Moreover, a further differentiation could be made across specific areas of activity so as to provide incentives in support of a profit-investment nexus that helps to influence the direction and speed of structural change (*TDR 1997*, chaps. V and VI). In developing countries, taxing consumption of luxury goods at a higher rate than mass consumption, besides having a progressive incidence, may also help in this regard.

It should also be noted, however, that an increase in the progressivity of a tax system may not always imply proportionally stronger public finances as a whole. This is the case, for example, when the tax yield from imposing higher taxes on high-income groups is channelled back to more or less the same income groups in the form of interest payments on government bonds, which are typically held in large

Chart 5.3

STATUTORY CORPORATE INCOME TAX RATES AND GROSS FIXED CAPITAL FORMATION IN SELECTED DEVELOPED COUNTRIES, 1982–2005

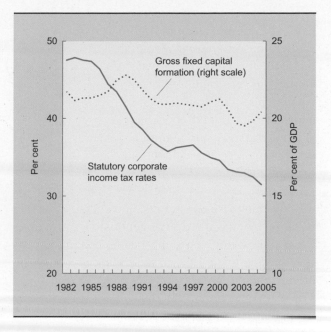

Source: UNCTAD secretariat calculations, based on an updated version of Devereux, Griffith and Klemm, 2002, at: http://www.ifs.org.uk/corptax/internationaltaxdata.zip.

Note: The data refer to the average of the following countries: Australia, Austria, Belgium, Canada, Finland, France, Germany, Greece, Ireland, Italy, Japan, the Netherlands, Norway, Portugal, Spain, Sweden, Switzerland, the United Kingdom and the United States.

part by the wealthier segments of a population. By the same token, an individual regressive tax may not necessarily contribute to greater inequality if the tax yield is spent in such a manner that it has a progressive effect, for example through social transfers and improved public services. What matters, therefore, is the progressivity of the fiscal system as a whole in terms of the structure of both taxation and public expenditure.

3. Fiscal space in developing countries

The considerations in the preceding section are relevant for developed countries, emerging market economies and other developing countries alike, even though there are large differences in the structure of their public finances and in their administrative capacities to effectively raise certain types of public revenue. A major difference is also that fiscal space in most developing countries is more strongly influenced by international factors that are beyond their control, such as fluctuations of commodity prices and international interest rates, and the availability of external financing in the form of either private capital inflows or ODA. And fiscal space in low-income and least developed countries is smaller almost by definition (i.e. owing to their low level of national income).

Within these constraints, however, fiscal space is largely determined endogenously. A proactive fiscal policy influences the macroeconomic situation and the overall tax base through its impact on private sector incomes (see also *TDR 2011*, chap. II). Where private consumption and investment are weak, an appropriate expansionary fiscal policy can boost demand expectations and the willingness to invest, thereby enlarging the tax base. This will also enhance the scope of governments to raise additional revenue to finance expenditure that reduces inequality, or to restructure the pattern of taxation across different income groups. By contrast, general fiscal retrenchment, as currently pursued in many developed countries, but also under adjustment programmes in developing and transition economies, owing to its negative impact on aggregate demand and the tax base, will lead to lower fiscal revenues and thereby reduce the scope for such fiscal action.

Suitably designed reforms of direct taxation can simultaneously achieve the goals of lowering income inequality and boosting growth of output and employment creation in developed and developing countries alike. The low degree of progressivity in developing and transition economies' tax systems and the large differences between regions and countries in this regard suggest that in many of these countries there is considerable scope for tackling income inequality effectively through more progressive taxation. Of course, this requires not only a change in perspective regarding the role of public

> Appropriating a greater share of commodity rents could benefit the entire population, and not just a few domestic and foreign actors.

> Strengthening international cooperation in tax matters could help avoid a downward spiral in competition for FDI and reduce tax evasion.

finances, but also a relatively high degree of formal employment and suitable administrative capacity. In this regard, developing countries' capacities to raise specific revenues vary greatly, depending on their level of development, the size of their informal sector and the composition of their GDP.

On the other hand, there are a number of potential sources of revenue that can contribute to improving equality while increasing government revenues, including in low-income countries. Taxation of wealth and inheritance is one such potential source that can be tapped in many developing countries for these purposes. This demands less administrative capacity, is harder to circumvent and has a progressive effect.

In resource-rich developing countries, income from the exploitation of natural resources and gains from rising international commodity prices are other potentially important sources of public revenue. By appropriating a greater share of commodity rents, governments can ensure that their countries' natural resource wealth benefits the entire population, and not just a few domestic and foreign actors. There appears to be considerable scope in many countries for collecting a larger amount of royalties and taxes, especially from companies active in the oil, gas and mining sectors. This is particularly important because the revenue potential from natural resources has grown significantly over the past decade owing to higher commodity prices and the discovery of new sources of energy, especially in Africa.

When terms-of-trade gains from commodity prices are expected to be temporary, they cannot serve as a solid basis for a sustained increase in government revenues and, in parallel, in public spending. However, even if temporary, the higher rents or windfall profits in the primary sector can still be used to help accelerate productivity growth and job creation elsewhere in the economy. This requires special taxation of the windfall profits and channelling them into productive investments elsewhere in the economy. The accumulation of unstable income of this kind in sovereign wealth funds or national development banks and spreading the use of these funds over time for specific social purposes may help to prevent a further increase in income inequality. High taxation of such windfall profits is especially justified since those profits are not the result of entrepreneurial success but of gyrations in international commodity prices that are beyond the influence of the individual commodity producer.

Another issue with regard to tax policies in developing countries is the treatment of TNCs and FDI, not only in the mining sector but also in the manufacturing and services sectors. While the activities of TNCs and FDI inflows have the potential to strengthen the productive capacity of host countries, this potential is not always fully exploited when the linkages with domestic producers remain weak. Nevertheless, developing countries often try to attract additional FDI by offering investors far-reaching – and sometimes excessive – fiscal concessions. Although these strategies have often been successful in attracting FDI, they may be worth reconsidering, because offering large tax concessions to attract FDI to the manufacturing sector generally involves competing with other potential host countries that are also offering concessions. This is problematic, since it creates a downward spiral in taxation that reduces the fiscal space of all the countries concerned. Moreover, any initial tax advantages will erode over time.

Strengthened international cooperation in tax matters could help avoid such tax competition, while preserving both the fiscal space of governments in countries that compete for production locations and the relative advantage that can be had from FDI on the basis of labour cost differentials (see also chapter VI below). Governments of the home countries of foreign investors could help prevent such tax competition by taxing profit remittances from FDI at a higher rate than domestic profits while deducting from the tax charge the typically much lower taxes already paid on the corporate profit in the host country. Taking into account the large differences in unit labour costs between the home and host countries, this could be done in such a way that the profits of the foreign investors from their production in the developing country would still be a multiple of those that would result from the production of the same goods at home.

Strengthened international cooperation on taxation is also necessary to reduce tax evasion. For this purpose, the current United Nations Committee of Experts on International Cooperation in Tax Matters could be made into a truly intergovernmental body. A new treaty based on the *United Nations Model Double Taxation Convention between Developed and Developing Countries: 2011 Update*[17] would support the interests of developing countries better than the one based on the current OECD model, since the former gives more taxing rights to developing countries.

Increasing public revenues with measures such as those discussed above would be important, though not sufficient, for enhancing the impact of fiscal policy on income distribution; much will also depend on how the increased revenues are spent, as discussed in the next section.

In several low-income and least developed countries it may be difficult or impossible to promptly implement any of these measures to increase fiscal space, because of their limited administrative and tax collecting capacities. In these cases, the multilateral financial institutions and bilateral donors would need to help by providing additional resources for social spending, as well as the appropriate technical and financial support for strengthening those capacities.

4. Public spending to reduce inequality

External financial support to low-income countries for social spending is all the more important for reducing inequality, since the lower the level of a country's income, the more limited is its scope for achieving some redistribution through progressive taxation. For many developing countries, increasing the progressive incidence of the public budget is probably best achieved through well-targeted redistributive spending, but also through growth-enhancing public investment.

Public investment in infrastructure, health and education, as well as environmental protection can create the conditions for higher productivity, diversification of production and decent formal employment in the rest of the economy. This also holds for the provision of fiscal incentives and improved public services within the framework of industrial policies aimed at diversification of economic activities. Generally, these measures may not reduce inequality directly, but they could contribute to strengthening a dynamic process of structural change through which fiscal instruments, and incomes policies (as discussed in chapter VI of this *Report*), would become more effective.

Taxing the rich to provide better public education may reduce inequality and promote faster growth. However, the provision of public services should also include the middle classes in order to raise overall skill levels, which will ultimately also contribute to a more equal income distribution and to an enlarged tax base in the future.

Increased government transfers may help reduce criminal activities as well, thereby alleviating social tensions and instability, and further stimulating investment and growth. There is evidence of a positive relationship between direct government transfers and growth. Public employment schemes, such as those launched in a number of developing countries in recent years (*TDR 2010*, chap. V), may have a positive effect on income distribution through several channels. First, they provide an income to workers who would otherwise be unemployed and who lack protection through any unemployment benefit scheme. Second, they help to establish an effective wage floor, similar to minimum wages imposed on employers in the formal private sector. Third, the additional demand for goods and services generated this way could help expand markets, and drive output growth and employment generation elsewhere in the economy, which in turn would contribute to enlarging the tax base. Fourth, they could be combined with projects to improve infrastructure and the provision of public services. Finally, such schemes could attract workers from the informal sector and provide them with professional skills, or enhance their existing skills, which would improve their employment prospects subsequently in the formal sector. There is evidence that public sector employment schemes can contribute to faster growth,

> A progressive income tax, income transfers of various kinds to low-income groups and improved access to education and skills acquisition may contribute to correcting income inequality ...

> ... At the same time, these measures can support domestic demand and boost growth and employment creation in the economy as a whole.

and that they can be successfully implemented even in low-income countries with a low administrative capacity (Weeks, 2010).

The capacity of countries to introduce social security schemes, such as old-age pension funds or unemployment benefits, also depends to a large extent on their stage of development. On the other hand, the existence of such institutions and the size of the population covered can have positive effects on the process of structural change, development, and in the case of unemployment insurance schemes, on macroeconomic stability. Similar to other fiscal measures, they can also provide incentives for the self-employed and for workers in the informal sector to join the formal sector, even if the wages there are not higher. For the lowest income groups in developing countries, social transfers of this kind need to be financed from overall public revenues so as to achieve the desired distributional effects and ensure as broad a coverage as possible. For the middle- and high-income groups, social security may be based on specific individual contributions that determine individual entitlements. Even if a progressive element is built into such schemes, establishing a link between contributions and entitlements would increase the motivation of the population to contribute to the fiscal base (Huber, 2009). International financial institutions and bilateral donors can support the creation of such schemes by allocating ODA for such purposes.

Governments may also use the proceeds from higher tax revenues for different forms of concessional lending and technical support in favour of small producers in both the industrial and rural sectors. Apart from supporting productivity and income growth in these activities, the provision of such financing could also serve as a vehicle to attract small-scale entrepreneurs and workers into the formal sector. They would thus become part of a socio-economic dynamic that builds on various institutions, including social and labour market institutions. Similarly, when governments manage to obtain gains from rents and windfall profits resulting from commodity exports in international foreign currency, they may channel these proceeds to national public financial institutions that provide foreign exchange credits to investors in other sectors for the acquisition of capital goods and technologies from abroad.

In conclusion, a progressive income tax, income transfers of various kinds to low-income groups and improved access to education and skills acquisition may contribute to correcting inequality in the distribution of incomes. At the same time, these measures can support domestic demand and boost growth and employment creation in the economy as a whole. However, there are limits to achieving greater equality in personal income distribution in this way. A comprehensive policy approach to reversing the trend towards greater inequality will require a broader reorientation of economic policy that takes into account the dynamics linking productive investment, growth and income distribution, which are influenced by labour market and macroeconomic policies. These aspects are discussed in the next chapter. ■

Notes

1   Econometric estimates confirm this interpretation of the charts. For chart 5.2A, the regression of the real per capita GDP growth rate over the entire period on the change in the top marginal income tax rate using robust standard errors gives a non-significant coefficient at the 10 per cent threshold (p-value = 0.126) and a very low R-squared (R-squared = 0.07). For chart 5.2B, the regression of the change in the top 1 per cent income share on the change in the top marginal income tax rate using robust standard errors gives a highly significant coefficient (p-value = 0.001) and a much higher R-squared (R-squared = 0.50).

2   A review of the system of government revenue collection in the United States until the 1930s shows that the government at that time relied primarily on tariffs, selective excise tax, and, eventually, a corporate income tax for its revenues. In addition, a century ago, United States tax revenues, measured as a share of GDP, were much smaller than they are at present (Hinrichs, 1966).

3   For further discussions on this issue, see Reddy and Vandemoortele, 1996; Devarajan and Reinikka, 2004; and Dupas, 2011.

4   In Latin America, it has been calculated that the increase in fiscal space after 2002 was largely due to higher commodity prices. Revenues from taxes, profits and royalties from commodities accounted for as much as 50 per cent of some countries' total increase in fiscal revenues as a share of GDP. The other main contribution to revenue growth derived from a new emphasis on progressive taxation (Cornia, Gómez-Sabaini and Martorano, 2011).

5   However, substantial anecdotal evidence suggests that local residents in many communities in developing countries contribute substantially to the construction and maintenance of local public goods outside the formal tax system, and thus their contributions are not recorded (e.g. Ostrom, 1991). People contribute to social welfare projects in the form of both money and labour, in often complex arrangements that determine how much each household should pay and what penalties apply to free riders (Olken and Singhal, 2011). Given the nature of these arrangements, it is likely that the contributions are quite progressive. For more information about such informal arrangements in developing countries, see Schneider and Enste, 2000.

6   Because there is a great variation in the composition of countries in Africa between the periods 1991–1995 and 2006–2010, the calculations were made for the periods 1996–2000 and 2006–2010 to avoid spurious computations reflecting changes in the composition of the sample.

7   UNCTAD secretariat calculations, based on UNESCO, *Institute for Statistics* database and World Bank, *World Development Indicators* database.

8   Data referring to secondary school enrolment and the number of years of education come, respectively, from UNESCO, *Institute for Statistics* database and ECLAC, 2011.

9   CCTs, which consist of small cash transfers to poor families, are conditional on certain behaviours, such as regular school attendance and ensuring health check-ups of their children of a certain age. They are widely used to address the problem of keeping poor children in school and to encourage greater access to health care. Originating in Brazil and Mexico, CCTs have become an increasingly popular tool for combating poverty, with more than 30 countries now providing such programmes (Fiszbein, Schady and Ferreira, 2009; Fried 2012; ILO, 2012).

10 The new wave of social transfer programmes includes: the Social Cash Transfer Scheme launched in 2003 in Zambia; the Orphans and Vulnerable Children Programme launched in 2004 in Kenya; the Productive Safety Net Programme launched in 2005 in Ethiopia; the Livelihood Empowerment Against Poverty programme launched in 2008 in Ghana; as well as the recent scaling up of the Food Subsidy Programme in Mozambique and the Mchinji (social cash transfer) Programme targeting the ultra poor and labour-constrained households in Malawi. Several smaller pilot programmes in other countries in West, Central and East Africa also exist, but remain at a more experimental stage (ODI and UNICEF, 2009).

11 The Government responded to the Asian crisis by strengthening the protection system, which was built on "five social insurance programs (Industrial Accident Insurance, National Health Insurance, National Pension Program, Employment Insurance Program, and Long-Term Care Insurance), one social assistance program (the Minimum Living Standard Guarantee), and public pension programs for special categories" (Kwon, Dong and Moon, 2010: 8). In addition, a minimum living standard guarantee scheme offers benefits to poor people, provided they participate in training, public works projects or community service (Kwon, 2005).

12 Measures included a three-year suspension of the debt of small farmers, which benefited 1.9 million families between April 2001 and March 2004 (Trakarnvanich, 2010), and the introduction of micro-credit schemes through the Thailand Village and Urban Revolving Fund (Boonperm, Haughton and Khandker, 2009). A similar project was introduced in 2005 at village level with the aim of helping each village to cope with their communitarian problems. To reduce migration to the city and to favour local income generation, the Government also introduced the One Tambon-One Product programme in 2001, which provides people with advice and technical assistance for the sale of their home-made products. Finally, in 2005, the Government implemented the Special Purpose Vehicle programme which focuses on the creation of a State enterprise for supporting agricultural activities through the provision of inputs.

13 To achieve these objectives, the Government supported the creation of a Malay middle class by promoting the acquisition by ethnic Malays of assets and access to well-paid jobs, supporting financial and management training for firms run by them, setting enrolment quotas in tertiary education, and supporting activities of the poorest households.

14 See Prabhu (2001) for a detailed review of the concept of socio-economic security and its translation into practice in the Indian context.

15 These include the Dhanalakshmi, or the Conditional Cash Transfer Scheme for Girl Child, launched in 2008; the Janani Suraksha Yojana launched in 2005, which aims to reduce maternal and neo-natal mortality through institutional deliveries; the Balika Samridhi Yojana launched in 1997, which aims at creating an enabling environment for the girl child to be born and become an educated and healthy adult; the National Programme for Education of Girls at Elementary-Level under the Sarva Shiksha Abhiyan, launched in 2003; the Kasturba Gandhi Balika Vidyalay Scheme launched in 2004, which seeks to arrest the dropout rate of girls in secondary education and ensure their retention in school up to the age of 18 years. See Prabhu (2009) for details about the many schemes at the state level.

16 This may complement regulations relating to remuneration structures in the financial sector, but also in the non-financial corporate sector more generally.

17 See: http://www.un.org/esa/ffd/documents/UN_ Model_2011_Update.pdf.

References

Aiyagari SR (1995). Optimal capital income taxation with incomplete markets, borrowing constraints, and constant discounting. *Journal of Political Economy*, 103(6): 1158–1175.

ADB (2008). *Social Protection Index for Committed Poverty Reduction*. Mandaluyong City, the Philippines.

ADB (2012). *Asian Development Outlook 2012: Confronting Rising Inequality in Asia*. Mandaluyong City, the Philippines.

Bakija J, Cole A and Heim BT (2012). Jobs and income growth of top earners and the causes of changing income inequality: Evidence from U.S. tax return data. Working paper, Williams College, Williamstown, MA. Available at: http://web.williams.edu/Economics/wp/BakijaColeHeimJobsIncomeGrowthTopEarners.pdf.

Barrientos A (2008). Cash transfers for older people reduce poverty and inequality. In: Bebbington AJ, Dani AA, De Haan A, and Walton M, eds. *Institutional Pathways to Equity: Addressing Inequality Traps*. Washington, DC, World Bank: 169–192.

Barrientos A, Niño-Zarazúa M and Maitrot M (2010). *Social Assistance in Developing Countries Database* (version 5.0). Manchester, Chronic Poverty Research Centre.

Besley T and Kanbur R (1990). The principles of targeting. Policy Research Working Paper Series 385, World Bank, Washington, DC.

Bird RM and Zolt EM (2005). Redistribution via taxation: The limited role of the personal income tax in developing countries. International Center for Public Policy Working Paper Series, Andrew Young School of Policy Studies, Georgia State University, Atlanta, GA.

Boonperm J, Haughton JH and Khandker SR (2009). Does the Village Fund matter in Thailand? Policy Research Working Paper Series 5011, World Bank, Washington, DC.

Cornia GA (2012). Inequality trends and their determinants: Latin America over 1990–2011. UNU-WIDER Working Paper No. 2012/09, United Nations University, World Institute for Development Economics Research, Helsinki.

Cornia GA, Gómez-Sabaini JC and Martorano B (2011). A new fiscal pact, tax policy changes and income inequality: Latin America during the last decade. UNU-WIDER Working Paper No. 2011/70, UNU-WIDER, Helsinki.

Chu KY, Davoodi H and Gupta S (2000). Income distribution and tax, and government social spending policies in developing countries. UNU-WIDER Working Papers No. 214, UNU-WIDER, Helsinki.

Devarajan S and Reinikka R (2004). Making services work for poor people. *Journal of African Economies*, 13(1): 142–166.

Devereux S (2007). Social pensions in Southern Africa in the twentieth century. *Journal of Southern African Studies*, 33(3): 539–560.

Devereux MP, Griffith R and Klemm A (2002). Corporate income tax reforms and international tax competition. *Economic Policy*, 17(35): 451–495.

Dodd R (2007). Tax breaks for billionaires: Loophole for hedge fund managers costs billions in tax revenue. Washington, DC, Economic Policy Institute. Available at: http://www.epi.org/publication/pm120/.

Dupas P (2011). Global health systems: Pricing and user fees. Stanford Working Paper, prepared for the *Elsevier Encyclopedia of Health Economics*.

ECLAC (2010). *Social Panorama of Latin America 2010*. Santiago, Chile.

ECLAC (2011). *Social Panorama of Latin America 2011*. Santiago, Chile.

Engel EMRA, Galetovic A and Raddatz CE (1999). Taxes and income distribution in Chile: Some unpleasant redistributive arithmetic. *Journal of Development Economics*, 59(1): 155–192.

Filgueira F, Molina CG, Papadópulos J and Tobar F (2006). Universalismo básico: una alternative possible y necesaria para mejorar las condiciones de vida. In: Molina CG, ed. *Universalismo básico. Una nueva política social para América Latina*. Washington, DC, Inter-American Development Bank.

Fiszbein A, Schady NR and Ferreira FHG (2009). Conditional cash transfers: Reducing present and future poverty. Washington, DC, World Bank. Available at:

http://www.worldbank.iccbox.ingenta.com/content/wb/bk17352.

Fried BJ (2012). Distributive politics and conditional cash transfers: The case of Brazil's Bolsa Família. *World Development*, 40(5):1042–1053.

Gassmann F (2011). Protecting vulnerable families in Central Asia: Poverty, vulnerability and the impact of the economic crisis. Innocenti Working Paper No. 2011-05, UNICEF Regional Office for CEE/CIS, Geneva, and UNICEF Innocenti Research Centre, Florence.

Gelbach JB and Pritchett LH (1995). Does more for the poor mean less for the poor? The politics of tagging. Policy Research Working Paper Series 1523, World Bank, Washington, DC.

Gemmell N and Morrissey O (2003). Tax structure and the incidence on the poor in developing countries. Research Paper No. 03/18, University of Nottingham, Centre for Research in Economic Development and International Trade, Nottingham.

Gemmell N and Morrissey O (2005). Distribution and poverty impacts of tax structure reform in developing countries: How little we know. *Development Policy Review*, 23(2): 131–144.

Giovannetti G and Sanfilippo M (2011). Social protection in sub-Saharan Africa: Learning from experiences. *VoxEU*. Available at: http://www.voxeu.org/index.php?q=node/6041.

Goñi E, López HJ and Servén L (2011). Fiscal redistribution and income inequality in Latin America. *World Development*, 39(9): 1558–1569.

Gordon RH (2010). Public Finance and economic development: Reflections based on experience in China. *Journal of Globalization and Development*, 1(1): Art. 7. Available at: http://www.degruyter.com/view/j/jgd.2010.1.1/jgd.2010.1.1.1024/jgd.2010.1.1.1024.xml.

Haavelmo T (1945). Multiplier effects of a balanced budget. *Econometrica,* 13: 311–318.

Heady C (2001). Taxation policy in low-income countries. WIDER Discussion Paper WDP 2001/81, UNU-WIDER, Helsinki.

Hinrichs HH (1966). *A General Theory of Tax Structure: Change During Economic Development*. Cambridge, MA, Harvard Law School International Tax Program.

Huber E (2009). Including the middle classes? Latin American Social Policies after the Washington Consensus. In: Kremer M, van Lieshout P and Went R eds. *Doing Good or Doing Better: Development Policies in a Globalizing World*. Amsterdam, Amsterdam University Press: 137–155.

Hungerford TL (2011). Changes in the distribution of income among tax filers between 1996 and 2006: The role of labor income, capital income, and tax policy. Washington, DC, Congressional Research Service.

ILO (2010). Extending social security to all: A guide through challenges and options. Geneva.

ILO (2012). Social protection floors for social justice and a fair globalization. Report IV (1), International Labour Conference, 101st Session, 2012. Geneva, ILO Publications.

Jomo KS (2012). Transfer pricing is a financing for development issue. Friedrich-Ebert-Stiftung. Available at: http://library.fes.de/pdf-files/iez/global/08938.pdf.

Khattry B and Mohan Rao M (2002). Fiscal faux pas? An analysis of the revenue implications of trade liberalization. *World Development*, 30(8): 1431–1444.

Koskela E and Vilmunen J (1996). Tax Progression is good for employment in popular models of trade union behavior. *Labour Economics*, 3(1): 65–80.

Kwon H (2005). Transforming the developmental welfare state in East Asia. *Development and Change*, 36(3): 477–497.

Kwon H, Dong G and Moon H (2010). The future challenges of the developmental welfare State: The case of Korea. Paper presented at the conference on Social Policy in Times of Change of the Social Policy Association at University of Lincoln, 5–7 July.

Leung JCB (2006). The emergence of social assistance in China. *International Journal of Social Welfare*, 15(3): 188–198.

Lindert K, Skoufias E and Shapiro J (2006). Redistributing income to the poor and the rich: Public transfers in Latin America and the Caribbean. SP Discussion Paper No. 0605. Washington, DC, World Bank.

Lopez-Calva LF and Lustig N (2010). Explaining the decline in inequality in Latin America: Technological change, educational upgrading and democracy. In: Lopez-Calva LF and Lustig N, eds. *Declining Inequality in Latin America: A Decade of Progress?* Washington, DC, Brookings Institution Press and UNDP.

Martorano B (2012). The impact of Uruguay's 2007 tax reform on equity and efficiency. Working Paper No. 06/2012, University of Florence, Florence.

McLure CE (1984). The evolution of tax advice and the taxation of capital income in the USA. *Government and Policy*, 2(3): 251–269.

Mesa-Lago C (2004). Evaluación de un cuarto de siglo de reformas estructurales de pensiones en América Latina. *Revista de la CEPAL*, 84, December: 59–82.

Mkandawire T (2007). Targeting and universalism in poverty reduction. In: Ocampo JA, Jomo KS and Sarbuland K, eds. *Policy Matters: Economic and Social Policies to Sustain Equitable Development*. Hyderabad, London and Penang, Orient Longmans, Zed Books and Third World Network: 305–333.

Møller V and Sotshangaye A (1996). My family eats this money too: Pension sharing and self-respect among Zulu grandmothers. *Southern African Journal of Gerontology*, 5(2): 9–19.

Musgrave RA (1959). *The Theory of Public Finance*. New York, McGraw Hill.

Musgrave RA (1990). Comments. In: Slemrod J, ed. *Do Taxes Matter? The Impact of the Tax Reform Act of 1986*. Cambridge, MA, MIT Press: 315–321.

Musgrave RA and Thin T (1948). Income tax progression: 1929-1948. *Journal of Political Economy*, 56(6): 498–514.

Narayan D, Chambers R, Shah MK and Petesch P (2000). *Voices of the Poor: Crying out for Change* (Conference edition). Washington, DC, Poverty Group, World Bank, June.

Niño-Zarazúa M, Barrientos A, Hickey S and Hulme D (2012). Social protection in sub-Saharan Africa: Getting the politics right. *World Development*, 40(1): 163–176.

ODI and UNICEF (2009). Strengthening social protection for children: West and Central Africa. Regional Thematic Report 1. Dakar, UNICEF West and Central Africa Regional Office and London, Overseas Development Institute. Available at: http://www.odi.org.uk/resources/docs/4573.pdf.

OECD (1989*). Economies in Transition: Structural Adjustments in OECD Countries*. Paris, OECD Publications.

OECD (2011*). Divided We Stand: Why Inequality Keeps Rising*. Paris, OECD Publications.

Olken BA and Singhal M (2011). Informal taxation. *American Economic Journal: Applied Economics*, 3(4): 1–28.

Ostrom E (1991). *Governing the Commons: The Evolution of Institutions for Collective Action*. Cambridge, Cambridge University Press.

Palacios R and Pallarés-Millares M (2000). International patterns of pension provision. World Bank Social Protection Discussion Paper Series no. 9. Washington, DC, World Bank.

Piketty T (2010). Commentary on 'Taxation of Wealth and Wealth Transfers' by Boadway R, Chamberlain E and Emmerson C. In: Institute for Fiscal Studies, eds. *Dimensions of Tax Design: The Mirrlees Review*. Oxford, Oxford University Press: 825–831.

Piketty T and Saez E (2007). How progressive is the U.S. federal tax system? A historical and international perspective. *Journal of Economic Perspectives*, 21(1): 3–24.

Piketty T, Saez E and Stantcheva S (2011). Optimal taxation of top labor incomes: A tale of three elasticities. NBER Working Paper No. 17616, National Bureau of Economic Research, Cambridge, MA.

Pissarides CA (1998). The impact of employment tax cuts on unemployment and wages: The role of unemployment benefits and tax structure. *European Economic Review*, 42(1): 155–183.

Prabhu KS (2001). Socio-economic security in the context of pervasive poverty: A case study of India. SES Discussion Paper, International Labour Office, Geneva.

Prabhu KS (2009). Conditional cash transfer schemes for alleviating human poverty: Relevance for India. Discussion Paper No. 1, UNDP, New Delhi. Available at: http://www.undp.org.in/content/cct/CCT_DP.pdf.

Ragayah HMZ (2011). Malaysia's new economic model: An assessment of its strategies for inclusive growth. Paper presented at the Asian regional workshop on Social Inclusiveness in Asia's Emerging Middle Income Countries, in Jakarta, organized by the Asian Development Bank, the International Labour Organization Regional Office for Asia and the Pacific, and the International Poverty Reduction Center in China, 13 September.

Reddy S and Vandemoortele J (1996). User financing of basic social services: A review of theoretical arguments and empirical evidence. UNICEF Staff Working Paper Series, UNICEF, New York.

Rodrik D (2006). Goodbye Washington Consensus, hello Washington confusion? A review of the World Bank's "Economic Growth in the 1990s: Learning from a Decade of Reform". *Journal of Economic Literature*, 44(4): 973–987.

Sáinz P and Calcagno A (1992). En busca de otra modalidad de desarrollo. *Revista de la Cepal*, no. 48. Santiago, Chile, Economic Commission for Latin America and the Caribbean, December.

Sandford C (1993). *Successful Tax Reform: Lessons from an Analysis of Tax Reform in Six Countries*. Bath, Fiscal Publications.

Schneider F and Enste D (2000). Shadow economies: Size, causes, and consequences. *Journal of Economic Literature*, 38(1): 77–114.

Skoufias E, Lindert K and Shapiro J (2010). Globalization and the role of public transfers in redistributing income in Latin America and the Caribbean. *World Development*, 38(6): 895–907.

Son HH (2012). Evaluating social protection programs in Tajikistan. *Journal of Asian Economics*, 23(2): 179–188.

Steinmo S (2003). The evolution of policy ideas: Tax policy in the 20th century. *British Journal of Politics and International Relations*, 5(2): 206–236.

Sung MJ (2009). The effects of taxes and benefits on income distribution and poverty rates in Korea. Paper for presentation at the 65th Annual Congress of IIPF at Cape Town, 13–16 August.

Tang J, Sha L and Ren ZX (2003). *Report on Poverty and Anti-poverty in Urban*. China, Beijing, Huaxia Press.

Tanzi V (1987). The response of other industrial countries to the U.S. Tax Reform Act. *National Tax Journal*, 40(3): 339–355.

Tax Justice Network (2011). The cost of tax abuse – A briefing paper on the cost of tax evasion worldwide. Available at: http://www.tackletaxhavens.com/Cost_of_Tax_Abuse_TJN%20Research_23rd_Nov_2011.pdf.

Toder E and Ponoman D (2012). Distributional effects of individual income tax expenditures: an update. Urban-Brookings Tax Policy Center.

Trakarnvanich B (2010). Performance based budgeting system: A study of poverty reduction policy implementation in Thailand. PhD thesis, National Institute of Development Administration, School of Public Administration. Bangkok.

UNCTAD (2002). *Economic Development in Africa: From Adjustment to Poverty Reduction: What is New?* United Nations publication, Sales No. E.02.II.D.18, New York and Geneva.

UNCTAD (2008). *Economic Development in Africa: Debt Sustainability: Oasis or Mirage?* United Nations publication, Sales No. E.04.II.D.37, New York and Geneva.

UNCTAD (*TDR 1997*). *Trade and Development Report, 1997. Globalization, Distribution and Growth.* United Nations publication, Sales No. E.97.II.D.8, New York and Geneva.

UNCTAD (*TDR 2005*). *Trade and Development Report, 2005. New Features of Global Interdependence.* United Nations publication, Sales No. E.05.II.D.13, New York and Geneva.

UNCTAD (*TDR 2006*). *Trade and Development Report, 2006. Global Partnership and National Policies for Development.* United Nations publication, Sales No. E.06.II.D.6, New York and Geneva.

UNCTAD (*TDR 2008*). *Trade and Development Report, 2008. Commodity Prices, Capital Flows and the Financing of Investment.* United Nations publication, Sales No. E.08.II.D.21, New York and Geneva.

UNCTAD (*TDR 2009*). *Trade and Development Report, 2009. Responding to the Global Crisis: Climate Change Mitigation and Development.* United Nations publication, Sales No. E. 09.II.D.16, New York and Geneva.

UNCTAD (*TDR 2010*). *Trade and Development Report, 2010. Employment, Globalization and Development.* United Nations publication, Sales No. E.10.II.D.3, New York and Geneva.

UNCTAD (*TDR 2011*). *Trade and Development Report, 2011. Post-crisis Policy Challenges in the World Economy.* United Nations publication, Sales No. E.11.II.D.3, New York and Geneva.

UN/DESA (2008). *World Economic and Social Survey 2008 – Overcoming Social Insecurity.* United Nations publication, Sales No. E.08.II.C.1, New York.

UN/DESA (2012). *World Economic and Social Survey 2012 – In Search of New Development Finance.* United Nations publication, Sales No. E.12.II.C.1, New York.

Webb S and Shariff K (1992). Designing and implementing adjustment programs. In: Corbo V, Fischer S and Webb S, eds. *Adjustment Lending Revisited: Policies to Restore Growth.* Washington, DC, World Bank: 69–92.

Weeks J (2010). Active macro policy for accelerating achievement of the MDG targets. New York, UNDP, September.

World Bank (1991). *Lessons of Tax Reform.* Washington, DC, World Bank.

Xiulan Z and Yuebin X (2010). From social insurance to social assistance: Process and development in China's urban social welfare policy. *Asia Pacific Journal of Social Work and Development*, 20(1): 41–51.

Chapter VI

THE ECONOMICS AND POLITICS OF INEQUALITY RECONSIDERED

A. Introduction

It is often believed that an efficient outcome of market processes in an increasingly globalized economy requires greater inequality between capital and labour incomes and a greater dispersion of personal income distribution. This chapter argues that such a belief is misguided.

Chapter IV of this *Report* has examined how globalization and technological change, and their interplay, have exerted pressure on income distribution. In this chapter it is argued that the apparent impact of these forces on inequality in many countries must be understood in the context of macroeconomic and labour market policies which have caused unemployment to rise and remain high. It suggests that neither globalization nor technological improvements inevitably require a shift in the distribution of income that favours the rich and deprives the poor of the means to improve their living standards. The rise of inequality observed in many countries could have been mitigated, if not prevented, by more appropriate macroeconomic and labour market policies without adversely affecting their international trade and technological progress.

> The measures being proposed and implemented in several countries in response to the crisis are tending to increase inequality even further.

A particular school of thought – which does not reflect economic reality – has dominated perceptions over the past few decades. It considers rising inequality as being a "normal" result of globalization and the use of more capital and advanced technologies in the production process. This chapter challenges that view and suggests that economic policies and institution-building based on a different understanding of the way a market economy evolves over time could lead to a more equitable as well as a more efficient form of economic development and structural change.

The tremendous influence of mainstream economic theory on the thinking of a majority of economists and policymakers about growth and development is reflected in the current public debate on economic policy in many countries. Public opinion and many policymakers are increasingly concerned about the trend of rising inequality in a large number of developed and developing countries. But at the same time the measures that are being proposed and implemented in several countries to overcome the current economic crisis are tending to increase inequality even further. Growing income gaps, high unemployment in many countries and increasingly frequent shocks and crises over the past 33 years raise serious doubts about the appropriateness of the theoretical foundations of the macroeconomic and labour market policies traditionally pursued in many countries. Indeed, the observation that it has not been possible to reduce unemployment by means of greater income inequality necessitates a fundamental policy reorientation.

Rising unemployment due to slow growth of an economy has a dual impact on inequality. First, it has a direct impact on inequality through lower – or no – incomes for the unemployed compared with their potential income from employment. Second, high and persistent unemployment tends to weaken the negotiating power of labour, thereby exerting downward pressure on real wages.

This chapter addresses inequality in terms of both functional and personal income distribution. Section B discusses the link between rising unemployment and the fall in the wage share. It shows that it is erroneous to apply the simple neoclassical supply-and-demand model that underlies widespread calls for greater wage flexibility in the labour market. Such a model neglects to consider the negative effects on domestic demand that result from a downward adjustment in the level of wages in response to initial demand shocks. Policies based on this model lead to greater inequality as a result of a falling share of wages, and they fail to generate additional employment or prevent a rise in unemployment. Rather, they tend to worsen the employment situation further by depressing consumer demand and reducing the incentives for fixed investment. On the other hand, regular adjustments of average nominal wages in line with average productivity growth would prevent a fall in the share of wages while generating additional domestic demand, which would induce increased output and the creation of new employment.

Section C of this chapter goes on to challenge the proposition that greater flexibility of wages at the firm or sectoral level (i.e. the greater differentiation of wages for similar occupations across firms or sectors) contributes to reducing so-called structural unemployment. It argues that in a dynamic and efficient economy, it is not flexibility of wages, but flexibility of profits – both overall and across firms – that helps to absorb shocks and leads to faster growth and employment creation.

Drawing on the analysis of the macroeconomic interaction between wages, productivity and employment in the earlier sections, section D of this chapter develops policy proposals for labour market and macroeconomic policies aimed at achieving better outcomes, not only in terms of income distribution but also in terms of growth and employment creation. Essential elements in this regard are the strengthening of institutions in support of collective wage bargaining and the addition of an incomes policy to the macroeconomic policy toolkit. This would allow the linking of real wage growth and the resulting rise in household demand – a key determinant of output growth in most economies – to the trend in productivity. At the same time, it would broaden the choice of combinations of instruments for macroeconomic management, and allow monetary policy to be geared, more than in the past, to stimulating investment and growth.

> Developing countries have considerable scope to reduce inequality by distributing the productivity gains more equally and in a way that boosts domestic demand.

This is a particularly important concern for developing and emerging economies. Developing countries may need to achieve a more drastic reduction of income inequalities than developed countries. Traditional social inequality, inherited power and commodity bonanzas in these countries often obstruct the creation of what is sometimes called "equality of opportunity", which is a precondition for a successful and dynamic division of labour. On the other hand, there is considerable potential for productivity growth in these countries as a result of increased specialization and division of labour. They also have the possibility to draw on the advanced technologies developed in other countries and combine them with relatively cheap domestic labour. This means that they also have considerable scope to reduce inequality by distributing the productivity gains more equally, and in a way that boosts domestic demand.

Clearly, preventing a further increase in inequality or achieving its reduction in developing countries requires additional policy measures, especially in favour of the lowest income groups and the rural areas. By absorbing a greater share of the gains from productivity growth and commodity rents, governments can also widen their "fiscal space", and increase infrastructure investment and spending on equality-enhancing public services, especially in education and professional skills formation. But for deepening the division of labour, many developing countries will need to increase their fixed investment in the formal manufacturing sector and attract a large number of the self-employed poor and those employed in the informal sector into formal employment with the promise of reasonable, rising and reliable wage incomes.

In addition to these issues related to national policies, section D addresses the international dimension of the employment-wage-growth nexus. It draws particular attention to the necessity of an appropriate currency regime for preventing misalignments of the real exchange rate. It also calls for greater cooperation among developing countries in determining the conditions for FDI. This cooperation should aim at a more equitable sharing of the huge productivity gains that can result from the combination of advanced technologies with relatively low real wages in developing countries.

B. The interaction between unemployment and the wage share

1. The traditional approach: employment creation through wage restraint

Mass unemployment has accompanied growth and development over the past few decades. Since the mid-1970s the unemployment rate in developed countries has never fallen much below 6 per cent (chart 6.1). The hope that the market mechanism would generate full employment and reward labour with at least a constant share of rising income has hardly materialized anywhere. In a number of developing countries, even though official unemployment has declined in recent years, it has remained relatively high overall. Indeed, absorbing a rapidly growing workforce into productive employment continues to be a major development challenge (*TDR 2010*, chap. IV).

The apparent inability of economic policy to deal with rising and persistent unemployment after the mid-1970s motivated the return of economic thinking to what had been a mainstream economic model in the 1920s. The unwillingness of workers to accept lower wages was considered to be the main

reason for unemployment inertia (see, for example, Hayek, 1960). Consequently, many economists and policymakers believed that too little inequality and the resistance of unions to accept lower wages were the main culprits of the new unemployment problem (see, for example, Nickell, 1997; Siebert, 1997; Elmeskov, Martin and Scarpetta, 1998).

Since the end of the 1980s, the OECD has championed the revival of this old approach based on the simple neoclassical model of the labour market. Indeed, the policies designed in many countries in line with its recommendations explain, to a large extent, the rise in inequality observed in developed countries during the past three decades. In 1994, the *OECD Jobs Study* described the mechanism that, according to traditional neoclassical theory, should lead to superior results on the labour market as follows:

> The adjustment process itself depends on the interplay of employers' demand for labour, which will be negatively related to the level of real wages, and the desire to be employed, which will be positively related to the level of real wages. In principle, there will be a real

Chart 6.1

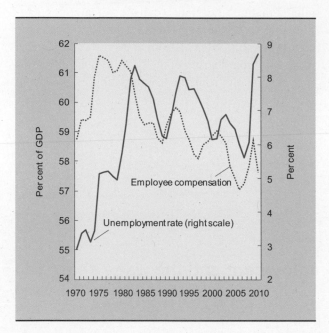

EMPLOYEE COMPENSATION AND UNEMPLOYMENT RATE IN DEVELOPED COUNTRIES, 1970–2010

Source: UNCTAD secretariat calculations, based on *OECD. Stat Extracts* database; European Commission, *Annual Macro-economic* (*EC-AMECO*) database; United States Bureau of Labor Statistics; and ILO, *Key Indicators of the Labour Market* (*KILM*) database.

Note: Developed countries exclude Eastern European countries. Employee compensation is calculated as a percentage of GDP at factor costs. There is a break in 1991 due to German reunification.

wage level – or, more correctly, a level of real labour costs – that ensures that all who want to work at that wage will find employment (OECD, 1994, Part I: 69).

It further noted: "Self-equilibration in the labour market requires, in addition to a negative relationship between labour-demand and labour costs, that wages respond to market conditions: labour-market slack putting downward pressure on real wages and vice versa" (OECD, 1994: Part II, 3).

This position is exactly what Keynes had attacked in his *General Theory* some 60 years earlier as follows:

> Thus writers in the classical tradition, over-looking the special assumption underlying their theory, have been driven inevitably to the conclusion, perfectly logical on their assumption, that apparent unemployment … must be due at bottom to a refusal by the unemployed factors to accept a reward which corresponds to their marginal productivity. A classical economist may sympathise with labour in refusing to accept a cut in its money-wage, and he will admit that it may not be wise to make it to meet conditions which are temporary; but scientific integrity forces him to declare that this refusal is, nevertheless, at the bottom of the trouble (Keynes, 1936/1973: 16).

Clearly, whatever the reasons for the rise in unemployment, the existence of a large number of unemployed workers exerted a downward pressure on wages as the balance of power in wage negotiations shifted towards employers. In this environment unions and social movements were weakened, or could not be strengthened. Mainstream economists were united in their attempt to do away with what they considered to be the downward stickiness of wages, overly tight social safety nets and many other ingredients of the so-called "welfare state". The policies generally adopted over the past 25 years have sought to keep wage increases low in comparison with overall productivity gains and accepted a concomitant increase in the share of capital income.

Workers facing the permanent threat of prolonged unemployment are often willing to accept lower wages in the hope of keeping their jobs. Such an outcome gives the appearance of being the result of a normal market process where an excess supply of a good is expected to induce a fall in its price, which would then lead to increased demand. However, from a macroeconomic point of view of the labour market in the context of the entire economy, application of this simple supply-demand mechanism is not as straightforward as it appears at first sight; indeed it is fallacious (*TDR 2010*, chap. III).

The explanation that high and rising unemployment was the result of real wages exceeding their equilibrium level could not be easily rejected in the 1970s, when the wage share reached historical highs in developed countries. However, in the subsequent decades, unemployment rose while real wages lagged far behind productivity growth. This suggests that the idea that reliance on the simple market mechanism can prevent unemployment is erroneous. Just ahead of the new big jump in unemployment in developed countries – from less than 6 per cent in 2007 to close to 9 per cent in 2010-2011− the share of wages in overall GDP had fallen to the lowest level on record since the end of the Second World War (i.e. to 57 per cent, down from more than 61 per cent in 1980). This should be a wake-up call. If unemployment rises more than during any other recession that occurred during the last three decades, even though the share of wages in GDP has fallen, there must be something fundamentally wrong with an economic theory that justifies the rise of inequality mainly in terms of the need to tackle persistent unemployment.

The neoclassical approach to employment theory assumes that falling nominal wages signal a lasting fall of real wages and a change in the relative prices of labour and capital. This would give firms an incentive to alter the production process by employing more labour and less capital in the future. However, this process would have to be extremely rapid, and all firms would have to engage in it simultaneously: only an instantaneous transition from one production structure to the other would prevent overall demand from falling. In a scenario of falling demand, however, the conditions under which firms adjust to the change in relative prices of labour and capital are fundamentally different. If wages per head or per hour fall and the growth in the number of workers or the number of hours worked does not compensate for the fall in wages, the wage sum will fall and induce a further drop in demand. It is highly improbable that in such a situation companies will take strategic decisions and engage in a restructuring process using more labour and less capital based on the expectation of lastingly lower real wages and unchanged demand.

The crucial point in this reasoning is the sequence of events and not the a priori logic of a market with normal supply and demand curves. The widespread idea that wage reduction in a recession increases employment and output is based on the assumption that supply and demand are a given and are independent of each other. However, this view, based on partial equilibrium analysis, is not tenable for the labour market at the macroeconomic level (*TDR 2010*, chap. III.B).

Indeed, the recent experiences of some developed countries, such as the United States, suggest that the macroeconomic process works in the opposite direction of what is suggested by the neoclassical model of employment and the labour market. In the United States, wages have been lagging behind productivity for many years, but unemployment rose at least as sharply as in former recessions when the financial crisis occurred in 2008, and it seems to be more persistent than ever before. There is growing agreement that cutting wages in a situation of fragile recovery, as has been done in the United States since 2010, would be counterproductive.

For employers, a fall in wages would seem to bring relief from the recession-induced pressure on their profits. However, if further falling demand by private households depresses their business even more and exerts an additional downward pressure on prices, this relief will be short-lived. With reduced household demand, companies will have to cut their production correspondingly. As a secondary effect, lower capacity utilization will cause a downward adjustment in investment plans and additional lay-offs. On the other hand, the expectation of higher profits as a result of falling nominal wages is based on the assumption of unchanged overall demand. However, this assumption does not reflect reality. Again, the sequence of events is crucial. If demand falls immediately after the drop in wages,[1] the expected substitution of falling wages by higher profits will not take place, because a reduction of overall output in the first round will have a negative impact on profits.

> Cutting wages when the recovery is fragile would be counterproductive.

While this analysis holds for closed economies, it seems to be less clear-cut for open economies that have a large share of exports in total demand. Under certain circumstances exports may indeed react positively to wage cuts: if wages are cut only in one country, if the productivity trend of that country remains intact and if its exchange rate does not appreciate, the fall in wages may stimulate export demand (through increased price competitiveness) or lead to higher profits in the export sector. The overall effect on demand may still be negative if domestic demand is greater than exports, as in most economies, but the potential impact of improved competitiveness should not be underestimated. Even a one-off improvement in competitiveness of a country can have a lasting effect on export demand, as the producers in that country gain market shares and thus benefit dispro-portionally from global demand growth. A continued depreciation of the real exchange rate by means of wage cuts without an exchange rate mechanism to compensate through appreciation of the currency could massively distort international trade and create large imbalances, as the effects on competitiveness accumulate and create a huge absolute advantage for the country over time, as happened in Germany (see section D.5 below).[2]

Moreover, seeking greater competitiveness by translating part of the productivity gains into lower export prices creates a fallacy of composition: employment creation in one country at the expense of growth and employment generation in other countries is not sustainable. A similar strategy followed in countries whose producers compete with domestic exporters will tend to trigger a downward spiral in wages but without any positive employment effects.

2. The alternative approach: wage growth as the key determinant of demand growth

The foregoing analysis has important implications for the treatment of inequality. The labour market should not be analysed in isolation, but in relation to overall growth. This is because the creation of new employment is a positive function of output growth rather than a function of falling wages and a deteriorating share of wages in GDP. In developed countries, employment cycles and growth cycles are observed to be closely linked. Employment growth is typically closely associated with the growth of aggregate demand and output (chart 6.2). Differences in macroeconomic and employment performance among these countries over time result from their varying macroeconomic policy stances rather than from different degrees of flexibility of their aggregate wage levels. In the post-war period until the mid-1970s, when employment grew much faster, there was much less wage restraint than during the last two decades that witnessed meagre employment creation. A downswing like the Great Recession of 2008 and 2009 reduces employment despite wage flexibility and very low wage shares in GDP. In order to reduce unemployment, all the developed countries need sustained recoveries based on rising mass incomes,

which, through their effects on imports, will also create additional export and income opportunities for developing countries.

The proposition that greater flexibility of the aggregate wage level and lower average wages are necessary to boost employment, as they lead to a substitution of labour for capital in the economy as a whole, can be directly refuted, given the strong positive correlation between investment in gross fixed capital formation (GFCF) and employment creation that exists in developed countries (chart 6.3). This correlation contradicts the neoclassical model: in the real world, companies invest and disinvest in capital and labour at the same time, and the level of their investment depends on the overall state of the economy, which determines their demand expectations. This implies that, in the macroeconomic context, capital and labour can be considered substitutes only to a very limited extent. Rather, they are used as complementary inputs in the production process which are combined – depending on the available technology at any point in time – to achieve a planned quantity of output, with little or no regard to their relative prices or functional income distribution.

Thus investment in real productive capacity and the rise in demand that motivates such investment are the main drivers of both income growth and employment creation. While the elasticity of employment in relation to growth is likely to differ from country to country, and from period to period, the evidence of the close link between growth, employment and investment belies the popular belief that unemployment can be remedied by shifting the distribution of income from labour to capital and from lower income groups – with a low propensity to save – to groups at the top of the income ladder, which have a relatively high propensity to save.

For developing countries and transition economies, statistical evidence suggests that the link between GDP growth or gross fixed capital formation and formal employment is weaker than in developed countries. This partly results from the fact that changes in informal employment and self-employment dampen the cyclical effects, as these two categories serve as buffers between formal employment and what can be defined and measured as unemployment. Indeed, in developing countries more than in developed countries, workers who are laid off in the formal sector of the economy in bad times often tend to move into

Chart 6.2

GROWTH OF EMPLOYMENT AND REAL GDP IN SELECTED COUNTRIES, 1981–2011

(Per cent)

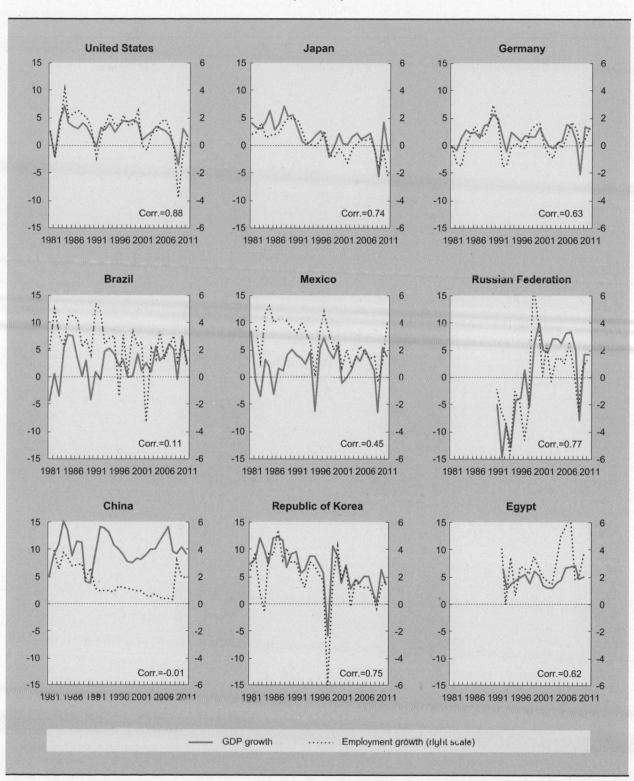

Source: UNCTAD secretariat calculations, based on table 1.1; UN/DESA, *National Accounts Main Aggregates* database; ILO, *LABORSTAT* and *KILM* databases; *OECD.StatExtracts*, *Annual Labour Force Statistics* and *Main Economic Indicators* databases; ECLAC, *CEPALSTAT* database; and national sources.

Note: Corr. = correlation.

Chart 6.3

GROWTH OF EMPLOYMENT AND GROSS FIXED CAPITAL FORMATION IN SELECTED COUNTRIES, 1981–2011

(Per cent)

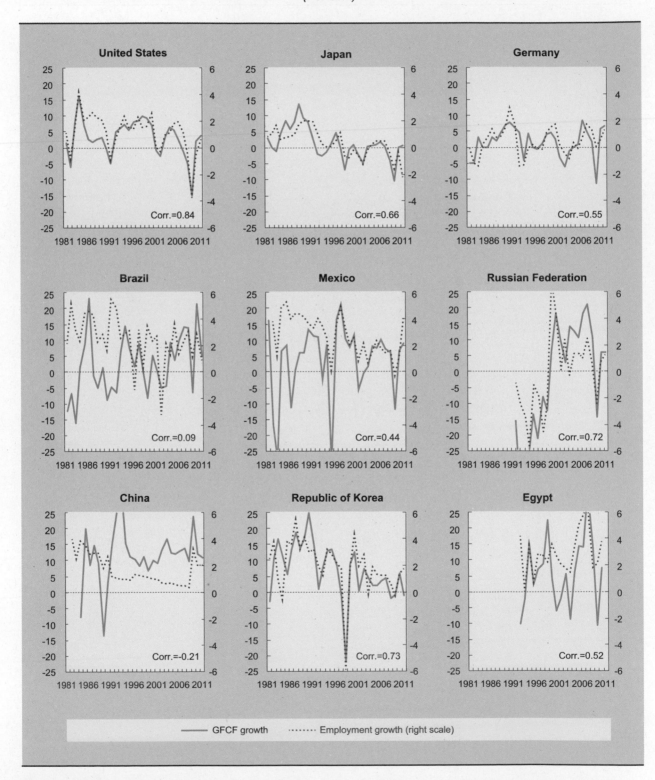

GFCF growth ········ Employment growth (right scale)

Source: UNCTAD secretariat calculations, based on UN/DESA, *National Accounts Main Aggregates* database; ILO, *LABORSTAT* and *KILM* databases; *OECD.StatExtracts*, *Annual Labour Force Statistics* and *Main Economic Indicators* databases; ECLAC, *CEPALSTAT* database; and national sources.

Note: Corr. = correlation.

the informal economy because of the lack of social safety nets (*TDR 2010*, chap. III.B.3). In developing and transition economies that are highly dependent on the production and export of primary commodities, there is usually a weaker link between growth and employment creation. This is because short-term growth can react strongly to internationally determined prices for their export commodities. In fact, the strong increases in commodity prices that occurred during the period 2002–2008 led to income growth without higher employment in the commodities or the formal sectors (UNECA, 2010). Nevertheless, in most other large developing countries and transition economies analysed in charts 6.2 and 6.3, with the exception of China, employment growth also remains positively correlated with growth of both GDP and investment in fixed capital. In the case of China, apart from the significant buffering effects of the informal sector and self-employment category, the demographic trend has played a significant role in the evolution of employment. In addition, the large stimulus package in response to the financial crisis helped boost employment when external demand for Chinese exports was weakening.

Whether a fall in unemployment can be achieved without an increase in inequality in a dynamic economy depends critically on how income gains generated by greater productivity are distributed. The crucial link is between nominal wages and employment at the macroeconomic level. From this perspective, it is not the factor-cost aspect that matters, but primarily the role of wages as the major determinant of aggregate demand (i.e. the consumption of wage earners). Higher wages and lower inequality can stimulate demand and output growth, which in turn can provide incentives for increased investment in productive capacity, with attendant effects on employment creation and productivity gains.

> Higher wages and lower inequality can stimulate demand and output growth ...

> ... which in turn can provide incentives for increased investment in productive capacity, with attendant effects on employment creation and productivity gains.

As continuous productivity gains increase the supply capacity of the economy, a rise in unemployment can only be avoided when companies can expect aggregate demand to expand at a similar rate. Since domestic incomes from wages are the main driver of domestic demand, regular adjustments of the level of real wages in line with the overall increase in productivity serve to stabilize demand expectations and generate sufficient effective domestic demand to avoid a rise in unemployment. This will feed a virtuous cycle of demand growth, investment, productivity increases and employment creation. The policy implications of this reasoning are discussed in section D of this chapter.

Regarding developing countries, there are a number of additional considerations. The main differences between developed and developing countries are not to be found in macroeconomic processes, but in corporate decision-making about production and investment, and in the structural and institutional factors governing the labour market. In many developing countries, the agricultural and services sectors are usually quite large and informal, and small-scale self-employment is common, though there are considerable differences across countries. In addition, formal employment in the manufacturing sector represents a relatively small share of total remunerative occupations, and unionization of labour and collective bargaining typically play a much smaller role than they do in most developed countries.

Following the almost universal adoption of export-led growth strategies during the 1980s and 1990s, the corporate sector in developing countries began to make decisions on production and investment primarily with reference to external demand and competition on global markets. Moreover, these countries import most of the higher end technologies from the more advanced economies. This appears to exacerbate the problem of combining technological progress, investment and productivity growth with employment creation. For this reason, it is even more important for developing countries to pursue policies and establish institutions that aim to prevent a further increase in income inequality and ensure that all kinds of productivity gains translate into higher incomes for all groups of their populations.

No doubt, in developing countries that are still highly dependent on the production and export of primary commodities, the link between growth and employment creation is less direct than in developed countries. Their growth performance is often strongly influenced by movements in internationally determined prices of primary commodities. Strong increases in commodity prices, as witnessed during the period 2002–2008, can lead to income growth without an increase in real output and employment in the commodities sector. This is all the more reason why governments should take measures to appropriate a substantial share of the higher commodity rents and channel them to other sectors where additional investment is urgently needed to advance diversification and the creation of formal employment (as discussed further in subsection D.3 below).

The situation is different in emerging market economies that have already reached the stage of having a more diversified production structure. In some of these economies, technological catching up has led to rapid growth in their tradable goods industries through an expansion of net exports. However, even countries with significant and growing exports of manufactured goods have sometimes found that this success has only a modest effect on aggregate employment in manufacturing. This may

be explained by the high capital intensity of much of their export-oriented production, combined with the loss of employment in production activities oriented to the domestic market that are outcompeted by imports. The challenge of ensuring that the growth process delivers more and better quality employment is therefore even more pressing in such countries.

In these countries, productivity growth is often passed on through lower prices, while keeping wages depressed in an attempt to maintain or improve external competitiveness. This explains why the export prices for certain manufactures produced in developing countries with relatively high productivity gains due to FDI have been falling relative to the prices of manufactures produced in developed countries (*TDR 2005*, chap. IV). It is understandable that countries pursuing a strategy of export-led growth and producers of manufactures in these countries seek to gain the competitive advantages just described. However, policymakers who support such a strategy should be aware that such practices may deprive a large proportion of their populations of a share in the productivity gains. Moreover, it leads to an overreliance on exports for income growth, which may have adverse effects in the long run and in particular during periods of crisis or slow global growth.

C. Wage flexibility at the firm level and the dynamics of a market economy

Although attributing rising unemployment to excessively high wages has proved to be seriously flawed and the attempt to reduce unemployment through wage restraint and greater income inequality has failed, few have questioned the theoretical foundations of this approach. Instead, the same theoretical reasoning has led to an increasing emphasis on greater "relative flexibility" of the labour market. This refers not so much to the aggregate wage level, as to the structure of wages for similar occupations across sectors and firms, and over time. It implies the

decentralization of wage setting and varying wages among and within firms according to their individual performance. The greater "relative" flexibility of wages increases inequality among workers employed in different sectors or firms. This is supposed to remove so-called "structural unemployment". Again, it was the OECD that spearheaded this approach, stating:

> In particular, greater wage flexibility, reductions in barriers to labour mobility and greater competition would make it easier for

the unemployed to find jobs at the going wage, although it is noticeable that profit shares are now at historically high levels. It may be that there has been insufficient relative wage flexibility or that excessive job protection has discouraged hiring even though there has been wage moderation" (OECD, 1994: Part I, 73).

It also noted:

Some of the key links between wage and price rigidities and employment and output performance have been explored in the context of various modeling exercises. These tend to show that differences in wage and price rigidities indeed have significant implications for the size and duration of trend and cyclical movements in unemployment. In particular, in the longer run, it is those economies with less flexible labour markets and greater wage rigidities which appear likely to experience greater persistence in both unemployment and inflation. Hence, policies to reduce labour market rigidities and improve flexibility are likely to reduce the size and duration of adverse movements in unemployment associated with exogenous disturbances and make it easier to close output gaps (OECD, 1994: Part I, 69).

In this view, in many developed countries there was not sufficient wage differentiation between the lowest and highest paid occupations to overcome structural unemployment. As noted by the OECD (1994: Part II, 2): "A fully flexible wage structure would ensure that abilities did not matter for employment: all ability groups could price themselves into work".

The belief that greater wage flexibility and a further weakening of institutions for collective wage setting at both the country and the firm level is the only way to adjust to changes in demand has persisted, despite growing concerns about inequality (Barkbu, Rahman, Valdés et al., 2012). For example, the President of the European Central Bank (ECB) hinted at the "fact" that the insistence of many countries to defend their welfare State was the main stumbling block to recovery of the European economies from the crisis when he called "for labour market reform that increases flexibility and mobility".[3] Similarly, with reference to the crisis in the euro zone, the IMF suggested that the ability of economies to adjust to shocks could be improved by "a wage-setting mechanism that is more responsive to firm-level economic conditions" (IMF and G-20, 2012:1). This was based on the belief that even

cyclical movements of unemployment and inflation are driven by relative wage inflexibility. It means that even after a fall in the aggregate wage level, high "structural" unemployment may persist due to insufficient flexibility of the labour market.

Section B of this chapter has shown that labour as a whole cannot simply "price itself into work". A pertinent question is whether the adjustment of wages in specific sectors or individual firms at the microeconomic level is an effective way of dealing with shocks. And should shocks, whether of external or internal origin, be absorbed by flexible wages and rising inequality? What kind of adjustment enabled the superior performance of market economies in terms of growth, investment and development in the past? What kind of adjustment is consistent with the empirical evidence of a high correlation between changes in the employment of labour and of capital? In finding answers to these questions some preliminary considerations may be helpful.

In the traditional view, a fall in the demand for the goods or services produced by firms prompts them to lay off workers to avoid a cut in profits due to lower capacity utilization. The laid off workers, in an attempt to individually "price themselves back to work" are ready to accept lower wages to maintain their jobs or be hired by another employer as soon as possible. Thus, full employment can be restored even if a decline in production by the individual company is permanent. According to this reasoning, the fall in wages will allow the workers that were laid off in the first round to be reemployed, even if the level of production is lower than before. However, in a market economy, an abrupt fall in demand is *not* a typical shock experienced by an individual company. At any given level of aggregate demand, demand shocks to one company are typically triggered by strategic moves of competing companies and in response to changes in consumer preferences.[4]

It is in the logic of competition that if a certain firm is outcompeted in the market for the goods or services it produces, demand will shift to its competitors that have followed a more successful business strategy. The loss of jobs in the former firm will therefore be compensated by the creation of additional jobs in the firms that have been more successful in the competitive process and need more workers to boost production in order to meet the increased demand for their products. What is required in this process is not a downward adjustment of wages, but a temporary safety net for the laid-off workers to avoid pressure on wages, as well as the provision of possibilities for retraining and new skill acquisition.

If a winning company has achieved its success by applying a new production technology or introducing a new product, the eventual effects on employment are similar. A new technology that improves productivity in one plant and creates a temporary advantage for comparable products for the innovating company will tend to trigger a general fall in prices as the innovation is imitated by other firms. It will also lead to a general increase in real wages and domestic demand throughout the economy. This would allow those workers who are no longer needed in the innovating company to find jobs elsewhere in firms that are benefiting from the increased demand, without having to accept pay cuts. If real wages rise in line with productivity at the level of the overall economy, the rise in demand to absorb the abundant workers would be generated by the real growth of the economy.

The idea that more flexible labour markets and greater flexibility of wages at the firm or sectoral level can reduce unemployment is even less convincing if applied to situations where the business model of a company or sector becomes obsolete as a result of changing consumer preferences. In this case, downward flexibility of wages at the firm level would imply preserving the obsolete structure by what would amount to a subsidy provided by the workers. If, at the same time, other firms benefit from growing demand for their products, the reasonable response would not be falling wages but falling profits in the obsolete firm and a closing down of idle capacities. Meanwhile, firms benefiting from the change in consumer preferences would add new capacities and absorb the temporarily unemployed. Again, it is falling or rising profits rather than falling or rising wages that would be the main force moving companies or their branches in or out of business.[5]

Generally, wage adjustments at the level of the firm cannot be efficient because it is usually impossible to identify the concrete reasons for the shock to which the firm is exposed. In the vast majority of

cases, subsidies, be they provided by the government or by workers, are not an appropriate answer to the challenge posed by a fall in demand on a specific market. Considering that the wage reduction leads to lower demand at the macro level, there is no realistic scenario where the efficient reaction of a dynamic market system to supply or demand shocks would be falling wages and rising inequality.

Another important argument against greater wage flexibility at the micro level is that the labour force employed by firms has many different skills and qualifications. The ways in which the different segments of the labour market function for each of these skills depends on the interregional and intersectoral mobility of labour, and the degree of unionization and centralization of wage negotiations. Under conditions of a well-integrated economy and high mobility of workers or centralized wage bargaining, it can be expected that similar wages will be paid in each of these segments. This means that the individual firm has to accept the market-established wage for a given qualification. Thus the idea that firm-level flexibility of wages can increase overall efficiency by determining a level of remuneration for workers in line with their marginal productivity is an illusion. Marginal productivity is a theoretical concept based on the idea that the contribution from, for example, one hour of work of a certain type of worker is measurable and clearly identifiable. However, in most modern production settings, it is impossible to measure the contribution of each individual employee to the value added produced by its firm (box 6.1).

The individual firm is a price taker, as the prices are set in the different labour markets. Therefore, it cannot cut wages in case of a shock that affects it individually, as workers would simply leave and find work elsewhere. Admittedly, there may be a number of obstacles to the geographical mobility of workers, which may limit the equalization of money wages to a certain region or agglomeration, especially in developing countries. The argument against promoting greater wage flexibility at the level of the firm is even stronger when the case of a positive shock for an individual firm is considered. For example, if entrepreneurs implement innovative ideas that increase

> Falling or rising profits, rather than falling or rising wages, are the main force that moves companies in or out of business.

Box 6.1

WAGE DETERMINATION AND MARGINAL PRODUCTIVITY

Marginal productivity is a theoretical concept based on the notion that the contribution from, for example, one hour of work of a particular worker is measurable and clearly identifiable. If the same wage is paid to all workers in a given segment of the labour market, all of them would have to accept a wage cut if one additional hour were added to a work process and if in that additional hour a lower output were produced than during the previous hours (a production process with diminishing returns to scale). This concept would be valid only if the inputs of many different employees into the production process were highly standardized and could be clearly identified and measured. However, this is not the case in most modern production settings.

The large majority of employees work in an environment where neither the marginal contributions of individual members of a production team nor their relative contributions can be measured. What is the marginal productivity of, say, a nurse in a hospital and what is his or her relative contribution to the overall outcome compared with that of the chief surgeon or the chief of administration? Because this is unknown, most of the employees in modern societies are remunerated in a way that reflects roughly the scarcity or availability of people with a similar qualification but not their individual marginal productivity. Rising productivity in particular production processes adding up to the increase in the overall productivity of the economy is typically reflected in falling prices of the goods that are produced more efficiently. The lower price level implies that the real wages of all employees are correspondingly higher even though there has been no improvement in the productivity of every employee. It is the team – and, in this extreme version, the team of the whole economy – that is rewarded by the greater output of the team as a whole, and not that of the individual employee, in the production process.[a]

---

[a] Take the example of a teacher at an elementary school who teaches exactly the same things for 40 years without any innovation or increase in productivity and without any change in salary. The teacher will nevertheless enjoy rising purchasing power if economy-wide productivity growth leads to falling prices in the economy as a whole. If the economy has an explicit inflation target, all nominal wages have to rise by this target plus the productivity growth rate, but that is only a technical matter and does not change the substance of the adjustment process.

productivity so that they can offer their goods much cheaper than before, it would be counterproductive for them to renegotiate wages at the level of the firm. The expectation that workers in their company will immediately try to appropriate a part of the pioneer rent would reduce the incentive for a potential pioneer in the first place, and thus reduce the innovative dynamism of the economy. Although other workers may be willing to accept a lower wage than those already employed in such a firm, a more efficient arrangement would be one that keeps individual wages unchanged and rewards pioneer firms with a temporarily higher profit arising from the greater-than-average increase of the productivity of their firm. It will also enable them to use part of the pioneer rent to reduce the price of their product, which will lead to a fall in the prices

of competing products throughout the economy as the more efficient mode of production is imitated by followers and thus benefits all workers.

To the extent that the wage tends to be similar in each segment of the labour market, temporary differences in profits could be significant. As observed already by Keynes (1930/1971), these differences serve to redirect the resources of the economy from uses where they are no longer needed to those where the maximum benefit for the society can be expected. Wage flexibility at the sectoral or firm level does not contribute to such an outcome. On the contrary, flexible wages tend to preserve obsolete structures and dramatically reduce the ability of the economy to adjust to new circumstances and to exploit its innovative potential.

Intertemporal structural change, as discussed in the preceding paragraphs, is characterized by pioneering enterprises which are able to improve their productivity faster than their competitors or to attract additional demand by introducing new products. Hence their success is explained by a combination of firm-specific higher productivity and given wages for the economy as a whole.

The same principles apply to international structural change, especially as it involves developing countries – that is, when the initial change results from a developing country's catching up process or the relocation of production from a developed to a developing country. International structural change often results when the technology from a more developed country is used in another country where wages and the average productivity level are much lower. Consequently, investment behaviour that is focused on the international or interregional transfer and implementation of technologies that are already known leads to lower prices or higher profits. However, the shocks resulting from this kind of structural change are similar to the ones resulting from intertemporal change. Again, single firms or their branches face competition from other firms offering comparable goods at lower prices due to lower production costs. And again, the reaction of trying to defend market shares by reducing real wages is not supportive of growth, additional employment creation and the reduction of inequality.

For developing countries, the strategy of acquiring, one way or another, technologies developed and already used elsewhere is indispensible for catching up. A downward adjustment of wages by individual firms or sectors in developed countries which are competing with producers from developing countries using such technologies has a similar effect as a protectionist measure. This practice is frequently taking place with the benign neglect of governments and trade unions on the erroneous assumption that it preserves jobs. But this is as counterproductive as subsidies to declining firms that suffer from an internal shock. A more rational approach would be to consider that the developing countries will use the increased proceeds of their exports to buy more imports from the developed countries, thereby creating new opportunities for other firms and new jobs in the latter countries.

To sum up, from a macroeconomic perspective, downward adjustments of average real wages leading to greater inequality between profit and wage incomes is an entirely ineffective remedy for unemployment when an economy is facing the most frequent kind of shock, namely a demand shock. Flexibility of wages at the firm or sectoral level and the resulting increase in inequality of labour incomes are equally ineffective, because they reduce the potential dynamics of competition among firms and the incentives for innovative investment. It is flexible profits, rather than flexible wages, that fit the dynamics of modern market systems. In the real world, shocks are mainly absorbed by profits and not by wages. This applies also to shocks created by competition through international trade and FDI. The change in profits leads firms to adjust to the new situation instead of trying to restore the unrestorable. The static neoclassical model of segregated labour markets with flexible wages, which regularly produce inequality in case of adjustment to shocks – be they international or intertemporal – should not guide adjustment policies at any stage of development.

D. Economic policy and institution-building to reduce inequality

1. The participatory society and dynamic adjustment

As discussed in sections B and C of this chapter, successful strategies for economic growth, catch-up and sustained improvements in welfare for all groups of the population cannot be achieved through deregulation of labour markets. Indeed, in many countries, such deregulation has contributed to slower growth and higher unemployment.

As the division of labour advances and the dependence of every participant on its success increases, it is important that the benefits be shared in a manner that increases the demand for the goods and services produced in line with the resulting growth in productivity. This is the only way an economy can avoid the danger of rising and persistent unemployment or the need to repeatedly adopt a "beggar-thy-neighbour" policy stance in order to create demand for its supply surplus. In developing and developed countries alike, the participation of the majority of the population in these gains is not only desirable for reasons of social justice and cohesion; it is also crucial for growth, because, as the main consumers of domestically produced goods and services, a rise in their income will result in higher demand, which will boost production.

Successful strategies for income growth and employment for all depend on investment in fixed capital. In economies with a dominant private sector, such investment is strongly influenced not only by the conditions for financing such investment, but also by expectations concerning the growth of demand for the goods and services that are produced with that capital. Therefore, investment can be expected to rise in a broad range of activities and greater diversification

achieved in the long run only if the proceeds from all productive activities are channelled through private households of all income groups. This requires appropriate economic policies and regulatory institutional arrangements to systematically balance the negotiating power between profit earners, who make decisions on investments, and wage earners who are the main drivers of consumer demand. Furthermore, resorting to additional, unorthodox, policy instruments would increase policy options and the number of possible combinations of policy instruments that can be employed to achieve the desired rate of output growth and higher rates of employment, while at the same time avoiding rising inflation and inequality.

2. Macroeconomic policies and institutional arrangements

Once it is recognized that the market mechanism cannot restore equilibrium between the supply of and demand for labour through rising inequality, the role of the government in stabilizing the overall economy becomes crucial for employment creation and income distribution. With appropriate policies, governments can prevent the huge additional costs that arise if the pressure on wages stemming from high unemployment is allowed to permeate the whole economy.

The euro area currently provides the most striking examples of the failure of wage restraint coupled with macroeconomic policies that are inimical to growth. In the Southern European members of the area, unemployment has soared despite large wage cuts. In order to absorb this surplus labour, additional employment opportunities need to be created by means of appropriate monetary, financial and fiscal policies aimed at achieving a strong growth dynamic based on fixed capital formation (see also *TDR 2010*, chap. V and *TDR 2008*, chap. IV). Governments that quickly and aggressively tackle rising unemployment with expansionary monetary and fiscal policies could also minimize the period of uncertainty and threat of job losses. Strong countercyclical policies in times of recession or below-potential growth are particularly important in countries where social safety nets are inadequate or absent. This is why it is justified to view the more aggressive economic policy stance of the United States as a substitute for the more advanced social safety nets in Europe. On the other hand, if Europe were to cut spending on welfare programmes during the crisis, it would have to change its attitude towards the role of macroeconomic policies. Cutting the safety net and withdrawing macroeconomic stimuli at the same time is bound to fail and will produce more unemployment and greater inequality.

In addition to employment- and growth-supporting monetary and fiscal policies, an appropriate incomes policy can play a significant role in achieving a socially acceptable degree of income inequality.

> Greater attention should be given to institution-building, including collective bargaining between unions and employers' associations, and related governance reforms.

Developing certain rules for determining the evolution of mass incomes in a growing economy would greatly facilitate the task of monetary, financial and fiscal policies. A well-designed incomes policy based on such rules could help prevent a rise of inequality in the growth process, while also contributing to employment growth by enabling a steady expansion of domestic demand. A central feature of an incomes policy should be to ensure that average nominal wages rise at the same rate as average productivity (plus the inflation target, see below). The implementation of such a policy requires an institutional framework adapted to the economic structure and the specific historical context of each country. Such a framework is all the more important, given that an incomes policy can serve not only as an instrument for employment generation, but also as a means of controlling inflation.

In order to preserve the wage share and ensure that real wage growth does not exceed the increase in an economy's supply capacity, the nominal wage adjustment should also take account of an inflation target. In this context, it should be borne in mind that in the absence of a major import price shock, the change in unit labour costs (i.e. the relation between wages and productivity growth) is the main determinant of the rate of inflation. There is empirical evidence for this in developed countries, in particular during periods when there was sufficient job creation and unemployment was on the decline (chart 6.4).

When wages in an economy rise, as a rule in line with average productivity growth plus the inflation target, the share of wages in GDP will remain constant and the economy as a whole will create a sufficient amount of demand to fully employ its productive capacities. In applying this rule, wage adjustment should be forward-looking. This means that it should be undertaken in accordance with the productivity *trend* and with the inflation *target* set by the government or the central bank for the next period, rather than according to the actual rates of productivity growth and inflation in the preceding period (i.e. backward-looking).

The medium-term productivity trend (for example, the average annual increase over five years) is preferable to the actual annual productivity growth, because the latter tends to be volatile and is influenced by cyclical movements of capacity utilization, and thus does not provide the basis for sustainable income growth. Moreover, wages should not be indexed according to past inflation, as has frequently been the practice. Such a scheme tends to perpetuate inflation without securing the desired level of real wages. This is because producers, faced with increasing labour costs, would be able to pass this cost increase on to prices as demand rises faster than output. By contrast, the application of the proposed scheme would ensure that the increase in unit labour costs – the major determinant of future inflation – does not exceed the inflation target.

The experience with backward-looking wage adjustments in response to the impact of the oil shocks in the mid-1970s and at the beginning of the 1980s is a case in point (box 6.2). Another is the experience of a number of developing countries that have a history of very high inflation. To be sure, in these countries nominal wage increases alone were

Chart 6.4

ANNUAL GROWTH RATES OF UNIT LABOUR COSTS AND INFLATION

(Per cent)

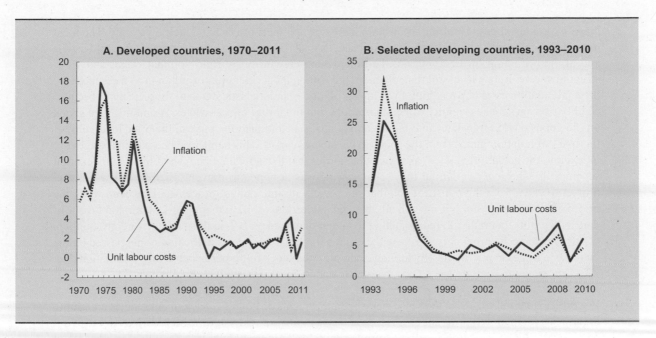

Source: UNCTAD secretariat calculations, based on IMF, *International Financial Statistics*, ECLAC, CEPALSTAT; UNSD, *National Accounts Statistics: Main Aggregates and Detailed Tables*; *EC-AMECO* database; and *UNCTADstat*.

Note: Unit labour costs refer to the total economy. Selected developing countries comprises Argentina, the Bolivarian Republic of Venezuela, Brazil, China, Honduras, Mexico, Panama, the Republic of Korea, South Africa and Tunisia.

not responsible for triggering inflation. However, bouts of accelerating inflation, often triggered by external shocks, spilled over into nominal wage increases. These fuelled a cost-price spiral as governments attempted to protect wage incomes from inflation by applying backward-looking indexation mechanisms. Such wage policies are costly, because for central banks to bring inflation down to the target level against permanent upward price pressures from the cost side, they are obliged, time and again, to raise interest rates. This deters real investment and employment for the sake of nominal stabilization.

Thus, linking wages to both productivity growth and the central bank's inflation target would also facilitate the task of the central bank in preventing inflation, while giving it greater scope to stimulate investment and growth. Investment in real productive capacity will also benefit from an adjustment of nominal wages according to the proposed scheme. This is because when domestic demand grows at a similar rate as the supply potential, it induces firms to invest and stimulates industrial growth and job creation.

Linking nominal wage growth to the productivity growth trend and to the inflation target would ensure that the share of wage income in total income remains constant, but it will not increase that share. And if wage restraint has been exercised over several years before the introduction of the scheme, the share may remain constant at a relatively low level. Therefore, it may be desirable for governments to correct the outcome of the primary distribution of income between capital and labour in an effort to redress inequities and national inequalities. However, it will be difficult to achieve this by raising nominal wages by more than productivity growth plus the target rate of inflation without prior agreement between trade unions and employers' associations. Employers unwilling to accept a reduction of their profits resulting from higher unit labour costs have no difficulty in passing on the higher unit labour costs to prices when there is growing demand from wage earners. Any attempt to increase the wage share will then turn out to be counterproductive: higher prices will restore profits, but at the same time higher inflation will tend to reduce the real value of workers'

Box 6.2

WAGE ADJUSTMENT IN RESPONSE TO AN IMPORT PRICE SHOCK

Negative supply shocks resulting from sharp increases in import prices have their own logic. The most quoted examples in the past have been the oil shocks that affected the world economy in the mid-1970s and at the beginning of the 1980s. At the time, countries with fairly rigid nominal wages and wage structures were more successful than others in preventing an acceleration of inflation as a result of the original inflationary shock resulting from higher oil prices and inelastic demand for oil. This is because rigidity of wages means rigidity of nominal wages, but flexibility of real wages. A one-off price shock on the goods market translates into higher inflation (i.e. a continued *increase* in the price level) only if the spark of inflation jumps from the goods to the labour market. This happens when nominal wages are indexed to the actual price level, as in many countries that had so-called backward looking indexation schemes like the *scala mobile* in Italy. That scheme was designed to prevent a fall in real wages and protect workers from the redistribution that can occur with inflationary processes. However, when the prices of imports rose sharply, as with oil, they did not lead to a shift in income distribution in favour of domestic profits, but rather to redistribution in favour of a third party – in this case the foreign suppliers of oil. The domestic producers who bore the brunt of higher import costs in the first round passed on the increase in wages to prices, thereby turning a one-off price shock into a permanently higher inflation rate. This prompted the central bank to take restrictive action and led to a fall in employment.

Rigidity of nominal wages, in the sense that wage adjustments do not reflect actual inflation, is preferable for adjustment to import price shocks, as it provides flexibility of real wages, which is necessary to avoid permanently higher inflation resulting from the initial inflationary bout. This may help to prevent an additional demand shock of restrictive monetary policies, which compromises growth and job creation.

accumulated savings. Moreover, it will prompt the central bank to adopt a more restrictive monetary policy, with attendant effects on investment, growth and employment. The only way to avoid this would be by imposing price controls.

In any case, policies that try to increase the share of wages require a high degree of social consensus if major social and economic disruptions are to be avoided. However, governments may seek to improve income distribution by using other instruments to correct the market outcome in favour of those with weak negotiating power. Possible government policies include progressive taxation (as discussed in chapter V) and the use of the proceeds for greater social transfers in favour of certain target groups. Public spending designed to improve the provision of essential goods and services and make them more affordable may also be increased.

The analysis of the different causes of greater inequality discussed in this *Report* suggests that a number of institutional arrangements are necessary

for implementing the recommended rule for the setting of nominal wages. Most important is government support for the creation and empowerment of unions with a nationwide mandate, which can be instrumental in implementing a successful incomes policy. Equal wages for similar occupations across an economy are essential for reducing income inequality and increasing mass demand in line with productivity growth. This can be achieved much more easily through collective bargaining between strong unions and employers' associations. And their behaviour can be influenced by government recommendations or guidelines for wage adjustments.

In this way a process of domestic-demand-led growth can be nurtured, while ensuring that wage growth neither substantially exceeds nor substantially falls short of a rate that supports stability of both prices and employment. Greater attention may need to be given to such institution-building and related governance reforms, particularly in developing countries that are in the process of enlarging their manufacturing sectors.

Additionally, for successful adjustment to demand shocks it is crucial that workers who are under pressure to quickly "price themselves back into the market" – which, as shown above, is not possible anyway – be given protection. It is also desirable to protect workers against prolonged phases of unemployment, not only for social reasons but also from a macroeconomic perspective, which may be even more important. To prevent the "pass through" to wages of high unemployment following shocks on goods or financial markets, a tight safety net is needed. This would allow temporarily unemployed workers to search for jobs being created elsewhere in the economy without having to substantially lower their standard of living and their demand for goods and services.

3. Specific aspects of incomes and employment policies in developing countries

Developing countries have huge potential for productivity growth. Hence they also have considerable scope to reduce income inequality by distributing the productivity gains more equally. This requires an incomes policy that takes into account a number of additional elements, depending on the characteristics of each economy (*TDR 2010*, chap. V). These include, in particular, the large number of self-employed workers in agriculture and those engaged in informal activities. Another aspect concerns the distribution of rents accruing from the exploitation of natural resources and from the large productivity gains resulting from combining imported advanced technologies with locally abundant cheap labour, especially through FDI and in export-oriented industries. A third aspect relates to nationwide collective bargaining and regulation mechanisms, which tend to be weaker in most developing countries. These aspects are discussed below.

(a) Reducing inequality in the context of a large informal sector and small-scale self-employment

Depending on the level of industrial development, informal employment and self-employment account for a large share of total employment in many developing countries. Moreover, the number of self-employed has been growing in many countries because of inadequate employment creation in the modern formal sectors. In these countries, it is therefore important to complement an incomes policy for the formal sector with measures to increase the incomes and purchasing power of informal workers and the self-employed. Mechanisms that link agricultural producer prices – and implicitly the earnings of farmers – to overall productivity growth in the economy would gradually improve the living conditions of rural populations. Developed countries have used such mechanisms for decades, enabling those employed in agricultural activities to share in the productivity growth occurring in the rest of the economy. Equally important, since these segments of the population tend to purchase locally produced consumer goods, such mechanisms would also contribute to increasing the demand for those goods. Productivity and incomes in the agricultural sector could also be enhanced through public investment in agricultural research and rural infrastructure development, publicly assisted agricultural support organizations and concessional public lending to small-scale farmers (see also *TDR 2010*, chap V).

While there can be no doubt about the desirability of improving living standards in rural areas, including through better remuneration for farmers, it should be borne in mind that economic development is associated with a process of a deepening division of labour. In this process, many of the self-employed poor and those employed in the informal sector need to be attracted into formal, dependable employment with the promise of reasonable, rising and reliable wage incomes. Strengthening the social safety net in parallel with a sustained expansion of the formal sector could help prevent workers from returning to activities in the informal sector if they lost their jobs in the formal sector.

(b) Commodity prices, rents and inequality

Another challenge, confronting many commodity-dependent developing countries, concerns the management of revenues from the exploitation of natural resources and of the gains from rising international commodity prices. In order to ensure that commodity rents (i.e. the difference between the sales price and the cost of exploitation of natural resources) serve to reduce inequality in developing countries, the relevant authorities in those countries should conclude appropriate contractual arrangements with companies – frequently large foreign TNCs – engaged in exploiting their natural resources. In most cases, these contracts will require the collection of higher royalties and taxes from these companies, a substantial share of which could then be channelled into the domestic economy (see also *TDR 2010*, chap. V, sect. D).[6]

Some of the gains in the terms of trade resulting from substantial increases in commodity export prices may be shared in a similar way as the productivity gains discussed earlier. However, the scope for raising the general level of real wages in response to terms-of-trade gains is circumscribed by the supply available to satisfy growing domestic demand. Therefore, such a policy needs to be accompanied by measures for lowering the costs of financing domestic investment and improving access to credit for a large number of domestic entrepreneurs in order to increase fixed investment for the production of domestically consumed goods and services. This is of particular relevance when terms-of-trade gains from commodity prices are expected to be temporary.

(c) Productivity rents from a combination of advanced technology with abundant cheap labour

As discussed in section B above, producers of manufactures in developing countries often use imported advanced technologies, especially when the production is for export. The transfer of such technologies and the introduction of more capital-intensive production techniques typically occur through FDI which is attracted by low labour costs in the host country. Such investment may contribute substantially to raising the average level of productivity in the low-wage country. The gains from this combination of advanced technologies with relatively low labour costs are generally captured by employers – be they domestic or TNCs – in the form of higher profits, or by foreign consumers in the form of lower purchasing prices. As unit labour costs are the most important determinant of competitiveness between countries and regions, the rents or the gains in market shares that the employer is able to realize by cutting prices can be extremely high.

The policy challenge for the low-wage countries is to ensure that an appropriate share of the productivity gains arising from this combination of capital and labour accrues to domestic wage earners. This cannot be achieved by leaving wage determination to a deregulated labour market. Here again, an incomes policy can play an important role. In the catch-up strategies of some successful industrializers in Asia (e.g. Japan and the Republic of Korea), domestic producers who obtained most of such productivity rents used a large share of those rents for reinvestment in export-oriented activities, thereby creating new employment opportunities. However, this process was sustainable only until a new generation of high-productivity, low-wage competitors emerged. Consequently, it became clear that faster overall wage growth was necessary to sustain the expansion of effective demand through an increase in domestic mass income and consumption (*TDR 1996*, Part Two, chap. I).

Therefore, the general rule for nominal wage adjustment should be based on the average productivity increase in all sectors, including industries with very high productivity increases resulting from the combination of advanced technologies with low domestic wages. This would help achieve a sustained increase in domestic demand and reduce income inequality between sectors and regions. Where this rule is difficult to implement, a similar result could be had by governments in the countries concerned by adequately taxing quasi-monopoly rents appropriated by TNCs and using the proceeds to increase domestic demand for domestically produced goods. Boosting domestic demand could be achieved either directly through purchases by the public sector or indirectly through temporary wage subsidies, public employment programmes and/or financial support for local private investors.

4. Legal minimum wages

In developing countries the degree of labour protection and organization of the labour force and employers is low, and structured negotiations for determining wages and employment conditions are rare. It is therefore especially difficult to establish an institutional framework for an incomes policy based on nominal wage adjustments in line with productivity growth plus the inflation target. Since it may take considerable time to create responsible institutions that can represent workers and employers effectively, a measure that could be implemented more rapidly for reducing inequality could be the establishment of minimum wages (*TDR 2010*, chap. V). In other countries, setting minimum wages may be a useful complement to collective bargaining.

Legally established minimum wages exist in most developed countries and in many developing countries, although a number of developing countries with large informal sectors may not always fully enforce such legislation. In particular, countries that lack a tight social safety net have frequently and for a long time chosen to use legal minimum wages to protect low-skilled workers from exploitation by powerful employers. Yet, despite considerable empirical evidence showing that legal minimum wages have only a minor or no effect on unemployment, such legislation has been criticized by those who view wage setting by the government as an intervention in an efficient market. These critics argue that since minimum wage legislation which seeks to protect low-skilled workers may set a wage level that exceeds the equilibrium price of labour, there is a higher risk of those workers remaining or becoming unemployed than in the absence of such legislation. They have been challenged by over 650 economists, including 5 Nobel laureates, who have stated that "a modest increase in the minimum wage would improve the well-being of low-wage workers and would not have the adverse effects that critics have claimed" (Economic Policy Institute, 2006).

In the neoclassical model underlying the reasoning of the critics, minimum wages are determined by the marginal productivity of workers with specific qualifications, but in most occupations neither the marginal contributions of individual members of a production team nor their relative contributions can be measured (box 6.1). Therefore all societies have a wide range within which they can determine the level of a legal minimum wage without violating any law of the market or the principle of supply and demand. If, for example, there was a rule that the minimum wage should always be half of the average wage of the economy under consideration, it is hard to imagine how such an arrangement would increase the risk of some groups becoming unemployed. Some labour-intensive goods and services would probably become more expensive, but the purchasing power of a large group of employees would rise, thus helping to create additional income and employment throughout the economy (see also G-20, 2012: 12).

Most minimum wage schemes have some indexation to inflation. Developing countries, in particular, tend to choose indexation mechanisms based on past inflation instead of an inflation target, and in many cases adjustment to productivity growth is not part of the mechanism. This kind of indexation is problematic for the same reasons as those discussed above in the context of general wage adjustments, especially since it creates inflation inertia. Again, when legal minimum wages are adjusted regularly in line with the average productivity growth of an economy and the targeted rate of inflation, rather than arbitrarily in response to the varying influences of interest groups on political decisions, they can have a positive effect on the investment-productivity-growth dynamic. Poverty will then be reduced not only by raising the income of those that earn the minimum wage, but also by the additional employment that is created in response to higher demand and higher profits in firms where productivity growth exceeds the average. Moreover, legal minimum wages and their regular adjustments can provide an important reference for wage negotiations in the private sector.

5. The international framework

In the discussion of national policies in the preceding sections it is implicitly assumed that the processes of adjusting to different changes in the overall economic setting are not affected by adverse external macroeconomic and financial developments or by divergent policies pursued in other countries.

However, in a world of increasingly interdependent open economies, a country's macroeconomic performance is increasingly influenced by external developments and policies in other countries. These can have a strong impact through international trade and financial relations. An individual country – comprising all its companies – may run persistently high current-account and trade surpluses based on greater price competitiveness, for various reasons. It can be the result of an increase in the unit labour cost that is not reflected in the valuation of its currency if the exchange rate is fixed unilaterally or multilaterally. Germany in the EMU is a classical example (box 6.3). On the other hand, an overvaluation of a country's currency resulting in its loss of competitiveness has been a feature of many developed and

Box 6.3

LABOUR MARKET FLEXIBILITY, GERMANY'S RELATIVE SUCCESS AND THE EURO CRISIS

Coinciding with the establishment of the European single currency area in 1999, Germany began to pursue new ways to fight high and persistent unemployment. As schemes such as reducing the work time and other measures had failed to reduce unemployment, in a tripartite agreement in 1999, policymakers, employers and union leaders agreed to abandon the traditional formula that based wage growth on equal participation of workers in productivity growth plus the inflation target. In its place, they opted for a strategy whereby redistribution in favour of capital was regarded as a means of reducing unemployment, based on the hope that this way productivity growth would translate into employment creation.

The new German labour market approach, in combination with the abolition of national currencies in the member States of the euro area, brought about a huge divergence in the growth of unit labour costs – the major determinant of prices and competitiveness – among these countries. Unit labour costs barely rose any more in Germany, whereas in most countries in Southern Europe, nominal wage growth slightly exceeded national productivity growth and the commonly agreed European inflation target of 2 per cent. France was the only country to exactly meet the agreed path for nominal wage growth since the introduction of the euro: French labour costs rose in line with national productivity performance and the euro zone's inflation target of 2 per cent.

Although the divergence among EMU members represented a low but fairly stable margin, and price and wage increases were small, they persisted over many years, so that a huge gap accumulated over time. At the end of the first decade of the EMU, the cost and price gap between Germany and Southern Europe had grown to around 25 per cent, and that between Germany and France to 15 per cent. In other words, Germany's real exchange rate vis-à-vis most of its euro area partners depreciated quite significantly, despite the absence of national currencies.

The growing gap in unit labour costs and prices had a strong impact on trade flows. While at the time of the establishment of the euro they were fairly balanced, as they had been for many years before, the first decade of the euro zone was a period of dramatically rising imbalances. As Germany's exports grew much faster than its imports, its current-account surplus widened. Meanwhile Southern Europe and France experienced widening trade and current-account deficits. Even after the shock of the financial crisis and its devastating impacts on global trade that affected German exports, in 2010 and 2011 Germany's surplus was quickly restored, to about €150 billion per year, of which exchanges with other EMU countries accounted for around €80 billion.

The current deep recession and the austerity programmes in the deficit countries have tended to reduce the visible deficits. However, without a fundamental turnaround in competitiveness, these countries lack the required growth stimulus. This experience shows that absolute and accumulating advantages of one country against other countries with similar trade structures are unsustainable; the huge gap in competitiveness has to be closed sooner or later. Failure to do so creates uncertainty on the part of lenders that have to finance the current-account deficits, as a result of which interest rates tend to increase. In order to be able to make net repayments of any debt that has been accumulated as a result of current-account deficits, the indebted country has to achieve a swing in its current-account balance at some point. A debtor thus has to be given the possibility to generate a current-account surplus. However, if the surplus countries use all means to defend their surplus positions, default by debtors is unavoidable.

The experience of the euro zone also shows that the conditions for competition among countries are different from those among firms. Individual firms are able to achieve a competitive advantage by increasing their productivity through innovation, which enables them to produce at lower unit labour costs than their competitors. But this mechanism does not work at the level of countries. Competitiveness among countries trading mainly in manufactures is strongly influenced by their relative average wage

Box 6.3 (concluded)

levels. In a world of national currencies and national sovereignty over monetary policy, a country supplying comparable manufactures at much lower prices than others would gain market shares and accumulate trade and current-account surpluses. However, political pressure to adjust wages and prices in international currency would mount, and sooner or later the country would be forced to adjust its wages, measured in international currency, through a revaluation of its currency.

In a currency union, however, member countries explicitly or implicitly agree not to opt for deflationary or inflationary policies (i.e. maintaining nominal wage growth below, or above, national productivity plus the commonly agreed inflation target). With an inflation target of close to 2 per cent (as set by the European Central Bank) the implicit agreement among EMU members is that unit labour costs would not rise by more than this rate. This implies that each country should use its productivity increase – be it 1 per cent as in Germany or 2 per cent as in Greece – for augmenting real wages or reducing working hours, or a combination of both. If, in any of the member countries, unit labour costs or inflation deviate from the commonly set inflation target, no matter whether this deviation is upwards or downwards, an unsustainable external position will arise.

The German approach to promoting its competitive position by keeping wage growth below the rate of its productivity growth plus the EMU inflation target not only led to intra-euro area imbalances; it was also unsuccessful at the national level. While exports from Germany began to rise sharply soon after the launch of the currency union, domestic demand remained as flat as real wages. This undermined the dynamics of its own domestic markets and increased the vulnerability of its trading partners (see chart).

CONSUMPTION AND INCOME IN GERMANY, 2000–2011

(Index numbers, 2000 = 100)

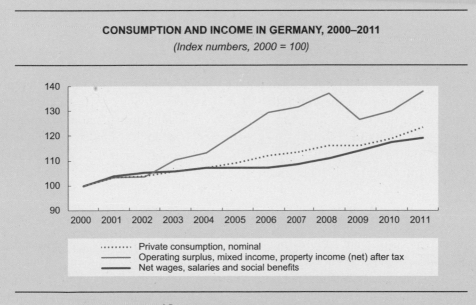

········· Private consumption, nominal
——— Operating surplus, mixed income, property income (net) after tax
——— Net wages, salaries and social benefits

Source: Federal Statistical Office of Germany, January 2012.
Note: Income in fourth quarter of 2011 estimated.

The hope for a substitution of capital by labour and for rising employment at given output growth did not materialize. Moreover, the result of the German experiment was disastrous for several other EMU members which lost market shares. Without a substantial increase in German wages, these other countries will now need several years of falling wages to restore their international competitiveness. However, time is not on their side: lower wages are causing domestic demand to fall and the current recession to deepen, especially in countries with relatively small export shares (in the order of 25 per cent of GDP), such as Italy and Spain. The resulting depression is, as Greece has amply shown, politically untenable.

emerging economies leading to a trade deficit. There can be many reasons for such an overvaluation, but the major one is carry trade – currency speculation based on interest rate differentials between currencies of countries – which recently has increased considerably as a result of very low interest rates in the United States and Europe. Overvaluation may lead to a severe financial crisis when the current-account deficit and foreign debt grow quickly; but it can also severely weaken a country's ability to diversify its production structure.

The macroeconomic shocks that arise from such mispricing in currency markets affect the economy as a whole, and therefore cannot be tackled at the level of the firm. The appropriate way to deal with such shocks is by revaluation or devaluation of the currencies concerned, rather than by wage cuts in the deficit countries. Recent examples in the euro area as well as many earlier examples in developing countries clearly show that attempts to redress huge trade imbalances through across-the-board domestic wage cuts do not work. The share of exports in overall demand is often too small for the expected effect of increased competitiveness on growth to be fast enough to prevent a deep recession triggered by the fall of domestic demand following wage reduction. Moreover, when wage cuts take place simultaneously in several countries that are trading partners, there is a fallacy of composition by which the competitiveness effect that could be had from wage compression is largely eroded. By contrast, devaluations favour exports of manufactures, but do not have a direct negative effect on domestic demand. Most importantly, they push back demand for imports and thereby stimulate demand for domestically produced goods.

Therefore, to be efficient, the adjustment process in developed and developing countries alike should be integrated into a rational global or regional monetary system; otherwise, external macroeconomic shocks will continue to threaten the smooth adjustment described above. In order to buffer macroeconomic shocks, changes in nominal exchange rates should reflect changes in fundamentals (i.e. the differential in the rate of inflation or in the rise of unit labour

> The appropriate way to deal with macroeconomic shocks is by revaluation or devaluation of the currencies concerned, rather than by wage cuts in the deficit countries.

costs) across countries. This way, changes in the unit labour cost at the country level can be equalized if measured in the currencies of the country's trading partners. This is the most effective instrument for preventing macroeconomic shocks stemming from misalignments of real exchange rates and countering the potential risk of overvaluation exerting downward pressure on wages, which would increase inequality. At the same time, a system in which the pattern of exchange rates follows nominal unit labour cost differentials is a necessary condition for avoiding beggar-thy-neighbour behaviour in international trade. In countries with open capital markets, exchange rates following inflation or unit labour cost differentials increase the scope for pursuing national monetary policies that foster growth by encouraging investment in fixed capital.

Another important aspect of the international framework is the way in which countries deal with the relocation of fixed capital. This may favour developing countries in the form of inward FDI when foreign investors are motivated by the opportunity to increase their profits by exploiting the wage differentials between rich and poor countries. The rule for real wage adjustment along the lines of national productivity growth, as proposed in this *Report*, is difficult to implement in developing countries as they frequently lack the labour market institutions, including trade unions and employers' associations, necessary for an effective incomes policy.

Therefore, principles that give due importance to adequate wage adjustments should play an important role when establishing the conditions for inward FDI. One of the conditions could be that the foreign affiliates of TNCs apply the principle of adjusting wages to the increase of overall productivity plus the national inflation target in the host country. In doing so, these firms would set a standard for domestic firms. To be more effective, these policies should be coordinated among all developing countries that are hosting or trying to attract FDI. This may be necessary in order to avoid excessive wage competition which in the end only benefits foreign firms in the form of higher profits or foreign consumers in the form of lower prices.

Observing such a rule for wage adjustments would by no means deprive foreign investors of their – often huge – extra profit arising from the combination of advanced technologies that boost absolute productivity with low absolute wages in the host country. The wage increase that they would guarantee would not be linked to their own productivity increase but to the average increase in the host economy as a whole. In a way, the application of such a rule would simulate conditions that exist in well-functioning labour markets. Foreign firms in low-wage countries not willing to adjust wages in this way would demonstrate that they are not respecting market principles.

The third area where more international cooperation is necessary relates to competition among countries. There is a widespread perception that accelerated globalization is compelling countries to compete in similar ways as companies. In this view, countries' wealth is considered to be dependent on each country's ability to effectively adjust to the challenges that are created by open markets for goods and capital. Countries with superior capital and technology endowments would come under competitive pressure from trading partners with a relatively large supply of labour and weak labour market institutions, and vice versa. In particular, the emergence of a huge pool of idle labour in developing countries like China and India would fundamentally change the capital-labour ratio for the entire world, and would bring about equilibrium of low and high wages somewhere in the middle.

As discussed earlier, declining wage shares are not a "natural" by-product of globalization, and the model describing competition among companies does not apply to countries, particularly not to countries with independent currencies. In a dynamic market economy, companies compete through differentiation of productivity and profits. They have to accept the price of labour, which is determined on the markets for different qualities of labour in the same way as the price of capital. Consequently, the success or failure of a company is determined by the specific value it adds to the goods and services traded on international markets. Companies that are able to generate higher productivity through innovation and new products produced at lower unit labour costs than their competitors can offer their goods at lower prices or make higher profits at given prices.

However, this mechanism does not apply at the country level. Regardless of whether wages are centrally negotiated for the economy as a whole or whether they are the outcome of a flexible labour market with a high degree of labour mobility, they will tend to be more or less equal for similar occupations. Thus countries, unlike companies, have to be considered as wage setters, not wage takers. Consequently, when productivity advantages are reflected in higher nominal and real wages, stronger growth of the average productivity of the entire economy does not increase the competitiveness of all companies against the rest of the world.

However, even if productivity gains, instead of being translated into higher real wages, were used to reduce prices, this would not necessarily improve the country's competitiveness or the competitiveness of all its enterprises. The prices in a country that consistently uses wage-dumping policies to improve its competitiveness would not necessarily be lower than in the rest of the world when expressed in the currencies of its trading partners. In a world of national currencies and national monetary policies, a country supplying its goods at much lower prices would gain market shares and accumulate huge trade and current-account surpluses. However, political pressure to adjust wages and prices measured in international currency would mount, and sooner or later the country would be obliged to undertake such an adjustment through a revaluation of its currency.

The principle to be applied is straightforward: given the increasingly open borders for trade and capital flows, the international trade and financial systems must be designed in such a way that in the global division of labour companies in different countries are not in danger of permanently losing out against those in the rest of the world. If nominal wage increases in one country consistently exceed the overall gain in productivity by a wider margin than in its trading partners, that country risks getting into an unsustainable position. This is because most of its companies either have to ask for higher prices and accept a permanent loss of market shares, or accept lower profits to avoid the loss of market shares. However, with open markets, the gap in price competitiveness compared with the rest of the world has to be closed one way or another.

In the present era of globalization, many countries have sought to defend their competitive positions by undervaluing their exchange rates. Although this strategy cannot be successful in the long run, there is always a risk that governments will use exchange-rate manipulation or wage compression, subsidies and lower corporate taxes to artificially improve the international competitiveness of their domestic producers. This kind of "new mercantilism" needs to be banned. All countries can simultaneously boost productivity, wages and trade to improve their overall economic welfare, but not all of them can simultaneously achieve current-account surpluses or higher market shares. Successive rounds of competitive devaluations or a race to the bottom in wages or taxes are counterproductive, and are likely to cause considerable harm. Therefore, there is a need for an international code of conduct that goes beyond the existing framework of international rules of trade policy, including the WTO's Balance-of-Payments Provisions (WTO, 2012). The code should oblige countries whose national policies have the potential to damage their trading partners and to destabilize the international economic system to adjust their nominal exchange rates in line with differential changes in inflation or unit labour costs.

E. Conclusions

The experience of the past few decades has shown that greater inequality does not make economies more resilient to shocks that cause rising unemployment. On the contrary, it has made economies more vulnerable. Pay increases below productivity growth and increased job uncertainty systematically destabilize domestic demand. Compensating the gap in domestic demand growth by increasing household debt or by gains from stock markets or housing bubbles, as in the United States in the run-up to the global financial crisis, is unsustainable.

A market economy cannot function by relying exclusively on a presumed efficient allocation of resources through flexible markets and flexible prices in all markets, including the labour market. Much more important are arrangements that allow investors in innovative activities to drive the economy towards higher levels of activity and structural change. Such arrangements include, in particular, measures for the proper functioning of the labour market, of which the most important are: first, linking the growth rate of average wages and, where applicable, the minimum wage to the overall performance of the economy as measured by overall productivity growth; second, adjusting this growth to a target rate of inflation; and third, ensuring, as far as possible, and according to the specific circumstances of each country, that the wage level for similar qualifications is similar throughout the economy, and is not left to the discretion of individual firms.

Such arrangements are in stark contrast to the dogma of labour market flexibility, which has re-emerged from the new spike in unemployment in the context of the financial crisis. But the obvious failure to return the global economy to a sustainable growth path after 2008, and in particular the failure to revive domestic demand in the developed world, should be taken as a warning sign. If a large majority of people lose faith in the willingness of companies and governments to provide them with a fair share of the collectively produced income, income growth itself will drastically suffer.

> A comprehensive incomes policy linking wage and productivity growth and including legal minimum wages and a tight social safety net for poorer families would favour investment dynamics and monetary stability.

Relearning some old lessons about fairness and participation is the only way to eventually overcome the crisis and pursue a path of sustainable economic development.

A comprehensive incomes policy, based on the principles and institutions outlined in this chapter and including legal minimum wages and a tight social safety net for poorer families, will not hamper successful economic strategies based on investment dynamics and monetary stability. On the contrary, it will help to stabilize income expectations of households and their consumption, thereby linking the most important determinant of effective demand in most economies to the expansion of the supply potential. Moreover, it will allow monetary policy to be more closely geared to the stimulation of investment and growth. Finally, it will provide the flexibility to handle negative supply-side shocks without major disruptions, as it will help to prevent additional downward adjustments of demand that are likely to result from restrictive monetary policies. ■

Notes

1 Demand could even fall before wages decline if consumer sentiment dims. For instance, if the prospect of falling wages is broadly discussed among union members or accompanied by strikes and demonstrations, private households may reduce consumption in anticipation of an expected wage cut.

2 In light of this, the idea that "profit-led growth" can lead to the same outcome as "wage-led growth" (falling or rising real wages), depending on the openness of the country concerned (Onaran and Galanis, 2012), is misleading.

3 *Financial Times*, Draghi urges eurozone to focus on growth, 4 May 2012.

4 Negative supply shocks have their own logic. However, even in such situations, it is preferable to link wage adjustments to the average growth of productivity rather than to the negotiating power of labour and capital in general or at the firm level (see section D.2).

5 This was also recognized by Keynes, when he wrote that in a market economy "[it] is by altering the rate of profits in general that they can be induced to produce this rather than that" (Keynes, 1936: 141).

6 When the prices of oil, mineral and metal products escalated after 2002, concerns grew that, while the resulting returns on investment of the companies involved soared, the share of the rents accruing to the respective host countries remained unchanged, or even fell (UNECA and AfDB, 2007; UNECA, 2009; *TDR 2010*, chap. V).

References

Barkbu B, Rahman J, Valdés R et al. (2012). Fostering growth in Europe now. IMF Staff Discussion Note SDN 12/07, June. Washington, DC, IMF.

Economic Policy Institute (2006). Economists' statement. Hundreds of Economists Say: raise the minimum wage. Available at: http://www.epi.org/page/-/pdf/epi_minimum_wage_2006.pdf.

Elmeskov J, Martin J and Scarpetta S (1998). Key lessons for labor market reforms: Evidence from OECD countries' experience. *Swedish Economic Policy Review,* 5(2): 205–252.

G-20 (2012). Boosting jobs and living standards in G20 countries. A joint report by the ILO, OECD, IMF and World Bank. June.

Hayek FA (1960). *The Constitution of Liberty.* Chicago, University of Chicago Press.

IMF and G-20 (2012). Euro area imbalances. Annex to *Umbrella Report for G-20 Mutual Assessment Process, 2012.* Available at: http://www.imf.org/external/np/g20/pdf/map2012/annex2.pdf.

Keynes JM (1930/1971). A treatise on money. In: *The Collected Writings of John Maynard Keynes,* Vol. V. London, Macmillan and St. Martin's Press for the Royal Economic Society.

Keynes JM (1936/1973). The general theory of employment, interest and money. In: *The Collected Writings of John Maynard Keynes,* Vol. VII. London, Macmillan and St. Martin's Press for the Royal Economic Society.

Nickell S (1997). Unemployment and labor market rigidities: Europe versus North America. *Journal of Economic Perspectives,* 11(3): 55–74.

OECD (1994). *The OECD Jobs Study.* Paris.

Onaran Ö and Galanis G (2012). Is aggregate demand wage-led or profit-led? Conditions of Work and Employment Series 31, International Labour Office, Geneva.

Siebert H (1997). Labor market rigidities: At the root of unemployment in Europe. *Journal of Economic Perspectives,* 11(3): 37–54.

UNCTAD (*TDR 1996*). *Trade and Development Report, 1997.* United Nations publication, Sales No. E.96.II.D.6, New York and Geneva.

UNCTAD (*TDR 2005*). *Trade and Development Report, 2005. New Features of Global Interdependence.* United Nations publication, Sales No. E.05.II.D.13, New York and Geneva.

UNCTAD (*TDR 2008*). *Trade and Development Report, 2008. Commodity Prices, Capital Flows and the Financing of Investment.* United Nations publication, Sales No. E.08.II.D.21, New York and Geneva.

UNCTAD (*TDR 2010*). *Trade and Development Report, 2010. Employment, Globalization and Development.* United Nations publication, Sales No. E.10.II.D.3, New York and Geneva.

UNECA (2009). *Africa Review Report on Mining.* E/ECA/CFSSD/6/7. Addis Ababa, United Nations Economic Commission for Africa.

UNECA (2010). *Economic Report on Africa 2010, Promoting high-level sustainable growth to reduce unemployment in Africa.* United Nations publication, Sales No. E.10.II.K.1, Addis Ababa, Ethiopia.

UNECA-AfDB (2007). The 2007 Big Table. Managing Africa's Natural Resources for Growth and Poverty Reduction. Summary Report. United Nations Economic Commission for Africa and African Development Bank, 1 February. Available at: http://www.uneca.org/thebigtable/.

WTO (2012). Understanding on the Balance-of-Payments Provisions of the General Agreement on Tariffs and Trade 1994. Geneva. Available at: http://www.wto.org/english/docs_e/legal_e/09-bops.pdf.

**UNITED NATIONS CONFERENCE
ON TRADE AND DEVELOPMENT**

Palais des Nations
CH-1211 GENEVA 10
Switzerland
(www.unctad.org)

Selected UNCTAD Publications

Trade and Development Report, 2011   United Nations publication, sales no. E.11.II.D.3
Post-crisis policy challenges in the world economy   ISBN 978-92-1-112822-2

Chapter	I	Current Trends and Issues in the World Economy
Chapter	II	Fiscal Aspects of the Financial Crisis and Its Impact on Public Debt
Chapter	III	Fiscal Space, Debt Sustainability and Economic Growth
Chapter	IV	Financial Re-Regulation and Restructuring
Chapter	V	Financialized Commodity Markets: Recent Developments and Policy Issues
		Annex: Reform of Commodity Derivatives Market Regulations
Chapter	VI	The Global Monetary Order and the International Trading System

Trade and Development Report, 2010   United Nations publication, sales no. E.10.II.D.3
Employment, globalization and development   ISBN 978-92-1-112807-9

Chapter	I	After the Global Crisis: An Uneven and Fragile Recovery
		Annex: Credit Default Swaps
Chapter	II	Potential Employment Effects of a Global Rebalancing
		Annex: Simulation of the Trade and Employment Effects of Global Rebalancing: A Technical Note
Chapter	III	Macroeconomic Aspects of Job Creation and Unemployment
Chapter	IV	Structural Change and Employment Creation in Developing Countries
Chapter	V	Revising the Policy Framework for Sustained Growth, Employment Creation and Poverty Reduction

Trade and Development Report, 2009   United Nations publication, sales no. E.09.II.D.16
Responding to the global crisis   ISBN 978-92-1-112776-8
Climate change mitigation and development

Chapter	I	The Impact of the Global Crisis and the Short-term Policy Response
		Annex: The Global Recession Compounds the Food Crisis
Chapter	II	The Financialization of Commodity Markets
Chapter	III	Learning from the Crisis: Policies for Safer and Sounder Financial Systems
Chapter	IV	Reform of the International Monetary and Financial System
Chapter	V	Climate Change Mitigation and Development

Trade and Development Report, 2008   United Nations publication, sales no. E.08.II.D.21
Commodity prices, capital flows and the financing of investment   ISBN 978-92-1-112752-2

Chapter	I	Current Trends and Issues in the World Economy
		Annex table to chapter I
Chapter	II	Commodity Price Hikes and Instability
Chapter	III	International Capital Flows, Current-Account Balances and Development Finance
		Annex: Econometric Analyses of Determinants of Expansionary and Contractionary Current-account Reversals
Chapter	IV	Domestic Sources of Finance and Investment in Productive Capacity
Chapter	V	Official Development Assistance for the MDGs and Economic Growth
		Annex: Details on Econometric Studies
Chapter	VI	Current Issues Related to the External Debt of Developing Countries

Trade and Development Report, 2007   United Nations publication, sales no. E.07.II.D.11
Regional cooperation for development   ISBN 978-92-1-112721-8

Chapter	I	Current Issues in the World Economy
		Statistical annex to chapter I
Chapter	II	Globalization, Regionalization and the Development Challenge
Chapter	III	The "New Regionalism" and North-South Trade Agreements
Chapter	IV	Regional Cooperation and Trade Integration Among Developing Countries
Chapter	V	Regional Financial and Monetary Cooperation
		Annex 1 The Southern African Development Community
		Annex 2 The Gulf Cooperation Council
Chapter	VI	Regional Cooperation in Trade Logistics, Energy and Industrial Policy

Trade and Development Report, 2006   United Nations publication, sales no. E.06.II.D.6
Global partnership and national policies for development   ISBN 92-1-112698-3

Chapter	I	Global Imbalances as a Systemic Problem
		Annex 1: Commodity Prices and Terms of Trade
		Annex 2: The Theoretical Background to the Saving/Investment Debate
Chapter	II	Evolving Development Strategies – Beyond the Monterrey Consensus
Chapter	III	Changes and Trends in the External Environment for Development
		Annex tables to chapter III
Chapter	IV	Macroeconomic Policy under Globalization
Chapter	V	National Policies in Support of Productive Dynamism
Chapter	VI	Institutional and Governance Arrangements Supportive of Economic Development

Trade and Development Report, 2005 United Nations publication, sales no. E.05.II.D.13
New features of global interdependence ISBN 92-1-112673-8

* * * * * *

Trade and Development Report, 1981–2011 United Nations publication, sales no. E.12.II.D.5
Three Decades of Thinking Development ISBN 978-92-1-112845-1

* * * * * *

The Financial and Economic Crisis of 2008-2009 and Developing Countries
Edited by Sebastian Dullien, Detlef J. Kotte,
Alejandro Márquez and Jan Priewe

United Nations publication, sales no. E.11.II.D.11
ISBN 978-92-1-112818-5

* * * * * *

The Global Economic Crisis:
Systemic Failures and Multilateral Remedies
Report by the UNCTAD Secretariat Task Force
on Systemic Issues and Economic Cooperation

United Nations publication, sales no. E.09.II.D.4
ISBN 978-92-1-112765-2

* * * * * *

These publications may be obtained from bookstores and distributors throughout the world. Consult your bookstore or write to the United Nations Publications Customer Service, c/o National Book Network, 15200 NBN Way, PO Box 190, Blue Ridge Summit, PA 17214, United States of America. Toll free telephone number: +1-888-254-4286; toll free fax number: +1-800-338-4550. Email: unpublications@nbnbooks.com. Internet: https://unp.un.org.

Regional Monetary Cooperation and Growth-enhancing Policies:
The new challenges for Latin America and the Caribbean
United Nations publication, UNCTAD/GDS/2010/1

Chapter I What Went Wrong? An Analysis of Growth and Macroeconomic Prices in Latin America

Chapter II Regional Monetary Cooperation for Growth-enhancing Policies

Chapter III Regional Payment Systems and the SUCRE Initiative

Chapter IV Policy Conclusions

* * * * * *

Price Formation in Financialized Commodity Markets: The role of information
United Nations publication, UNCTAD/GDS/2011/1

1. Motivation of this Study

2. Price Formation in Commodity Markets

3. Recent Evolution of Prices and Fundamentals

4. Financialization of Commodity Price Formation

5. Field Survey

6. Policy Considerations and Recommendations

7. Conclusions

* * * * * *

These publications are available on the website at: www.unctad.org. Copies may be obtained from the Publications Assistant, Macroeconomic and Development Policies Branch, Division on Globalization and Development Strategies, United Nations Conference on Trade and Development (UNCTAD), Palais des Nations, CH-1211 Geneva 10, Switzerland; fax +41-22-917-0274.

UNCTAD Discussion Papers

No. 206	Dec. 2011	André NASSIF, Carmem FEIJÓ and Eliane ARAÚJO	The long-term "optimal" real exchange rate and the currency overvaluation trend in open emerging economies: The case of Brazil
No. 205	Dec. 2011	Ulrich HOFFMANN	Some reflections on climate change, green growth illusions and development space
No. 204	Oct. 2011	Peter BOFINGER	The scope for foreign exchange market interventions
No. 203	Sep. 2011	Javier LINDENBOIM, Damián KENNEDY and Juan M. GRAÑA	Share of labour compensation and aggregate demand discussions towards a growth strategy
No. 202	June 2011	Pilar FAJARNES	An overview of major sources of data and analyses relating to physical fundamentals in international commodity markets
No. 201	Feb. 2011	Ulrich HOFFMANN	Assuring food security in developing countries under the challenges of climate change: Key trade and development issues of a fundamental transformation of agriculture
No. 200	Sep. 2010	Jörg MAYER	Global rebalancing: Effects on trade flows and employment
No. 199	June 2010	Ugo PANIZZA, Federico STURZENEGGER and Jeromin ZETTELMEYER	International government debt
No. 198	April 2010	Lee C. BUCHHEIT G. MITU GULATI	Responsible sovereign lending and borrowing
No. 197	March 2010	Christopher L. GILBERT	Speculative influences on commodity futures prices 2006–2008
No. 196	Nov. 2009	Michael HERRMANN	Food security and agricultural development in times of high commodity prices
No. 195	Oct. 2009	Jörg MAYER	The growing interdependence between financial and commodity markets
No. 194	June 2009	Andrew CORNFORD	Statistics for international trade in banking services: Requirements, availability and prospects
No. 193	Jan. 2009	Sebastian DULLIEN	Central banking, financial institutions and credit creation in developing countries
No. 192	Nov. 2008	Enrique COSIO-PASCAL	The emerging of a multilateral forum for debt restructuring: The Paris Club
No. 191	Oct. 2008	Jörg MAYER	Policy space: What, for what, and where?
No. 190	Oct. 2008	Martin KNOLL	Budget support: A reformed approach or old wine in new skins?
No. 189	Sep. 2008	Martina METZGER	Regional cooperation and integration in sub-Saharan Africa
No. 188	March 2008	Ugo PANIZZA	Domestic and external public debt in developing countries
No. 187	Feb. 2008	Michael GEIGER	Instruments of monetary policy in China and their effectiveness: 1994–2006
No. 186	Jan. 2008	Marwan ELKHOURY	Credit rating agencies and their potential impact on developing countries

* * * * * *

UNCTAD Discussion Papers are available on the website at: www.unctad.org. Copies of *UNCTAD Discussion Papers* may be obtained from the Publications Assistant, Macroeconomic and Development Policies Branch, Division on Globalization and Development Strategies, United Nations Conference on Trade and Development (UNCTAD), Palais des Nations, CH-1211 Geneva 10, Switzerland; fax +41-22-917-0274.

G-24 Discussion Paper Series
Research papers for the Intergovernmental Group of Twenty-Four
on International Monetary Affairs and Development

No. 59	June 2010	Andrew CORNFORD	Revising Basel 2: The Impact of the Financial Crisis and Implications for Developing Countries
No. 58	May 2010	Kevin P. GALLAGHER	Policy Space to Prevent and Mitigate Financial Crises in Trade and Investment Agreements
No. 57	December 2009	Frank ACKERMAN	Financing the Climate Mitigation and Adaptation Measures in Developing Countries
No. 56	June 2009	Anuradha MITTAL	The 2008 Food Price Crisis: Rethinking Food Security Policies
No. 55	April 2009	Eric HELLEINER	The Contemporary Reform of Global Financial Governance: Implications of and Lessons from the Past
No. 54	February 2009	Gerald EPSTEIN	Post-war Experiences with Developmental Central Banks: The Good, the Bad and the Hopeful
No. 53	December 2008	Frank ACKERMAN	Carbon Markets and Beyond: The Limited Role of Prices and Taxes in Climate and Development Policy
No. 52	November 2008	C.P. CHANDRASEKHAR	Global Liquidity and Financial Flows to Developing Countries: New Trends in Emerging Markets and their Implications
No. 51	September 2008	Ugo PANIZZA	The External Debt Contentious Six Years after the Monterrey Consensus
No. 50	July 2008	Stephany GRIFFITH-JONES with David GRIFFITH-JONES and Dagmar HERTOVA	Enhancing the Role of Regional Development Banks
No. 49	December 2007	David WOODWARD	IMF Voting Reform: Need, Opportunity and Options
No. 48	November 2007	Sam LAIRD	Aid for Trade: Cool Aid or Kool-Aid
No. 47	October 2007	Jan KREGEL	IMF Contingency Financing for Middle-Income Countries with Access to Private Capital Markets: An Assessment of the Proposal to Create a Reserve Augmentation Line
No. 46	September 2007	José María FANELLI	Regional Arrangements to Support Growth and Macro-Policy Coordination in MERCOSUR
No. 45	April 2007	Sheila PAGE	The Potential Impact of the Aid for Trade Initiative
No. 44	March 2007	Injoo SOHN	East Asia's Counterweight Strategy: Asian Financial Cooperation and Evolving International Monetary Order
No. 43	February 2007	Devesh KAPUR and Richard WEBB	Beyond the IMF
No. 42	November 2006	Mushtaq H. KHAN	Governance and Anti-Corruption Reforms in Developing Countries: Policies, Evidence and Ways Forward
No. 41	October 2006	Fernando LORENZO and Nelson NOYA	IMF Policies for Financial Crises Prevention in Emerging Markets
No. 40	May 2006	Lucio SIMPSON	The Role of the IMF in Debt Restructurings: Lending Into Arrears, Moral Hazard and Sustainability Concerns
No. 39	February 2006	Ricardo GOTTSCHALK and Daniela PRATES	East Asia's Growing Demand for Primary Commodities – Macroeconomic Challenges for Latin America

* * * * * *

G-24 Discussion Paper Series are available on the website at: www.unctad.org. Copies of *G-24 Discussion Paper Series* may be obtained from the Publications Assistant, Macroeconomic and Development Policies Branch, Division on Globalization and Development Strategies, United Nations Conference on Trade and Development (UNCTAD), Palais des Nations, CH-1211 Geneva 10, Switzerland; fax +41-22-917-0274.

QUESTIONNAIRE

Trade and Development Report, 2012

In order to improve the quality and relevance of the Trade and Development Report, the UNCTAD secretariat would greatly appreciate your views on this publication. Please complete the following questionnaire and return it to:

Readership Survey
Division on Globalization and Development Strategies
UNCTAD
Palais des Nations, Room E.10009
CH-1211 Geneva 10, Switzerland
Fax: (+41) (0)22 917 0274
E-mail: tdr@unctad.org

Thank you very much for your kind cooperation.

1. What is your assessment of this publication?

	Excellent	Good	Adequate	Poor
Overall	☐	☐	☐	☐
Relevance of issues	☐	☐	☐	☐
Analytical quality	☐	☐	☐	☐
Policy conclusions	☐	☐	☐	☐
Presentation	☐	☐	☐	☐

2. What do you consider the strong points of this publication?

_____
_____
_____

3. What do you consider the weak points of this publication?

_____
_____
_____

4. For what main purposes do you use this publication?

Analysis and research ☐   Education and training ☐
Policy formulation and management ☐   Other (*specify*) _____

5. Which of the following best describes your area of work?

Government ☐   Public enterprise ☐
Non-governmental organization ☐   Academic or research ☐
International organization ☐   Media ☐
Private enterprise institution ☐   Other (*specify*) _____

6. Name and address of respondent (*optional*):

_____
_____
_____

7. Do you have any further comments?

_____
_____
_____